AMERICAN ENCOUNTERS/GLOBAL INTERACTIONS
A series edited by Gilbert M. Joseph
and Emily S. Rosenberg

This series aims to stimulate critical perspectives and fresh interpretive frameworks for scholarship on the history of the imposing global presence of the United States. Its primary concerns include the deployment and contestation of power, the construction and deconstruction of cultural and political borders, the fluid meanings of intercultural encounters, and the complex interplay between the global and the local. American Encounters seeks to strengthen dialogue and collaboration between historians of U.S. international relations and area studies specialists.

The series encourages scholarship based on multiarchival historical research. At the same time, it supports a recognition of the representational character of all stories about the past and promotes critical inquiry into issues of subjectivity and narrative. In the process, American Encounters strives to understand the context in which meanings related to nations, cultures, and political economy are continually produced, challenged, and reshaped.

Georges Woke Up Laughing

LONG-DISTANCE NATIONALISM

AND THE SEARCH FOR HOME

Nina Glick Schiller & Georges Eugene Fouron

DUKE UNIVERSITY PRESS

DURHAM/LONDON

2001

To the memory of Arthur Eugene Fouron, my father, Ananie Colin Fouron, my mother, Artulia Eugene, my paternal grandmother, and Luce Peck Beauduy, my aunt, who nurtured and sheltered me for so many years.

To my wife, Maud David Fouron, my children, Seendy, Valcry, and Roselaine, and my wife's cousin, Fanchette Molin, whose support, understanding, and encouragement have been so important for the completion of this project.

—GEORGES E. FOURON

* * *

To the women who made this book possible: Rebecca Weissman Zaretsky, my paternal grandmother, who inspired the questions behind this book; Connie Sutton, my sister/teacher, who taught me how to answer them; Evelyn Rosenzweig Barnett, who helped me live the answers; and my daughters, Rachel and Naomi Schiller, who continue to ask questions. And to Stephen Perry Reyna, my hero, husband, and soul mate, who has provided unfailing intellectual and emotional support, patience, and humor, and understands the lessons of family.

—NINA BARNETT GLICK SCHILLER REYNA

Contents

Acknowledgments

We want to thank the large number of people who made this book possible: family members, colleagues, institutions, and interviewees. Our families have lived with this book. The disruptions were many. They range from Georges and Nina moving into each other's households so as to be able to write together, to us demanding that each member of our household define the terms *nationalism, patriotism*, and *transnationalism*. For their patience, moral and material support, and intellectual contributions, we would like to thank: Maud, Seendy, Valery, Fanchette, Gaelle, Maurice, Solange, Patrick, Fabiola, Farah, Leni, Kethly, Josette, Milou, Gerald, Miche, Manvyo, Pada, Guetty and family, Yvette, Berline, Closita, Fabienne, Magi, and Yvonne, Rachel, Naomi, Steve, Devan, Evelyn, and Warren.

This book was completed because of the perceptive and patient editing of Rachel Schiller, Naomi Schiller, and Richard Downs, the research and word-processing support of Natalie Elivert, Carrie Fisher, Rachel Price, Pierre Minn, Greg Osborn, and Carolyn Stolzenburg, and the computer wizardry of Dee-Ann Dixon, and we thank them. We would also like to acknowledge the research assistance of Jonas Frank, Max Guerrier, Fabienne Molin, Claude Monfiston, and Warren Silverzahn, whose help all proved invaluable. Institutional support has been provided by sabbatical leaves granted from SUNY Stony Brook and the University of New Hampshire, and grants from the Wenner Gren Foundation, the Rockefeller Foundation through the Instituto de Filosofia e Ciências Humanas, UNICAMP, the Mellon Foundation through postdoctoral fellowships at Yale University, and the Graduate Dean's Research Fund and the Center for the Humanities of the University of New Hampshire. Among the people who have offered encouragement and contributed intellectually to the book, and who are part of our extended family, we want to thank J. Yvonne Brown, Marie Lucie Brutus, Carolle Charles, Josh DeWind, Bela Feldman-Bianco, Grace Sciacca, Antonio Lauria-Perricelli, Hanna Lessinger, Betty Levin, Patricia Pessar, Eli Seifman, Dick Streb, Connie Sutton, and Chavannes Thomas. Our book builds on the framework about transnational migration and the deterritorialized nation-state developed by Linda Basch, Cristina Blanc-Szanton, and Nina between 1986 and 1993, and the insights of both Linda and Cristina continue throughout *Georges Woke Up Laughing*.

We have changed the names of people in Haiti whom we interviewed and of our family members, who willingly shared their life stories and opinions with us. We would have preferred to acknowledge them directly, but it seems best to protect their privacy. *Mèsi Anpil*.

Georges Woke Up Laughing

I

"At First I Was Laughing"

Georges woke up laughing.

In my dream I was young and in Haiti with my friends, laughing, joking, and having a wonderful time. I was walking down the main street of my hometown of Aux Cayes. The sun was shining, the streets were clean, and the port was bustling with ships. At first I was laughing because of the feeling of happiness that stayed with me, even after I woke up. I tried to explain my wonderful dream to my wife, Rolande. Then I laughed again, but this time not from joy. I had been dreaming of a Haiti that never was.

Georges stopped in his recollection, trying to come to terms with the sadness that had accompanied the joy of the dream. His dream would be familiar to immigrants from around the world whose days as well as nights are filled with memories of things past. In the pain of resettling in a new country, memory is often replaced by nostalgia. The economic deprivation or political repression that prompted migration frequently are put aside. In Georges's case, the dull ache of lifelong homesickness has become a part of him, although he had not confronted it fully until we began to write this book.

But for Georges and millions of contemporary immigrants, the longed-for homeland is not just a site of nostalgia; it is a location of ongoing experience. These immigrants live their lives across borders in a social world that includes not only the daily difficulties they encounter in their new land but also the often harsh realities of their homeland. Yet many immigrants continue, as does Georges, to dream of a homeland in which "the sun was shining, the streets were clean."

Before I left Haiti at the age of twenty-five, I had other kinds of dreams. Back then, I used to dream about travel and of the good life in the United States. I could even see myself driving a beautiful car, and I read all about the latest models. But the funny thing was, not only hadn't I traveled, I had never even been in a car. It was only after I had made a home for myself in New York that I began to have sweet dreams of Haiti, even though the Haiti of my youth had actually been more nightmare than joy. The Duvalier dictatorship was clamping down on all dissent. Wearing an Afro, speaking out at school, or joining any form of organization could lead to beatings, imprisonment, torture, murder, and disappearance. Besides being afraid, I was constantly anxious about how I would get an education and find some sort of a job. I couldn't even take my next meal for granted, even though my father was the director of a technical school, and my mother did sewing and fancy embroidery to supplement his very small salary.

Thirty years later, Georges is one of the immigrants to the United States who can say he has achieved "the American dream." While his car is not the latest model and he still owes money on the loans he borrowed to support his own graduate studies and put his children through college, he has made a place for himself in his new world. At first he could only find factory work, although he had arrived in the United States with a college degree and an advanced certificate in international relations. Over the years, Georges succeeded in obtaining a doctorate in education and becoming a university professor. He married Rolande, a woman from his hometown, and together they bought a home and raised a family. His daughter is now a corporate lawyer and his son is a computer engineer.

Still, through all their struggles to make it in America, Georges and Rolande have kept their connections to Haiti. In effect, they live simultaneously in two countries, participating in personal and political events in both the United States and Haiti. Georges is among the uncounted but large number of immigrants who, since the 1960s, have settled in the United States yet maintain a link to home. By retaining such ties, they defy the widespread assumption in the United States that immigrants are uprooted people who leave behind home and country to transplant themselves in a new terrain. They have forced scholars and political leaders to begin to reconceptualize the nature of immigration, and to create a new vocabulary and theory to describe the transnational connections of contemporary immigrants. A scholarship of transnational migration has emerged that defines these new immigrants as "transmigrants."

Transmigrants live their lives across borders. They settle in their new country while sending money and gifts back to family, and buying property, building houses, and participating in the activities of a land they still call home. Wherever their networks extend, transmigrants remain tied to their ancestral land by their actions as well as their thoughts, even though they may not frequently or ever travel "home" again. To describe the networks of social relationships that link together an array of transmigrants and individuals in the homeland connected to each other through kinship, friendship, business, religion, or politics, we speak of transnational social fields.[1] Transmigrants live within a transnational social field that extends into countries around the world in which family members or compatriots have settled. They live in two or more nation-states.

Not all immigrants become transmigrants. For a variety of reasons, some do indeed cut their home ties and remain out of touch with the life they left behind. While some immigrants abandon their connections in order to totally assimilate and live "the American dream," others do so because they lack even the minimal resources to fulfill their obligations to those they left behind.[2]

Georges is a transmigrant, but his relationship to Haiti extends beyond the level of personal ties and commitments to a deep love of country. As part of this love, Georges struggles to restore the glory of Haiti so that his homeland and all Haitians can obtain respect, dignity, and justice among the peoples of the world. Efforts to ensure that one's homeland stands as an equal in the world of nations is a form of nationalism.[3] In this sense, Georges is a long-distance nationalist, as are millions of immigrants from around the world who have settled in the United States yet remain committed to their native lands.

The Scope of Our Inquiry

This is a book about long-distance nationalism, and how and why both Georges and many other Haitians living abroad and in Haiti have become long-distance nationalists.[4] Long-distance nationalism is a claim to membership in a political community that stretches beyond the territorial borders of a homeland. It generates an emotional attachment that is strong enough to compel people to political action that ranges from displaying a home country flag to deciding to "return" to fight and die in a land they may never have seen. In order to explain long-distance nationalism and its reemergence within a world of increasingly globalized economies, we look to the experiences of transnational migration and connection.

Georges, as a long-distance nationalist, believes that the population of his homeland, Haiti, stretches across the territorial boundaries of two states. Therefore, our discussion of long-distance nationalism must necessarily include an analysis of how long-distance nationalists experience and think about states, and how this differs from the ways in which, since World War II, people around the world have been taught to think about government and citizenship. This, then, is a book not only about long-distance nationalism but also about people's relationship to states. There has been a growing debate among scholars about whether or not states continue to be significant in the lives of immigrants, now that manufacturing processes, corporate investments, the movement of capital, and all forms of media extend across state borders.[5] All these forms of border crossing, collectively labeled "globalization," seem to challenge the role and importance of nation-states and destabilize the meaning of national identities. Some scholars have begun to explore the implications of dual citizenship or the political practices of long-distance nationalists, interpreting these developments as signs and symbols of an era of globalization in which nation-states are of diminishing importance.[6] They have not, however, substantiated their claims by providing ethnographies of transborder citizenries.

In *Georges Woke Up Laughing*, we explore the continuing significance of nation-states in a world where state borders do not confine flows of capital, labor, culture, or political emotion.[7] We argue that the reemergence of long-distance nationalism reflects the tensions generated by the global reach of corporations and banks, continued political division of the world into separate and very unequal states, and longings of disempowered people to lead lives of dignity and self-respect. While scholars debate the significance of nation-states in the wake of globalization, most people in states continue to identify themselves, their political leaders, and the people and political leaders around the globe in terms of these nation-states.

We offer the Haitian experience of transnational migration to the United States and long-distance nationalism as entry points into a public discussion of a form of identity and political action that challenges the world as we know it. The Haitian experience is a case study and morality tale that speaks to what has become a central question today: At a moment in history when worldwide flows of media, fashion, and finance seem to mark the emergence of a global society, what motivates people to fight, kill, and die for ancestral homelands?

While this is a book about the ancestral loyalties of immigrants in the context of globalization, it is also about the histories and politics that link the United States to countries around the world. Haiti is one of the many countries in which the United States has maintained a strong military, political, and economic presence. The backdrop for so much of the contemporary immigration to the United States from places as disparate as the Philippines, Taiwan, El Salvador, Israel, and Haiti is the close association between these countries and the United States. The relationship between the United States and Haiti began shortly after Haitian independence in 1804 — a tie made real for Georges when he found in the library of Yale University the correspondence of the U.S. consul posted in Aux Cayes, Georges's hometown, in 1824. The relationship continued through two periods of U.S. military occupation in Haiti: 1915–1934 and 1994–1996. The U.S. influence in Haiti today takes both direct and indirect forms. Currently, some U.S. officials serve as advisers to the Haitian government, while U.S. congresspeople and the U.S. embassy in Haiti make pronouncements that have the tone of directives.[8] Thus, a book that examines the intimate ties linking Haitians in Haiti and the United States must explore the connection between Haiti and the United States as well. The lines of interconnection extend from the daily interactions between family members in the United States and those still in Haiti to the domain of U.S. foreign policy.

This is also a book about the United States because transmigrants, with all their home ties, do become a part of U.S. society. They work, pay taxes, participate in neighborhood activities, and read U.S. daily newspapers; they worry about crime in the streets, the proliferation of drugs, and the quality of the schools; and they become citizens and campaign for political office. Nevertheless, although many transmigrants strive for inclusion, they have daily experiences of exclusion from the U.S. mainstream. Migrants' stories, especially those told by newcomers who find themselves portrayed as racially inferior, rarely resemble the myths of immigrants succeeding solely because of their hard work and merit.

As a black man, Georges experiences racial differentiation as part of his life in New York. He weaves into his relationships to both Haiti and the United States what he has learned about who does and doesn't belong in America. Every time he is stopped by the police on his way home from work late at night because he is perceived to be an intruder in the white neighborhood that surrounds the university where he teaches, Georges learns once again that he is never fully an American. His "Americanness" is modified by his blackness; to be a "black American" is to live a life shaped by negative connotations and stereotypes. While Georges identifies with black American struggles, he cannot say that the United States is his home. Instead, he identifies with Haiti as his homeland, not only by celebrating his "roots" but also by maintaining ongoing connections "back home."

Georges's accounts of his reception in the United States are not foreign to the memories of settlement contained in Nina's family stories. Nina's grandparents were Jewish immigrants from Russia and Poland who arrived in New York at the turn of the twentieth century. Nina grew up surrounded by stories of migration. She felt that her second-generation parents were somehow different from other parents in the white Protestant suburban neighborhood of her childhood. Her father's mother, Rebecca Weissman Zaretsky, was coupled in an arranged marriage at the age of sixteen to a man from her hometown who was fleeing the czar's army and whose parents were afraid he would end up marrying a non-Jewish woman. Rebecca was sent to join him less than a year later and she never saw her parents or most of her siblings again. Nine years later, Rebecca's husband, Baruch, died in a flu epidemic, leaving her with three young children, little knowledge of the English language, and no means of support. It was Rebecca's history of rupture, loss, and struggle that engaged Nina's imagination as she was growing up. Nina's elementary school essay about the person she most admired was about Rebecca, and in high school, Nina wrote a history essay on immigration.

If Nina's family stories were about migration, loss, and adjustment, they were also about race. In 1931, Nina's father's brother Jack, although born in the United States and a U.S. citizen, was forced to seek a medical education in Germany. He had been denied admission to medical school in the United States because of quotas against Jews. Even though he was an "A" student at City College, Jack was not able to obtain all the opportunities open to "real" (meaning white) Americans. Then, in 1933, he fled the Nazi persecution of "the Jewish race" in Germany and finished his education in Switzerland, returning home just before World War II. After the war, Jack changed his last name from Zaretsky to Barnett. He was able to pass into U.S. mainstream culture as a successful surgeon using this guise, sustaining his claim to "whiteness" by becoming staunchly racist.[9]

Our Vantage Point

Our stand on immigration has, of course, been shaped by who we are: Georges, a first-generation Haitian immigrant; and Nina, the grandchild of Russian Jewish immigrants for whom questions of immigration and belonging in the United States had been a lifelong interest. Until the 1980s, both of us had understood our personal migration histories as variations on the story that is widely told about immigration to the United States. According to this tale, those who arrive in the United States must make a fundamental choice about where they belong. If you are an immigrant, you must uproot yourself and cut your loyalties to your former home and country so that you can fully embrace your new life, language, and nation. If you are not willing to do this, you remain an exile, waiting for the time you can return home.

Researching Haitian immigration together in New York, we began to rethink the immigrant experience. Georges seemed to be neither immigrant nor exile. His life was not on hold while he waited to return to his homeland of Haiti. He had settled in the United States, becoming a citizen and raising a family; he participates in daily life as a New Yorker to such an extent that he cannot begin his day without tackling the crossword puzzle in the *New York Times*. At the same time, he remains attached to Haiti. His ties are simultaneously personal and political. He is in frequent communication with family in Haiti, helping to support some relatives, while deeply enmeshed in patterns of gift giving and visiting with others. He also closely follows the political situation in Haiti, listening constantly to Haitian radio programs that combine live coverage from Haiti with heated debate among Haitians living in New York, Florida, Montreal, and Port-au-Prince.

We began to realize that Georges was living his life across borders. What he was doing did not fit the model of immigrant life as presented in the media and textbooks. We also realized that for Georges, the connection between family and nation was intimate and immediate. Somehow, his work to help his family members in Haiti and educate his children in the United States was about the building of the Haitian nation. This nationalism was not that of an exclusive, competitive ideology, however. Rather, Georges's loyalty to Haiti seems to be part of his desire to see the United States and the entire world become more just and democratic.

Our rethinking of the notion of immigration was part of a new wave of scholarship that began to reconceptualize how immigrants settle in a new land.[10] It also led Nina to reexamine her own family history. Had her grandparents actually cut all their home ties when they emigrated from Europe at the turn of the twentieth century? Suddenly Nina understood her family stories differently. Nina's paternal grandmother, Rebecca Zaretsky, although she had left Russia in 1904 at the age of seventeen, sent packages to the family she had left behind and received a flow of letters in return throughout her life. As her eyesight weakened, she brought the letters, handwritten in Yiddish, to her daughter-in-law, Evelyn, to read. In this way, Evelyn, born and raised in the United States, became part of this transnational connection. Nina remembers her mother struggling to regain her command of written Yiddish, a skill she had learned from her own immigrant parents, but had put aside in her effort to assimilate. In 1972, Rebecca's younger brother, whom she had not seen for sixty years, came to visit. After her death, cousins began to arrive and new transnational family networks were established, although many of these Russian cousins eventually settled in Israel.

As we wrote this book, Nina recalled going with Rebecca to a meeting of her hometown association (*Landsmannschaft*).[11] Rebecca had not only maintained ties to her family over the decades but continued to identify with others who came from her hometown. In Nina's family story, the kinship connections are not ones that extend from family to a nation in Russia. Like many Jewish immigrants and their descendants, Nina's family did develop transnational loyalties as well as family ties to the state of Israel. Yet there were Russian Jews who became supporters of the Russian Revolution and maintained some type of transnational loyalty, at least up until the time of the cold war.

When we began to look at U.S. immigrant history, we discovered that our family stories with their transnational identifications are not unique. Many of these cross-border connections had been recorded but forgotten as the myth of the uprooted immigrant developed. We found that at the beginning of the twentieth century, U.S. politicians, philanthropists, journalists, and of course, the immigrants themselves were well aware of the steady flow of money and goods that immigrants sent to their home country and of the movement of people back and forth. Those who were against immigration to the United States used the data on remittances as yet another reason why immigrants were harming the country and why immigration should be ended. Those who supported continuing immigration gave many reasons why such interconnections were beneficial for U.S. foreign policy interests.[12]

In the major migrations of the 1880s to 1930, a large proportion of the immigrants who arrived from Italy, Hungary, Poland, Russia, Greece, Turkey, China, Japan, Korea, Mexico, and Cuba kept their ties to home. These ties proved to be the foundation for transnational political loyalties and identities, drawing many of these immigrants into nationalist movements that extended between their ancestral land and the regions of immigrant settlement in the United States.[13] The majority of those who arrived from southern Italy, Poland, Lithuania, Hungary, Bulgaria, and Slovenia actually returned home, either to visit or resettle permanently.[14] They used their trip or trips to the United States as a way of buying land and raising their social position in their native land. Rapid steamships cut the Atlantic journey to little more than a week, and many of those recorded as "returning" probably moved back and forth, living their lives across borders. Others who stayed permanently in the United States continued to send money, gifts, and letters throughout their lives.

World War I, the 1920s' legislation that ended mass migration to the United States, the worldwide depression of the 1930s, World War II, and the initiation of the cold war all produced massive dislocations in emigrant-sending countries along with a growing suspicion in the United States of crosscutting political allegiances and dual nationalities. Despite these successive disasters, some immigrant families quietly kept the letters and packages coming. Many other immigrants in the United States, however, eventually lost the social networks that connected them to families and localities abroad. As these ties broke, the memory of their vitality, and of the transnational personal and political connections of immigrants that had cut across national borders, faded.

Until now. Immigrants from around the world are once again settling in the United States even as they live their lives across national borders. Since the 1960s, the United States has entered into a whole new period of immigration, and it is becoming clear that many contemporary arrivals, like the millions of people who arrived in the previous wave of migration, are intent on claiming the United States as their own, yet working to build their homelands. In response, scholars are beginning to investigate the history and significance of long distance nationalism.[15]

It's Not Just Haitians

Between 1960 and 1996, more than thirty-one million immigrants arrived in the United States from countries around the world. Overall, the new migration was motivated by changes in the global economy. These changes disrupted systems of production, distribution, and consumption in some localities, while simultaneously creating a demand for skilled and unskilled labor in others. The United States was facing a labor shortage in the 1960s. The 1965 U.S. immigration reforms ended the restrictions that kept many immigrants of color from Asia from entering the United States legally, and facilitated the migration of domestic workers and unification of immigrant families. At the same time, in Latin America, Africa, and Asia, the introduction of factory production for export (rather than national use) and modern agricultural production systems disrupted social and economic relationships in the countryside, spurring first rural-urban and then international migration. These economic changes were accompanied in many countries by the growth of military dictatorships, which led to migrations of political refugees.

In the 1980s, the number of legal immigrants to the United States totaled more than seven million a year—a figure approaching the yearly totals of the high-water mark of U.S. immigration between 1901 and 1910.[16] As in the past period of large-scale immigration, the dramatic rise in numbers resulted in an impassioned public discussion about immigration. The newer immigrants were criticized for refusing to assimilate and struggling to keep their native tongues in the same breath that they were categorized as unassimilable, racially inferior newcomers.[17] Calls to end immigration are again heard across the land in a language of race that resembles the rhetoric of exclusion popular in the 1920s. Only then it was Nina's Jewish grandparents, as well as Italian, Balkan, and Slavic immigrants, who were seen as unfit candidates for U.S. citizenship. Now the immigrants blamed for overpopulation, the strain on public services from education to health care, and the destruction of the national fabric are Hispanic, Asian, or black.

Lost in the intense debates about the most recent mass immigration is the response of many immigrants to both the strident, hate-filled voices that call for their exclusion from their new land and the poignant voices from home who plead with them not to forget those left behind. Many immigrants remain intimately linked to their homelands, even as they build new lives for themselves in the United States. They live in the midst of transnational connections. These ties link them to multiple political rhetorics and nation-state–building processes. In the past decade, increasing numbers of political leaders, candidates for political office, and public officials in migrant-sending countries are themselves transmigrants, having built their political careers by living and participating in both societies, and then returning home to hold elective or appointive office. Money sent home by transmigrants constitutes a significant sector of the cash flow of many of these states. In Haiti, the dollar value of these immigrant remittances exceeds the amount in foreign exchange earned by Haitian exports.[18] Surveys conducted in both New York City and Miami in the mid-1980s indicated that 90 percent of Haitian immigrants send money to Haiti.[19] Immigrants reported that they sent an average of $100 cash each month to Haiti, in addition to the value of other goods sent periodically. In a country where the average income was said to be U.S.$250 a year in 1995, the transnational ties that Haitian immigrants maintain help to sustain the Haitian economy.

Haiti is not alone in this dependency on immigrant remittances. In 1996, Dominicans in the United States sent $1.138 billion to the Dominican Republic, and an estimated one-third of the population depended on these remittances to survive.[20] The story repeats itself in the Philippines, Mexico, Brazil, and China. Whole countries if they are small, or regions of larger countries, count on the remittances sent by a sector of their population that has migrated but preserves its home ties. Meanwhile, transmigrants constitute important political lobbies, using their U.S. citizenship to support U.S. policies favorable to their homelands. The former president of the Dominican Republic, Leonel Fernandez, elected in 1996, is a transmigrant with significant ties among Dominicans in New York City.[21]

Both Haitians within the territory of Haiti and those of Haitian descent living abroad began to speak of the approximately million and a half persons of Haitian descent living outside the territorial borders of Haiti as "the diaspora." Haiti itself is home to around seven million people, less than the population of New York City. In 1990, Jean-Bertrand Aristide, as part of his campaign for the presidency of Haiti, portrayed Haitians living abroad as the tenth department, adding the Haitian diaspora to the nine geographic divisions of Haitian territory designated "departments." When he became president, Aristide created the Ministry of Haitians Living Abroad, which continued after his term as a symbol that the Haitian state now includes the Haitian diaspora. In maintaining this ministry, the Haitian government is declaring that Haitian emigrants, whatever their legal citizenship, remain Haitian.

Despite the widespread evidence of the political connections of its immigrant population that reflect and encourage long distance nationalism, most U.S. public officials, many political leaders, and the U.S. public have remained unaware of this aspect of immigrant life. Immigrants continue to be treated as uprooted populations, and the prevalence and significance of their home ties are not assessed, despite frequent news reports that note particular instances of transnational bonds.[22] Many still contend that immigrants should abandon their maternal tongue and identification with their land of birth, naturalize as Americans, and get on with life as part of the United States. They reason that if immigrants are not interested in belonging, then they should go back to wherever they came from. "You can have only one country, so either love America or leave it." People who hold this position often support their argument by pointing to past generations of immigrants who, they maintain, worked hard to become part of their new country.

Nevertheless, those who use images of the past to critique the transnational practices of contemporary immigrants are standing on shaky ground. Not only does it appear that transnational migration is as American as apple pie, but it is also becoming clear that long-distance nationalism has been an important, although little noted, aspect of the political history of the United States and emigrant-sending countries.[23]

This Particular Book

Georges Woke Up Laughing developed during a research trip to Haiti that we made together in 1996. This trip was the next step in our long-term exploration of the contemporary immigrant experience.[24] Our collaboration had begun in 1985 when Georges, who had just finished writing his dissertation about Haitian immigrant adaptations, walked into Nina's office. "I read your dissertation," he shouted, "and you've got it all wrong! How can you say that Haitians have no identity? Haitians never stop thinking about Haiti. Never." An hour or so later, we realized we had been writing about similar issues using a different vocabulary, and Nina invited Georges to join the research team that she was organizing to study Haitian ethnic identity. We embarked on joint research and writing, and traveled together to Haiti in 1991, but our trip to Haiti in 1996 was distinct for both of us. Georges had made many visits to Haiti since he first left in 1969, and this time, as always, was returning so he could walk the streets of his hometown, visit with his brother and sisters who have remained in Haiti, and assist his wife's father, who was ill.[25] On this journey, however, Georges was also returning "home" so that he could understand more fully the nature of and reasons for his continuing commitments to Haiti. He passionately identifies with Haiti, with an intensity that Nina found difficult to comprehend until we wrote this book. Nina had used her study of anthropology, with its identification with the global human experience, to remain emotionally distanced from all nationalisms. Nina had previously traveled to Haiti to research Haitian migration three times before, but this trip was a chance for her to revisit the question of nationalism. She remains proud of her participation in the movement against the U.S. war in Southeast Asia, and is estranged from her family's defense of Israel and their support for Israel's persistent anti-Arab discourse.

In the course of our joint research and writing, Nina came to understand how Georges's nationalism and that of many Haitians could unite them with people struggling around the world for a decent life. She found that many of the Haitians with whom we spoke linked their devotion to Haiti to their desire "to live like human beings." As a political activist in

Cincinnati, Ohio, Nina had heard this same phrase among white and black women on welfare, black women hospital workers, and trade union activists, black and white, men and women, who walked the picket lines. She heard it again when she worked as an ethnographer among the homeless in New York City and with people with AIDS in New Jersey.

In Haiti, we spoke with 109 people, almost all of whom had little money and no power. These interviewees were not the poorest of the poor, although some were homeless and many had no regular employment, searching each day for some means to feed their families. To better understand how these people differed from those with resources in their sense of family obligations, national identity, and relationship to the Haitian state and the United States, we also talked to a handful of individuals who had steady jobs and bright prospects, and a few who were wealthy yet not in power. Our sample was chosen to represent three different categories of relationships to the United States: people who had never lived in the United States but had ongoing ties with family abroad; those who had never traveled to the United States and had no meaningful connections with those abroad; and those who had lived in the United States but had returned to live in Haiti.

As is so often the case with anthropological research, both the researchers and direction of the study changed in the course of the project. We had expected to find that people who had family members abroad would differ from those without such connections, and did indeed discover some variation between the two groups. For example, we found that young persons who received support from abroad often were more optimistic about their own future, as well as Haiti's, and more fervently nationalist. What struck us, though, was the similarity in the way the majority of the people we interviewed spoke about Haiti. Haitians living in Haiti dreamed of "a strong, prosperous, secure, and beautiful Haiti," and shared a nostalgia for a past Haiti that had proved its worth to the world. This was a vision of Haiti we already knew well, since it was also shared by Georges. We found Haitians in Haiti and those abroad linked together not only by their insistence that those who had settled abroad remained a part of Haiti but also by a shared nostalgia for a proud Haitian past and shared dreams for a brighter Haitian future.

Still, we learned that dreams and transnational relationships can divide as well as unite. We explored not only the solidarities but also the disjunctures and contradictions that exist between transmigrants and those living in the homeland. Resentments and tensions can mark the relations between givers of gifts and recipients. People in Haiti deal with their daily grim realities by imagining that those who have fled have secured a happy and prosperous future in the United States. Jealousy can add to their misery. Haitians who have settled in the United States and face the daily burden of trying to live in a strange and different world while supporting family members back home dream of the Haiti they have left. The tensions between the Haitian diaspora and Haitians in Haiti are complicated, often exacerbated by divisions of class, gender, and generation. We realized that our book project had to examine the deep fissures that separate people in Haiti, along with the divisions between persons in Haiti and Haitians in the United States, noting at the same time that almost everyone spoke to us as nationalists, as persons who identified with and loved Haiti.

When we returned to the United States, and sat together to translate our interviews from Haitian Kreyòl and transcribe them, we came to other realizations.[26] As interviewees addressed Georges, they were using the conversations to speak to the Haitians living in the United States. Underneath the answers to our questions were other points that the speakers wanted to make, including the questions they had for us. Those interviewed were asking Georges and the Haitian diaspora to fulfill their obligations to Haiti. They were insisting that Georges, and all Haitians in the diaspora, could do more. Georges began to "get the point."[27] Soon, and without thinking about what he was doing, Georges began to answer back to the tape-recorded voices, recalling his own past and continuing struggles to live in the United States. Fascinated by the dialogue unfolding before her, Nina wrote down Georges's responses to the interviews. Then we realized that Georges was not the only one who was being addressed. Our respondents also spoke to Nina, not as a disinterested researcher but as a white American. They were using her as a messenger to stake their claims on the United States, as well as to address the American people and government. Moreover, and this was what Nina found most disconcerting, they were judging themselves and Haiti as they thought they must look through Nina's eyes. They mixed together a fierce love of Haiti with a sense that Haiti's failures were a judgment on the worth of its people. Nina, too, felt the need to reply. Nina's family history, not to mention her struggles to sort out her responses to nationalism, the role of the United States around the world, and anti-Semitism and Zionism, therefore became part of the story as well.

Our joint responses transformed this book project. We sought to explain the nature of the relationship between the United States and Haiti, and the lessons to be learned from the new form of citizenship—transborder citizenship—that this relationship has encouraged. We realized that some aspects of long-distance nationalism and transborder citizenship offer hope not just for Haiti but also for people throughout the world struggling to overcome their disempowerment and alienation from government.

Our writing process was constantly collaborative. We shared a fellowship in the Global Migration program of Yale University, and during that year, sat together at the computer. Most of the time, Nina recorded our conversation. Sometimes, Georges would make a statement and find that Nina, thinking along the same lines, had just entered the mutual thought into the text. Throughout this book, we move from Georges's direct recollections of his life experiences, which we set off in italics, to our joint analysis expressed in the pronoun "we." When Nina's recollections or experiences are counterposed to Georges, we italicize her words also. When we stand back and observe each other's responses, we describe them in the third person, "Georges found" or "Nina noticed," reflecting the processes through which each of us scrutinized the perceptions of the other.

We try as much as possible to directly present the statements of the people we interviewed in Haiti so that, as we promised them, their voices could be heard. Much writing in Haiti about the identity of Haitians in the United States, including our own work, has not drawn on the voices of ordinary Haitians. Statements about Haitian identity have focused on the writings or statements of Haitian political leaders, or spokespersons for and members of Haitian organizations. In this book, we build on and make reference to the views of political leaders, but our emphasis is on the vast majority of the Haitian people whose experiences and viewpoints are rarely described.[28]

We contrast the outlook and experiences of persons living in Haiti with Haitian transmigrants in New York, including Georges and his family. Preceded in his migration by two aunts, who provided him with a couch to sleep on and Sunday dinners when he first arrived in the United States, Georges subsequently helped his parents, two brothers, and a sister to migrate and settle in New York. He lives his life in the United States in a Haitian milieu of near and distant relatives of his and his wife, Rolande, as well as childhood hometown friends. Rolande's cousin Yvette lives in their household, and Georges and Rolande's connections to Haiti include the large network of nieces, nephews, and cousins that Yvette supports in Haiti.[29]

2

Long-Distance Nationalism Defined

Why am I so hung up on Haiti? In my house, in every room, I have a radio tuned to a Haitian station. I can't shake it. And yet I know better. Isn't that strange? I always say that people shouldn't have a blind allegiance to a country. But my love for Haiti is for Haiti. It is not for conquest; it is not against anyone else. In my case, I am looking for a place where I feel I belong, a place to retire later in life in peace. Haiti is my universe, the place I should have been all the time. I have a strong feeling and commitment to Haiti. I would love to see the country and the people having a decent way of life and receive respect in the world of nations.

We have declared that Georges is a long-distance nationalist and that long-distance nationalism is a potent contemporary political ideology. In order to explore the constructive energy Georges finds within long-distance nationalism, we must from the onset define nationalism, long-distance nationalism, nation-state, transnational nation-state, and transborder citizenship. We do so remembering that Georges's wife, Rolande, and Nina's mother, Evelyn, have requested a book without jargon that they can read and enjoy, so while we build our definitions on the scholarly literature, we will not review its intricacies.

Nationalism can be defined as a set of beliefs and practices that link together the people of a nation and its territory. The nation is understood to be people who share common origins and history as indicated by their shared culture, language, and identity.[1] Central to nationalism is the belief that a nation has the right to control the territory that is its homeland by having its own state, whose territorial boundaries stretch to the borders of the homeland. Therefore, it is difficult to speak of nations without also discussing states.

The state is generally understood to be a sovereign system of government within a particular territory. The apparatus of the modern state includes a head of state, legislative body, court system, and an armed forces. Increasingly, theorists of the state have begun to realize that the power of states resides not in the government institutions themselves but in the processes, routines, and everyday activities that operate together to create and legitimate social order and discipline.[2] Individuals may promote ideas about the state as much through critique as through unquestioning acceptance. When a person denounces a corrupt or venal public official, avoids taxes, decries the condition of the public schools, roads, or order, s/he circulates and endorses certain ideas about the state. When we put together the terms *nation* and *state* and designate a particular polity as a nation-state, we make the assumption that people who share an identity as a nation also contribute to the quotidian routines, ritual, and discourse that form the state within a particular territory. When people contest a particular set of leaders, they often do so in the name of the nation that claims a particular state and its territory. The government of each such state represents the nation that lives within its borders.

People around the globe settled into a pattern of thinking about the world as divided into territorially based nation-states only after two world wars were fought in the name of nation-states and colonial states in Africa, Asia, the Pacific, and the Caribbean were granted independence. This dominant, but still not totally hegemonic, model is exemplified and made concrete by the United Nations. This organization projects a view of the world in which each nation is located exclusively within its own separate national territory, demarcated by internationally recognized borders.[3] Inherent to this model's logic is the assumption that each individual can be a citizen of only one state and identify with only one nation.[4] Yet the world has never been completely organized this way, and now, in a new age of migration as well as a renewed and intensified period of globalization, long-distance nationalism is reconfiguring the way many people understand the relationship between populations and the states that claim to represent them. Currently, an increasing number of states are developing legal ways of reclaiming emigrants and their descendants, and those who have emigrated are publicly declaring their full-fledged incorporation into two or more states.

A new form of state has emerged that extends its reach across borders, claiming that its emigrants and their descendants remain an integral and intimate part of their ancestral homeland, even if they are legal citizens of another state. In some ways, this transborder state represents a resurgence of a form of nationalism and political practice that existed in the nineteenth and first half of the twentieth century. National leaders during that period saw their emigrants more as colonists than permanent settlers abroad. Benito Mussolini's efforts to mobilize Italians settled in the United States was one of the most visible efforts of the long-distance projects of a number of political leaders from states that included Greece, Hungary, Ireland, Korea, China, Mexico, and Japan.[5] In earlier cases, however, transmigrants were expected to eventually return home, and long-distance nationalism contained a call to come and rebuild the land. To accept permanent settlement elsewhere was generally defined as national betrayal. The current political moment is quite different. Political leaders and the emigrants themselves are increasingly ready to see emigrants as permanently settled abroad, but also continuing to be part of the body politic of their homeland.

In the course of the past decade, as we have mapped the emergence of this project to reconstitute nation-states so as to encompass populations well incorporated into the social, economic, and political life of other states, we have searched for the best term to describe these states. In 1994, Nina and her colleagues, Linda Basch and Cristina Szanton Blanc, employed the phrase "deterritorialized nation-state" for nation-states that define their population as extending beyond the state's territorial borders.[6] Yet the adjective "deterritorialized" evokes an image of a nation without borders or territory, and the states in question maintain a territorial base. Others have built on Arjun Appadurai's term "transnation," but this descriptor, although more felicitous, also often projects images of a world of nations without territorially based states. Consequently, we have decided to use "transnational nation-state." The dictionary defines transnational as "transcending or reaching beyond national boundaries."[7] When combined with the word nation-state, we believe this phrase represents the particular politics we examine in this book: the reconstitution of the concept of the state so that both the nation and the authority of the government it represents extend beyond the state's territorial boundaries and incorporate dispersed populations. This is not the only form of transnational politics. It is the one that concerns us here as we broaden the scholarship of everyday forms of nation-state formation so that it can encompass long-distance nationalism.[8]

An Approach to Long-Distance Nationalism

Our understanding of long-distance nationalism includes all five of the following specifications. First of all, it resembles conventional localized nationalism as an ideology that links people to territory. As in other versions of nationalism, the concept of a territorial homeland governed by a state that represents the nation remains salient, but national borders are not thought to delimit membership in the nation. Long-distance nationalists differ from local nationalists in their assertion that people living in various disparate geographic locations within different states share a common identification with an ancestral territory and its government. Hence, long-distance nationalism provides a justification for such a government to reconfigure itself as a *transnational nation-state*. Long-distance nationalism binds together immigrants, their descendants, and those who have remained in their homeland into a single *transborder citizenry*. Citizens residing within the territorial homeland view emigrants and their descendants as part of the nation, whatever legal citizenship the émigrés may have.

To legitimize the connection between the people who can claim membership in the transnational nation-state, long-distance nationalism highlights ideas about common descent and shared racialized identities that have long been a part of conceptions of national belonging.[9] For example, although Georges is a U.S. citizen living in the United States, he continues to see Haiti as his homeland; many people in Haiti agree and see him as Haitian, despite the fact that he is not legally a Haitian citizen. They contend that "his blood remains Haitian."

Second, long-distance nationalism does not exist only in the domains of the imagination and sentiment. It leads to specific actions. These actions link a dispersed population to a specific homeland and its political system. Long-distance nationalists may vote, demonstrate, contribute money, create works of art, give birth, and fight, kill, and die all for a "homeland" in which they may never have lived. Meanwhile, those who live in this land will recognize these actions as patriotic contributions to the well-being of their homeland.[10]

Georges is a long-distance nationalist not only because he dreams about Haiti but also because he takes actions on behalf of it while continuing to live in New York. He believes that when he assists family members in Haiti, speaks out about problems there, or counsels young people of Haitian descent born in the United States, he is working to reconstruct Haiti. People living in Haiti are long-distance nationalists as well if they continue to claim Georges as their own, and maintain that he continues to be responsible for Haiti and that his actions abroad reflect on the reputation and future of Haiti.

Third, long-distance nationalists have as their political objective the constitution of a transnational nation-state. Long-distance nationalists challenge established theories of states as well as nations. They endorse and in fact help to sustain the image of the world as divided into separate, sovereign, territorially based states, each representing a nation, yet they contest the notion that relationships between citizens and their state are confined within that territory. Instead, they envision transnational nation-states. While the concept of transnational nation-states contradicts conventional political theory, when we look at the way in which past and present generations of immigrants have actually experienced their ancestral states, transnational nation-states become not just thinkable but political realities that merit investigation.

Emigrants living outside the territory controlled by the state not only continue to see themselves as part of an ancestral nation; they also take political action in relationship to those states. And they take these actions as representatives of the nation from which they are descended. Meanwhile, for their part, government officials of these states often claim to continue to represent their dispersed populations, no matter where such persons live and no matter what legal citizenship they may hold. In effect, they declare that their government as well as their national population is transnational. For example, a number of emigrant-sending states such as Mexico, Colombia, the Dominican Republic, Ecuador, and Brazil have adopted policies that turned them into transnational nation-states. Many have changed their laws and created government agencies to ensure that transmigrants remain incorporated in their native land. Some governments have granted dual nationality so that emigrants can carry two passports; others have extended voting to emigrants who have become U.S. citizens. Through these changes, as well as the establishment of special ministries responsible for diasporic populations, the political leaders of these countries signal that transmigrants, and their children, remain members of the nation of their birth.

Whether localized or long-distance, nationalism brings together those who share a sense of "peoplehood" based on a common culture and history with the political project of building or defending a territorially based state that speaks for its people. Nevertheless, long-distance nationalism differs from localized nationalism in that it situates people in an ancestral homeland and persons settled in other lands within a single political project. Although in many instances, government officials embrace or reshape this political project, long-distance nationalism cannot be seen as a "top-down" fostering of elite beliefs. The vision of the nation as extending beyond the territorial boundaries of the state frequently springs from the life experiences of migrants of different classes, whose lives stretch across borders to connect homeland and new land.[11] It is also rooted in the day-to-day efforts of people in the homeland to live lives of dignity and self-respect that compel them to include those who have migrated in their definition of their national community.

Fourth, conditions in the homeland or new land may encourage or subvert the beliefs and practices that contribute to long-distance nationalism. Certain political circumstances make it difficult for persons abroad and those at home to engage in transnational projects that contribute to building the homeland. For instance, under dictatorships such as that of the Duvalier regime in Haiti or the Salazar government in Portugal, or when revolutionary governments such as Cuba see themselves under siege by foreign powers, transnational political projects may be discouraged or forbidden. Those who left were labeled as traitors, defectors, or betrayers of the nation. Similarly, states that receive immigrants may be suspicious of their transnational ties, especially if they wish to remain connected to a country perceived to be an enemy nation. After World War I, the United States not only closed its borders to most immigration but also launched an assimilationist policy that demanded that homeland identities and loyalties be abandoned. During World War II, Japanese and German long-distance nationalists in the United States were forced to renounce their homelands. On the other hand, if after even several generations it has been difficult for immigrants to obtain legal citizenship in their new land—which has been the experience of Turkish immigrants in Germany—or if immigrants and their descendants find that access to their legal citizenship does not guarantee them the full protection of the law—as has been the case for immigrants of color in the United States—long-distance nationalism as a set of both beliefs and practices may flourish.

Finally, long-distance nationalism must be distinguished from other forms of collective belonging. There is now a plethora of scholarly writing that uses "diaspora" to describe transborder belonging and identification, past and present.[12] We find this approach confusing because it confounds very different historical experiences and forms of consciousness. Instead, we differentiate between identification with a particular, existing state or the desire to construct a new state, which we call long-distance nationalism, and other forms of transborder ideas about membership, such as those based on religion or a notion of shared history and dispersal. Dispersed populations that share an ideology of common descent and a history of dispersal, racialization, and oppression, but make no claim to nation-state building, are probably best categorized as diasporas. Accordingly, we would speak about an African diaspora. The Jews in ancient times or the Middle Ages praying for the messianic age in which the temple in Jerusalem would be restored can best be understood as a diaspora.

It is only when a diasporic population begins to organize to obtain its own state, as Jews did in the twentieth century, that we would designate them as long-distance nationalists. In the case of Israel, this linkage between a concept of the Jewish people and a specific state has been written into Israeli law, which extends citizenship rights to the Jewish diaspora. Individuals who have never even set foot on Israeli territory but whose genealogies establish Jewish identity have citizenship rights in Israel.[13] When Serbs in Chicago and those in Belgrade work together to oust Muslims from Bosnia and build a greater Christian Serbia, they express long-distance nationalism by their actions as well as their words. The German law that made it possible for persons of German descent who had lived for generations outside of Germany to return as citizens because they were "ethnic Germans" was an expression of long-distance nationalism. Portugal's effort to redesign itself as a "global nation" and reclaim persons of Portuguese descent settled around the world is an instance of a transnational nation-state encouraging long-distance nationalism.[14] Long-distance nationalism is the motivation that stands behind headlines about U.S. citizens of Chinese, Israeli, Kosovar, Irish, or Korean descent who lobby, spy, fight, and raise funds for a homeland in which they may never have lived or in which they may no longer feel "at home."[15] Haitians who live in the United States as citizens or permanent residents yet contribute to development projects that they deem crucial to improving Haiti are long-distance nationalists.

Despite the intensity of the passion engendered by long-distance nationalism and the prevalence of this ideology in the world today, we know relatively little about it. Apart from Benedict Anderson, most theorists of nationalism have not addressed the question of long-distance nationalism.[16] This is because it is a political ideology that falls outside of what has become the standard-issue model of how the world is presently supposed to be organized. Long-distance nationalism calls into question the common understanding of the current structure of political and economic relationships in the world. It allows us to address current debates about the relationship between globalization processes that are knitting the world into a single economic system and the significance of state structures. It helps us to better explain the roles that various nation-states are playing within the changing structure of the global economy.

The Question of Citizenship

Everyone relates to states, the political units into which the world is divided, by means of both law and emotion. The government of each state creates laws that define who has a right to citizenship in that state and what those citizenship rights entail. The word "citizen" is now generally understood as a person who is a full member of a modern state and as such has legal rights in that state, including the right to vote, hold political office, and claim public benefits. Citizens of states also have certain responsibilities, which vary from country to country.[17] But this clear-cut, textbook-style definition gets extremely muddy in practice, and in different states, people actually conceive of citizenship somewhat differently.

Moreover, as scholars of citizenship have noted, not all people who are legal citizens receive the same treatment from a state or are able to claim the same rights.[18] There are often categories of people who are legal citizens according to the laws of a state, yet who face various forms of exclusions and denials of civil rights because they are not considered to be truly part of the nation. For long periods of U.S. history, for example, people of color and women, even when they were acknowledged to be citizens, were not granted equal rights—and questions of equal treatment by state agencies are still points of contention. In Haiti until recently, individuals who lived in the countryside had the word *paysan* (peasant) written on their birth certificates and were referred to as *moun andeyò* (people outside the city) to imply that they were not considered to be part of the political classes. Participation in politics was reserved, in essence, for the elite and highly educated in Port-au-Prince.[19]

Because of the contradictions between the legal status of citizen and the actuality of state practices, some scholars focus on the "substantive" rather than the legal status of citizenship.[20] When people make claims to belong to a state through collectively organizing to protect themselves against discrimination, gain rights, or make contributions to the development of that state and the life of the people within it, they are said to be substantively acting as citizens, whether or not they have the legal documents that recognize such a status. This substantive approach to citizenship gives us a way to describe the behavior of long-distance nationalists who participate politically in states and make claims on more than one state, even when they are not living within the territory or are not legal citizens of a state. It also allows us to designate long-distance nationalists as "transborder citizens." The phrase transborder citizenship reflects the relationship that people who live within transnational social fields have with more than one government. We use "transborder" rather than "transnational" citizenship to highlight the fact that while these "citizens" cross territorial borders, they do so in the name of only one nation.

Transborder citizens may act as substantive citizens in more than one state, but only as long-distance nationalists who are engaged in claiming a single national identity.[21] As we note in chapter 8, however, because transborder citizens participate in the political processes and cultures of more than one state, they may draw on concepts of the state and ideas of civil and political rights of more than one polity. In the Haitian case, this has led many poor people to become a new politically engaged citizenry with repercussions in both the United States and Haiti. While we speak of a "transborder citizenry," we do not assume that these citizens speak with a single political voice. As with any other citizenry, a transborder one will have political divisions based on differences in party or ideology. Such a citizenry is, at the same time, united by a shared identity.[22]

Still, although "transborder citizen" proves useful in describing the political behavior of persons who live their lives across the borders of two or more nation-states, this use of "citizen" suffers from the same drawbacks as all approaches to citizenship that are not based on legal definitions. Whatever their claims to membership, people who are substantive but not legal citizens face legal restrictions and lack legal protections. Haitian transmigrants living in the United States may participate as members in the societal and political processes of both the United States and Haiti. Yet, if such people remain Haitian citizens, making their presence known publicly may have repercussions, especially if they are undocumented. At the same time, if Haitian transmigrants become U.S. citizens but still participate in the Haitian political system without Haitian citizenship, their commitment to Haiti or right to hold office in Haiti may be challenged.

Increasing numbers of states, including Greece, Ireland, the Dominican Republic, and Colombia, are recognizing long-distance nationalism by changing their laws to allow for dual citizenship.[23] Some countries, such as France and Israel, have had dual citizenship for many decades. Others, like Mexico, find a legal middle ground by recognizing those who have emigrated and their descendants as "nationals" of their homeland, without granting them full citizenship rights such as voting. The state in a sense grants honorary membership just as a university may grant an honorary degree. This form of membership confers respect but few, if any, political privileges.[24] Many Haitian emigrants claim membership in their ancestral land and also engage in politics designed to shape the future of their homeland. Haiti does not allow dual citizenship but dual nationality is assumed by most Haitians, as we demonstrate in chapter 5. The Haitian government has found ways to recognize these claims without changing its citizenship laws.

Sometimes, the political actions of transborder citizens living outside the territorial boundaries of the state can affect its political direction. In the Israeli election of 1999, it was generally assumed that if the election for prime minister had been close, the votes of Israelis living in the United States who were U.S. citizens would have proven crucial. Indeed, plane loads of persons of Israeli origin, many of whom were U.S. citizens, returned to Israel to vote in that election.[25] The long-distance nationalism of the returning Israeli/American voters was translated into much more than an emotional tie. These people were transborder citizens, asserting their political rights in two different states, and participating in both with political understandings shaped by each political system.

As we will show, even though transmigrants challenge the concept of the bounded nation-state through their long-distance nationalism, they paradoxically reconstitute a concept of national sovereignty. When they make certain demands on the government of their homeland, they reinforce the older vision of a nation-state as a sovereign power. For example, Haitian transmigrants living in the United States continuously join with people in Haiti in a critique of Haitian political officials based on their failure to lead Haiti into a period of economic development that could provide for the common welfare. Yet these leaders, confronted by the pressures on them from "donors" of foreign aid and transnational corporations whose capital far exceeds the worth of many states, are unable to respond to the demands of their people. To speak about this confusing situation of independent nation-states with little actual national sovereignty, we have developed the concept of the "apparent state." Apparent states are structures of government that have a distinctive set of institutions and political procedures, but have little or no actual power to meet the needs of the population.

The concepts of long-distance nationalism, transnational nation-state, transborder citizenship, and the apparent state allow us to explore the ways in which the life experiences, family values, self-esteem, and political identity of someone like Georges are intimately linked to conditions in both the homeland and country of settlement. Our approach, which is ethnographic and autobiographical, demonstrates how the desires, ambitions, and mundane needs of women and men to give a brighter future to their children may still be intertwined with nationalism and states. To do this, we trace the lines that connect self, family, nation, and poor and rich states. We bring together and analyze the interconnections of subjects usually researched as separate topics: family obligations and anger, emigration as desire and immigration as discontent, race as stigma and pride, and the reconfiguring of nationalism, citizenship, and state sovereignty within a global economy. Clearly, because our book is a case study of a particular setting of long-distance nationalism and the transnational nation-state, we can do no more than open the discussion of the significance of long-distance nationalism in a period of globalization.

Nationalism as a Floating Signifier

In the wake of the rise of Hitler and Mussolini in Europe in the 1930s, and of post–World War II dictators around the world who built support for their regimes by fanning nationalist emotions, Western scholars tried to distinguish between what they saw as the good nationalism of democracies such as England, France, and the United States, and the destructive nationalism of authoritarian regimes. The emergence of a new wave of nationalism after the breakup of the Soviet Union and Yugoslavia in which genocidal actions are being justified in the name of love of country has revived efforts to make such distinctions. Much of this debate has been waged in terms of whether the state that claims to speak for a nation of people is democratic in the sense that it holds free and fair elections for its leaders and legislature. From the Left came a different categorization of nationalist politics. Nationalisms were judged to be progressive or reactionary depending on whether they were used to unite populations in struggles against imperialist powers or whether nationalist ideologies were used by these powers to rally the populations of imperialist countries to suppress struggles for national liberation.[26]

In the current era of globalization, in which most countries around the world are formally independent and democratic but intertwined with the institutions of global capital, another approach to nationalism is more fruitful. Ideologies such as nationalism can be understood productively as "discursive formations" in which shared sets of symbols contain multiple and conflicting meanings and messages.[27] Nationalism as an ideology has succeeded in the breadth of its appeal because it can be used by different sectors within a state to organize around fundamentally different agendas. Here we build on insights offered by James Scott's work on "hidden transcripts." Scott has noted that disempowered people maintain a sharply dissonant political culture expressed outside the intimidating gaze of the powerful. He also observes that there is a "politics of disguise and anonymity that takes place in public view but is designed to have a double meaning . . . [so that] a partly sanitized, ambiguous, and coded version of the hidden transcript is always present in the public discourse of subordinate groups."[28]

Nationalist rhetoric holds within it a hidden transcript of the disempowered within a nation. The nation is in many ways a "floating signifier"—that is, it means many contradictory things to people who organize to obtain diametrically different views of the future, all waving the national flag.[29] The word "polysemous," defined as "having a multiplicity of meanings," is also a useful way to understand the power of nationalist ideologies. It also highlights the flexibility of nationalism that can readily encompass religious messages about personal or collective salvation within discussions about the future of the nation. The embedding of religious belief within nationalist rhetoric can either legitimate an oppressive political system or challenge it.

Approaching nationalism in this way allows us to move beyond the opposition between nationalist ideologies and religious beliefs that has been made by Western social science. Many theories of nationalism factor out any exploration of religion. When nationalist struggles are waged in the name of religious beliefs, analysts call such struggles "fundamentalist." This labeling does not explain how religious beliefs and nationalism can reinforce and define each other.[30]

As long as the nation-state system continues to be the dominant model of political organization, people with vastly different outlooks and experiences within each state are frequently drawn into a politics that engages them with some form of national identification. Even if sectors of a population within a state struggle to reject identification with that particular state and the nation it claims to represent, they may find themselves identifying with another nation or sense of peoplehood. This was, for example, the only alternative that seemed possible to people who lived through the breakup of Yugoslavia and the Soviet Union. Those sectors of a population whose experiences of subordination in a particular state do not mesh readily with a concept of nation—for example, women, the poor, gays and lesbians, members of a religion, people of color—often embed their struggle in claims to rights within a specific nation.[31] They fight for a different representation of the nation and equal rights within the state rather than extending resistance globally. This is because by the end of the twentieth century, nationalist ideologies had been introduced, propounded, and legitimated as part of the history of particular people in every location of the world. In other words, in most places, nationalism is the dominant political ideology at this point in time. Its basic assumptions about identity are accepted by most people as normal and natural, even as the meaning of the nation and its representations are constantly contested, redefined, and reconstituted.

Long-distance nationalism continues the ambiguities and multiple messages of localized nationalism. Like all nationalisms, the long-distance version can contain and be used to express a myriad of political agendas. In the face of ever-increasing globalization, long-distance nationalism plays a particular role in nation-state building. It obscures the degree to which many contemporary states have become apparent ones. When scholars first began to study transnational migration and other transnational processes in the 1980s, several prominent voices such as Arjun Appadurai and Mi-

chael Kearney argued that this was the start of a postnational period.³² They
predicted that people around the world would no longer identify with
nation-states, but rather become "postnationalists" who looked at the
world in different terms. Now, many scholars acknowledge that nation-
states seem to continue to be important, despite the salience of transnational processes. Our book enters into this discussion by explaining the role
of long-distance nationalism in maintaining a form of nationalist ideology
in the context of transnational processes and globalization.

Nina began this book distrusting nationalism in general, seeing in its
equation of blood and nation a foundation for racism and genocide. She believed that political leaders and theorists alike used an imagery of citizenship to hold in check the class and cultural tensions inherent in projects to
build nation-states. She perceived of nationalism solely as a means by which
the rich and powerful convince those who suffer from the inequalities of
the existing structure to support the system. In Haiti, where the handful of
rich live lives of great leisure among the vast majority who wake up and go
to bed hungry, she saw classic territorially situated as well as long-distance
nationalism as an especially cruel diversion. Nina knew that in the mid–
twentieth century, nationalism had been an ideology of liberation, used to
unite colonized people to struggle for independence from imperial powers.
But she agreed with writers such as Franz Fanon, the black revolutionary-
minded psychiatrist, who in the 1960s warned that postcolonial nationalism often served the interests of elites.³³

It was as she came to understand the different ways in which women, the
poor, and racialized Haitian immigrants in the United States used their
identification with Haiti that Nina changed her view about nationalism.
She finally became convinced of what Georges had been trying to explain
to her for years: there are other aspects of nationalist ideologies in locations
such as Haiti. She began to recognize the usefulness of an approach to nationalism that sees it as a discursive formation, a shared way of speaking
that has multiple and contradictory meanings that change depending on
the time, place, and speaker. Nina had to admit, in some ways despite herself, that many people in Haiti were linking their identification with Haiti
to global struggles against injustice. In the midst of globalization, long-
distance nationalism could mobilize people to demand liberation from
hunger, poverty, malnutrition, and political oppression. At the same time,
nationalism, as it extends into long-distance nationalism in the midst of a

globalizing economy, takes on new meanings for both the dominant classes and people resisting oppression.

We have filled this book with the voices of poor men and women who use a Haitian nationalist rhetoric to struggle against their daily misery and suffering. Rather than despair at the fact that nationalism is so deeply rooted in so many locations around the globe, we look at the ways in which in a setting such as Haiti, some sectors of the population use it to develop an agenda for resistance. And we note that the path they choose under the signpost of nationalism constitutes a challenge to global structures of power. They follow this path toward an alternative vision for Haiti, and this vision situates Haiti in a world where social justice is triumphant. We found this alternative vision not just among the poor, and certainly not held by all the poor, although the poor of Haiti have been the main force there struggling and dying for social justice. But students, professionals, priests, nuns, church laypeople, and artists in Haiti also contribute to the efforts to move Haiti in a different direction. And so do many transmigrants, whether they are service workers, domestic workers, clerks, professionals, or small business owners.

We do not want to romanticize the power of this vision. Even as people declare their commitment to Haiti, they confront the jealousies and distrust that underlie ongoing family ties and cooperation between neighbors, the vast divisions in experience between rural and urban people, and between those in Haiti and those living abroad, and the profound divisions created by class and the disillusionment with political leaders. Yet just as real are the daily experiences of the collectivity expressed in family life and transnational networks, and the memories of the excitement and even joy that accompanied the grassroots movement of the 1980s as well as the election of Jean Bertrand Aristide, a leader of that movement, in 1990. As people in Haiti spoke to us of their past efforts at social transformation, their voices echoed Georges's longing for a world in which struggles for social and economic justice are victorious.

The Questions Before Us and the Structure of the Book

In the wake of both the new immigration and resurgence of transnational connections between immigrants and their homelands, it is time for all of us, immigrants and nonimmigrants alike, to explore the implications of long-distance nationalism. In such a world, what are the meanings of home, country, nation, and nationalism? How different or similar are the past experiences of immigrants, who engaged in transnational relations that stretched from family ties to political parties, from that of contemporary long-distance nationalists such as Georges? Does Georges's dream of his youth in Haiti represent a case of prolonged homesickness or does it have roots in his life in the United States? Who exactly is Georges? Haitian? American? Haitian American? Black? African American? And what about his children, who were born in the United States? As an immigrant and a U.S. citizen, how should Georges relate to the land and people of his ancestry? What is he to Haiti or Haiti to him? How do those people in Haiti whom he left behind view him? And just as important, what is the United States to Georges and the people to whom he is connected who continue to live in Haiti but dream about New York?

When we question the meaning of membership in nation-states, we initiate a discussion about loyalties and identities, about nationality and citizenship. Such an exploration raises the issue of who has been considered an American, both in the past and present. These queries lead us to a cascade of further questions. Is it only immigrant nostalgia or ethnic pride that fuels the St. Patrick's Day or Columbus Day parades and so many "ethnic festivals" that dot the U.S. cultural landscape? Even when past generations of immigrants lost their family ties, didn't many retain some sort of political loyalty? Why do the descendants of Irish, Italian, German, and Eastern European immigrants serve as political lobbies that represent the interests of their ancestral lands within U.S. congressional and presidential politics? How are we to understand the transnational connections of American Jews such as Nina's relatives? Nina's relatives do not identify as Russian or Polish but they do have transnational loyalties and links to the state of Israel. Their identities motivate both action and emotion, leading them to donate money to projects in Israel, visit this "homeland," and keep up ties with cousins who emigrated from Russia to Israel. Although they have been having this debate for more than thirty years, Nina's mother, Evelyn, still begins to sob when Nina refuses to feel a bond as a Jew to Israel.

The questions continue. Once we begin to think about transnational migration, our perception of how the world is organized stands challenged and in need of revision. If Georges and millions of others are living simultaneously in more than one country, what do we understand about the boundaries of nation and state? Can we accept the view projected by the media, political leaders across the ideological spectrum, and the United Nations that the world is made up of separate independent nation-states, each with their own territory, language, history, and culture? Is it possible for a person to have two or more homelands? And if it is possible, is it desirable? Who benefits and who loses when large numbers of people in the current global economy have dual citizenship and live their lives across international borders? Can some form of long-distance nationalism help connect people struggling for social justice or does it only increase the degree of hatred and violence in the world?

Our answers begin with the emotions and obligations that surround the "return of the native." Chapter 3 traces Georges's visits to members of his family in Haiti, and describes the rituals of distributing "commission"—or presents of money, food, clothing, and other necessary or desirable commodities—from Georges and his friends and relatives to a widespread network of people in Haiti. As Georges gives out goods that allow for the subsistence of those in Haiti, he is the recipient of admiration, social recognition, and jealousy. By introducing the members of Georges's extended network of kin and neighbors, the chapter explores both the sweetness and bitterness that pervade these continuing relationships between members of the Haitian diaspora and their family and friends in Haiti.

Chapter 4 begins our look at the links that Haitians in Haiti and the United States are forging between family, nation, and transnational nation-state. We ask whether the transnational terrain on which Georges builds his politics is shared by others in Haiti and find our answers in the poignant statements of the people we interviewed. Exploring the family connections that are maintained between the Haitian diaspora and the people who continue to live in Haiti, we discover a "morality of knowledge." Many of the persons to whom we talked insisted that those who live abroad are obligated to help their kin because "they *know* the conditions in which we live." Underneath this morality of knowledge lies an ideology of blood ties that links all Haitians.

In chapter 5, Georges responds to the racial discrimination that affects his daily life experiences in the United States through transforming transnational family obligations into long-distance nationalism. Coming from their own different but difficult life experiences, people of various classes in Haiti extend the obligations of family to the Haitian nation, and define the nation as existing wherever persons who share "Haitian blood" settle. Even when people migrate and change their legal citizenship, their blood is said "to remain Haitian."

Within the shared language of family, blood, and nation, we discover the multiple meanings of nationalism, a topic we begin to examine in chapter 6. Because of her lifelong anger generated by the subordination that women face in Haiti, Georges's mother, Nadine, first rejected him, and then, fleeing to the United States, rejected her native land of Haiti as well. Many other Haitian women, as they have struggled to contribute to their families in Haiti or as transmigrants, have nevertheless been drawn into a broader political discourse and activities that link family and nation through common "blood." They use nationalist language, including the rhetoric of long-distance nationalism, in ways that destabilize the established meanings of nationalism while fueling social movements for justice and equality. The long-distance nationalism of Haitian women sheds further light on our finding that long-distance nationalism is a polysemous narrative that can be adapted both by the powerful to legitimate the intensification of poverty that accompanies globalization and the most oppressed to struggle against these conditions.

Continuing our study of the many paths toward long-distance nationalism, chapter 7 raises the issue of the second generation. We argue for a definition of the second generation that includes sections of Haitian youth in Haiti and the United States. We note the sharp disjunctures in daily circumstance, ideologies of race and nation, and political experiences that separate young people of Haitian descent who grow up in the United States from those who come of age in Haiti. Yet we find that a vocal sector of young people of Haitian descent in both locations are long-distance nationalists.

In chapter 8, we begin to explore the relationship of long-distance nationalists to the state. Georges finds himself introducing the 287 U.S. students in his course on U.S. law and education to their Constitution as well as constitutional rights and responsibilities. Returning to Haiti, Georges discovered that his own interest in the relationship between a state and its citizens is shared by many of the individuals he interviewed, including young people. Despite two centuries of disappointment, people in Haiti expect the state to be "responsible" and take care of the people. We continue this discussion of the state in chapter 9, asserting that, as articulated by many Haitian leaders, long-distance nationalism and the concept of Haiti as a transnational nation-state perpetuate an image of Haiti as a sovereign state at a time when Haitian political leaders are actually constrained from implementing any form of policy that can meet the needs of the majority of the Haitian people. At the same time, the failures of the Haitian political leadership to produce any meaningful changes in Haiti have led to a general political demoralization. This demoralization, however, is often expressed using the metaphors and symbols of nationalism.

In chapter 10, we examine the utilization by Haiti's disempowered of nationalist ideology to critique oppression and legitimate struggles against it. We look more closely at the disparate political agendas contained within the shared rhetoric of long-distance nationalism. Chapter 11, in conclusion, returns us to the global arena in which Haitian long-distance nationalism is but one example of a worldwide trend. Although the Haitian experience of building a black nation has created a particularly strong sense of national identity, contemporary globalization has produced variants of long-distance nationalism among populations from all over the world. We use the metaphor of a two-way street to think about the very different political directions political movements can take using nationalist rhetoric.[34] Rather than decry its resurgence in the twenty-first century, we suggest examining the direction chosen when people use nationalism to motivate action. On the one hand, the language of nationalism may be used to justify an exclusive claim to territory and resources alleged by others in the name of cultural and biological superiority. On the other hand, as we found in the grassroots women's movement or among the poor of Haiti, the language of nation may be a means of linking one's own struggles to those of people around the world for social and economic justice.

The nationalist passions of persons who live within transnational social fields generate feelings of belonging, as well as identities strong enough to live and die for. It is urgent that all of us understand how and why fierce loyalties, whether to ancestral lands or the United States, are being produced in the midst of a globalized economy, rapid flows of capital, goods, and services, and mass migration. The globalization of the economy, the ways in which migrants relate to countries of settlement such as the United States and their native lands, and the ways in which the United States and other countries of settlement relate to the ancestral homes of these migrants, all call on us to reconsider our understandings of home and country. A rethinking of loyalty, membership, nationalism, and citizenship is clearly in order. We offer this book as a case study with which to begin this collective process.

3

Delivering the Commission:
The Return of the Native

The phone keeps ringing. Rolande's mother calls collect from Haiti with a list of last-minute things that she needs. Rolande's cousins call. To prepare to leave, I call my brother in Haiti. You know it's part of your obligations to call them to let them know you are coming and not to refuse a request. Every time I go home to Haiti, there is a certain tension because everyone imagines that Rolande and I are extremely wealthy. In reality our resources are limited, our budget is tight, and our bills barely paid.

Georges was recalling his departure for Haiti in the summer of 1996. Suitcases, packages in gift wrapping, and clothing and electronic appliances still to be wrapped are strewn around the living room. The room, ordinarily immaculate, is usually used only to formally entertain guests. It is decorated to announce the material and intellectual achievements of the family—diplomas, photos of weddings and graduations, and objects of art. Some of these objects, which signal that the family has money for more than just life's necessities, reflect the style of middle-class interior decoration in Queens, New York, while others are conspicuously different, chosen to celebrate Haitian roots. But on days when a family member leaves for Haiti, the room is the center of activity. Relatives and friends call to ask about sending packages or money to their family waiting in Haiti. Then they arrive to deliver the presents that everyone terms "commission." Meanwhile, phone calls are made to Haiti to announce the exact time of Georges's arrival. For some in Haiti, the presents are more a symbolic renewal of the transnational extensions of family than the fulfillment of pressing needs. For others, the commission is a lifeline that pays for their housing, clothing, schooling, food, and medication.

Packing is a science. Although the airline allows only two suitcases, each weighing seventy pounds, and one carry-on bag of the proper size, it is impossible to refuse a request to carry commissions. It is impossible because for much of the year, the members of the household— Georges, Rolande, and Rolande's cousin Yvette—rely on the same network to carry essential goods, medications, and money to their family members in Haiti. It is also impossible because complete refusal is a violation of one of the most basic of norms that bind friends and family. To refuse would be to deny the relationship. When a cousin arrives with heavy goods to stock a store in Haiti, delicate negotiations ensue about how much Georges can possibly carry. Suitcases are then packed, locked, and weighed so as to ensure against the disaster of challenge at the airport. In such an eventuality, Georges would have to leave part of his personal belongings behind instead of eliminating friends' and relatives' commissions—commissions already announced and awaited.

At the airport, long lines of people stand waiting, surrounded by their own commission-filled luggage. As the line moves slowly toward the check-in desk, Georges visits with a friend he has not seen for more than ten years. Around him are other people also renewing acquaintances and finding friends who are traveling. The sense of community is enhanced by the cluster of friends and family who have brought each traveler to the airport. These people will stay until the travelers move to the boarding area. Georges stands with Rolande and Yvette, who are both emphasizing to him the urgency of delivering the commissions as soon as he arrives. They bombard him with last-minute reminders of whom to call, whom to visit, and what package goes where. They speak loudly in order to be heard over the din of voices.

A degree of tension and anxiety about ticketing and arrangements cuts through the sense of communal assembly and good-natured banter. The tension increases as each traveler and his or her companions approach the check-in desk. Will the luggage size, shape, and weight be found acceptable? Had the Haitian travel agent from whom the ticket was purchased confirmed the seat on the plane? Is there even room on the plane for all those with confirmed reservations? The airport personnel, who are few in number, do little to explain procedures to the passengers during the long wait. They meet each passenger with a chilly, if not disdainful demeanor. The standard security questions, "Did you accept any packages from someone you don't know?" seem to be personalized and threatening, rather than routine airport procedure. At the airport, most ticket agents speak only in English, although a good portion of the travelers are Haitians who had been visiting family members in New York and only speak Kreyòl. Those who do not speak English rely on fellow passengers and their entourage for explanation and encouragement. The authoritarian style of the airport personnel, which echoes the military and political authorities that Haitians know well from their experience with dictatorial regimes in Haiti, contributes to the feeling of community created among those engaged in the project of connecting to Haiti.

His luggage approved and accepted, Georges boards the plane. Almost every passenger on the plane is Haitian. Most of the others are linked to the nongovernmental organizations that are found everywhere in Haiti and bring a constant stream of foreigners, many of whom are white Americans engaging in a new form of philanthropic tourism. These people and the returning Haitian immigrants are currently the only form of tourism Haiti can sustain.

Although Haitian immigrants who return to Haiti to visit are called "*Kreyòl touris*," signaling both their connection and distance from Haiti, most see their trips as part of their pattern of family life and obligation. At the same time, they use these visits to escape the constraints of their life in the United States, and to seek spiritual and emotional renewal. As one of Georges's friends who goes to Haiti every January and July said, "I am somebody only when I am in Haiti."

To be "somebody" means to carve an identity in Haiti that separates you from the experience of blackness in the United States—the stereotypes on television and in film, and the constant scrutiny when you walk down a street, enter a store, or drive your car. It means also to affirm and build a place in Haitian society, announcing with the clothes, goods, and gifts that you are a person of consequence. In a peculiar way, as black immigrants, Haitians are both visible and invisible in the United States. They are visible as the embodiment of the U.S. black/white divide, but invisible as blacks who have their own specific history and culture. Georges constantly faces this contradiction:

In the United States, I am just another black man, a person others may fear and disdain, someone other people cross the street to avoid on a cold, dark New York City night. When that happens, I remember that I am from Haiti, the nation that won its independence by defeating the armies of Napoleon, the sweet Haiti of sunshine and warm breezes, the Haiti of my dreams.

Although our particular trip in 1996 is precipitated by our research on the continuing connection between Haitian immigrants and Haiti, Georges is also embarking on his own voyage of affirmation and renewal.

Meanwhile, in Haiti, Georges's brother, Alfred, waits for a glimpse of Georges with Nina, who had arrived several weeks earlier. They stand behind a chain-link fence with several hundred other anxious relatives and friends of arriving passengers. Those who wait to pick up passengers are not allowed into the airport, and the only waiting areas are cement-covered spaces exposed to the relentless sun and occasional hard rain. The only shade available is a lone tree, and as the sun rises higher in the sky, all who can get near the tree press closer to its diminishing area of shade. Everyone stands except one elderly woman who had lived most of her adult life in New York and then retired to Haiti. Having grown accustomed to more comfort, she waits for her grandchildren while sitting on a folding chair and holding an umbrella. Vendors circulate with small plastic bags of warm "Culligan" water, cups of soda on ice (you take a drink and return the cup), chewing gum, and crackers. Without any announcement of which plane has arrived, and with most planes hours late, Alfred and Nina strain to identify Georges as people, laden with suitcases, boxes, and bags, continuously stream out of the small airport building. Two hours after the plane was due, Alfred asks one of the porters carrying baggage whether the most recently arrived plane was from New York or Miami. "You must not be from here," the porter answers. "Don't you see how these people are dressed?" he says disdainfully. "People coming from New York don't arrive in old clothes."

As she stands waiting for Georges, Nina recalls her own flight to Haiti. For several years, Georges and Nina had been writing that many immigrants from Haiti and numerous migrant-sending countries live their lives across borders, so that they live simultaneously in two or more nation-states. Aboard the plane, Nina saw evidence of this form of migration, not only in the flow of people and goods on the plane but in the conversations around her as well.

When the steward handed out immigration cards to be stamped by Haitian officials on arrival, a young woman in jeans queried, "What address should I put on the card, my address in New York or Haiti?" The steward replied, matter-of-factly, "Whichever address is your permanent address." The passenger continued to be puzzled, and said, "But they are both my permanent addresses."

Another fellow passenger, a dark-skinned woman in her sixties wearing a churchgoing hat, explained that she was headed to Haiti on a religious pilgrimage with other members of her Protestant church in New York. The pastor organized the trip each year to visit a number of congregations. Many of these congregations had churches built for them by Haitians in the United States. She herself had just finished erecting such a church, paying thousands of dollars for the construction and furnishings. She was also going to Haiti for business reasons. Her sons, both professionals and employed full-time in New York, owned a car rental agency in Haiti. It was difficult for them to make the business profitable because vehicles are quickly destroyed by the terrible condition of Haitian roads. She planned to return to Haiti to assist with the selling of old vehicles and buying of new ones. One of her sons made such a visit almost monthly to ensure that their business affairs were in order.

Next to Nina on her flight sat a teenager who was returning with his father to live in Haiti. His mother and younger siblings remained in New York. The teenager's family had planned his education carefully. He began in a prestigious school in Haiti, and then came to New York for high school in order to learn English and receive a U.S. high school diploma. He then returned to Haiti to obtain his baccalaureate, the degree awarded in Haiti, France, and Canada after a fifth year of high school and a competitive exam. On receiving this degree, he would be able to apply for a university education in both the U.S. and francophone worlds, and function successfully in both milieus.

The airport scenes Nina witnessed in New York and Port-au-Prince, as well as her casual conversations in the airplane, convey to her the intensity of the interconnectedness between Haitian immigrants and Haiti. Only as the months pass and the research proceeds, however, does she fully comprehend the extent to which Haitians in Haiti and the United States are separated yet connected and distant but close.

Finally, Georges arrives. Alfred loads Georges's bulging suitcases onto the back of the truck, and we drive the six miles from the airport to Alfred's house on La Plaine. As soon as dinner is over, Georges unpacks the presents he has brought for Alfred's family. Prior to coming to Haiti, Georges and Rolande had contacted Alfred to inquire about what type of goods his household needs, and thus, Georges brings gifts of convenience rather than survival. He carries lightbulbs that save electricity and extra fans to make the nights more comfortable. But in bringing gifts for this household, Georges and Rolande did not only rely on requests. During each of her visits, Rolande surveys the types of modern electronic appliances owned by Alfred's family and decides what would be useful. She left behind her pocket calculator in 1995, and after her return to the United States, sent a cordless phone.

Unlike many middle-class houses in Haiti that flaunt the latest in consumer fashions imported from Miami, the Fouron house is not elaborately decorated. There are no tile-lined Jacuzzis or theater-type televisions. This is not a household that has stressed conspicuous consumption, and the family has invested any available money into expanding the size of the house rather than in furnishing it or utilizing elaborate building materials. When they purchase food, clothing, and household goods, the family tries to buy goods produced in Haiti, if at all possible. But gifts from abroad, which expand the level of practical convenience, are accepted and appreciated.

Alfred is Georges's older brother. He is thin and lithe, with a bounce to his step and a ready grin. He looks younger than the bearded, graying, professorial Georges. Alfred is currently the director of a nongovernmental organization funded from abroad. His wife, Andrea, teaches sewing in a trade school. Over the years, they bought land and slowly constructed a house that currently has fourteen rooms and three bathrooms. The solar panels, wells, and pumps ensure that there is always electricity and water. The size of the house and its facilities means that Alfred's home is now able to serve as a base area for visits from both Georges and Rolande's family, as well as any of the friends they bring with them to Haiti. Alfred and Andrea's household includes Andrea's ailing father, three adult children (ages twenty-seven, twenty-five, and twenty-one), and one younger child, Andrea's niece, Stephanie. Stephanie had been taken in as a daughter when Andrea's sister died soon after childbirth. Such adoptions and rearrangements of household membership following the death of a woman in childbirth are commonplace in Haiti. The statistic that the average Haitian life span is only fifty-five years is shaped by frequent deaths of women in childbirth, as well as an infant mortality rate of 13 percent.[1] The household also includes a live-in maid. Because so many people are desperate for food and shelter in Haiti, middle-class families are almost always able to afford live-in domestic servants.

Although Georges has been traveling all day, he gets back in Alfred's truck a few minutes after dinner. There are people to be visited, kinship ties to be confirmed and renewed, and commissions to be delivered. However, the road into Port-au-Prince, always difficult and slow going, is almost completely blocked this night. Delivering the commissions has to be spread throughout the week. Only four weeks later Rolande arrives, and the circuit of visiting, renewal of ties, and distribution of commissions is retraced, this time with increased emphasis on Rolande's kinship connections.

Reconnection and Redistribution

The circumstances of the various households within Georges and Rolande's visiting and distribution circuit are a microcosm of the various forces that link emigrants and the people and countries they left behind. The ties between each household we visit as Georges delivers his commissions in Haiti place us on the terrain of transnational interconnection. It is a domain that is well-known to migrants and their dependents back home, but remains an unexplored vista to the majority of people living in the United States. It is a realm in which questions of family values, economy, politics, and the relationship between self and nation merge.

The first few days of formal visiting are not orchestrated by Georges but by Alfred. It is often the case that the traveler's visits reflect the host family's own agenda in addition to the circuit of the migrant's connections. During Georges's visit, Alfred, as host, takes him to people who are not presently receiving gifts or are not emotionally close to Georges, Rolande, or Yvette. In fact, the very first night Alfred brings Georges to households that Alfred wants included in the support network, although nothing was specifically said about this at the time.

Among these people is Elizabeth, a younger sister of Georges and Alfred. In her thirties, her face still young yet becoming weary, Elizabeth's body lines and language are softer and her demeanor less assertive than

Georges's other siblings, perhaps because her parentage and links to the Fouron family are rather newly established. Elizabeth is a daughter of Georges's father but not by his wife and was only acknowledged by him when she was a teenager and Georges had already settled in New York. So Georges had only met Elizabeth on his trips back to Haiti. Now Elizabeth is struggling to support herself on the salary of a day care teacher. This means that she has so little money she can't afford even a rented room and cannot find an acceptable husband. Alfred pays Elizabeth's rent in a boarding house, and it is to this house that Alfred brings Georges. By prioritizing the visit to Elizabeth, Alfred is calling Georges's attention to the dilemma. The visit expresses, without words, the widespread conception that those who have emigrated have the resources to support all family members left behind. And if the emigrant is a college professor, then of course he must have enough funds to meet their needs. Those who live the daily realities of Haiti cannot comprehend Georges and Rolande's monthly struggles to pay their bills.

Some of my family in Haiti see me as the big professor and know that my children went to the best universities. They don't understand that we borrowed from our pension to pay the tuitions, which were more than my entire university salary, even after financial aid. So they think Georges has it, so let Georges do it. I wanted a family meeting to find a way to help Elizabeth.

Over the course of Georges's visit, Alfred and Georges decide that a possible solution to Elizabeth's troubles would be for her family abroad and Alfred here in Haiti to provide Elizabeth with money to start some kind of very small business venture. Buying charcoal from the rural areas as a wholesaler and distributing it through retailers in Port-au-Prince is one option. This could supplement her job. She would need one thousand dollars in order to begin. This seems a better plan than if Georges were to send money to support her every month, which would make Elizabeth dependent on remittances. As it is, Elizabeth is receiving sporadic remittances from Georges and Alvin, one of Georges's brothers in New York. Georges delivers some money from Alvin as part of the first night's visiting.

Next, Alfred takes us to visit Yvette's sister-in-law, Mirelle, and her family in the poorer section of Delmas, a middle-class settlement near Port-au-

Prince. Mirelle's household is almost entirely dependent on remittances from abroad. Mirelle is a widow. The only legacy Yvette's brother left his wife and five children when he died in 1984 was his connection to two siblings, Yvette and Candio, who had been able to migrate and settle in the United States. Candio lives in Boston, where he established his own household with his wife and children. Since their brother's death, Yvette and Candio have been struggling to help Mirelle raise her children. Yvette and Candio pay rent on a house, and send clothes, consumer goods, and money for food and water. The household boasts a color television and cassette sound system with large speakers. Yvette and Candio also have paid Mirelle's children's school tuition, with the hope that the youngsters would succeed, and thus be able to support themselves and the rest of their household. Even when children are grown into adults in Haiti, they may remain unemployed and need continued support from family abroad, unless they have adequate education, connections, and luck.

So far, Yvette and Candio's strategy of investing in the education of their nieces and nephews has been of little avail, and the sending of commission continues. The oldest niece, educated through high school and secretarial school, has moved in with a man in the neighborhood and is not contributing to the family. Another niece married and had an elaborate wedding financed by her family abroad. A few years later, she died giving birth to her second child. A nephew who still lives in the household does have a job as a clerk in a private maritime operation, but the salary from this type of job cannot even pay the 5,000 Haitian dollars a year (U.S.$1,666) that it takes to rent Mirelle's small house.

Yvette and Candio's plan to increase the self-sufficiency of Mirelle's family in Haiti has now focused on the youngest daughter, Lourdes, who is just finishing high school. Only nineteen, yet well educated and assertive, Lourdes is currently the major recipient of gifts. Her education, together with gifts of stylish clothes, toiletries, purses, and jewelry, enhances her presentation of self that her family hopes will facilitate the necessary contacts to get into the university or to obtain a job or visa. This special treatment, however, has led her to believe that she has a superior status and makes her unwilling to look for occupations that she considers to be beneath her. In the meantime, despite all the efforts of family abroad, Mirelle's household continues to depend almost entirely on remittances. The flow of money makes it possible for the family to lease a home in Delmas.

Although the modest house is in one of the less prosperous corners of the neighborhood, it is still Delmas, a respectable address.

Delmas is a municipality that extends between Port-au-Prince, the capital, and the wealthy suburb of Petionville. In all its startling contrast, Delmas stands as a monument to the ongoing connections between Haitian immigrants and the world they left behind in Haiti. Many of the houses are new, having been constructed in the last twenty years by Haitians who live or have lived abroad. Most of these houses, surrounded by elaborate walls and gated driveways, seem rather substantial from the outside. Their size, design, and the quality of their building materials announce the prosperity attained by their owners. But many are dream houses, seemingly frozen halfway between aspirations and materiality. Several stories high, with glass windows and multiple rooms, they are raw and unfinished, surrounded by rusting iron rods and other pieces of building materials. Their owners often find that they cannot achieve the degree of economic security that would allow them to live in Haiti permanently. Therefore, they either install relatives in their half-built homes or rent them to tenants. These tenants spend most of their income on rent or obtain rent, as Mirelle does, from family who live abroad. Even houses that are no more than shells are usually occupied, frequently in such cases by "guardians" rather than formal tenants. Guardians are, in fact, usually squatters, whose residence in partially completed houses is acknowledged by the owner. In exchange for some rudimentary shelter, guardians take on the responsibility of ensuring that other squatters don't overrun the house, and that thieves don't tear it apart and sell the pieces to other would-be returnees.

In Mirelle's section, most of the streets are unpaved. There is no sewer or public water system, the bottled water sold in Delmas is expensive, and the electrical connections are often only available by jury-rigging wire to tap into the few legal electricity lines. Moreover, at the end of the street, there is an entire squatter settlement called Site Okay with houses of cement blocks or scrap material erected on state lands. Mirelle's three-room leased house has a wall and gate around the yard. But a flow of neighbors come through the gate and depend on the small amenities that the home offers: the rain-collecting cistern that is used for bathing and washing clothes, electricity, a color television, and a gas stove. Neighbors look over the wall, call out greetings, exchange gossip or advice, and witness the arrival of guests carrying packages. Since guests frequently are not invited into the house but are seated instead in the yard, their numbers and characteristics are readily observable to the neighbors who routinely come into the yard or look over the wall. Thus, the very house and its cistern, together with the resources delivered to Mirelle, become part of what economically sustains a broad network of people.

The next stop on the commission route was Agenisse's house. Agenisse is distantly related to Rolande in terms of genealogy, but is close to her in terms of the cultivated ties that create mutual obligation. Agenisse's mother is Rolande's mother's niece. Rolande's parents took in Agenisse and her parents and other siblings when Agenisse was a child. When François Duvalier became president of Haiti in 1957, Agenisse's father abandoned his job in a distillery and swore not to work as long as Duvalier was in power. Duvalier became president-for-life, remaining Haiti's dictator until 1971. Agenisse's family would have starved if her mother had not provided for the family by sewing and if Rolande's parents had not taken them in. Hence, Rolande and Agenisse, second cousins, grew up in the same household.

Agenisse, a secretary with a decent-paying job, is married to Antonio, an engineer who was educated in Haiti and works for a local company. Her household maintains strong ties to family in the United States, Germany, and Canada, where members of her family have settled. Agenisse's household reflects the security of steady middle-class incomes and its decor speaks of several types of transnational connections. Built on a street in Delmas, full of new and relatively completed houses, Agenisse's home has flagstone outside walls and louvered glass windows. The house is furnished with solid, stylish, wooden furniture, and has modern toilet and kitchen fixtures. The neighborhood has no piped-in water, so the plumbing did not work until special arrangements were made to bring water into the house— first by tanks on the roof, and later through the construction of an underground cistern to store both rainwater and purchased water. The material to build the house came from Agenisse's husband's family in New York, as did the two expensive vehicles parked inside the gates of the house. Unlike the situation in Mirelle's house, where the delivery of commissions was watched by and redistributed to neighbors, the delivery of Agenisse's presents takes place behind the carefully locked high gates that close off the house and yard.

Given the employment status and transnational connections of Agenisse's household, the gifts from Rolande and Georges are meant to cement social relations rather than provide substantive support. They include small items of clothing and toys. While Georges was brought to visit Agenisse as part of the first round of symbolic visits, it was Rolande who sent the gifts. Agenisse is part of Rolande's, not Georges's, kinship network. Underneath the connections that link households in the United States with those in Haiti, Haitian immigrant men and women have their own set of kinship ties that draw both genders into specific commitments and obligations.

As Georges drops off commissions and renews ties during the evenings of his first week in Haiti, he continues to experience the differing degrees of prosperity, status, economic hardship, and political insecurity in the lives of the people in his network. His visit to another sister, Janine, brought him to Petionville, which sits on a mountain overlooking the urban sprawl of Port-au-Prince. Janine lives in a beautifully furnished, stately old house. Her home is typical of the former elegance of Petionville, which was once an exclusive suburb, and still has shops, clubs, and neighborhoods that cater to those with wealth and power. Janine is as elegant and stately as her house. She was educated (as a health administrator and nurse) in the United States and Canada. This summer, she is working in a clinic for slum dwellers, supported by the U.S. Agency for International Development.[2]

Janine is divorced and supports a teenage daughter at a private school of sufficient excellence to prepare students for the highly prestigious secondary school degree sanctioned by the French government. Janine's income is not enough to maintain her elegant style of life in her rented house and deal with emergencies such as the breakdown of an automobile. On his first visit, Georges delivers money from his brother, Alvin, to Janine. As the summer proceeds, Georges, Alfred, and Nina contribute money to fix Janine's jeep, which we borrow to go visit Rolande's parents and proves to need major engine work.

While we were able to visit Janine in the cool and quiet of her own home, the same was not possible for other persons in Georges's network. For example, Mimrose, one of Yvette and Candio's sisters, lives in a house with no number on a street with no name. Her meager dwelling is down a back alley that is an addition to an addition to an official street. Even the configuration of city streets signals Mimrose's lack of social standing, her insignificance to the world around her. To locate the dwelling of any person who lives there, you have to find someone who already knows where that person lives. At any rate, Mimrose did not want to receive us in her single rented room, which barely provided shelter for her and her children. So we located Mimrose at the shop in the center of Port-au-Prince where she sells fritay-fried bananas, plantain, fish, pork rind, and conch. Fifty-five years of age, Mimrose's style is quite different from Yvette's quiet, modest manner. A plump woman with dark skin and a warm, contagious smile, her welcome to Georges was friendly, in a Kreyòl filled with double entendre jokes about sexuality that were not an invitation but a shared conversation about the ironies of life. Before she accepted the money and gifts we had brought from Yvette, Mimrose made sure that she treated each of us to a cool bottle of soda, and showed us pictures of a son, a fine-looking young man dressed in cap and gown, who had just graduated from high school.

The shop where Mimrose conducts her small business is neither owned nor rented by her. She has an arrangement with the owner of the building to sell her cooked snacks in front of the shop at night. Mimrose and her common-law husband, Henri, who lives in the United States, developed this commercial activity so that she would not be entirely dependent on remittances sent by family abroad. Yet most of the money to support Mimrose and her six children continues to come from her siblings and common-law husband living in the United States. Georges brings Mimrose money from Yvette.

Mimrose would like to join Henri in the United States. Henri's legal status as a permanent resident helped him obtain employment and begin the process of application that will eventually bring his children to the United States as permanent residents. Henri cannot apply to have Mimrose join him in the United States as a permanent resident, however. He is blocked by U.S. immigration law because, although she is the mother of his children, Mimrose was never legally married to Henri. He is afraid to return to Haiti and marry her. Under the Duvalier regime, Henri was a street *macoute*—a member of Duvalier's paramilitary—who was equipped with a gun but no salary, and lived by the extortion and intimidation of his neighbors. Henri fled Haiti after the fall of the Duvalier dictatorship in 1986 and has not visited his family for ten years, fearful that if he returns his former victims will take revenge. He came to the United States without papers, apparently receiving some kind of assistance from powerful people so that he was able to regularize his legal status by claiming asylum as a political refugee. If those he harmed learned about his refugee status, their anger would increase, since most of the people beaten, raped, and robbed by the macoute during the Duvalier regime and subsequent military governments were not given asylum by the United States.

Like so many transmigrants, even though he has legal papers, Henri has been able to lead only the most marginal of existences. He works for minimum wage at a supermarket collecting shopping carts in the parking lot. His job offers him no health benefits, and in the winter of 1996, he continued to work despite the fact that he had pneumonia. Pressed by his family obligations in Haiti and bills in Boston, he could not afford to be sick, and therefore lose wages and probably his job. When he passed out in the frozen parking lot and was rescued by his fellow workers, he feared the bills for an ambulance and took a bus to the hospital. Because the job was full-time and he became ill at work, he was able to receive workers' compensation. The compensation, however, was even less money than the $160 a week he was taking home, and he returned to work almost immediately. Soon he was sick again.

Because he was a permanent resident, Henri was eligible for Medicaid. But his efforts to bring his children to the United States could have been negatively affected if he received such federal services. Recent changes in U.S. immigration law prevent those who have received government benefits from sponsoring the immigration of other family members. The emergency room and daily hospital bills were each more than his weekly wages. The two hospitalizations that Henri experienced in 1996 were disasters for his family in Haiti. Meanwhile, because he cannot afford long-distance service on his telephone, his family in Haiti was unaware that he was not working and money would not be forthcoming. By 1997, Henri had developed a stomach ulcer.

At the same time that Henri was sick in Boston, Mimrose and one of her children became ill in Haiti. She had an abscessed tooth. One of her children also had some form of infection. Without money from her husband, Mimrose and her child could not afford to go to a medical doctor. They did go to a local healer, though, and both recovered.

Mimrose's current ability to support herself through her small business is constricted by the political situation in Haiti. Politics and personal survival are intertwined themes that form part of the daily experience and consciousness of persons of all classes. In Mimrose's case, the food products she is trying to sell are ones that are usually purchased and consumed from early evening to late at night. Unfortunately, there has not been much nightly traffic in Port-au-Prince for years because of the insecurity of the political situation. Moreover, street crime is on the rise, filling the nights with danger and death. Each morning, the dead bodies in the streets are testimony to the growing violent crime that accompanies the lack of employment and desperate search for income. Young men, whose despair leads them to commit small crimes, compete in the streets with disgruntled former macoute who are armed and equally without hope. They are increasingly joined by youth with criminal records in the United States who have been shipped back by the U.S. government. The only world they know is that of U.S. inner-city neighborhoods. Among the many U.S. exports to Haiti is the crime wave brought by these youthful deportees. In the general atmosphere of insecurity, there is no one to look to for safety. The criminal justice system does not function, and people use violence to settle personal vendettas, misdeeds, debts, and disputes. So when Georges arrives in Haiti, Mimrose's business is providing little support to the family, and she and her children are even more dependent than usual on remittances from Yvette, Henri, and Candio.

Georges's circuit of distribution brings him to visit another business that is faltering under Haiti's terrible economic conditions. It is a gift shop owned by Georges's cousin's husband, Harry. In this case, the commissions take the form not of gifts but of small bits of merchandise to replenish the stock. Georges's cousin Julienne had been one of the numerous transmigrants who establish businesses in Haiti, and then alternate between returning to run them and trying to manage them while living abroad. Harry and Julienne began the gift shop when they returned to Haiti in 1983. Trained as an engineer, Harry was lured back to Haiti by a chance to work in his profession, something he could not do in the United States, and a longing for the leisurely life of a professional position in Haiti, which includes a house, servants, and new cars. But, knowing government employment is insecure and the salary inadequate for the lifestyle they desired, Julienne opened a gift shop. The couple took trips to the United States and Canada to stock the store. Through all the family's losses, dislocations, and pain—Harry lost his job; Julienne developed breast cancer, returned to the States and died; and Harry moved to New York with the children—the gift shop remained open and continued to be stocked by the delivery of commissions.

Hometown

Although members of their family have settled in the capital city of Port-au-Prince, Georges and Rolande did not grow up there. Many family members remain in their hometown of Aux Cayes, a small city in the south of Haiti.

Therefore, the round of visiting is not complete until both Georges and Rolande return to Aux Cayes. Towns and hamlets throughout Haiti, although almost unreachable by road, have become linked to the United States by the steady stream of money and gifts from people who have settled abroad. Most of these gifts originate in family networks, but many small towns and hamlets also receive support from their residents who have settled abroad and then band together to form "regional associations" that sponsor small development projects to benefit their hometowns.

In the summer of 1996, Georges and Nina wait for Rolande, Leah, and Leah's friend Cynthia to arrive from New York before they make the almost-five-hour trip to Aux Cayes. The road to Aux Cayes is one of the few paved routes connecting Port-au-Prince to its provinces, but the difficulty of the trip makes Aux Cayes feel much more remote than 180 kilometers. Only the first half of the road should actually be called paved. After that, potholes are more frequent than pavement. Vehicles loaded down with passengers and cargo zigzag back and forth in the path of oncoming traffic to try to find areas of solid roadway. Sport utility vehicles, trucks, and jeeps are much more likely to make it to Aux Cayes than cars.

Still, reaching Aux Cayes by road is easier than it was in Georges's youth, when the road was not paved at all. During the rainy season, the trip took more than a day and required an overnight stop. Georges had never made the trip until he left Aux Cayes to take his high school final examinations, which were only given in the capital. Today, daily buses carry passengers and goods between the two cities. Yet, in some ways, Aux Cayes seems more closely connected to Miami and New York than Port-au-Prince. For a short period of time in the 1970s and 1980s, because of their local building activities and coastal locations, the seaside towns around Aux Cayes were able to send extremely poor people to the United States. Usually, the poor or landless cannot emigrate unless they receive money from more prosperous family members who have preceded them abroad. As a result of the migration of family members and the establishment of transnational family networks, many poor people from the rural areas near Aux Cayes were also able to move to the city, build houses, and start small businesses. The city is no longer the bustling port of Georges's youth; its sugar refinery and other local industries were shut down by the Duvalier regime, and were not replaced by other productive activities. Nonetheless, the population of Aux Cayes has grown from perhaps 25,000 in the 1950s to approximately 75,000 in 1996. An entire marshy area that once separated the center of the city from the sea has been partially drained to provide space for the poor people who once lived by growing crops in the rural areas around Aux Cayes. Georges, Rolande, and Yvette are among the thousands of former residents who send and bring remittances. These remittances have taken over the former role of industry as fuel for the economy.

Recently, Rolande has been using her vacation from work almost every summer to come to Haiti and visit Aux Cayes. While her mother, who everyone calls Man-Nana, age eighty-six, travels back and forth between Haiti and the United States, her father, affectionately known as Papa-Dyo, eighty-eight years old, insists on staying put in his hometown. Tall and thin, with a commanding presence, Papa-Dyo was a tax collector for most of his life. Rolande's parents' home was built primarily with money sent by Rolande and Georges a decade after they settled in New York. It has a telephone and electricity. An electric pump brings water to a tank on the roof to provide running water for an indoor kitchen as well as a bathroom, shower, and toilet. There is an additional kitchen for charcoal cooking and an outhouse for servants in the backyard.

Built in the traditional style of architecture of Aux Cayes, the house was constructed to bestow prestige on its residents by becoming a seamless part of the old high-status neighborhood that stands next to the cathedral. Its very similarity with the rest of the neighborhood marks its residents as persons of substance. This architectural style stands in sharp contrast to that of the homes built by prosperous transmigrants in other sections of Aux Cayes and in Port-au-Prince. The newer remittance houses announce the owner's wealth and ties to the diaspora through an architecture that is more reflective of suburban Florida than Haiti.

We arrive at Papa-Dyo and Man-Nana's house with vast suitcases filled with gifts. Many are practical. There is sugar, powdered milk, batteries, canned milk, clothes, radios, towels, and soap. There is also perfume for Man-Nana, and candy and high-calorie milkshakes for Papa-Dyo, who is ill with a slowly progressing throat cancer for which he has refused treatment, fearing that any kind of intervention will shorten his life. Some of the goods in the heavy suitcases are stock for Man-Nana's small business. From her front room, Man-Nana sells a narrow range of food products. She buys cans of evaporated milk, fresh rolls, sugar, and rice in bulk, and then resells them in small amounts—one six-ounce can of milk or a roll at a time—to people in the neighborhood. Because she has a refrigerator and electricity, when there is electricity in Aux Cayes, she can sometimes provide ice and cold soda. Man-Nana's profits amount to a few dollars, but the little she does earn allows her to stretch Papa-Dyo's small government pension along with the remittances of money and goods she receives from her daughter.

Some of the gifts Georges and Rolande bring include lovely dresses and hair clips for Annette, a ten-year-old girl who Georges and Rolande are in the process of adopting. This year's visit to Aux Cayes is not only to maintain ties but also to formalize a new link of kinship by finalizing Annette's adoption. Annette and her brother were left orphans in Aux Cayes. She is the niece of one of Man-Nana's live-in maids, who is actually also a distant relative of Man-Nana's. The children have closer relatives than Rolande, but these relatives cannot afford to feed two more people. The relatives kept the young boy; Man-Nana took Annette. Children such as Annette are often taken into households as servants. Sometimes they are abused, physically or sexually, and sometimes they are educated and become a form of poor relation. Man-Nana generally insists that some of her servants' small salaries be used to pay school fees so that these young people become literate and have some opportunity for future social mobility.

Papa-Dyo and Man-Nana's household already had three young women servants, including Annette's aunt, who all take care of their aging employers. The relationship is both tender and tyrannical on the part of the elders; it is affectionate and resistant on the part of the young women. In Annette's case, Georges and Rolande decided on adoption. Their two children are almost grown, and although fluent in Kreyòl, their current ties to Haiti are weak. Georges and Rolande plan to bring Annette to the United States when she is older; she will be a daughter who can provide a strengthened connection to Haiti and to family in Aux Cayes. She will also be a daughter who can provide assistance and companionship as Georges and Rolande age; in the meantime, her presence in the family's household in Aux Cayes keeps the elders young.

In taking Annette into her household and in urging that some of her young servants' salaries be invested in their schooling, Man-Nana—like Rolande and Georges—continues a cross-class pattern of maintaining solidarity and sponsoring social mobility. Man-Nana herself was a beneficiary of such cross-class ties. As a young girl, she came from a rural hamlet to live with Madame Gerald, a rich woman in Aux Cayes. Madame Gerald had been born into a very poor family. A striking beauty, she had married the son of one of the leading families of Aux Cayes. He had wed her despite the opposition of his family. Madame Gerald had then taken over her husband's business, become wealthy, and used her wealth to educate her family. She educated Man-Nana and ensured that she make a good marriage to Papa-Dyo, a man with an education and a prestigious government position as a tax collector. Her connection to the family deepened when Madame Gerald's sister became Rolande's godmother. During our trip, we all paid a visit to Rolande's godmother.

Georges has one sister, Marianne, who remains in Aux Cayes, where she has lived her whole life. Visits with Marianne are part of his round of delivering commissions and maintaining family ties. Marianne has never traveled abroad. She differs from Janine, her urbane sister in Port-au-Prince, in the style of her house, clothes, and appearance. Darker in color, plainer in dress, Marianne, a public school teacher, lives with her husband, Pierre, and five children. They reside on the edge of town in a house that the couple has slowly built. Although it is solid and roomy, their home is located in a neighborhood without status. The house is reached by crossing a stream that has become an open sewer. Marianne and Pierre's home was built not from remittances but through a loan program sponsored by the Haitian Agriculture Department, where Pierre is an agricultural technician. Until recently, he was doing rather well by leasing state lands for a minimal sum of money and growing rice, which he stored in his house and sold. Rice growing had been lucrative before the current flood of cheap rice imported from the United States entered Haiti. Many Haitians blame the increasingly desperate situation in Haiti on the influx of imported food and food assistance that provides cheaper food yet also destroys Haitian agriculture, making the country even more dependent on foreign aid.

The worsening situation has made Marianne and Pierre eager to emigrate. This was not previously the case. As soon as Georges became a U.S. citizen in 1980, he offered to apply for visas for his parents and siblings. At that time, Marianne and Pierre were doing fairly well in Haiti and did not want to leave. In addition, being Jehovah's Witnesses and believing that the world was coming to an end, they did not see a reason to migrate. Georges begged them at the time to "do it for your children, if not for yourself." Another sister and two brothers accepted the offered visas in the 1980s, and now live in Brooklyn.

Times are harder now, and the sporadic assistance that Marianne and Pierre receive from family abroad is welcome, if bitter in taste. These days, Marianne perceives herself as the poor relation compared to her siblings who live abroad, and whose lives seem full of wealth and glamour in comparison. It will now take ten or more years for Georges to get a visa for his sister. U.S. citizens can get visas to bring siblings to the States, but there is a ranking of the types of relatives who can be brought and siblings are a low-ranked category. By the time Marianne arrives, she will be too old to work. Georges and Rolande will have to support her while she goes through the lengthy and expensive procedure of bringing her husband and children to the United States.

Rolande is an only child and the extended family to whom she is closest is Agenisse's in Port-au-Prince. Consequently, she did not make many family visits in Aux Cayes. Nevertheless, both Georges and Rolande find themselves providing food and small amounts of money to a broad circle of dependents who supply various forms of assistance and companionship to Rolande's parents in return. Many of these people are aware of Georges and Rolande's visit, as well as the money and goods they have brought. As a result, each day a stream of visitors comes into the house. They greet Georges and Rolande, and then proceed to the back of the house, where Man-Nana receives her lesser-status neighbors.

Man-Nana will call me on the side and say, "Se youn ti kichoy yo vin chèche" *[It is a little tidbit they are looking for]. And I will ask,* "How much should I give?" *And she will say,* "Five dollars or twenty dollars." *Twenty Haitian dollars is about six U.S. Not too much. But if it is someone who is really someone she is close to, she will say,* "You know how deep your pocket is. Give her whatever you can afford." *Then I know I am in trouble. I can't give that person just six U.S. dollars.*

Some of the people Man-Nana and Yvette support used to render assistance to the household but are no longer able to do so. In Haiti, there is no system of social security. In addition, few jobs other than government employment offer any type of pension. The old and disabled are thus generally dependent either on their kin or the charity of persons they have previously served. Asefi, for example, is now in her sixties, and her body is thin and weak; she is no longer able to perform the hard labor by which she made a living. She has a daughter in Port-au-Prince, but the daughter has abandoned her. Asefi used to do laundry for Man-Nana, picking up clothes and taking them to the river. So that she will not be homeless, Yvette pays the yearly lease money for Asefi's room. On this visit, Georges and Rolande deliver the lease money, adding some of their own to ensure that Asefi has something to eat. Man-Nana pays for Asefi's food and regularly sends her money for medicine. The money that Man-Nana uses for this purpose comes from the funds sent to her by Rolande and Georges.

Asefi is not the only disabled person that Georges and Rolande support. They also help two Pauls.

When I was a boy, I used to hang out at the shop of cabinetmaker Boss Duchamel. He had been a student at the vocational school that my father headed. During that time I got to know Paul, who was an apprentice in the shop. One year, I went to Aux Cayes and inquired about Paul, and I learned that he had suffered a stroke and had no means of support. So I looked for him and I found him. What flashed in my mind was my father, who had also had a stroke, and so I decided to send money every month for him. Because I adopted him, Rolande's mother, Man-Nana, adopted him, and if I don't send money, she sends money. But he moved, and she became concerned and sent someone to look for him. Another Paul who had suffered a stroke heard that Man-Nana was looking for a Paul with a stroke. He passed for the real Paul. Man-Nana would give the money to a servant, who gave it to Paul. She thought she was giving it to the first Paul, and it was the second Paul. Then I returned and sent the word out that I would like to see Paul. The second Paul showed up, and I said, "But you are not the real Paul." Paul the second said, "But my name is Paul, and I had a stroke and I was a cabinetmaker. I have no support and I didn't have anything." There was no point in getting mad at him. I said, "What the heck," and gave him the money. The next day the real Paul came, so now I am supporting two Pauls.

As shown above, the distribution from the diaspora spreads small bits of cash and goods through a network that extends far beyond the immediate families of those who live abroad. Haitians in the diaspora provide vitally needed resources to a wide range of people in Haiti. The different family units are connected to the Haitian diaspora to form a transnational social field—a terrain of personal networks that connect people in Haiti, the United States, and countries such as Canada.

The questions we came to Haiti to answer were informed by an understanding of the dependencies and anger, discord and jealousies, as well as strength and resiliency, of family ties. As researchers, we needed to know whether, when we looked beyond Georges's family, we would find similar dynamics of connection and disjuncture. We wanted to know how those living in Haiti and hoping for remittances viewed Haiti, the Haitian diaspora, and the United States. Did those with little or no connection with persons abroad differ in their views from persons who had close ties with family and friends in the United States? Did those with few or no ties have a more critical or idealized view of the diaspora and its relationship to Haiti, and a different relationship to the United States? We needed to know more about the width and depth of the transnational social fields being built on a foundation of distribution networks. And we needed to know if there was a relationship between the very personalized reciprocities and the broader political questions of citizenship, views of the state, loyalty, and identity. So, having delivered Georges and Rolande's commissions, we began to conduct our interviews. As we spoke with people in Port-au-Prince and Aux Cayes, a narrative of the connections between transnational family experiences and identification with Haiti as a nation began to emerge. As they described their relationship to Haiti and the Haitian diaspora, they also told us about their vision of the United States.

GEORGES'S FAMILY PHOTOS

Georges's father and two of his sisters in Aux Cayes, Haiti, in 1962. Courtesy of Fouron family.

The year before Georges left Haiti, he was a student at Ecole Normale (Teachers College) in Port-au-Prince, which entitled him to use the French · Institute library. Courtesy of Fouron family.

Georges's passport, 1969.

Shortly after his arrival in New York during his first trip to the United States in 1969, Georges posed on the top of an apartment building for this picture, which he sent home to Haiti. The inscription on the back speaks of his "nostalgia" for Haiti, a theme that has marked his more than thirty years of settle-ment in the United States. Courtesy of Fouron family.

Georges's parents' passport, which they used when they left Haiti in 1978.

Georges's parents in 1988, after they had arrived to live with him in Brooklyn, New York. Georges's mother immediately adopted the dress style of the United States. In Haiti, women of her generation generally did not wear pants. Courtesy of Fouron family.

Georges stands in front of Teachers College, Columbia University, New York City, in 1980 after receiving his master's degree in education. Fouron family photograph.

Georges, waiting for his daughter to arrive for a visit to Haiti, stands hot and tired in a crowded, unshaded area outside the airport in Port-au-Prince, 1996. Courtesy of Fouron family.

INTERVIEWS

Georges interviewing a Haitian
woman in Delmas, Haiti, summer
1996. Photo by Fabienne Molin.

Nina interviewing a Haitian woman
in Delmas, Haiti, summer 1996.
Photo by Fabienne Molin.

WALL PAINTINGS

The Haitian people cheer from the sidelines as the U.S.-led military force returns Aristide to power in an operation called "uphold democracy." Wall painting, Port-au-Prince, Haiti, 1994. Photo from collection of Georges Fouron.

There are many levels of meaning in this wall painting. The drummer provides the African rhythms of Vodou, the rhythms of Africa that blend with other elements of the Haitian people. Together, the figures express the aspirations of the grassroots movement for a brighter future. The map of Haiti in the center of this wall painting speaks of a "Haiti for Tomor-row." Photo from collection of Georges Fouron.

The poor—portrayed as crying, silenced, and faceless—saw in the return of Aristide the resolution of the problems of poverty and misery. Wall painting, Port-au-Prince, Haiti, 1994. Photo from collection of Georges Fouron.

The grassroots movement's demands for justice, work, liberty, reconciliation, and democracy are surrounded by a map of Haiti, a rooster (a symbol for Aristide), mulatto and black reconciliation, and a lamp that may represent either enlightenment or Vodou. Photo from collection of Georges Fouron.

The wealthy Haitian mulattoes and the *Makout* rip Haiti apart, under the caption *ace* (enough). Wall painting, Port-au-Prince, Haiti, 1994. Photo from collection of Georges Fouron.

The Diaspora Bar, Aux Cayes, Haiti, summer 1995. Many Haitian businesses, supported by funds from family abroad, are named Diaspo or Dyaspora (Diaspora) to signal the continuing ties between those abroad and those in Haiti. Photo by Nina Glick Schiller.

The sign advertises the benefits of transnational telephonic communication, advising passersby to "Call the United States collect. Everyone, everywhere is close by." Graffiti on the sign denounces privatization. Photo by Nina Glick Schiller.

Signs such as this have proliferated in Haitian rural areas linking development to the actions of foreign states and nongovernmental organizations from abroad. This project was building outhouses with funding from the European Community. Photo by Nina Glick Schiller.

DEMONSTRATIONS OF TRANSBORDER CITIZENS

In 1980, tens of thousands of Haitians marched across the Brooklyn Bridge while calling the U.S. Food and Drug Administration a liar, coward, and racist for linking Haitians to the AIDS epidemic. Haitian nationalism and a sense of U.S.-based civil rights fueled the protest. Photo by Georges Fouron.

Demonstrators waving Haitian and U.S. flags march to a police precinct in Brooklyn, New York, to protest the police assault on Haitian immigrant Abner Louima, 29 August 1997. Photo by SELA (Haitian Information Center).

A face-off between demonstrators holding a Haitian flag and New York City police over the police shooting of Patrick Dorismond, a thirty year-old Haitian man who refused to buy drugs from an undercover officer, Manhattan, 1999. Photo by SELA (Haitian Information Center).

4

"*Without Them, I Would Not Be Here*": *Transnational Kinship*

It was only when I passed the exam to the university in Port-au-Prince and won a scholarship that my mother told me about the other branch of my family. My mother was the poor side of that family, and she saw them as doing better than her because they had a house in Port-au-Prince. But now that I needed help, she turned to them. I had a scholarship, but it only provided twenty [U.S.] dollars a month to live on. And my family expected me to send some of that home to help support them in Aux Cayes. Although the university tuition was free, there were books to buy, and there was no way I could pay my room and board in Port-au-Prince on that scholarship.

My father had a name, status in Aux Cayes, but not money. So my mother sent my father to talk to my Aunt Eva to see if she would take me in. Eva's mother was my mother's father's sister. So Eva and her sisters, Lilianne and Keysha, were actually my mother's cousins and my second cousins, not my aunts. But because they were of my mother's generation, I called them "aunt" and I called their children "cousins." Although I could not pay, Eva took me in. The household was being supported by remittances sent to support her sister's children and other cousins who were also living there. Being there, I benefited from that. It was a big house and had a basement. All the boys slept in the basement, dormitory style. The house had a modern toilet and shower, but I was not allowed to use them. I had to use the outhouse with the servants. The kids who received money from New York and the relative who could pay could use the shower and toilet. Upstairs was for visitors and big people. But they were very nice to me. In a sense, my situation was like the Haitian proverb says, "In the middle of the rice, the little rock tastes some grease." Without them, I would not be here.

We were sitting listening to the tapes of our 1996 interviews when Georges began to revisit his past. He spoke not as the transmigrant with endless numbers of people to support but as the young man whose family abroad could fulfill his dreams or crush his hopes. We sat at our desks in Luce Hall, the new state-of-the art building of the Yale Center for International and Area Studies. Until we turned on the tape recorder, the space had been dominated by the gleaming glass, polished wood, and powerful computer, all emblems of our status as fellowship recipients at a major U.S. university. Then the voice of Emilia, a young Haitian woman we interviewed in Haiti in the summer of 1996, filled the small office with gloom. "Look at the other students of my age already living abroad. They are already working and making money. Even when I finish my studies, I won't have anything to do in a country that doesn't offer you anything. Three of my mother's children are already finished with school and none of them is working or doing anything. What a sad story. Alas. Sometimes I sit and cry and cry because there is no future for me." Georges stopped the tape, and suddenly he was back in Haiti and twenty-four years old.

I was the same age when that happened to me. At the time, I was finishing my studies at the school of international relations in Port-au-Prince and living with my Aunt Eva. I looked at my cousins who were leaving to live abroad, and I could see no future for me in Haiti and no way out. Once my cousins all went, the remittances that my aunts, who were living in New York, sent to Port-au-Prince would be drastically cut. The families in the United States would have their own responsi-

bilities. My cousins planning to leave also created a need for me to leave. My anguish began in 1967 when I knew that my cousin Gregory would be leaving for Canada; the others had already left. My aunt Eva, whom I was living with, would not have asked me for money, but I would have been very uncomfortable because she only was able to provide for me because she was receiving money every month for my cousins. I could not ask my aunt to support me. She was only a dressmaker. After the money stopped, she would only have her sewing shop. I would have to leave. That was the year I got my ulcer. I knew that if I went back to Aux Cayes I would be stuck. I didn't have the money to live on my own in Port-au-Prince. I had to get out. What would I do?

Family in Haiti continues to be experienced not as a small residential unit of mother, father, and children but as a tree with underground roots, not always visible yet capable of giving sustenance and support to the various branches extending in different directions. When faced with a desperate need to carve out a future, Georges found assistance—first in getting a college education and then in emigrating to the United States—from persons he called aunts and cousins whom he had not even known about during his childhood. Close to thirty years later, we found young people such as Emilia who saw no future for themselves in Haiti and dreamed of migration to the United States as a solution to their problems. Only those who had family connections saw a way to realize these aspirations, however. We also discovered that the obligations of family, including those that stretch across national boundaries, are still the pervasive fabric of daily life.

Here, we trace those transnational patterns of obligation, as Haitians stake their claims on family settled in the United States. Family ties extending across national boundaries is a critical aspect of the ways many Haitians experience long-distance nationalism. This is because for both Haitians in Haiti and the Haitian diaspora, the fates of family and nation are directly and intimately related.

The theme of family ties and obligations strong enough to span national borders reverberated through the responses of those we interviewed, young and old, poor and middle class, and men and women. The rich, "the bourgeoisie," in Haitian terms, also spoke of family connections. Though they have infinitely more possibilities, they count on family ties and businesses to make their way in the world. As person after person told us their life stories, we could see that the circuit of distribution that we traced as we delivered Georges and Rolande's commissions was far from unique. Men and women spoke of family obligations in a tone of moral judgment that resonated with Georges's belief that who he is as a person is expressed through his ties to family in Haiti and to Haiti as a nation.

I represent the whole nation, not just my family. So whatever I achieve, good or bad, will mark the nation. If I succeed, the nation will be proud of me; if I fail, I will bring disgrace to the nation. Your obligation to the nation begins with the obligation to improve yourself and your family. As you improve yourself and your family, you are contributing to Haiti. If you abandon your family and it is known, then you bring shame to your nation.

To understand Georges's identification with Haiti, it is first important to explore the Haitian sense of family as it has been experienced by Georges and the people we interviewed in Haiti. The Haitian experience of family is certainly shaped by the economic situation in Haiti. In their search for the few resources available for survival, people locate any possible ties of family that might yield some assistance. A person might reach out and reclaim family members they have never met, renewing bonds that have been dormant for decades or even generations. Georges's mother, looking for a way to provide support for her son in Port-au-Prince, revived ties with her second cousin who had a household in the capital city, aided by her other second cousins living in New York.

Rediscovering and revitalizing family connections is a transnational strategy. Those who are looking to survive in Haiti will turn to dormant family links in Haiti and abroad. For instance, desperate to find a way to leave Haiti, Georges wrote to the Fouron family in Canada to request that they send him a plane ticket.[1] His father was somehow able to locate the address. Georges's paternal grandfather was Dr. Fouron, a medical doctor and person of some social position in Aux Cayes. Georges's father's mother was not married to Dr. Fouron but claimed the name Fouron for her son, Gilbert. By so doing, she gave Gilbert, Georges's father, a social resource; the Fouron name signaled that Gilbert was a person with a certain prominence, despite the failure of his father to acknowledge his son. This name assisted Georges's father in his own efforts to secure a respectable social position—a goal he obtained when he became the head of the technical school in Aux Cayes. The acknowledged descendants of Dr. Fouron had left Aux Cayes for Canada. In Georges's case, the attempt to claim paternal blood ties failed; he received no response. But the dormant family ties his mother asserted, in the name of her own father, did prove to be a resource, making it possible for Georges first to live in Port-au-Prince and then to leave Haiti.

I had to get out. I began writing to foreign consulates stationed in Port-au-Prince asking for help. And that is when a friend from school, who had connections, returned from a conference in Trinidad and she told me, "There is a golden opportunity. Why don't you write to them? You are doing international relations, and they have a scholarship for someone who is doing international relations." I wrote, and they answered back. It turned out that the Swiss government gave me a scholarship to study in Trinidad at the University of the West Indies, which was fine with me because all I needed was to get out of Haiti. Of course, the university courses there were in English, and I didn't speak English, but I was sure I could learn.

But the scholarship didn't have transportation. I told my Aunt Lilianne in New York whom I had never met that if she would get me to the United States for the summer, I would pay her back and earn money to go to Trinidad. With the scholarship, I obtained a visa to Trinidad. This made it possible for me to go to the U.S. consulate and get a tourist visa to come to the United States. Lilianne then sent me a ticket to come for the summer. I worked in New York in a factory all summer until I could pay back the price of the ticket to New York and Trinidad.

I was able to save because my aunts didn't charge me room and board, and so all I needed was lunch money.

And so the ties that kept me alive in Port-au-Prince were there for me in New York. The same mechanism of support continued. I had a place to stay, people to guide me to get jobs, and a Social Security card.

The conception of family as a resource must be understood in the context of the Haitian economy. The gross national product per capita was reported to be U.S.$400 a year in 1998, and the life expectancy was 55 years. Haiti is still primarily rural, with 70 percent of the people living in the countryside.[2] Yet because of erosion, the lack of water, an increased population, and the importation of cheap agricultural products, an ever-increasing number of people abandon their efforts to make a living in the rural areas. They move to larger towns or the capital city of Port-au-Prince, which has seen the greatest degree of growth. In 1969, during the Duvalier repression, the city contained several hundred thousand people, and had one central marketplace and little traffic. Today, Port-au-Prince is a city of more than a million. The whole city has now become a marketplace; tens of thousands of people have something to sell and almost no one has money with which to purchase these goods. Cars, sports utility vehicles, trucks, and buses extend from one end of the city to the other in endless traffic jams. People migrate from the countryside to Port-au-Prince, and from Haiti to the United States, in response to a rural economy that can't compete with global agricultural markets and to an urban economy where only a fraction of the people can find steady employment.

Belfort, age twenty-eight, was one of the migrants to Port-au-Prince whom we interviewed. He had come to the capital city from a hamlet near Aux Cayes in 1991 in search of something to do. Both his parents are "cultivators," and have land and a house, but the agricultural policies of foreign lenders and U.S. "food assistance" make small-scale farming unprofitable.[3] As Belfort explained:

There is no return for the efforts. I used to be a cultivator, but I realized after a while I was not getting anywhere. I invested my efforts and yet earned nothing from the harvest so I came [to Port-au-Prince]. If I could have found some aid to learn a trade that would have been better for me. If you have the means to get some training in a profession, it is better.

In the 1980s, development experts predicted that employment in Haiti's "unproductive" agricultural sector would be replaced by factories producing goods for multinational corporations attracted to Haiti because of cheap labor.[4] When these predictions were made, Haiti had developed a small manufacturing sector producing goods for export. Some wealthy international corporations such as Disney have been attracted to Haiti because they do not have to follow U.S. minimum wage laws there. In 1994, employers could pay women U.S.$1.85 *a day*.[5] Even these low-paying factory jobs in the industrial sector are far too few to provide employment for any significant sector of the population. And the salaries are so low that they cannot support even the workers, much less their entire family. In reports about Haiti and countries in similar situations, the unemployment rates are given in a matter-of-fact fashion that offers no indication of what sustains people. The U.S. Central Intelligence Agency, for example, reports that in 2000, 70 percent of the labor force was unemployed.[6] Forty-four percent of the people we interviewed in Port-au-Prince and Aux Cayes said that they had no work. This was as true of persons in their twenties as it was of persons in their sixties. Many of the older people had not had a job in years or decades. Numerous younger people had never had a job, even if they had a high school diploma or technical education.

If this is true, how do people survive in Haiti? As we witnessed, many Haitians live by *grapiyaj* (scrambling) — that is, they keep themselves alive by becoming involved in many small activities. These Haitians get help from different people, making wide use of family ties and connections, pooling tiny pieces of resources together to make a whole, or enough on which to survive. Those who have any type of work are called on to distribute their small earnings among a broad network of people.

We must point out that not everyone in Haiti faces economic difficulty and insecurity. There is a small group of families described by Haitians as the bourgeoisie or elite who live lives of luxury and who have gotten considerably richer as the general situation of the rest of the population has worsened. Composed of a few thousand families (less than 1 percent of the population), the Haitian bourgeoisie controls more than 47 percent of the country's wealth.[7] Although many of these families do own land, their major wealth continues to be based on their control of the economic transactions between Haiti and the rest of the world. They were the major Haitian beneficiaries when Haiti was an important exporter of coffee and other tropical products. Today, they profit from the production or importation of building materials, the importation of food and used clothing, and factories that produce and export goods for international corporations. Their wealth is enhanced by the fact that they pay little or no taxes, and their enterprises often do not pay for the electricity and telephone services supplied by the state-owned utilities. Living in richly decorated houses behind secure gates, protected by armed private security guards when they travel between home and office or to their private beaches, the members of the Haitian bourgeoisie live lives of privilege and conspicuous consumption in the midst of poverty and misery. While historically many members of this class were mulattoes, since the Duvalier era, increasing numbers are black. Family connections also bolster the economic interests of bourgeois families. For the majority of people in Haiti, however, family ties are vital to their day-to-day survival.

"Every Little Bit Helps": Family Support within Haiti

Jerome is an alert, verbal man in his thirties who works as a mechanic in a small "garage." The garage consists of a shack that houses a telephone and chair, and an open lot that contains neither lifts nor large tools. It is filled with clusters of men who labor over battered cars and trucks in various states of disrepair. This job and his considerable skill as a mechanic make Jerome a person of substance in his family. Jerome described to us the relationship between his job and the survival of other members of his family.

> I have been living in Port-au-Prince for six years, since 1989. I give money to many to spend, but it is never enough, and they always come back for more because in a family you have very few people working and every little bit helps. I have a father here. In Jacmel [a town in southern Haiti], I have younger sisters and brothers, cousins, an aunt. I support them, not in the same way I support those who live in my house. But each month or every other month I send them whatever I [can] send them. In addition to sending money to those who are left in Jacmel, a distant relative will just come to the garage and they may not ask directly but I won't let them go empty-handed when they "just drop by." You are obligated to find the $20

or $30 [Haitian], especially if he or she is from the province. I am in a better position than my friends who grew up in the same neighborhoods. They are still catching hell. . . . [Y]ou help those people who live with you, around you, or people who you know in your circuit [*pwòch-ou*]. When you are in a position to make money, not big money, you would have to be very hard-hearted, not at all human, not to help a lot of people. Once you are living in this environment, . . . you are obligated to help them.

Two themes emphasized by Jerome became a refrain we heard repeatedly. First of all, he stated that those who have more are obligated to help those whom they know have less. Second, and just as important, a person's humanity is defined by their acts of helping others. Those who have greater needs depend on you to survive. By assisting them, you affirm your humanity. These themes continue to resonate when Haitians emigrate and settle abroad. The support that Haitians in the diaspora give to family in Haiti continues established patterns within the homeland. The few with work or any money support the many who have even less. Many in the first generation of immigrants such as Georges fulfill these obligations. As for the next generation, the connection to Haiti remains to be seen. We discuss some of the various relationships that the generations born in the United States have with Haiti and their relatives there in chapter 7.

It was because of this system of redistribution that Mathieu, who had come to Port-au-Prince from the countryside to seek his fortune, was able to survive at all. Mathieu left his two children, ages four and six, with his mother to search for a trade or work in the city. He has thus far been unsuccessful, so he lives with a cousin who has built a "house" on state-owned land where a number of people have begun to squat. The land is near an open gully or sewer, and at times of flooding, the water overflows and sewage covers the land where people have built their homes. The cousin's wife conducts some kind of small trading and a portion of that money also goes to help Mathieu survive. Mathieu explained: "My cousin doesn't work. I may be friendly with him and he may give me fifty gourdes [U.S.$3.33] today, but he can't give me money every day." With no family or friends abroad, Mathieu has no one to provide him with remittances or to assist him in emigrating. But if he did "find the opportunity to go, if I had the chance, yes, I would go."

"My Family Helps Me": Family Assistance from Abroad

Life is very different when a person has a family member abroad. Pedro, age twenty-nine, resembles far too many people in Haiti who struggle to obtain a high school education or technical training yet still can't find work. His life has some measure of security because Pedro receives remittances sent to him by family living in the United States. As Nina sat in the house that Pedro, his brother, and his three sisters had built with help from family abroad, Pedro told of his effort to find employment in Port-au-Prince:

> I came to Port-au-Prince in 1985, and I have been here eleven years. Here it is very difficult to find work because to find work, you must have contacts in the enterprise. We don't have anyone in this house who works because all the other people from my hometown left and live in the United States so I have no contacts. But my relatives [who live in the United States] help me and my sisters and brother. The two sisters who are abroad work . . . and send money to my house every month. If the family here needs $150 [U.S.$50] each month for school, they send the money. If we need $600 [U.S.$200] each month for food, they send it. They send clothes. As soon as someone is visiting Haiti, they make a suitcase for us. They even send milk. Each month they also send cassettes [news of the family recorded on tape]. My older sister has been there for fifteen years. The other one has been there nine years. On arriving in the United States, they were obliged to work as home attendants to older people. They went to nursing schools and after that they earned a better living.

Despite the fact that he is able to live on the remittances sent by his family, Pedro is planning to emigrate so that he can himself work and make use of his technical training. Because of the family unification provisions of the U.S. immigration law, he will be able to obtain a visa as a sibling of a citizen. This, however, takes years. So meanwhile, Pedro remains unmarried and waits—a man with plans and hope who is "waiting for the residence to come."

What is striking about people such as Pedro is the sense that they are living their life on hold. They look to their transnational family connections to serve as a bridge to a future life in the United States, putting up with much of the political corruption and economic deterioration around them because they can picture themselves elsewhere. Those we interviewed who have family abroad who send remittances experience a flow of resources that assures their day-to-day survival, as well as providing them with consumer goods that differentiate them from peers whose family bonds do not stretch transnationally. But although they reap multiple benefits from these connections, many of these people plan to migrate. Those with a commitment from family members to supply them with visas and travel money were among the only people we spoke to in Haiti who were optimistic about the future. Yet the future they were optimistic about was not in Haiti.

Families survive through their transnational ties, but not without pain and loneliness. Giselle is a young woman who lives in Aux Cayes with her brother and sister in her aunt's household. Giselle's face became taut when she explained that her father left when she was three and her mother had been away for seven years, earning her living by taking care of other people's children. Her voice, generally clear and confident, became softer, and she looked down: "My mother is a home care worker at night and during the day she does day care for children."

Giselle has other relatives in Miami. One uncle drives a taxi, and an aunt and uncle are factory workers. Therefore, she has the additional security of living in a household supported by many paychecks earned abroad. The household in which she lives in Haiti is a collective family enterprise; Giselle's mother's sister is raising both her own and her sister's children with resources that come from a kin network of siblings and their spouses in the United States. Giselle noted that she has "three aunts and four uncles. They live in Miami, Chicago, Boston, and New York. Every month they send money. They send us to school. They pay for food. They send money to see the doctor. Money to use every day and for us to put in our pocket. If we need something they can't send from abroad, they send us money to buy it in Haiti. Someone abroad [parents, aunts, or uncles] pays the electricity, telephone, and taxes on the house where I live. They send money for my aunt's sons and daughters. They send clothes, too. The house we are living in belongs to my aunt and uncle [who live abroad]." Because of her strong transnational family network, Giselle's daily life has been secure, although the current poor health of the aunt with whom she is living may upset the entire arrangement.

Despite her relative security, however, Giselle plans to leave Haiti to obtain an education and perhaps settle abroad. As with so many of the people we interviewed who dreamed about or were in the midst of actually leaving

Haiti, Giselle believes her country has failed "the people who are on the bottom." She feels a sense of betrayal, almost as if a loved one had rejected her.

"My Husband Sends Merchandise": The Family as a Transnational Business

The large-scale legal and illegal emigration of Haitians to the United States is, in part, a response to a broad penetration of the Haitian economy by agricultural products and manufactured goods produced elsewhere. These products are produced by poorly paid workers in vast agricultural enterprises or factories located all over the world. They are controlled by multinational corporations based in powerful countries such as the United States.

Haitian agriculture and manufacturing cannot compete with goods produced within this global economy. The penetration of food products and manufactured objects, both new and used, into even the small cities and rural areas of Haiti has destroyed an array of small-scale economic activities that previously provided livelihoods for people. These people, whose source of income used to come from their own labor, now live by migration and remittances sent through family networks. As we have seen, these networks become a conduit for the distribution of food and manufactured objects from abroad. This distribution, while necessary for immediate survival, also weakens Haiti's productive economic sector and destroys the viability of Haitian agriculture and skilled trades.

Like many, Rose's husband supports her household by working in the United States and sending money home. While both of Giselle's parents had become part of the diaspora, Rose and her husband utilize a different form of household management in which one spouse stays in Haiti and uses the resources from abroad to establish a business at home. Although many couples employ this strategy, these businesses do not provide an income large enough to sustain a family without also receiving money from abroad. Instead, the incomes from these small businesses offer a small safety net in case circumstances abroad delay a monthly transfer of cash. Money invested in building or expanding a house in Haiti can thus simultaneously become money invested in creating a place from which to conduct business. In this situation, it is more likely that the woman will be the one remaining in Haiti since small-scale commerce conducted from a home is seen as part of the female domain.

Rose's husband sends her a variety of goods, which she then sells from a well-kept house whose cement-block construction is plastered over. The house has smooth, newly painted walls, both inside and out. Rose sells not only manufactured items such as used cutlery but also agricultural goods that her husband ships from Miami to the Haitian port of Miragoâne. Down the street, her younger sister Elvire, age thirty-three, also has a business in her well-built, rented house. She used the income from remittances from her husband to finance this small enterprise. From the front of her house, she also sells imported products such as evaporated milk and soap. As Elvire maintained, "You just don't eat the money that he sends. You put it to work. I had a business before my husband left, but now it has gotten bigger. When my husband sent money for school or the house, I set aside money for the business so we won't be completely dependent on him. My husband sends me money to expand the business. The reason why he did it was because if a month comes in which he cannot send money to me, the children will not suffer. If I need to pay for the children's schooling, I take the money out of the business and when I receive the money transfer I put the money back." Despite the income from such projects, most of the major expenses of the household are paid by the remittances from her husband, who visits often. "He pays for the leased house and the school for the three children. I depend on my husband for everyday living expenses. I call him on the phone from time to time, and I have his address. He sends money via money transfer houses, and people who are traveling bring suitcases and gifts. He sent the television and VCR."

Her siblings, too, contribute to her household and keep in close contact. Elvire has multiple links to the diaspora through four siblings abroad, all of whom work in restaurants. "They keep in contact regularly. They write and send money, gifts, provisions, and commissions. My husband's mother is living abroad in Miami and she sent for him. He left in 1988. Now he has permanent residence and is applying for citizenship so it will be easier to get papers for his children. Before his mother, my sister went. My sister is now an American. She has four children in the United States and left three children in Haiti. She sent for two. My sister returns and visits me. When they come, they stay with me, and bring goods and gifts." The presence of kin abroad sometimes helps those left behind get credit for businesses they have started. In talking about her business, Elvire emphasized this useful aspect of her extensive kin network living in the diaspora. "It is easier for me because once you have a relative living abroad it is easier for me to find money to borrow." In emergencies, she is also able to sell the many gifts from abroad that fill her house.

Elvire's current commercial activities replace her former occupation as a skilled dressmaker. Because in the United States, exporting old clothes to poor countries has become a large and profitable business, Elvire's dressmaking skills are no longer a marketable commodity. The clothing she used to make and sell has been replaced by the readily available cheap second hand clothes from abroad, referred to in Haiti as Kenedi or *pèpè*. "I do commerce and I am also a dressmaker. But I don't do the dressmaking now because it doesn't really bring me any income [because of the pèpè]. But I benefit from pèpè because I buy it for my children and myself. But yes, it takes away from my getting jobs. . . . When they have a special occasion, they are not going to buy pèpè but will buy cloth and ask people to sew for them."

Dressmaking is only one of many occupations that have disappeared in Haiti. Most shoemakers now only repair footwear. One woman described why her cousin, a skilled shoemaker, developed a "persistent urge to travel to New York. . . . Now people don't learn that trade anymore. In the old times, my cousin used to buy leather and make shoes to sell. So they used to make the shoes and display them on the wall, and people used to come and buy them. He used to fix them and resole them as well. At a point he wasn't making any money. To live well he had to go to New York."

Both Rose and Elvire's narratives provide evidence of the way in which the penetration of cheap products from First World nations has obliterated Haitian economic self-sufficiency. Rose's husband ships U.S. agricultural products to Haiti. Haiti is a country where the majority of the people live off the land. But cheap imported food increasingly makes Haitian-grown products unprofitable to sell and market. While her sister sells fresh imported vegetables, Elvire sells small imported packaged goods and snacks, many of which also replace products that Haitians did or could produce. Moreover, many Haitian occupations such as Elvire's trade as a dressmaker are disappearing in the flood of imported secondhand objects.

"We Are Now Middle Class": Families as Sources of Social Mobility

The current manner in which Haiti is incorporated into the larger world economy contributes to the well-being of particular individuals and families, at the same time that it devastates the country as a whole. Even as the importation of goods destroys various forms of Haitian economic activity, individual families may dramatically improve their life circumstances by the emigration of one or more of their members who then provide money and small business activities for those left behind. The improvements are both material and social. On the basis of the remittances, families in Haiti find they have access to capital in the form of money from abroad and loans. Moreover, they may be able to obtain higher social standing. Some of this comes from the status that is obtained through building a better and bigger house, filling it with imported electronic objects, and wearing finer clothing. Yet if at all possible, remittances are also invested in education. Historically in Haiti, families have achieved social mobility through educating their children. As they extend their family ties transnationally, Haitians continue to see education as both a means and marker of social mobility.

Raymond Perrin, age twenty-four, a student at the Faculty of Social Sciences of the University of Haiti, sat with us under a tree near the college and traced with great satisfaction the progress of his family. The university building nearby is shabby and neglected, the unfinished facade exposing a concrete staircase that leads nowhere. This bleak exterior stands in sharp contrast to the energy and ambition of students such as Raymond. Despite its graffiti, broken doors, and limited number of classrooms, this university still signifies to these students that they are becoming part of Haiti's intellectual elite. Those who have family abroad see possibilities opening up before them. Raymond, with five of his siblings already educated and in the United States, and one about to leave, spoke to us only of achievements and not of the barriers ahead. Certainly, the Perrin family has come a long way from their beginnings in Aquin, a little rural hamlet about twenty-five miles from Port-au-Prince.

Raymond's father migrated first to St. Martin, a Caribbean island with a growing Haitian population. He then made his way to the United States, where he was able to obtain legal papers, probably through the 1986 amnesty program that gave permanent resident visas to people who had fled the political repression and economic devastation of the Duvalier regime. With the money Raymond's father sent from the United States, most of Raymond's siblings were able first to attend school and then to emigrate.

> Currently, I have my father and five brothers and two nephews and two sisters, all in Brooklyn. My father has been there fourteen years. When he first left, he didn't have his papers. Then he got his residence. It took him a long time. He works at a place where they work

with plywood. He was a cabinetmaker in Haiti. I have a sister who studied medicine in Haiti and is studying for the matching exam [that will allow her to practice medicine in the United States]. One of my brothers is an electronic engineer, and he went abroad and left the field and is studying psychotherapy right now. I am a student at the university and another brother is abroad. He needs one more year before he goes to college, and then I have another little brother who is in Haiti with me. He finished his secondary education and is studying English now. He is waiting to leave. Now, with a child in medicine, if we consider the family all together, I will say we are in the middle class.

Raymond's father's migration and the U.S. amnesty program of 1986 made higher education and social mobility possible for the entire family. More recently, however, the U.S. government refused to accept people fleeing the Haitian military dictatorship that was in power from 1991 to 1994. In 1996, Congress along with the U.S. Immigration and Naturalization Service proceeded to tighten immigration laws and procedures, making refugee status more difficult to attain, and curtailing the possibilities of Haitians legally emigrating and therefore permanently settling in the United States. These changes have not eliminated the flow of illegal immigrants or hindered the plans of those who live within transnational social fields to emigrate. If Raymond's father had not been able to regularize his status, he would have still emigrated and sent money home to educate his family. Once educated, though, his children would have either been forced to remain in Haiti or follow their father into illegal migration. They would have had little chance to regularize their status, and the opportunities to use their education would have been limited by their undocumented status. In either case, their aspirations would have been blocked and their discontent might have grown, despite the fact that their transnational family ties would have continued to allow them a middle-class existence in Haiti. But Raymond and his siblings, unlike growing numbers of children of immigrants, were able to obtain visas.

This transnational family strategy of mobility can be impeded if the transmigrant faces unemployment, sickness, and disability. In such instances, the flow of support may cease, temporarily or even permanently. Death is the most complete abandonment. Family members in Haiti may find themselves accustomed to a lifestyle and status that they suddenly cannot maintain. Often, they are plunged into a desperate situation, unwilling to exchange the social status they have gained from having relatives abroad for an income obtained by methods such as selling in the market or other low-status occupations that they may have found acceptable if remittances had not launched them onto a trajectory of social mobility. In one such situation, a young man whose family was stranded by an aunt's death told us that to support his lifestyle, he had turned to illegal activities, or as he put it, "all kinds of things that nobody knows about."

The Transmigrant Perspective: Keeping a Foothold in Haiti

When we look at the economic situation in Haiti, we can see how family ties function as a lifeline for those left behind. What about the transmigrants? What are the rewards for a life of constant giving, of trying to provide for family members whose needs can never fully be met? First of all, transmigrants obtain increased social status through their giving. This is a reward that cannot be overemphasized. In the United States, a migrant with a low-paying position, or even working as a professional, may face racial discrimination or sexism that denies the person the recognition she or he deserves. Living as a transmigrant who distributes life-sustaining resources or prestigious gifts to family back home, however, provides much needed self-esteem. The hardships that Haitians face abroad—laboring at exhausting factory work; driving a taxi cab for a living sixteen hours a day; working two minimum wage jobs so that family both in the United States and Haiti can be supported; changing bedpans and suffering verbal abuse in home health care work—all remain invisible. They are concealed behind the facade of large homes built in Haiti, the display of fine clothes and jewelry on return visits, the renting of cars at exorbitant costs to drive home on impassable roads, and the flow of money and goods back to Haiti. More often than not, the difficulties experienced in the United States do transfer into social status, but the social status and even social mobility that transnational networks of obligations yield are achieved only back home. It is there that the transmigrant becomes a person of note.

Georges lives amid family and friends caught up in this status system, yet he often rails against it. When he does, he judges peoples' behavior in terms of whether or not what they do helps Haiti. His long-distance nationalism provides him with a standard against which to measure transnational transactions.

When I see what people do to appear important in Haiti, I understand it, but at the same time I think it is crazy. I know a taxi driver in New York. He was able through endless hours of work to save and purchase two taxi medallions. But instead of continuing to save and invest, he began to travel to Haiti and act like a wealthy man. He would rent a car during each trip for the exorbitant cost of U.S.$150 a day. He distributed money left and right. But now he is broke. He had so many debts that he had to lease his medallions to a cab company. This sense of having to be superior is destroying Haiti.

Georges also questions the actions of Candio, the brother of Rolande's cousin Yvette, whose endless commissions we delivered in the summer of 1996. Candio lives in Medford, Massachusetts. Although he earns very little at the supermarket where he works, Candio did have access to the best cuts of meat at a cheap price. On his way to Haiti to bury his niece who died in childbirth, Candio packed up six suitcases full of things for distribution: fine clothes to validate his supposed prosperity in the United States and one bag loaded with meat.

He first came from Boston to New York. We told him, "You will not be able to take all those things on the plane." He didn't believe us because he had brought them by plane from Boston to New York. When he got to Kennedy airport in New York to go to Haiti for the funeral, they would not let him on the plane and he had to leave suitcases behind. He could only take two suitcases, so he brought the meat and gifts, and left all his clothes behind. He didn't even bring his underwear, and in Port-au-Prince, he had to buy all new clothes for the funeral. To show off his wealth, he chartered a bus for $500 [U.S.$150] to take his gifts and the mourners from Port-au-Prince to Tibouk [a small town in the south].

One does not have to achieve social and occupational mobility abroad to be thought of as a success at home. Instead, it is the distribution of goods and displays of wealth in Haiti that marks returning immigrants as successful among those who are their dependents. If you obtain education abroad or succeed in a profession or business, you can of course add this to your legend, but these gains are not necessary to receive status and respect back home. Time and again in our interviews, those who received remittances could tell us what they received, but had no idea what kind of work the members of their family were doing in the United States, Canada, or Europe. The very fulfillment of one's duties to one's family members and personal network reflects the immigrant's success abroad.

Still, the motivation to achieve social status in Haiti is not the only reason why transmigrants continue to meet the urgent needs of people in Haiti with a constant flow of money and goods. Transmigrants who support their family can facilitate their return if they are unable to live in the United States because of illness, disability, unemployment, or old age. At the same time, those who spend money building a house in Haiti are pulled back to their homeland by this investment. Those who have actually built homes in Haiti can sell them at the time of retirement and live elsewhere, but the price of a house sold in Haiti is only the price of down payment in most other countries. Yvette, Georges, and Rolande plan to retire in Haiti, if conditions stabilize.

The restructuring of the U.S. economy at the end of the twentieth century has contributed to the difficulties that transmigrants face in trying to live their lives across national borders. As well, the economic restructuring has made it imperative for immigrants to construct and maintain their transnational networks while attempting to live within transnational social fields. The U.S. economy after "corporate downsizing" and the export of industrial production to low-wage areas of the world offers much less in the way of secure employment for most people. Service sector jobs—such as home health care attendants, store clerks, or delivery workers—are increasing in number, and tend to offer few or no benefits for illness or retirement. And the jobs themselves are often temporary or part-time. In the current U.S. economy, transmigrants find that if they lose their job, the next one may well be much worse, despite the fact that they have more years of experience in the United States and have become more comfortable with English. Because of the value placed on education in Haiti and the status it brings, Haitian immigrants have a higher level of education than many new immigrant populations. Yet, in a world where legitimate work increasingly requires credentials, responsibilities both in Haiti and the United States make it difficult for people to take the time to obtain sufficient formal training to achieve occupational advancement or even secure future employment. Although the cultivation of transnational networks may limit social mobility in the United States, many immigrants thus continue to nurture their home ties as a source of financial security, a form of personal capital, and a type of hedge fund in an extremely insecure world.

"If They Know What They Left Behind": The Morality of Knowledge

When they spoke to us about family, most people stressed that support from family members is an obligation. Indeed, the primary family value is obligation rather than love. This does not mean to say that there are no deep emotional bonds among Haitian family members. Rather, it is to observe that with or without love, there is obligation. This obligation led Georges to assist family members he barely knew, once he succeeded in the United States. Such duties are expressed in a form of morality that links individuals not only to their families but also to the nation. People tend to speak more readily about love of Haiti than love of family, although the two are intimately connected.

Some people in Haiti not only expect that improvements in their life depend on assistance from family members abroad but have also come to believe that they are unable to change their conditions on their own. The political setbacks to the grassroots movement in Haiti that followed the overthrow of Aristide in 1991 reinforced these notions. Rose, the woman in Aux Cayes who prospers because of the constant stream of goods sent by her husband in south Florida, stated this assumption clearly: "I am not a problem without a solution. Those who left have the obligation [to help] because those who are left behind can't do anything by themselves. So those abroad have to watch over those in Haiti. They can't leave them to die so they have to support them. If they don't do it, you just resign yourself." For Rose, the solutions to her problems can be found through family members in the United States.

Family ties express, re-create, legitimate, and are sanctioned by a morality that stands outside the profit motive, yet nonetheless has its own dynamic of calculation. There may well be love, warmth, and mutual respect, but whatever the degree of affirming emotion, there is accountability. Because the central family value is one of obligation, family can be experienced as a series of "debts" that must be paid and can be collected. The debts to family cannot be reduced to a sum of money borrowed or lent. Instead, there is a sense that family ties come with a set of claims that those in need can make on those who have more. A refusal to acknowledge these debts will never be forgotten.

After transmigrants settle in the United States, they are expected to provide support, if they are aware of the difficult circumstances that a family member faces. Maurice, age twenty-seven, stated this ethical value as follows: "If a Haitian lives abroad and you know in what conditions you left your family, it is an obligation, maybe, to help them. Because in Haiti, you don't live but you survive."

Repeatedly, people in Haiti explained to us that kin who leave are obligated to maintain their ties to home because they are aware of the suffering they escaped. Awareness of suffering is thought to compel action. For example, as Berthony, a young man whose ambitions were thwarted by the death of his mother's sister in New York, explained to us: "If they know what they left behind, their convictions, their conscience, they must say to themselves, Haiti has nothing so they must send some money."

This is a morality that cuts across age groups. It also holds true for many Haitians with different types of migration experience. At seventy-one years of age, Leopold returned to Haiti to live on his social security in 1986 after an absence of sixteen years. During that time, working successively as a factory worker, taxi driver, and delivery truck driver, he had maintained his ties to his wife and eight children in Haiti. Eventually, he brought all of them to the United States. His morality of knowledge was expressed in the same language as that of the young people we interviewed. "Naturally, it's an obligation. It is because you left your close relatives here in poverty. The people you left behind must survive, and you must have certain humanity in your heart. You are obligated to send a little something for that person to survive. . . . That is a necessity because you left them and you know what conditions they are living in."

The logic of this morality links the reason for migrating to the situation of one's family. One of the main reasons to leave Haiti is to support a family. Hence, one leaves with an understanding of what the situation is and what one must do. This duty to support kin is presented in many of our interviews as a pattern of behavior that distinguishes those who are fully human from those who are abnormal.

Cazeau, a fifty-eight-year-old man, is an acquaintance of George's in-laws. He left Haiti for political reasons, living in the United States between 1977 and 1992. As he forcefully put it: "In the case of someone who leaves Haiti and doesn't help the family s/he left behind, I would send him/her to a doctor to see if s/he is sick. Because a brother, father, mother, [or] sister who takes care of you since you are a little baby, and gives you an education, and when you reach a certain age sends you abroad, and when you go abroad and forget about them, this kind of individual, don't criticize them outright. You can say, for sure, s/he is not normal. That person should go get a check up."[5]

Thus, you assert your humanity by fulfilling family responsibilities. To neglect this obligation is an indicator of bad faith, a violation of trust. In our interview, we found that the phrase "bad faith" is key in the transnational moral vocabulary of Haitians.[8] Josaphat, age twenty, lives with his sister in a house owned by his mother's mother, and also occupied by his mother's sister and brother. The entire household survives on remittances from Josaphat's mother, who left for the United States when Josaphat was just a child. Josaphat tells us that "if a person travels, and has the opportunity to make money, in that sense s/he is obligated to help. If you don't do it you have bad faith because you know the condition in which people are living."

Georges, who lives under the burden of exactly such knowledge and its concomitant obligation, wondered if the responsibility attached to knowledge extends both ways. Are people living on remittances in Haiti compelled to modify their expectations based on the conditions migrants face in the diaspora? Georges asks, "Do people abroad always have the means to help? What if s/he says I would love to help you but I can't?" Josaphat's response was emphatic: "If that person knows what s/he went abroad for, s/he is obligated to have the means. Even if s/he says that s/he can't, I will always say that s/he can. Take my case for example. I don't have means, I don't have anything. Now if I call on members of my family and I say I want to study agronomy, and the person says, 'I don't have the money,' I would demand, if you work ten hours a day then work twelve hours a day to help me. S/he is obligated to work overtime to help me."

The preceding statements describe the moral system, not its actual implementation. Some people ignore their blood ties and abandon their family members. As with any dominant value system, not everyone agrees. Despite the predominance of the sense that kinship is lived as obligation, not everyone concurs that the obligation is unceasing, persists across distances of time and space, and must be fulfilled under any conditions. Among the people with whom we spoke, however, only 25 percent thought circumstances beyond the immigrants' control might mitigate these obligations. Most of those who didn't make kinship responsibilities an absolute value weren't in desperate straits. They had some resources of their own and did not depend at all or fully on those who live abroad. Also, even those who uphold these values may not be willing or able to live by them.

"He Was a Responsible Person": Immigrant Obligations and Unmet Expectations

If a family member who has been helped to go abroad does not support family in Haiti, anger resonates throughout a broad network. Esmeralda, sitting in her modern, elegant rented house in a walled though unguarded development in Petionville, described this to us. Her living room, with its pastel colors and imported furniture, seemed to indicate prosperity. The fact that all was not well only became apparent when Esmeralda tried to serve us refreshments and there were neither glasses nor silverware. Because the previous maid had not been paid, she had stolen them. Esmeralda could neither pay the maid nor replace the kitchenware on her husband's salary as a technician. Although she has a degree in psychology, Esmeralda last worked as a secretary in the Office of the President. She lost the job when there was a change in government. Her anger, however, was directed neither at the government nor the maid. She was instead upset with her relatives abroad who had abandoned their obligations to their family.

> I know children who were idolized by their parents, who were the sole resource that their parents had. I am thinking about my cousin who is in Philadelphia. The parents borrowed money and they took loans on their house to send him abroad to help the parents with the other children. He left twelve years ago and has never been back, and we lost communication with him. But we know he works there, and that he married, had two children with his wife, and is divorced now. He bought a house in Philadelphia, and now the house belongs to the wife and children. He lives alone in an apartment. Another cousin . . . got involved with other women, he rented apartments, and his wife and children don't even have his address or telephone.

Nothing. They change. . . . They change their telephone number so you can't get in touch with them. Even if you have an emergency and you call them, they tell the operator that they are not home. . . . When you call them and they have a problem, they change their voice and say that it is not they who answered the phone.

As we transcribed the interview and listened to Esmeralda recounting the betrayal and abandonment of her family abroad, Georges became increasingly disquieted.

She doesn't understand. She is imagining life in the United States as bountiful. Whenever you leave home, people think that you have money. When I got the scholarship for tuition and room and board in Trinidad, I still was expected to send money back home. And I did that. Instead of buying books I needed, I borrowed them from the library. And instead of eating three times a day, I would eat twice. Not only that, I also sold my return plane ticket and sent the money to help my family in Aux Cayes. In order to get into Trinidad as a student, I needed to have a plane ticket showing that I would be able to leave at the end of my studies. But after I arrived, I cashed in the return ticket, so at the end of the school year I was stuck. The point is that sometimes you just have no money to meet your obligations and then you are forced to cut ties.

Sometimes the demands are so great and not realistic. They are not in line with the conditions that you find yourself in as an immigrant. While people think you are living the good life, you may have no money at all. I finally got to New York because Alex, who was not family but is a boyhood friend who had become like family, sent me a ticket. Because I did not have papers, the only job that I could find was stacking merchandise in a warehouse near the Westside Highway on 34th Street. I only earned the minimum wage—maybe it was $1.25 per hour. I lived in a hotel room with Alex and another friend. We ate out only on Friday nights when we got paid. The other days, we would fry eggs at night and boil plaintains *to reduce our expenses. But the point is that we had little to live on, and even by living together in a single room, at times you were unable to meet the expectations of home.*

I managed to send money but sometimes I would skip months. But I would receive letters from my dad talking about all the sacrifices they had made, scolding me for not sending money regularly enough, and asking for an increase in the monthly remittances. And other times, I would receive letters requesting help for emergencies. So I thought I was meeting my obligations, but they didn't see it that way. In those days before there were money transfer houses, what I would do was to send checks before I had the money in the bank. My father would go to a local merchant who needed U.S. currency and he could cash the check. But sometimes the check would bounce. Then he would write and scold me, and say that I was being wasteful and not managing my money. Meanwhile, I could not go to school, which was my goal, because I didn't have the money.

The morality of obligation also carries an expectation that the family members already living in the United States will render assistance to newly arrived kin. It is not sufficient to help a new immigrant buy a plane ticket or obtain documents for migration. When they arrive, the new immigrant must be provided with shelter and food. Those in Haiti monitor the reception of newcomers by those who are already settled. When the welcome is foreshortened or constrained in any way, there is censure, criticism, and resentment. Because family members in Haiti assume that those living abroad are prosperous, no allowances are made for the strained resources of the host's household, a lack of space, or the high cost of living in the United States. Esmeralda, having told us about the sacrifices that family members make to send a relative abroad, gave voice to the discontent of an entire family network at the treatment a newly arrived person sometimes receives when they join the diaspora: "My husband's family sent him to Miami to study broadcasting. He went to live with his aunt. . . . She told him, it is not a question of family anymore. When you live here, you are responsible for your own upkeep. And [after] . . . two or three weeks, they start looking at you as a burden and nuisance. They locked their doors and didn't give him the key; [if he came home late] he had to sleep outside. His mother's sister did that to him. She said that you came here to study. This is your problem, not my problem. . . . She would not feed him. So they are not responsible for you."

While we were transcribing this portion of the tape, Georges was again carried back to his past. In this recollection, he was not the one burdened by supporting those back home. He became once again the new arrival, shocked by the harshness of the reception he receives from some of his family in New York.

My Aunt Keysha did that to me. Since my other aunt, Lilianne, did not have room for me to sleep in her apartment, I was sent to spend the night with Aunt Keysha. However, she refused to give [me] a key to her apartment. So, in the cold of the fall nights, I had to wait for her, sitting on a bench on Eastern Parkway until she came [home] from work. Keysha didn't feed me either. She said to me, "I am not your servant." Finally, one day, frustrated with my continuing presence in her apartment, she said to me: "You have been here three months. How much longer do you plan on staying here? Since you came, you have given me no time to have sex with my boyfriend."

Dependencies Have Their Bitterness

In some ways, I hate to walk around Aux Cayes. Everywhere, there are people I used to know. Some are old friends, but they act like they don't know me. They stay away for the simple reason that they don't want others to think that they are asking for help or flattering the returnee. To make things worse, there is another group who I either don't recognize or don't remember, and so I pass them by. They think that I am snubbing them because I have become too grand.

Transnational family ties continue the lines of connection and division that exist within families in Haiti. On the one hand, to understand the foundations of long-distance nationalism, it is important to remember that when family obligation extends between Haiti and the United States, a transnational terrain on which shared identities and divisions can be inscribed is constantly being planted, nurtured, and harvested. On the other hand, a crop of bitterness is sown and reaped because the obligations and dependencies engendered by the morality system just explored can leave a bad taste.

When transmigrants return to Haiti, they partly expect to step into old roles within families and friendships, just as one might anticipate going home and finally putting on old and comfortable clothes. But when they return, they and those who had stayed behind discover that a process of change has been occurring. While those who have gone back and forth yearly may experience little disjuncture, many who cannot afford or do not wish to travel frequently often feel a certain degree of culture shock when they visit "home." Home is not what they remember it to be, and they find that a process of transformation has been going on in both themselves and their family and friends in Haiti. It is as if the old clothes no longer fit or are too tattered to be worn at all. Whether or not they feel at home when they return to Haiti, however, they don't always find a warm reception and don't always feel welcome.

In return for their distributions of presents, Georges, Rolande, and Yvette gain social status and prestige. They also obtain a sense of well-being that comes from a commitment fulfilled. Yet dependencies have their bitterness. Georges, Rolande, and Yvette face anger and resentment, too. Those who stayed behind chafe at the real and imagined disparity between their life circumstances and that of their relatives, friends, and acquaintances who have gone abroad. The very giving of gifts connotes this inequality. Those members of the Haitian diaspora who arrive to vacation in Haiti and distribute commissions are visibly wealthier than those they left behind. When Georges walks through his hometown of Aux Cayes, he is greeted by some with respect or requests for funds, and by others with anger because he went away.

The distribution of commissions, remittances, and simple greetings brings pain as well as pleasure. While they may unite those abroad with those who remain in Haiti, these distributions can also create enmity and division. There is enmity between those who receive from relatives and those who don't obtain support. A person who receives a gift may compare him or herself to others receiving support and argue that he or she is more deserving because of a greater need now or a favor done decades before. Marianne, Georges's sister, measures herself not against those who have nothing but against others of her own kin whom she perceives as having received more, and against other families who provide their kin in Haiti with grander kinds of gifts. She sees herself as the neglected child of the family, the lowest among siblings because she has never been abroad. This feeling is heightened by the question Marianne's neighbors constantly ask her, "When are you going to New York to join your brother?" Each time Georges visits, they expect that he has arrived to take her back with him, and when he leaves they inquire, "Why are you the only one in your family who was left behind?" She feels abandoned, even though at a certain point she could have left Haiti and chose not to go.

Yvette's broad network of kin and dependents in Haiti are always asking for more. When her niece, whose wedding she had financed, died in childbirth, Yvette paid for the funeral and flew to Haiti to attend it. Two years later, a nephew died. This young man was a son of a sister whom Yvette barely knew because the sister had been sent to live with a distant relative before Yvette was born. Despite this, Yvette paid for a large portion of the funeral including a band, imported flowers, and a videotaped record of the events so that she could sit in New York and experience the funeral as if she were in Port-au-Prince. But because Yvette did not personally attend the funeral and had attended her niece's, Yvette's sister felt slighted.

The pressure to send remittances also divides members of a family. Competition and tensions between siblings are expressed through differential patterns of support. Who gives and who doesn't, who gives more and who gives less, who gives to one and who gives to another—all of these are observed, commented on, and remembered. Even the style of the giving can become a point of contention. When Georges's sister, Karolle, went to Haiti with money for Marianne from their brother, Alvin, Karolle stayed in Port-au-Prince in Janine's fancy house. Karolle sent word to Marianne to come by bus to get the money. Marianne was incensed by the lack of respect. She called Karolle and said to her, "How dare you, you are my younger sister. You should come and visit." Although Marianne needed the money, she refused to journey to Port-au-Prince. She felt that she was being treated as a suppliant by her younger sister. The sisters had been apart for eight years. Karolle, for her part, refused to send the money as a commission with some other traveler to Aux Cayes or through a money transfer house, and so returned to Brooklyn with Alvin's money. The family was still talking about this quarrel five years later, and Marianne recounts her side of the story whenever Georges visits. As he tells it:

Every time I see Marianne, she complains to me about Karolle, and I tease her and tell her, "But you are a Christian, and this is not the way a Christian behaves." But Marianne insists that she will never forget and both her sisters are responsible for the slight. That is why, when you go home, you try to be sure to visit every single person and slight no one. That is why Man-Nana sits me down every time I go and says to me, "You have to visit this one and that one." Because after I go, those who feel slighted take it out on Man-Nana. They wait until after I leave, and then they come and report. "He didn't talk to me, he didn't visit with me, he didn't bring anything for me." But if you do visit, the ties are strengthened. The person says, "He visited, he acknowledged me." It is not so much the gift that you give them. It is the fact that you went to their house, you went to their place, and you talked to them.

In which household the transmigrants choose to stay on return trips to Haiti can also be a source of friction within families and networks. Just as the transmigrants validate their success abroad through their gift distribution, those in Haiti use the occasion of hosting transmigrants to mark their social and material achievements. Now that Alfred has a spacious house, Georges has begun staying with him rather than Janine. In 1996, when he brought five people to live at Alfred's house, Janine made a point of inviting Georges's daughter Leah and her friend Cynthia to stay the night. On previous visits, Georges often stayed with a range of relatives so as not to stir up family animosities. Transmigrants visiting relatives in Haiti face pressures to stay with many people, sleeping here one day and there the next, to show no favoritism. Similarly, when people living in Haiti visit the United States, they also move between the households of various family members, trying not to play favorites.

Some recipients of remittances who live in Haiti have been able to secure visas to travel to the United States. A smaller number of people who have U.S. permanent residence visas move back and forth between Haiti and the United States each year, but actually spend most of their time in Haiti. In fact, to keep those visas, they must live for part of every year in the United States. Their commuting between two countries is shaped by the requirements of U.S. immigration law. Whether they enter the United States with visitors' or permanent residence visas, these people, like those who have settled in the United States, are obliged to return to Haiti laden with gifts and commissions. They, too, become the givers of goods and receivers of status. Many of them, like Man-Nana are parents whose adult children have migrated and settled abroad. Their children assist them in obtaining permanent resident visas in the United States, not because the parents desire to emigrate but because both parents and children fear the time when an aging parent can no longer live on his or her own or is in need of medical care unavailable in Haiti. Without such visas, children may not be able to nurse their parents.

Man-Nana has been traveling to Queens for many years because Rolande wants to ensure that if her mother can no longer live on her own in Haiti, she will have the documents to reside legally in the United States in the Fouron household. In addition, the yearly visits serve as an occasion for Man-Nana to stay in contact with her two grandchildren and purchase gifts for her network in Haiti. She arrives in New York with a list, and after each trip, brings back all types of small presents: clothes and shoes (both used and new), rice, meat, sugar, watches, and batteries. For some people, she fulfills requests; for others, she brings a little something to be sure not to slight them. Rolande does the shopping.

Of course, not everyone in Haiti has family members who have managed to successfully emigrate and settle abroad. Whole sets of people either have no relatives, supporters, or friends abroad, or have been abandoned by their family members who have emigrated. They watch the distribution of commissions with envy. Because of this, the return visits of transmigrants can spread waves of disharmony throughout a neighborhood, even though these visits provide resources that are distributed beyond the household.

As we have seen, people without family abroad are not entirely shut off from the distribution. Many of those who watch, also wait. In Lourdes's yard and Man-Nana's kitchen, a stream of people comes to both greet and receive. Those who live off Yvette's largess to Lourdes include individuals who come to eat, and others who come to use her cistern to wash their clothes and shower. Just as remittances are redistributed among the networks of persons who receive support from the diaspora, the pattern repeats itself within Haiti. Those who distribute goods and money obtain prestige, yet are also the targets of jealousy and discontent. Many have no place at all in the distribution circuits, even though remittances are spread within networks that reach far beyond the ties of the transmigrant bringing the commissions. Even those who receive some small present through the redistribution of remittances by those directly linked to peoples abroad may harbor bitterness. Their resentment may, in fact, be intensified by the paucity of the presents they receive. Such persons receive little and their needs are great. They compare the small bits of resources that come their way to the larger houses and fuller stomachs of persons who have family abroad.

Whether the transactions produce pride or bitterness, whether they assuage or generate desires, the flow of money and goods shapes decisions about daily life for those who live within transnational distribution networks. This is just as true for immigrants living their daily lives in New York, Miami, Boston, or Montreal as it is for those in Port-au-Prince or Aux Cayes. Whether Annette, Georges and Rolande's adopted daughter, or Lourdes, Yvette's niece, can go to school depends entirely on whether Georges and Yvette send sufficient money regularly to Haiti. Whether Georges, his siblings in New York, or Yvette can return to Haiti to visit or live depends on whether they have fulfilled their never-ending obligations and sent money and gifts.

If I look at my family and I compare myself with Jean, my younger brother, who is a factory worker who now lives in Brooklyn with his wife and children, I am better off. But, also, it is a personal decision about what to do with your money. Jean has not been back for ten years nor has he sent money. He used to send money to support his children who stayed with his wife's mother. He did send for his five children who were born in Haiti. The last two children just arrived. But he left debts behind, money he borrowed to support his family. For him to go back would be a social disgrace because he left debts that he didn't settle. He never even contacted these people after his whole family left Haiti.

The situation is even worse for a person who has abandoned family members. It is extremely difficult for such people to return. On the other hand, sending money constantly means that transmigrants might not have sufficient funds to return and reap the psychological and emotional rewards of their constant sacrifice. They can't return unless they not only have enough money to pay for their plane ticket that costs about $600 from New York, but also have money and gifts to distribute. Yvette's network of kin and friends is so large that she rarely has been able to afford to go to Haiti. Two of her five trips there during the thirteen years since she arrived in the United States were made to attend funerals. Funerals require less visiting and distribution. You come, you mourn, and you leave. Although there is less pressure, funerals can be an occasion for display and distribution, bestowing status to both transmigrants and those related to them.

The circumstances of transmigrants' lives abroad can be severely constrained by their networks of obligation. To send remittances and provide money for family members to migrate to the United States limits the possibilities for prosperity for the majority of transmigrants. The burden never ends. Yvette can afford to support Mimrose, Lourdes, and a multitude of others on her salary as a mail room clerk because she lives with Georges and Rolande. Georges looks for additional work besides his full-time job and thus has much less time for academic pursuits, let alone recreation. Rolande also seeks out extra sources of income beyond her full-time employment as a hospital administrator. They have two layers of responsibilities: They must sustain many people in Haiti even as they repay the loans they obtained to send two children to elite universities in the United States.

It's not just the money. It's that the responsibilities are unending. You cannot project a time when you know that you will be free of these responsibilities. Most of those who depend on you have no skills or education, and even if they did, there are no jobs in Haiti. And life is getting more expensive in Haiti.

For both the transmigrants in the United States and those living in Haiti, the apparent solution to the problem of never-ending responsibility would seem to be to bring those who are dependent to the United States, where they can then find jobs and support themselves. Certainly, those who live on remittances often see the United States as a place where all dreams come true and everything is possible. Yet it is difficult to bring relatives to the United States because of U.S. immigration laws. Moreover, even when relatives are brought over, they frequently continue to need to be supported, and at a higher cost than in Haiti. The newcomers also often have their own dependents who expect to be supported in Haiti while the newly arrived person is adjusting to life in the United States.

And the complications continue. Transmigrants who spend their money obtaining status for themselves in Haiti fuel expectations among children left behind that they have rich parents and so belong to the leisured class. This can backfire.

That taxi driver I told you about, who spent all his money showing off in Haiti, now has more problems because of the daughter he "found" on one of his trips to Haiti. He had fathered this daughter before he left Haiti, but when he came to Haiti and presented himself as a wealthy man, the girl's mother presented him with his daughter. He then sent money to support her in Haiti, but she wanted to come to the United States. She thought her father lived in a palace. Finally, when she arrived, she found that he lives in a crowded apartment in Brooklyn. He has never invested anything to buy a house or fix up his apartment. All of his money has gone into building up his social status in Haiti. She has been brought up to believe that she is too good to work with her hands so she won't do factory or domestic work. Her father has to support her.

And he does support her. To meet the obligations of family means to do much more than preserve the good opinion of people in Haiti. At the same time, through fulfilling these responsibilities, Haitian transmigrants preserve their claim to be nationalists who love their motherland, even though much of this love is expressed long-distance.

Like the harmonic echoes of a melody, the theme that the nation is an extension of the family, and that both family and nation can extend long distances and across the borders of states, ran through the plaintive, yet proud explanations of the morality of transnational family obligation. Both in Haiti and among Haitians in the United States, as people spoke to us of family, they also talked about their nation. Bad faith to family is therefore disloyalty to the nation. If Georges continued to identify himself as a part of the Haitian nation and claim that he loved his country, he had to assist the person to whom he spoke.

5

"The Blood Remains Haitian": Race, Nation, and Belonging in the Transmigrant Experience

"Where are you going?" The police officer asks, after stopping my car in a neighborhood near the university.

"I am going home," I say.

"Where are you coming from?" The voice in the darkness demands.

"I am coming from Stony Brook. I am a professor," I reply. Then, I show the officer my university identification that indicates that I am Professor Georges Fouron.

"Ok, Georges, be careful," comes the response. Suddenly, the police officer is all smiles and his tone of voice becomes too familiar.

"What did I do, officer?" I ask, although I know all too well that my transgression is being a black man driving through a white suburb at night.

Back comes some cockamamy excuse.

"You crossed the yellow line."

Georges sees himself as someone who has been crossing lines for a long time. In traversing borders and living his life in a transnational field that includes two nation-states, Georges experiences the lines of race and nation as they are drawn in both social orders. Haitian transmigrants live their lives within both Haitian and U.S. understandings of blackness. These perspectives are not the same. The bitter lesson that Georges and other Haitian migrants learn as they strive to become incorporated into life in the United States reinforces their affectionate recollections of the sweetness of Haiti. In his longing for Haiti, Georges combines his daily experiences with the U.S. racial divide and his own ongoing relationship to Haiti. In turn, Haiti reaches out and embraces him across national territorial borders as well as the divisions created by his legal status as a U.S. citizen. This embrace contains the hopes of those left behind who have seen the Haitian diaspora as embodying a brighter future for Haiti.[1]

We have discerned three strands of Haitian long-distance nationalism. Haitian transmigrants weave one strand of their border-crossing nationalism in response to the way they experience "race" in the United States. This has a common thread, made visible in Georges's encounter above with the police officer, who is sworn to serve and protect the U.S. public. On such occasions, persons of color, whatever their legal status, find themselves on the wrong side of the color line.[2] A second strand that makes up the warp and woof of long-distance nationalism is the complex relationship that Georges maintains to Haiti—one in which family obligation, memory, pride, and despair are intertwined. Georges's experiences in the United States shape his memories of and longing for Haiti. At the same time, he remains directly connected to Haiti through his transnational ties of family, the Haitian media—whose radio broadcasts fill his house in New York with Haitian voices, many directly from Haiti—and periodic visits that place him once again on Haitian soil.

The third and final strand of Haitian long-distance nationalism is produced by those who remain in Haiti. Throughout our trip, and the writing of this book, the fervent nationalist appeal that nineteen-year-old Marjorie made to Haitians living abroad stayed with us, compelling us to understand and explain such passion. Boldly, Marjorie had taken our tape recorder in her own hands and said: "Those who are listening to my voice, I urge them to concentrate and remember what country they left behind. It is not for you to ally with other countries. My brothers, see the one on the ground, see the one who has nothing, help him out. Those who are sick, help them as you can. All the bad ideas and bad things, remove them from our lives. Change your heart and then the country will find a solution."

Marjorie lives in a household that is connected to the United States through a flow of remittances. Yet her appeal was based on a broader sense of kinship than the boundaries of her family network. Note that Marjorie identifies those who are "left behind" as a "country" and she speaks to Haitian migrants as her "brothers." She defined all those living abroad as family members who continued to have obligations to those they "left behind."

There is much that is uniquely Haitian in Marjorie's statement about family and nation, as well as in her use of kinship metaphors to construct Haitian long-distance nationalism. It is also the case that some of the roots of Haitian long-distance nationalism spring from U.S. soil. Moreover, the personal networks in Haiti to family members living abroad are becoming a form of intimate political connection to the United States. Many in Haiti are beginning to define migration as an expression of their nationalism. They see settlement in the United States as necessary to both their personal well-being and that of Haiti. The United States, therefore, becomes a location that Haitians can rightfully claim as part of their birthright because of their connection to it through family, history, and political economy. In the emerging transnational realities and long-distance nationalism of Haitians, the United States is becoming the path to the future for Haiti.

In examining the experiences that have led Haitians in Haiti and the United States to develop a transnational concept of nation and make it part of their personal identity, it is important to observe that the Haitian ideology of family, blood, and nation reflects and contributes to nationalism as a set of ideas that motivates political action in countries around the world. Haitian conceptions of nation emerged as part of a more global development of nationalist ideologies that link individuals to states through notions of descent and race.[3] Haitians participated in and were influenced by this global dialogue. Today, long-distance nationalists who engage in transnational politics based in a diverse array of states all draw from a core identity narrative. In this narrative, each person inherits membership in and becomes a representative of her or his ancestral nation. Georges's story, therefore, can tell us about more than his and Haiti's particular situation. As we trace Haitian links between family and nation that extend transnationally, the tale we have to tell provides insights into the fervent attachments so many migrants claim to homelands halfway around the world.

"You Are Different"

Between 1959 and 1993, 302,458 Haitians entered the United States with permanent resident visas and 1,381,240 Haitians arrived with nonimmigrant visas. Most of those entering as nonimmigrants came with tourist visas and arrived by plane.[4] In addition, beginning in about 1971, many tens of thousands of Haitians arrived in south Florida via small wooden sail-boats.[5] Until the 1990s, a great number of the migrants who came by plane as "tourists" did so for much more than a brief visit. Once in the United States, these migrants were able to find employment as factory operatives, janitors, nannies, and domestic workers. With one of these jobs in hand, newcomers could then obtain permanent resident visas on the basis that workers in these occupations were in short supply. Although this use of tourist visas between the 1960s and 1980s differed from the official intent, it provided for a period in which migrants and employers could find each other and establish whether a newcomer had the skills to stay and prosper. Most did.

Individuals who arrived with visitors' visas generally had a network of family members who assisted them in purchasing a ticket and obtaining travel documents. In the 1960s and 1970s, most of those who followed this route came from the middle or upper classes of Haiti, but some were skilled urban workers. Except for the so-called boat people, few came directly from the countryside. While many of the boat people were less educated and came from poorer families than the majority of other Haitian migrants, even boat people tended to arrive with some skills and education.[6] In most cases, it took some resources to be able to buy a place on a crowded, unseaworthy sailboat. Increasing numbers of people from more varied origins began to emigrate by the 1980s, assisted by family members who had preceded them. Most Haitians settled in south Florida and the New York metropoli-tan area, but there are also established Haitian populations in Chicago, Philadelphia, and Stamford, Connecticut, as well as the Washington, D.C., area. New York City was the initial location of settlement, and in 1994, 30 percent of the newly arrived legal migrants continued to settle there.[7]

Georges is one of the many Haitians who arrived in New York with a tourist visa in the 1960s. After receiving his advanced certification in in-ternational relations from the University of the West Indies in Trinidad, Georges got off the aircraft in 1970 knowing that he could not go home, al-though his visa and plane ticket indicated that he was only stopping off on the way home to Haiti.

I knew that in Haiti young men were being tortured, imprisoned, and killed. Some of my friends were disappearing. And even with university degrees, there

was no chance of employment unless you were a supporter of the Duvalier dictator-
ship. Meanwhile, my parents and siblings were looking to me for support. They saw
me as the lucky one, since I was the one with the education and passport. So I got
off the plane in New York City and looked for a job.

Despite his ability to speak English and several university diplomas, Georges sought a low-paying factory job because he lacked one crucial piece of paper: a permanent resident visa that would have allowed him to legally remain in the country and work.[8] Working in a succession of small factories, Georges received his first education about race in the United States. His bosses differentiated him from people they termed "American Negroes" and "Spanish." "You are different," they told him. "You are educated and you work hard. Just stay away from the others and you'll do fine."

But things were not so fine. Georges discovered that racism in the United States could vary with the setting and situation. He gained some immediate advantage when employers made distinctions between black migrants from the Caribbean and African Americans, believing that Caribbean migrants were superior to U.S. blacks.[9] But he quickly learned that when black migrants apply for professional jobs, seek decent housing, or walk down the street, they are suspected simply because they are black. He also discovered that black men are particularly feared and avoided, whether or not they are citizens of the country. Even after Georges obtained his permanent resident visa, although he was well educated and jobs were available, he could only find factory work.

Finally, his old friend Alex and another old school friend who came from a well-to-do family made Georges an offer. They set him up as the manager of a newsstand. Georges would live off some of the profits and send them the rest, so they could go to medical school in Mexico. When the friends in Mexico finished their studies, they would come to the United States and send Georges to graduate school. It all worked for a while. Georges married Rolande, settled in an apartment in Brooklyn, and their daughter Leah was born. The hours in the newsstand were long, but the business was good. In fact, business was too good. The mob moved in and took over the store. Georges was told to "leave the keys and don't look back."

I didn't know what I was going to do next. I didn't know what I was going to tell Rolande. I still had to send money to everyone in Haiti, and now I had a family. I took a factory job for three years and became convinced I would never be able to raise enough money to go to school. I applied for master's degree programs at the public colleges because they were less expensive than the private ones. But the public colleges would not consider my credentials from Haiti and Trinidad. They told me I would have to start college all over again. Rolande encouraged me to apply to Columbia University Teachers College. They accepted me and told me I could pay in installments. I began a master's program in education there, even though I knew that we didn't have enough money in the bank to cover the first check that I gave them. But I got a job in the college library, and Alex paid for part of one semester as he had promised when I ran the newsstand and sent him to medical school in Mexico. We managed somehow, and the next semester I was awarded a fellowship.

With U.S. credentials in teaching, Georges was sure that he could at last be the professional educator he had struggled so hard to become. He wanted to teach poor black children, with whom he identified. But it was difficult for a black man without connections or experience to find a teaching job in the United States in the 1970s, even though there was a teacher shortage. It still is true in New York City that to turn your degree into a job in the school system, it helps to know the principal of a school. There are now Haitian school administrators who are willing to hire Haitian teachers, but in 1980, Georges had to wait until the day before school opened before anyone offered him a job. It turned out to be in a town two hours north of New York.

As soon as I got there, I knew there was something strange about them hiring me. However, it was only months later that I learned that the school district faced legal sanctions for having consistently refused to hire black faculty. That is why they called me. The town was too far for me to commute each day from Brook-

lyn, but no one in the town would rent me a room. Finally, the janitor, who was the only black employee of the school district and who happened to be Haitian, took me in. But he only had a small one-bedroom apartment, and [so] I slept on his living room couch. Then a widowed Jewish Holocaust survivor who lived in the next town called me up and invited me to share her house. I moved in with her, and she insisted that I stay, even when she began to receive threatening phone calls because of my presence. The faculty sympathized with me, but they would not invite me to their homes. They explained, apologetically, that they were certain that I would be gone the next year and they had to continue to live in the community.

The next year Georges did leave. He found a teaching job in Brooklyn. After several years, he won a doctoral fellowship in education at Columbia. When he finished his advanced degree, he was able to find a faculty position at the State University of New York at Stony Brook. But that first bitter year teaching in upstate New York had served as an initiation into the experience of blackness in the United States. The lessons have continued over the years. He has had students walk into his university classroom, look right past him, and ask for the professor. Students have told him that growing up on Long Island, New York, the only other black person they have ever known was their maid.

And then there are the police. Nina, who is always late and in a hurry, often becomes impatient with Georges, who never speeds. But Georges's care in obeying every traffic regulation goes beyond his efforts to be a good citizen; he has learned that no matter how long he lives in the United States and whatever his legal status, his right to belong will always be open to question.

In all of these encounters, Georges remembers that he is a descendant of African slaves who rose up and created the new black nation of Haiti, crossing the line that defined the governance of an independent state as a whites-only privilege. He becomes a part of that black nation that continues to challenge the idea that only whites are deserving of personal and political sovereignty. In this context, his successes and the accomplishments of his family belong to Haiti and all black people. Haiti's failures similarly reflect on his self-esteem—a self in which he is a representative of his family, race, and nation.

Doing What Comes Naturally

Georges takes a chair into the small courtyard in front of his brother Alfred's home, and sits on it so that the chair leans back and rests against the wall of the house. He smiles as he looks around him, his body resting contentedly in the Haitian version of a recliner. The sky is a vivid blue, the sun is bright, and there is a lovely breeze. It is Georges's first day back to Haiti after an absence of four years. He is in a state of euphoria.

This is home and I don't see myself spending the rest of my life in the United States. It is only here that I feel really alive. It's something in the air—the smells, the tastes, the sounds. It's something about the way things look and feel. I just finally feel right. Wow!

All his youthful memories come rushing back: the desperate days of trying to find money to leave Haiti are mixed together with the longing he has experienced ever since for the lost solidarity of close-knit friendships. He remembers the good times: hunting birds with slingshots, bathing in the river, and sitting up late and talking with friends. He also recalls the bad times: the fear that there would be no future for him in Haiti, his fear of the macoute, the scarcity of food and clothing, and the rage of his mother directed toward him because she could not provide for him. Despite these painful memories, he feels a sense of peace. Coming home as a successful professional, his sense of achievement and the differences between his past and present circumstances heighten the delights of return.

By the second day, Georges's tone has changed. He has begun to notice things. First, he sees the roads. "They are a disgrace," he tells Nina and anyone else who will listen. Even the paved ones are full of potholes so that you can't drive without zigzagging as if you were drunk. There is also the dust. It makes everything and everyone look dirty. And there is the disorder everywhere. Automobile and truck drivers respect no rules. There is garbage in the streets, too. The government doesn't repair the roads or pick up the trash. As each day goes by, Georges's discomfort with the situation in Haiti increases.

A week later, Georges goes to the airport to pick up Alex, his boyhood and best friend who comes to Haiti every summer. Georges returns muttering, "*Se pa posib. Se pa posib*" ("It's not possible. It's not possible"). After a week in Haiti, he sees the airport differently than he did in the euphoria of his arrival. He notices that the electronic sign that is supposed to flash the next flight's time of arrival continually announces that it is Thursday afternoon. He is incensed that family members are forced to stand for hours outside the terminal in the relentless sun, waiting for arriving passengers. The disorder and confusion at the airport fill him with shame. Nina is puzzled. As she records in the field notes that she writes after each day's work:

It seems so unlike Georges to put the conditions of the pavement before the conditions of the people? Just why do these particular aspects of Haiti upset Georges so much? Why at the airport did he see the lack of order and public facilities? Why didn't he comment on the hungry women and children asking for money? Why is it that it was only after this visit to the airport that he began worrying about the impressions a white American friend who is coming for a first visit to Haiti later that summer will have about Haiti?[10]

Months later, as we sit listening to the tapes of our interviews and reading Nina's field notes, we are able to explore the complexity of Georges's feelings for the country of his birth and the United States.

When we were in Haiti, I wanted to point to something that would make me proud. It was supposed to be a new time for Haiti, now that there was democracy and a popularly elected government. Here is a government that denounced the neglect of the country by dictators and yet they allow the same neglect. I expected a sense of renewal. And I also saw that the current leaders don't really care about Haiti. And the airport was upsetting because this is the first thing that foreigners see. I felt that foreigners use the disorder and decay as a justification for racism.

They could look at everything falling in disrepair and say: "These people need for-
eigners to come in and run things for them." I felt ashamed, especially at a time
when a new government was in control.

It is not that the poverty didn't bother me. But couldn't the government at
least get a few people together and pick up the garbage and make the streets clean?
With the garbage, you have diseases and all kinds of things. And I felt that the con-
dition of the airport and the roads made it clear that these people were not responsi-
ble leaders. And I felt it even more when we went for a trip to the Dominican Re-
public that summer and I saw the museums, the roads, the modernization, and
the national monuments. There, you have the sense that someone is doing some-
thing in the country. Where are the museums in Haiti? Port-au-Prince was
founded in 1749. Where are the historical sites? I kept thinking, we have been inde-
pendent for nearly two hundred years. What do we have to show the world?

Georges's reaction to the condition of Haiti was shaped by the fact that
since the Haitian revolution, European and white American leaders have
devalued the culture and national independence of Haiti.[11] The white gaze
that he constantly experiences in the United States reinforces his longing
for Haiti and becomes part of his relationship to Haiti. When he returns to
Haitian territory, the political and economic situation in Haiti becomes a
source of personal shame. Nation, race, and self are tied to his experience of
Haiti, whether he is on Haitian soil or in the United States.

Blood Ties

In 1804, the national identity of Haiti was forged in a successful slave rebel-
lion that defeated the armies of Napoleon and led to Haiti becoming the
first black republic. Before the Haitian Revolution, the vast majority of the
population in the French colony of Saint Domingue had been enslaved Africans. The colony had also contained a vocal population of educated free
mulattoes, the offspring of black slave mothers and white plantation owners. Many among the mulattoes were claimed by their wealthy fathers and

educated in France. They became owners of plantations and slaves. Some of these men participated in the French Revolution and its fiery debates about liberty and equality. They expected that Haitian mulattoes would be granted full citizenship rights in France. Black slaves in Haiti heard of the talk about the "rights of man" as well and expected an end to slavery.

By the close of the eighteenth century, political theorists seeking a way to legitimate state power over the people without reference to the divine right of kings promoted the concept of the "natural rights of man." These rights were said to be the common possession of persons who inhabited the territory controlled by the state. The state drew its authority from "the people." Inhabitants of a territory governed by such a state were said to be a "people" or "nation." As this theory was popularized, the word "nation" became transformed from earlier meanings of localized descent groups to a "fundamental political category."[12] But certain questions about "the people" remained. Were all persons living within the borders of a state to be included equally in "the people" and therefore regarded as citizens? Both the U.S. founding fathers and the French revolutionaries struggled over whether "the people" encompassed persons of African descent.

The French revolutionary government abolished slavery, but was divided as to whether persons in their colonies, and especially those of African descent, could claim the rights of French citizenship. Some held that black people could become French citizens if they spoke the French language fluently and assimilated into French culture. But within a few years, this position was defeated, slavery was reinstituted, and even the sophisticated slave-owning mulattoes were denied French citizenship.[13]

Underlying the arguments on both sides was a conception of the nation as a community of blood.[14] Ideas of blood as a basis for citizenship were debated by Haitian and French intellectuals during the years of the French Revolution when mulattoes from Haiti claimed the rights of French citizens. There was an organized faction within the French revolutionary government that repudiated these claims. This group contended that "blacks and mulattoes, whatever they may say, are not true French" because "they are not tied by any tie to France. . . . they have no blood ties from France, and they don't have patriotic feelings toward France."[15] The opposition wanted to recognize the French citizenship of Haitian mulattoes on the grounds that they had fathers of French descent so that they were indeed connected by birth to France.

In the French concept of citizenship that developed in the wake of the

French Revolution, mastery of the French culture and language rather than lineage were taken to be gauges of who was sufficiently civilized to be accorded French citizenship. Nevertheless, the French discovered, as did the American revolutionaries, that one could talk about human rights yet still have slavery and colonization. To justify this seeming contradiction, U.S. and French political theorists began to categorize all people of color as not fully civilized, and perhaps even incapable of civilization. They equated civilization, in short, with whiteness.[16]

These debates about whether or not black people were to be included in "the rights of man" helped spark the Haitian Revolution, and contributed to the conflation of concepts of family, blood, and nation that continue to be part of Haitian daily life today. In conceptualizing the newly emerging nation after the French Revolution, Haitians adopted the language of peoplehood and nation. Various declarations signed by Jean-Jacques Dessalines, the victorious general who led Haiti to independence, read "in the name of the Haitian people." In the Act of Independence of 1804, reference is also made to liberty "consecrated by the blood of the people of this island."[17] Liberty was being won through the sacrifice of the people's blood.

The Haitian state was founded on 1 January 1804. The way this moment is remembered is informative. According to Haitian historian Beaubrun Ardouin, whose 1853 accounting of the founding of the nation both reflected and became incorporated into Haitian written and oral histories, "Dessalines asked the audience and generals and the troops to swear that they would defend the freedom of the people, of the entire race of people that had up until now been vilified as slaves. As a response to that appeal made to the people, the population of Gonaïves, men and women, representing the young Haitian nation and the entire black race, pronounced also this oath, which tied it to its future descendants from that moment into all generations as a distinct fatherland."[18]

The first Constitution of Haiti declared the Haitian people to be black, introducing the language of race into the nation's formation. In fact, in defiance of the values of the powerful cultures of Europe and their equation of civilization with whiteness, Haitians defined the "black" (*nèg*) to mean both a Haitian citizen and human being. No matter what your skin color, you could become a Haitian citizen if you lived in Haiti. Thus, the use of the word black for Haitian citizens did not initially equate Haitian citizenship with ancestry. The white Polish soldiers who fought on the side of the slave uprising were granted Haitian citizenship, and over the centuries,

Middle Eastern Arabs and Jews, German Jewish refugees from Nazism, and various Europeans seeking their fortunes have settled in Haiti and become citizens. In so doing, they became nèg. Nonetheless, over the years, as a concept of the Haitian people developed, it became linked with a concept of a community of blood that shares, as a common ancestry, the revolutionary heroes who rose up against slavery and founded the nation.

Generally, whenever and wherever in the world new political leaders come to power through the force of arms, they face the problem of obtaining political recognition from abroad and winning acceptance from the international community. The challenge confronting the political leaders of Haiti from the beginning was of a more fundamental nature, however, and one that has engaged the poorest peasant and most urbane of the elite in a common struggle. The entire population of Haiti and its leaders found themselves marginalized because of their color.

Since its founding in 1804, Haiti has come up against various forms of exclusion or punitive treatment by the United States and the European states. By the nineteenth century, Europeans used a concept of race to distinguish between those they judged fit to rule and those they considered only capable of being ruled. Haitians—even the mulatto elite, fluent in French, dressed in the latest Parisian fashions, well read and well bred—were by these standards considered unable to govern a country. Haitian diplomats and scholars were ridiculed because they dared to assert their equality with whites. Over the years, Haitians came to understand that their claims to acceptance as human beings in the eyes of the white world were linked to the degree to which the leaders of other governments acknowledged the sovereignty of the Haitian state and accorded honor to the Haitian nation.

In struggling to win respect for their nation, Haitians found that they were ridiculed because of the religious practices of the majority of the Haitian people. The many religious beliefs of Africa and the Christianity brought from Europe had been brought together in Haiti as a new religion, which has come to be called Vodou. This syncretic religion recognizes the power of an almighty god (*Bondye* or *Gran Mèt*) as well as numerous ancestral and natural spirits (*lwa*) who are often represented by the images of Catholic saints. Beginning in 1865, the Catholic Church, which had broken its ties with Haiti after the revolution, established a formal relationship with the Haitian government and began to import European priests. These priests condemned Vodou and organized anti-Vodou campaigns. The vari-

ous Protestant denominations that became increasingly important in Haiti
in the twentieth century also supported campaigns against Vodou. As a result, the Haitian elite and educated people of all class backgrounds have
publicly repudiated Vodou, although many privately practice it. European
and U.S. governments and intellectuals used Vodou to discredit the viability of Haiti as a black sovereign state and as a key indicator of the failure
of black people to achieve civilization. Until the U.S. occupation, though,
many rural Haitians were removed from these challenges to their sense of
pride and identity.

All these slights to national honor, and to the capacities and intelligence
of the Haitian people, became known to the general populace when the
United States invaded and occupied Haiti for nineteen years. From 1915 to
1934, the United States governed Haiti, justifying its presence in terms of
the inability of Haitians to maintain order in their own country. The occupation ensured that the United States, rather than competing European
powers, obtained access to Haitian bauxite and tropical products such as
rubber and sugar, all seen as essential for U.S. industrial development. The
Haitian Constitution was rewritten by the U.S. military forces to allow foreigners to own property in Haiti. Attempts were made to build an infrastructure of roads, railroads, and sanitation facilities and services conducive
to the extraction of profits for U.S. corporations.

The occupation favored the mulattoes, putting in place light-skinned
presidents and creating an army led by light-skinned officers. At the same
time, the U.S. occupiers tried to draw racial lines between themselves and
all Haitians. Even the educated elites were characterized as racially different
and incapable of civilization. For instance, Colonel Littleton Waller, a Ma-
rine Corps commander who became the senior U.S. military officer in
Haiti, wrote to a friend in the United States expressing his views of the Haitians among whom he worked: "Thes [sic] people are niggers in spite of the
thin varnish of education and refinement. Down in their hearts they are just
the same happy, idle, irresponsible people we know of."[19] As the occupation
became organized, the United States racially segregated all Haitians. The
Catholic Church established separate masses for white North Americans.
Local hotels, which catered to whites from the United States, adopted Jim
Crow regulations. White U.S. social clubs were established that excluded all
Haitians, even the president of Haiti.[20]

Haitian intellectuals responded to the racism of the U.S. occupation by
defending the intellectual capacities of all people of African descent. The

U.S. occupation ended in 1934, but the efforts of Haitian leaders and writers to defend the capacities of black people continued. They used examples of Haitian achievements in the white world as evidence. For example, Daniel Fignole, a populist political leader in the 1940s and 1950s, edited a journal *Chantier* that popularized the achievements of Haitian intellectuals such as Louis Joseph Janvier, a Haitian who had obtained distinction for his studies both of medicine and political science in Paris in the nineteenth century. Janvier's achievements were said to prove that "the brain of blacks has great elasticity, and it has the facility to acquire all sorts of knowledge without becoming exhausted."[21] Similarly, noting the death of a prominent intellectual, Dr. Justin-Chrysostome Dorsainvil, an article in *Chantier* stated, "The country, the black Race, especially our black Community, has lost in J. C. Dorsainvil one of the 'astonishing products' that you see only once every fifty years and that proves that this African Branch (section of the African race) has at its disposal an inexhaustible reservoir of intellectual and moral worth capable of flourishing in all areas of endeavor, if the natural and human obstacles are removed."[22]

Throughout the twentieth century, Haitian political leaders also have popularized a language of blood and ancestry that evokes the imagery of the nation of Haiti standing independent as a sacred patrimony of all Haitians. *Chantier* asserted, "We must remember that to break the chains of slavery our fathers had to shed their blood. In creating the Haitian Nation they dreamed, before everything else, to transmit to their children, a little corner of land where freely, they could earn their living through hard and conscientious work. Haiti is thus the inheritance of our forefathers."[23]

Duvalier took up this portrait and used it to legitimate his rule when he came to power in 1957. In taking on the name "Papa Doc," he gained patriarchal authority and legitimacy. He also transformed portions of the Catholic liturgy into a statement of obedience to be recited by all schoolchildren and at public occasions. Prayers that were well-known even to the illiterate majority and incorporated into the opening rituals of Vodou services were converted into pronouncements of patriotic faith. Duvalier's version of the Lord's Prayer began: "Our Doc, who art in the Palais National for life, hallowed be Thy name, for by past, present, and future generations, Thy will be done in Port-au-Prince as it is in the provinces."[24] In this way, Duvalier surrounded his regime and its representation of the nation with an aura of the sacred. He built on the ideology of the inherent relationship between self and nation, ancestry and Haiti. His contention, "I am the flag," was widely ridiculed by foreign observers of Haitian politics. Yet, this equation of self with nation resonated with a sense of identity that he shared with both rural and urban Haitians who saw their ties to Haiti as formed from blood and inheritance. To the Haitian poor and elite he was also saying, "you/we are the flag," the nation.

In order to legitimate his regime, Duvalier made numerous and seemingly contradictory connections between the sacred, the religious beliefs and practices of people in Haiti, and an identification with the nation. He surrounded himself with symbols of the spirits of Vodou so that as he linked himself to the nation, he was simultaneously projecting himself as an embodiment of spirit. He wore black suits and top hats, the symbols of Baron Samedi, the guardian of cemeteries who stands between life and death, controlling movement between the world of the living and that of the spirits. Many people in Haiti believed that Duvalier had these same supernatural powers. If he was the flag/nation, then there was no division between the nation and the realm of the spirits. Duvalier also rejected the white foreign church hierarchy appointed by the Vatican to serve in Haiti, and appointed in their place Haitian bishops and other church officials. In so doing, he fanned nationalist sentiments in Haiti by claiming that the Catholic Church was part of the Haitian nation.

If, in the Haiti of Georges's childhood, the conflation of self, ancestry, blood, and nation was promoted by both political and religious functionaries, these same notions were also embedded in the oral traditions and literature of Haiti. The idea of Haiti as a nation united by a common ancestry—a nation that was won through bloodshed and united by blood—was reiterated constantly in Haitian stories, songs, and writings. Haitians of all classes and colors came to define themselves as heirs to the founding ancestors of the Haitian Revolution. These founders are known to literate Haitians through school textbooks. To illiterate Haitians, they are known through oral traditions and Vodou. Several of the revolutionary heroes became *lwa* (spirits); Ezili Danto, one of the most important of the lwa, is said to have participated in the Haitian Revolution.[25]

In the Haiti of today, revolutionary ancestors and a language of blood that links family, God, and nation continue to provide a basis for community as well as a linkage between past and future. Aristide built on this legacy in his sermons, using references to national pride and religious faith to promote the agenda of the poor: "If you are a Haitian and you have Haitian blood that runs in your veins, if you are a real Haitian, stand beneath the flag of conviction and sing the national anthem. Link your faith with your commitment . . . like the proud Christians that you are."[26] We found echoes of this message that projects the Haitian people as a Christian family in our interviews. Twenty-seven-year-old Maurice, who had been a participant in a church-based organization, told us:

> We will see if Haiti is to make any progress. Only God will say something. There is much to be done yet. I would like to add that we would like to see that all those people who think that they are Haitian, everyone who would like to have a life, all those who have some sense of responsibility, who have love as Christians, to put their heads together to help Haiti, to help their brothers and sisters, especially those who are worse off. Those with possibility and those with goodwill. Those who do good may not find their reward on earth but life is not over when you die since we have to live again in another world, maybe we may not think it exists but it does exist because we have a creator.

To tie together the concept of family and nation, we found people in Haiti constantly using a language of blood. "Blood, that's blood that makes you a true Haitian," we heard repeatedly. "I am Haitian because my parents are Haitian. . . . It is in the blood" was the way family, blood, and nation were connected by Dimase, a thirty-three-year-old man who received support from his three brothers and two sisters in New York and California. When asked to define what it meant to be Haitian, 82 percent of the people we interviewed spoke of descent. Half of the respondents began their exposition by speaking of "Haitian blood."

While the shared mythology and rituals of nationhood have been common to all classes in Haiti, linking them to a pride of nation, this mythology has not necessarily connected them to each other. Class divisions in Haiti have historically been expressed through distinctions of color and language: the dominant classes spoke French and were portrayed as mulattoes; the rural poor spoke Kreyòl and were identified as black.[27] Through most of Haiti's past, elites spoke of their pride in the Haitian nation. They also argued that Haitian culture was fundamentally French. Haitians' ability to master French culture proved to the world that black people had the capacity to participate in the highest levels of civilization. The black middle class that emerged as significant political actors after World War II generally valued French culture, too. Georges remembers that although there was no money in his house for food, his father, a poorly paid head of a vocational school in Haiti, subscribed to *Paris Match* and several other French periodicals.

Although the Haitian poor have in many ways accepted the value of French culture and whiteness, they have also created their own definitions of what it means to be Haitian, seeing Haitian culture not only as one of pride but also of proud suffering. In our interviews, we were told, "A Haitian is someone who knows poverty, suffering, and who is full of anger/resentment, and is ready for all eventualities, who embraces life the way s/he finds it." This idea of Haiti as a nation, defined not by the fact that its people share a culture and territory but by a historical experience of pain and persecution, was echoed by Vico, age twenty-one. Vico was supported by his mother, who had emigrated to the United States and was sending money to allow her son to finish high school. As he explained, "The word Haitian means someone who is part of Haiti; finally, a Haitian is someone who has been mistreated."

The class divisions and tensions are not seen by the poor to negate the unity of the nation; their anger and illiteracy has not meant that they have been isolated from or alien to the language of national identity and unity. Rather, they have accepted the metaphor of Haitian blood as uniting the nation. They use this language to critique the ever-widening class divisions in Haiti and the use of color distinctions to justify such divides. For many of the poor, all Haitian people have the same blood, and it is black. Jeremie, who grew up in the countryside and had never been to school, had worked for years as an artisan within Haiti's tourist sector. At the age of fifty-six, with tourists no longer coming to Haiti, he had been surviving for many years on remittances. Sitting in the yard of his house, surrounded by grandchildren he was tending for family living abroad, he said: "There really is *ti wouj* [mulatto] and *ti nwa* [black]. The reason why that exists is because a lot of them do not . . . realize that if I cut myself and they also cut themselves, the blood would be the same color. But because they are looking at the skin color they are saying there is mulatto and black. But in reality we are the same nation of the same color—black, black, black—and we are the same blood." Sedye, an unemployed, impoverished musician who serves the lwa, emphasized this same theme to us. His barely habitable one-room apartment has rotted staircases and floors. While perched on a balcony that gave him a wonderful but precarious view of Port-au-Prince, he remarked: "All of the colors are from Guinea [Africa] and have value, and God created all of them. . . . When Cedras [the head of the military coup that ousted Aristide in 1991] took power, they said that all of those who are in the lower class are called black pigs [*nèg nwè kochon nwè*]. . . . The mulattoes, with the black blood in their veins, are saying these stupid things."

Changing Locations of Haiti

The language of nation as a family of persons who share a common ancestry and blood that the poor use to critique the rich, and that all classes use to unite the nation, is currently providing Haitians with a potent ideology to link emigrants and their descendants to the Haitian nation-state. When Haitians arrive in the United States, they come with a clear sense of their own national identity.[28] While they may claim a tie to a small rural hamlet, large town, or Port-au-Prince as part of their sense of self, they also firmly identify with the Haitian nation. In the late 1950s through the 1970s, however, when Haitians first began to arrive in significant numbers in New York City, they certainly did not see themselves as part of a transnational nation-state. Haitian nationalist ideology at the time portrayed those who left Haiti as having abandoned their nation.

Until the 1990s, Haitians in the United States, whether they participated in organized Haitian activities or remained distant from formal groups, tended to believe that you had to choose either to be loyal to Haiti and eventually return or "forget about Haiti" and become an American.[29] Permanent emigration was defined as an abandonment of home and family.[30] You might have multiple identities, but you could have only one political loyalty. That loyalty would ultimately determine where you physically resided. Most Haitian migrants believed that each person could have only one nation, and that to be part of that nation, you had to live within its territorial boundaries.

In this political outlook, Haitians reflected the understanding of nation-states that had become hegemonic after World War II, as well as a distinction between native and foreign that has deep historical roots in Haiti. All persons who were born on Haitian territory of Haitian parents were defined as Haitian, and all Haitians were defined as black. Blackness carried with it the sense of being human. All foreigners, whatever the color of their skin, are by definition white and therefore capable of inhuman behavior. Those Haitians who left their homeland became in a certain sense foreign; that is, they became white and could not be trusted. This division between native and foreign was reinforced and popularized by François Duvalier, when his relentless pursuit of all internal political opposition precipitated a large-scale exodus from Haiti. The Duvalier regime was able to mobilize nationalist sentiment against those who had fled. The Haitian government labeled emigrants as traitors, scum, and enemies of the nation. Organized contacts with Haitians abroad were discouraged, and Duvalier's spies were rumored to monitor Haitian migrants in New York to ascertain if they were conspiring with persons in Haiti.

Similarly, Haitian anti-Duvalier activists in the United States embraced a political rhetoric that drew a sharp line between Haitians living abroad and those in Haiti. They criticized remittances to families or hometowns and scolded any migrant organizations that contributed to projects in Haiti. These contributions, they claimed, maintained the oppressive Haitian government and thus harmed the nation. They portrayed the diaspora as political refugees in exile from repression, rather than as permanent residents.[31] These leaders feared that as Haitians became incorporated economically and socially in the United States, they would abandon the struggle against the Duvalier regime. Consequently, most Haitian migrant leaders preached a "politics of return" that called on Haitians abroad first to work for the overthrow of the Duvalier regime and then to return to rebuild Haiti. Haitians could realize their loyalty to their homeland, according to the politics of return, only by going back to Haiti. Becoming a U.S. citizen was seen as a shameful betrayal of the Haitian homeland.

This was the political climate that greeted Georges when he arrived in New York in 1969. He, his best friends, and his close family members, who readily confided in each other about sexual trysts as well as other personal triumphs and failures, did not tell each other when they became U.S. citizens. Nina, observing the pressures to return in the 1960s through 1980s, thought it all sounded familiar. But it was not until the two of us began systematically studying long-distance nationalism that we put together the Haitian nationalist exhortations "to return" with the Zionist appeals to American Jews "to return" to Israel. We began to realize that both the Haitian and Jewish nationalist language echoed the nationalist literature at the turn of the twentieth century. At that time, European political leaders made the same call to their compatriots settling in the United States: "Return home and rebuild your homeland."[32]

Sitting in living rooms among a circle of family and friends, men of all class backgrounds debated whether it made more sense to plan to return to or "forget about Haiti." Did they see themselves as exiles waiting for the end of the Duvalier dictatorship when they would return to rebuild Haiti, or as uprooted immigrants who had cut their ties to home? Women rarely entered into these living room debates, but they also considered the question of return as they participated in church, school, and family settings in discussions about the preservation of Haitian culture and the future of the next generation. Haiti remained the point of reference among the hundreds of Haitians we interviewed or spoke with in informal conversations in New York from the 1960s through the 1980s. Meanwhile, of course, most Haitians were intimately engaged in the life of Haiti, monitoring news from Haiti, debating the current situation, and searching for ways to sustain their family networks. What Haitian transmigrants lacked was a political language that made visible and validated their sense of continuing to be part of Haiti.

Both the Duvalier regime and the anti-Duvalier activists began to use the word *diaspora*, which until that time had not been part of the Haitian political vocabulary. For the Duvalierists, the diaspora was those Haitians who had abandoned the nation by emigrating, and hence, were outside of and against the nation. Haitian leaders abroad labeled Haitians living outside the United States as "the diaspora" as a way of communicating that all Haitians abroad were exiles and political refugees whose goal was to return home to rebuild Haiti. Until the 1990s, however, most people in Haiti or most Haitians abroad either did not know the word or avoided using it because it was seen as being too politically charged. In our 1985 interviews with ninety-three leaders of Haitian organizations in the New York metropolitan area, only the leaders of anti-Duvalierist organizations acknowledged being familiar with the word *diaspora*.

Given the legacy of the political disconnection of emigrants from their homeland and the new realities of being categorized as black Americans, no matter what their culture or the color tone of their skin, it is not surprising that in the first decades of settlement, Haitian migrants adopted a multiplicity of alternative identities and kept a low profile. At first, many publicly identified themselves as French. Our interviews with Haitian migrant leaders in 1985 introduced to us people who, although identified as Haitians in our research, had many other identities as well. For these leaders, Christian, Haitian nationalist, Haitian American, American, Masonic, French, black, African, African American, and hometown identities could all be overlapping, noncontradictory public identities.[33]

During these first decades of settlement in the United States, Haitians did not see themselves as a distinct ethnic group or "Haitian community" in the United States. The dissemination of the concept of the Haitian community, and the different meanings imparted to this term by Haitians and non-Haitians in the United States, is a result of four decades of interaction with U.S.-based institutions and their efforts to incorporate black migrants into the U.S. social fabric. The first organizational identities embraced by Haitian migrants of upper- or middle-class origins in the 1960s were those of class not community. As they tried to make it in the United States, their old world beckoned, and it was not the old world of memory but that of transnational family connection to which they continued to belong. For people from the elite mulatto families or the educated middle class, there was much at stake. As they bent over a factory assembly line, parked cars, or pushed a broom, it was important to hold onto the fact that in Haiti they were people who commanded respect. To preserve their social position in Haiti, they had to maintain Haitian class divisions in the United States. This meant that persons of high status in Haiti avoided interacting in the United States with Haitians whom they saw as their social inferiors. Upper-class Haitians built elite social clubs rather than community organizations and did not speak or act in terms of a united Haitian community. They identified with Haiti, not with other Haitian migrants. Over time, many of the mulatto elite families quietly withdrew to the suburbs, where they continued to keep their distance from other Haitians.

It was only as they encountered the civic culture of New York City that Haitians began organizing as a community. The newcomers, arriving in the New York metropolitan area in increasingly large numbers in the 1960s, found no public recognition of their transnational connections and continuing identification with Haiti. They were, however, encouraged by politicians and church officials to organize as Haitians, with the connotation that they were a new U.S. ethnic group. Before the 1960s, black migrants had not been perceived by the white mainstream as having distinctive ethnicities; they were seen simply as black. But in the wake of the civil rights and black power movements, public authorities in the 1960s began to not only recognize but actively foster black ethnic differences. Haitians were offered occasions to distinguish themselves from African Americans.[34]

To understand the meaning of this sponsorship of black ethnicity and the Haitian response, it is crucial to separate, as well as acknowledge the connections between, ethnic identity and long-distance nationalism. There is tremendous variation in the academic literature and everyday conversational practices in the English-speaking world between these two terms. Part of the confusion arises from the rapidly changing uses of the words *ethnicity* and *nation* in the course of the twentieth century. To understand the U.S. migrant experience, we find it most useful to link both terms to the ways in which U.S. political leaders, academics, and white mainstream institutions such as political parties and major foundations have approached the task of incorporating immigrants into the United States. These public opinion makers currently deploy both *ethnic group* and *ethnicity* as a means of acknowledging cultural difference within the fabric of U.S. society. To the extent that they affirm the right to cultural difference, they abandon the efforts to assimilate immigrants that require newcomers to give up all other forms of identification in order to become genuine Americans. They move from a melting pot model of society in which all cultures blend into a single, unified, uniquely U.S. culture to one of cultural pluralism or multiculturalism. Multiculturalism accords immigrants compound ethnic identities, so that Haitians become Haitian Americans.[35] While the U.S. model of multiculturalism projects a culturally diverse society made up of multiple ethnic groups, it does not allow for long-distance nationalism. The celebration of culture within multiculturalism is one of ancestral roots, not ongoing political relationships and loyalties.

In the 1960s, the National Democratic Party created a special slot for Haitians on the All-American Council, a clustering of European ethnic groups, and encouraged the formation of the Haitian-American Citizens Society based in New York. U.S. Catholic dioceses began to employ Haitian priests and establish special masses for Haitians. By the 1970s, the New York City Community Development Agency, an offspring of President Johnson's War On Poverty, began to fund separate Haitian community centers. Protestant organizations such as the American Baptist Convention advocated the creation of separate Haitian congregations. In the 1980s, the Ford Foundation funded the Haitian Centers Council, an umbrella group of New York community centers. The Catholic Church and Ford Foundation also supported Haitian community organizations in south Florida in the 1980s. Currently, in the various localities of Haitian settlement, Haitian priests, ministers, educators, newspaper reporters, and radio broadcasters routinely appeal to and speak in the name of the Haitian community. They portray Haitians within a U.S. ethnic mosaic and celebrate Haitians' contributions to the "cultural diversity of America."[36]

This perception of Haitians as a new U.S. ethnic group has been popularized in a variety of ways. The public school system has played a major
role. For example, the Haitian patriotic songs that Rolande and Georges
learned during their childhood in Haiti were taught to their children Leah
and Jacob in their elementary school in New York City in the 1980s. During
their school assemblies in Brooklyn, their teachers dressed the Haitian children in the red and blue of the Haitian flag and marched them onstage.
They pledged allegiance to the Haitian flag and sang the song, *"Nous Tè
Voulons Chère Patrie"* ("We Love You, Dear Fatherland"), to remind them
of their Haitian identity. The "Hispanic" children also sang the national an-
thems of their countries of origin.

More recently, school administrators in south Florida began to teach
Haitian children Haitian patriotic rituals and rhetoric. Palm Beach County
adopted a seventh-grade curriculum in 1998 that included the teaching of
Haitian history from 1400 to 1987. Students are taught to "compare information about Haitian politics and language before and after Haiti became
the first independent nation in the Caribbean."[37] The Broward County
schools have started to celebrate the Battle of Vertières, a decisive 1803 contest at the end of the Haitian Revolution that has long been commemorated
in Haiti. According to a Florida newspaper, local schools observed the Haitian national holiday "with patriotic songs, dance, and Haitian food" in order to "promote recognition of the holiday among Haitian-American students and awareness of Haitian history to the public."[38]

U.S. institutions, organizations, and political leaders—including local
school systems, the Ethical Culture Society, and members of the New
York City Council—also have sponsored or endorsed celebrations of Haitian Flag Day for two decades. In 1982, for instance, the United Haitian Association (UHA), which had been formed in 1978 with the support of the
program director of the New York Council of Churches, organized such a
celebration. U.S. lawyers were present to provide legal advice about immigration. The Haitian founder and head of the association told his audience
that his organization conducted activities "to promote the Haitian culture
in the heart of the other ethnic groups living in the United States and
abroad." But he went on to make an appeal on behalf of Haiti: "UHA requests your time, your participation, your enthusiasm to continue the big
fight which undoubtedly will result in the liberation of the refugees and the
liberation of Haiti." The evening closed with the singing of the Haitian
national anthem and shouts of "Unity, Victory, Long Live Haiti." A UHA

newsletter concluded its reporting of the event with a "Patriotic Appeal to the Community. . . . On this commemorative day of the creation of our bi-color symbol of the sacred Union of our ancestors who forged our nation, the UHA reminds the Haitian community that the land is a continued cre-ation, that all the Haitians should feel agitation in them, the noble feeling and the great emotions capable of feeding their patriotic flame."[39]

In 1997, 18 May was celebrated as Haitian Flag Day in New York City, as it has been for many years. The festivities began with an ecumenical service at a Catholic Church in Brooklyn that has been a center for Haitian activi-ties since the 1960s. The same day there was a cultural fair, a theater presen-tation, a basketball tournament, Haitian Flag Day programs in three high schools and two colleges in Brooklyn, and a walkathon at Medgar Evers, a branch of the City University of New York that has been a center for African American and Caribbean studies. The Brooklyn Society for Ethical Cul-ture, together with the Haitian Cultural Society, hosted an all-day event at which several Haitian intellectuals were invited to speak about the signifi-cance of Haitian Flag Day in a program titled "Haiti: The Making of a Nation."

Throughout the first decades of settlement, despite all the celebration of Haiti, there was no public acknowledgment that Haitian migrants were maintaining and reinforcing transnational familial, economic, religious, and organizational ties to Haiti. But organizations formed to represent the Haitian community as an ethnic group in the United States increasingly became engaged in activities in Haiti. Catholic parishes in New York and Miami emerged as some of the public faces of the Haitian community in the United States, advocating for Haitian refugees and providing immi-grant services. At the same time, they became a catalyst for political change in Haiti. Haitian Americans United for Progress (HAUP) typified this de-velopment. Based in a Catholic Church in an area of dense middle-class Haitian settlement in Queens, New York, and led by Catholic priests and lay church leaders, HAUP received funding in 1969 from a federal antipov-erty program to "empower" the Haitian community. In the following de-cades, the organization obtained grants for community development, as-sisted Haitian boat people, and provided job training and English classes. It also became a founding member of the Haitian Centers Council, an or-ganization funded by several philanthropic groups in order to unite Hai-tian organizations in New York. Following what would appear to be a clas-sic immigrant path into U.S. politics, HAUP created ties with local political clubs along with links to state and federal elected representatives from Queens. But HAUP had another face, less visible to funders and more prominent among Haitian migrants. It served as a center for anti-Duvalier activity, hosting meetings where men and women debated the political situation in Haiti, and the "American plan" of restructuring the Haitian economy to foster export processing and agribusiness. Growing strength in local-level politics in the United States went hand in hand with an increasing political engagement in Haiti.

In the eyes of many school administrators, U.S. politicians, and philanthropic organizations, the various community activities and celebrations of Haitian national holidays are part and parcel of U.S. identity politics. Although the flags, songs, and dances are Haitian, they teach Haitian adults and children alike to identify with a diverse, multicultural United States. Still, Haitian transmigrants and their children may experience these "ethnic" rituals in a different light. Their growing identification with the United States may not preclude or supersede their identification with Haiti. The public celebrations and discussions of Haitian history, symbols, and politics mesh well with the transnational ties and obligations of Haitian families.[40] In response to both continuing transnational connection and the experience of publicly identifying with Haiti, although they live in the United States, Haitian transmigrants have begun to see Haitians in the United States and Haiti as living in a single social and political terrain.

Religion has played a particularly significant role in this transformation. Starting in the 1970s, Haitian Catholic priests in both Haiti and the United States, influenced by liberation theology, emerged as important leaders of the poor and began to build a transnational grassroots movement that demanded social justice. Responding to the call for prayer in indigenous languages and cultural idioms, these priests used their prestige and literacy to legitimate Kreyòl, thereby bringing the African-based culture of the rural poor into the Catholic Mass.[41] In the United States as well as Haiti, Catholic masses became occasions for discussions of the state of the Haitian nation and need for fundamental change. Haitians in both localities participated in the same political discourse, within the context of Catholic prayer. In Haiti, this developed into the *Ti Legliz* (grassroots churches), congregations of the poor that challenged both the Catholic hierarchy that remained linked to the elite and the Duvalier regime. In the United States, the same transnational religious movement influenced community organizations such as HAUP, so that it served simultaneously as a community group immersed in local ethnic politics and an extension of the movement for social change in Haiti. The Haitian Catholic Church had become fully transnational by the year 2000, regularly sponsoring activities in both the United States and Haiti. The Church continues to link saving souls and saving Haiti, although there are sharp political differences within the institution on what kind of politics saving Haiti entails.

On the surface, the Haitian Protestant churches seem to have followed a different trajectory. These churches, which range from established mainstream denominations to evangelical fundamentalists, have grown in number and significance in both Haiti and the United States in the past two decades. From their pulpits and widely disseminated radio shows, many ministers warn their congregants against political activism. They also preach that "only God can save Haiti." In these messages, religious prayer brings national as well as individual salvation. In actuality, these churches have not only promoted transnational connections but have infused into the transnational space they foster a concern for the Haitian nation.

The Haitian media, too, have played a vital role in legitimizing the concept of Haiti as a transnational nation-state. Beginning in 1986, Haitian newspapers founded by political exiles in the United States set up publishing operations in Haiti. Their coverage included the activities of the diaspora as well as political developments in Haiti, and their advertisements were for businesses and property in the United States, Canada, and Haiti. A few years later, Haitian radio programs began live broadcasts from Haiti or call-in shows where people in Haitian localities such as Montreal, New York, and south Florida could participate in the same discussion. When they turned on the radio, Haitian migrants found not simply entertainment in a familiar language. By listening to Haitian radio, they were able to identify with Haiti on a daily basis. Those living in Haiti, meanwhile, were learning to think about their national life as extending beyond the borders of their ancestral state. To legitimate this new frame of mind, Haitians formulated an ideology of long-distance nationalism.

Embracing Prodigal Sons and Daughters

Even before Haitian political leaders acknowledged Haitians living abroad as a continuing part of the Haitian body politic, impoverished people in Haiti who survived on remittances sent by family were making such claims. This became evident to us when, cognizant of the political language of the

1990s, we went back and looked at what people in Haiti had been trying to communicate to us in the 1980s, which at the time we were not able to hear.

In 1989, our research assistant in Haiti interviewed several networks of people living in the vicinity of Port-au-Prince who were supported by remittances sent from family members abroad. The thirteen people he spoke with used an ideology of blood to explain the ongoing connection between Haitians living abroad and those in Haiti. They also asserted that Haitians living abroad remained a part of Haiti, even if they became naturalized U.S. citizens. For example, Petit-Fils, a fifty-nine-year-old painter, declared: "A person is still a Haitian [if he becomes a citizen of another country]. His blood is still Haitian blood. It is only the person's title and name that is changed. The person's skin is still Haitian, and besides that, the person was born in Haiti and even if that person doesn't consider himself Haitian the whites in the country where he's living still consider him Haitian. Therefore, I don't think a person should reject his country."

In 1990, Haitian political leaders echoed this rhetoric when Aristide, a Catholic priest who had emerged as one of the leaders of the grassroots church movement, began to campaign for president. Initially, Aristide, who had himself lived and studied abroad but had returned to Haiti, had repeated the call to the diaspora to return. As he declared in 1987 in one of his books, *In the Parish of the Poor*, "My generation is running away from Haiti, with its dark corners and byways. I want to call them back before they begin their fruitless travels. . . . I say to them come back and make a new Haiti."[42] Yet, in 1990, while building grassroots support for his candidacy, Aristide reconsidered the politics of return in light of the part that the diaspora was playing in Haiti.

It was clear that remittances from transmigrants to family members had helped a significant sector of the Haitian population weather the most difficult periods of the Duvalier dictatorship. Meanwhile, Catholic priests—many with substantial bases in Miami, the New York metropolitan area, and Montreal, but who were part of a growing grassroots movement in Haiti, too—had transformed the political life and consciousness of the growing numbers of Haitian transmigrants. They brought transmigrants from diverse class backgrounds into a strong, public, anti-Duvalier movement that made its voice known in the United States through frequent demonstrations and political lobbying. This U.S. movement had become part of a Haitian transnational political struggle to rebuild Haiti. Such activities continued after the Duvalier regime ended in 1986. Individuals seeking the Haitian presidency began to campaign for the office in New York and Miami, even though Haitians living abroad could not vote. Aristide solicited the diaspora's support during his 1990 presidential campaign by asserting that Lavalas, the grassroots movement he was leading, encouraged "the participation of all citizens from all social classes. A special place will be reserved for peasants, women, all patriotic movements, and all Haitians in diaspora."[43]

Aristide, as well as many of those in his government, looked on Haitian transmigrants' financial resources and professional skills as crucial for Haiti's renewal. He spoke of the diaspora as a "bank." Haitian transmigrants could fulfill their responsibilities toward their homeland by continuing to live and work abroad while sending money back to rebuild Haiti. Their trips to Haiti should be as "Kreyòl tourists," bringing tourist dollars.[44]

The diaspora proved to be a key source of funds and personnel for political activities in Haiti. The campaign manager for Aristide's 1990 presidential bid reported that two-thirds of the three hundred thousand dollars raised for the race came from the diaspora.[45] In 1991, to provide the newly elected Aristide government with much needed funds, Haitians in Haiti and throughout the diaspora organized a "marathon of dignity" called Send Haiti Upwards (*Voye Ayiti Monte*, known by Haitians as VOAM). In less than a week, despite their dire economic conditions, overseas Haitians raised more that one million dollars for various projects in Haiti. The Family is Life (*La Fanmi Se Lavi*), a benevolent association founded by Aristide to help orphans in Port-au-Prince, received numerous contributions through minimarathons organized by various overseas Haitian communities.

Through this rhetoric, Aristide, acting as Haiti's head of state, was reclaiming all Haitian migrants and all persons of Haitian descent living abroad, no matter what their legal citizenship or place of birth, as part and parcel of the Haitian nation-state. On the day of his inauguration as president, Aristide dubbed Haitians living abroad the "Tenth Department." The territory of Haiti is divided into nine geographic divisions called departments. Aristide spoke as if they were an equivalent of France's overseas departments, although the Haitian Constitution had not been changed and Haitians abroad live within the territorial boundaries of other countries. In his first New Year's message to the Tenth Department, Aristide welcomed Haitian overseas communities anew, as Haiti's prodigal children, in the fold of the Haitian community, "under the aegis and the protection of the political power of the Haitian nation-state."[46] The diaspora was redefined. It was no longer a location of exile but an integral and vital part of Haiti.

In return for their support, Aristide pledged to the diaspora that the Haitian government would be their spokesperson and protector. Speaking at the United Nations in 1991, he deplored the negative treatment Haitian migrants had been subjected to and the lack of compassion expressed by countries that had received them. From the United Nations's podium, Aristide declared:

> **The sixth commandment of democracy: legitimate defense of the diaspora, or tenth department**. Driven out until 1991 by the blind brutality of the repressive machine or by the structures of exploitation erected in an antidemocratic system, our Haitian brothers and sisters have not always had the good fortune to find the promised land. Illegal because the brutes have not had the forethought to give their victims certificates of torture properly signed; illegal because they have had to travel as boat people without being provided with legal documents, they have nevertheless made great contributions to the economic prosperity of their patrons, preferring to do all the hardest work rather than to take charity.[47]

Aristide summarized his changed view of the diaspora in his autobiography, published in 1993. In a chapter with the revealing title "May the Peace of the Dollar Be with You," he wrote: "With Lavalas' rise to power, Haiti had grown greater, extending far beyond its 27,000 square kilometers and nine departments. Even before February 7, 1991, we had created a tenth department encompassing our compatriots outside, who had multiple roles. Without them, what would become of some of the families on the island? . . . Honorary ambassadors of Haiti, ties between the mother country and the rest of the world, enthusiastic supporters of renewal, the avant garde of a new definition of citizenship. . . . A new citizenship was being forged, together with a new society that cooperates with its branches overseas."[48]

In response to their new welcome, many Haitian organizations that had focused their attention on the conditions faced by Haitian migrants in the United States now launched transnational activities. They began to sponsor activities to rebuild Haiti. The phrase "building Haiti" combined a collective nostalgia for an imagined past of Haitian accomplishments with a commitment to contribute not only to family but the nation. Within a very few years, the ethos of Haitian life in the United States had changed. Increasing numbers of people both in Haiti and the diaspora began to believe that emigrants could remain settled in the United States and still be patriots. With the election of Aristide in 1990, long-distance nationalism became the order of the day as both young and old contributed to Haiti by sending donations, organizing projects, or making short trips. Haitian organizations based in New York sent members to Haiti to participate in various projects, from clinics to literacy campaigns, to rebuild Haiti. The rhetoric of rebuilding was shared by those in Haiti. They embraced the project of national construction as a transnational project to restore their country.

Nevertheless, it was the political mobilization of the diaspora on behalf of Aristide, when he was exiled by a military coup after only seven months in office, that firmly implanted the concept of the Haitian people as a transnational nation among Haitians in Haiti. We found that the idea was shared in Haiti among both persons who did and did not have personal ties to the diaspora. From 1991 to 1994, the military government that overthrew Aristide carried out a reign of terror. They were responsible for massacres in poor neighborhoods, random shootings with dead bodies left in the streets to spread terror, attacks on grassroots organizations of the poor, rapes and sexual tortures of women activists, and assassinations of political leaders.[49] During these grim times, the opposition of the Haitian diaspora to the military junta and its call for the restoration of the democratically elected Aristide government provided hope to the population of Haiti. We were repeatedly told that the diaspora had "helped Haiti" by returning Aristide to office: "They are the ones who fought in Miami. They screamed for help so that Aristide could return to Haiti to rebuild the country. To build the country. To make it a smooth/silky country."

Demonstrations, statements of protest placed as paid advertisements in the *New York Times*, patient lobbying with U.S. congresspeople, and the press of Haitian refugees seeking to enter the United States did keep the issue of Aristide's presidency alive in the United States.[50] After three years of officially condemning the Haitian military but actually providing it with various kinds of economic and military assistance, the United States changed its stance, leading a United Nations military intervention and occupation in October 1994 that restored Aristide to office.[51]

Aristide returned with a coterie of advisers and ministers who were transmigrants, adept at lobbying within the U.S. political system, and convinced that they could help Haiti through hobnobbing with U.S. congressional members, businesspeople, and bankers. They popularized the political inclusion of the diaspora as part of Haiti. Their presence personified Haiti as a transnational nation-state. Their political practices and transnational political networks contributed to this new conception of Haiti. The possibility and necessity for Haitian migrants to remain politically engaged in Haiti, while permanently settling in the United States, also became a central theme of Haitian transnational newspapers and radio. Broadcasters spoke not as political exiles or ethnics but as the Haitian diaspora—an influential section of the Haitian people.

Even If You Naturalize . . .

By the 1990s, poor and middle-class people in Haiti were routinely referring to blood ties to explain the long-distance nationalism of the diaspora. The fervor with which many individuals spoke about the links between those living in Haiti and those who had emigrated and lived abroad matched the intensity of the most fiery political leader.

It was this intensity that can be felt in the appeal that Marjorie made to the diaspora. Marjorie, the young woman who took our tape recorder into her hand to speak directly to her "brothers and sisters" in the diaspora, is a slender, determined nineteen-year-old whose father is a cultivator, whose mother sells meat in the market, and whose sister in the United States sends remittances to support the family she left in Aux Cayes. Readily responding to our request to define the term Haitian, Marjorie stated: "A person who is living abroad for a long time is a Haitian. Even if you are naturalized [as an American], you keep Haitian blood. The only way they can keep you from being Haitian is if they cut your meat and took all your blood."

The continuity of Haitian identity was said to hold even after persons became legally naturalized. Dimase is the thirty-three-year-old man who is supported by his five siblings in the United States. They consistently send money for the rent, clothes, and shoes. This income is supplemented by the work his wife does cooking and selling food to an engineering company. They have one child and live in a poor, though not totally impoverished, neighborhood right outside Port-Au-Prince. For Dimase, nationality is a matter of descent, so that "even if you naturalize [as an American], you are still Haitian." He went on to apply this to his siblings. Of his brother who has become a U.S. citizen, he said, "Inside of him, my brother stays Haitian. He is Haitian even if he changes his nationality."

Those who did not receive remittances could be equally as adamant. The response of an impoverished, unemployed young man designated by his friends as *Resigne* (Resigned) was typical. He is so poor that he sleeps in a tree and uses the washing facilities in the house of Yvette's sister-in-law—a house for which Yvette pays the rent. "They don't change even if they naturalize because they have the blood. Even if they naturalize and become citizens [of another country], they have Haitian blood in them. They love Haiti."

To Resigne, the disapora, organically a part of Haiti but with resources, "can come here and build schools. They make health centers. All these things could help. There are many children. You have five fingers, each has its own height." To express his belief that the diaspora is part of Haiti, Resigne used a folk saying that has often expressed the unity of the Haitian nation, despite the divisions of class. In this unity, each is obliged to contribute what they can, as the fingers of a hand that are unequal in size, but that all contribute to completing a task. Marc, a man in his sixties who lives in the same neighborhood and is also struggling with daily survival, echoed the affirmation of the organic link between the diaspora and Haiti, utilizing the same metaphor. "Those abroad can help. . . . You have your five fingers, they are not of the same height." Ninety-three percent of the people we spoke with thought that individuals born in Haiti remained all or part Haitian, wherever they lived or whatever their legal citizenship, although 7 percent of this group insisted that to claim their membership in the nation, those abroad had to contribute to Haiti.

By 1996, there was a widespread and nearly uniform knowledge of the word "diaspora" that has now become incorporated into Kreyòl to mean Haitians living abroad. The implication that those abroad were obligated to return home generally had been abandoned. Respondents differed in their judgment of the effectiveness of this assistance to Haiti. Many told us that the diaspora did help family, but had failed to help the nation as a whole. Underlying this critique was the view that it was the responsibility of the diaspora to help rebuild Haiti.

Those living in poor housing and without education envisioned the rebuilding of Haiti as a process of physical construction. For them, Haiti as a transnational nation based on the symbolic solidarity of blood ties was a visible force they could see around them. As an exhausted mother of six in Port-au-Prince told us: "Yes, the diaspora helps Haiti. They build schools, now they are talking about building houses for those who can't afford them. Those who can't send their children to school, they will give them half scholarships to send them to school, they have done many things. Even though I did not benefit from them, there are many people who do benefit from that help."

In the years since our interview, as it has been clearer that the diaspora has not provided the leadership or resources to rebuild Haiti, anger at the diaspora has grown. Many of these critics, however, are not repudiating the ties to the diaspora but admonishing the diaspora for neglecting its obligations to the nation. Depending on the context, "diaspora" can be used as a statement of solidarity or reproach, imparting into the term a pejorative undertone suggesting a person who is vain, crass, and a self-centered upstart. This negative evaluation of the diaspora speaks to some of the tensions between those who left and those who remain in Haiti, but such tensions do not amount to a severing of ties.

There also is a counternarrative to the embrace of the diaspora. The educated middle class who remained in Haiti and faced competition from those educated abroad tend to stress the differences between those abroad and in Haiti, arguing that those in the diaspora don't understand Haitian realities. The bourgeoisie, although many are transmigrants with luxurious houses in both Haiti and south Florida, have tended to see members of the diaspora as a threat to their entrenched interests. The poor and disempowered with whom we spoke were able to embrace the diaspora as part of Haiti through ties of blood and simultaneously mark the social distance created through migration. They did this by referring to visiting members of the diaspora, or those who had migrated and abandoned their family obligations, as *blan*, white. We found Georges referred to as white often.

When Nina asked Linda, age sixteen yet having had only two years of schooling, about Georges, she said, "No, he is not Haitian. He is white." And when she talked about the role of the diaspora in Haiti, she observed that "yes, the white can help Haiti." Return migrants who come home with education, English fluency, and the look of money also reported to us they were perceived as white. Pierre-Antoine, a young man of twenty-four who had been brought by his family to the United States to finish high school in 1985, had been in the U.S. military, and had returned to Haiti shortly before we interviewed him. He told us, "I've heard people from the masses labeling me as 'white,' which to them means 'foreigner,' or he's from the outside. Which is a connotation of the same thing. . . . They're probably thinking money-wise or whatever."

In discussions of the diaspora among the disempowered, blan is used as a form of social commentary about distances in education and resources, rather than nationality. Mary-Jo, who had worked in factories but currently had no work at all and five children to support, told us, "Yes, I have heard of diaspora. It is someone who is living abroad. Someone who is living in Haiti is not the same. It is not a bad thing [to be diaspora]. Like when a person comes from abroad, s/he is not the same person as you. Here . . . nothing is happening. And that person was breathing a different air and therefore s/he is different from you. S/he takes on another smell. S/he breathes another air. S/he changes her or his face, her or his characteristics, but s/he is still Haitian." Here Mary-Jo was signaling some of the dissonance, distances, and life experiences that separate those in Haiti from those abroad. Whether those abroad were labeled "outsider," "foreigner," or "white," or were seen as having "a different face," these speakers were not using such distinctions to sever their connections with the diaspora. The assertion of distance can serve as an appeal for closeness, an argument within rather than an abrogation of family.

Similarly, the recent trend of Haitians living in the United States toward becoming U.S. citizens cannot be interpreted as a rejection of Haiti. In the 1990s, migrants from many parts of the world, including Haiti, began to become U.S. citizens at much greater rates than in the previous several decades.[52] Yvette, Rolande's cousin, worked to improve her English and became a naturalized U.S. citizen. She returned from being awarded her citizenship papers, triumphant, and declared that she would now study even more English so that she could speak like a "real" American. Nevertheless, Yvette does not see her efforts to become incorporated into the United States as a repudiation of Haiti. Her assumption of U.S. citizenship does not mean that she has abandoned her obligations to family in Haiti or her identification with her homeland. In part, Yvette and the myriad of other transmigrants who have become naturalized were responding to a series of punitive measures that the U.S. Congress passed against permanent residents. These measures denied Medicaid care to elderly permanent residents and mandated that permanent residents must be deported as a result of any conviction, past or present, including traffic violations. In addition, the growth of naturalization among Haitians was an indicator that they had come to see obtaining U.S. citizenship as an expression of their continuing commitment to Haiti. They are better able to help Haiti by taking political action as a U.S. citizen. They are beginning to think that they may have to participate in Haiti while remaining physically in the United States.

By the millennium, the political chaos unleashed first by the coup and then U.S. intervention, which further displaced the authority of the Haitian state, meant that it was becoming too dangerous for transmigrants to return to Haiti to settle. Even visits began to be too dangerous. In the summer of 1999, a wedding that Yvette sponsored in Haiti for a niece was attacked by robbers. The thieves cut the lights, and in the darkness, made off with all the wedding presents and the video camera being used to document the event for family in the diaspora. That winter, Rolande and a family member were robbed at gunpoint in broad daylight in the middle of a traffic jam. The robbers took Rolande's passport and her rings, the car, and all the money that Rolande had brought to pay for private hospital care for her mother, who had just experienced a stroke while visiting Haiti. They also stole Rolande and Georges's dreams of retiring in Haiti, or even their ability to visit Haiti without fearing for their lives. The loss was immeasurable. However, for Georges and many in the Haitian diaspora, despair at the violence and disorder that plagues Haiti has yet to prompt a repudiation of their identification with and willingness to act on behalf of Haiti.

Even anger, bitter disappointment, demoralization, and denouncements of Haiti are often stated in nationalist terms, ones that fuel rather than abate the emotional pull of long-distance nationalism. A statement made on Haitian Flag Day in 1997 by Monsignor Darbouze, a Haitian priest who had been promoted to a leadership position in the Catholic Diocese of Brooklyn, expresses the complex relationship with Haiti—the intertwining of nostalgia, political critique, and ongoing identification—that compels transmigrants to adopt U.S. citizenship as a statement of both love of and despair for Haiti:

> "Long live the Haitian flag!" There used to be a time when I [used to say] these words with pride. It was the time of my youth when they celebrated May 18 [Haitian Flag Day] with pomp and circumstance. I recall the parade of primary and secondary schoolchildren in school uniform, singing and marching to the sound of music. The vibration of the marching drums still resonates in my ears. In those

days Haiti was still sweet, the worth of our flag was respected. Patriotism was more than just a word that one uttered. I want to speak
about the period before the macoute [the armed thugs of the Duvalier regime,] the "grands mangeurs" [the corrupt officials of the Aristide and Préval regimes], and the betrayers of the nation. . . . In
those days, there was a certain sense of the country and the common
good. Democracy didn't exist, but there existed, nonetheless, security and order. The Constitution wasn't respected but they did not
completely trammel it under foot.

Are these the words of a resentful Haitian? No! Rather these are
the words of a true son of Haiti who made the choice to become an
American citizen because he could no longer stand to see his dear fatherland being sullied without taking a stand. The only way for him
to react was to become an American citizen. **Long live the Haitian
flag!**[53]

As heirs of Africans whose enslavement was justified by Europeans on
the grounds that black people were less than human, many Haitians believe
that they are never subject to only individual success or failure in the eyes of
the world. Father Darbouze's or Georges's accomplishments and setbacks
are those of Haiti; Haiti's achievements or shortcomings are theirs. All of
this feels familiar to Nina, who grew up in a family that examined both heroes and villains in the news to see if they were Jewish. Nina's parents
stressed that the public successes of Jews reflected well on all Jews, while a
Jewish scoundrel reinforced the anti-Semitic stereotypes that justified the
Holocaust. When memories of racial, religious, or cultural persecution are
transmitted across generations, one's identification with an entire nation
feels like a normal and natural response. When discrimination is an ongoing daily experience, national identities are strengthened. Those who live in
Haiti experience exclusion and scorn within the terrain of world public
opinion. The Hollywood transformation of Haitian religious life into a
realm of voodoo dolls and zombies is one source of pain. The refusal of the
United States to accept most Haitians who fled from repression from
Haiti's brutal governments in the 1980s and 1990s, even when refugees'
bodies were scarred from torture, is a continuing denial of Haitian human
rights claims, and hence a denial of Haitians' claims to be human.[54] Much
of the developing Haitian long-distance nationalism is a shared emotional
state that sustains the Haitian poor as well as middle class, women as well

as men, young and old—notwithstanding the differences of class, gender, and generation.

Haiti has become a transnational space that extends beyond territorial boundaries, encompassing persons of Haitian ancestry wherever they are located and whatever legal citizenship they may hold. Among those in Haiti, this reconceptualization of their nation builds on widely held ideas of blood ties and has provided a living bridge that can connect them to other lands of greater opportunity. Meanwhile, Haitian migrants living in the United States who face the racial barriers of daily life in an unwelcoming country establish links to their ancestral homeland using a concept of nationality and descent that links them to Haiti as a black nation. As the situation in Haiti becomes ever more desperate, their nostalgia for the sweet Haitian past carries them through the pain of their current situation, in which they are unable to either abandon or reclaim Haiti.

6

"She Tried to Reclaim Me": Gendered Long-Distance Nationalism

It wasn't until I brought her to New York that I began to understand her. And it wasn't until after she died, and I began to write about Haiti, that I began to feel her pain. I had brought her to the United States out of obligation; she was my mother, and I had a duty to assist her. But I never felt about her the way people are supposed to feel about their mothers. I just didn't feel any deep affection for her. After I graduated from college, she tried to reclaim me and say that I was her favorite son. She was so proud of me all of a sudden. And then she was frustrated because I couldn't reach out to her.

I had no love for her because when I was small and needed her, all she gave me was her anger. When people talk about maternal love, I can't relate to that because I never felt that. I didn't hate her because otherwise I would never have sent for her. But I first began to understand something about her from her reaction to the United States. She was totally transformed in New York. I brought her to Brooklyn and she settled in, first with me, and later on with my brother, learned her way around, found a job as a home health aide, and earned her own income.

One day, she sat and talked to me. "This is my country now," she told me. "I will never return to Haiti."

And as she spoke to me, I could see my mother yelling and screaming at me and carrying on when I was a child in Haiti. And every time she passes me, she slaps me. And I am sitting there wondering why she is attacking me like this. I was sent there to get my meals, even after I was taken out of the house by my father and sent to live nearby with his mother and sister, so her blows were something I felt every day. At the first opportunity, I was out of that house and back to my grandmother and father's sister's house, where I was safe. Now, I can see that it was not that she was a bad person. But her social condition, her gender position, made her do those things. Writing this chapter is my reconciliation with her, even though now she is dead. I can say to her, "Now I understand what you did to me. It was because you were a woman in a repressive society that you took your anger out on me."

When my mother cried, "This is my country and I will never go back," she meant, "Here, I can be independent. Here, I am not confined within the limits of a marriage—if I break it, where do I go?" But my mother's experience of marriage was not that of all Haitian women. Her relationship to my father and to Haiti was about class as well as gender. I can see that when I look at other Haitian women who have migrated and at the women we interviewed in Haiti.

Georges's reminiscences about his mother, Nadine—Nanie is what she was called—had come abruptly as we listened to our recorded interview with Rose, a forty-five-year-old woman who lives in Aux Cayes. Rose was describing the small businesses that she maintains with the help of her husband, who had emigrated to Florida. Although the freshly painted walls of the family house and presence of new furniture made it clear that Rose's husband's migration had improved the living standard of his family in Haiti, Rose was eager to migrate to the United States. She told us, "I want to leave because I am not doing anything here." Yet even though Rose saw her future as life in the United States, she did not voice the same anger toward Haiti that Georges's mother, Nanie, had expressed so forcefully. Instead, she shared with the majority of the women we interviewed in Haiti, and most of the Haitian women we have known in the United States, a fierce identification with Haiti. As Georges sought to reconcile his own complex emotions toward his mother and Haiti, he opened for both of us an exploration of the fissures of gender, geographic location, and class that underlie the shared Haitian "narrative of the nation."[1] We began to see that shared national narratives contain within them multiple meanings and ambivalences. By exploring why Nanie expressed her anger at a difficult marriage and an oppressive system of gender by rejecting her nationality, we came to understand the different ways in which Haitian women and men, Haitians of different classes, and Haitians in Haiti and the diaspora, come to identify with and understand the nation.

As an oppressed sector of the Haitian population, women experience their lives through the divides of class and gender. Haitian women find that some aspects of the national narrative lead them back to a gender hierarchy that reinforces the exploitative class system of contemporary Haiti. Yet the contradictions embedded within the gender and class systems of Haiti, as they are lived within a transborder domain, simultaneously lead women to become active participants in ongoing struggles against all forms of oppression. In so doing, women destabilize the established meanings of nationalism and help forge an alternative political direction within the shared nationalist rhetoric.

Women, Class, Nation, and Long-Distance Nationalism

To understand Georges's mother, Nanie, who brutally rejected her first-born son and then proudly rejected Haiti, we need to put her story together with that of women like Rose, who when they migrate, do not look back in anger. We must also consider Yvette, Rolande's cousin, who with no children of her own, nurtures relatives' children and sees their successes as both hers and Haiti's. Just how close that identification is became clear to us the day Georges's daughter Leah graduated from law school. Yvette sat next to Nina together with eighteen Fouron friends and relatives who had come to watch the graduation ceremony. Other graduates also had their family members present, and as the names of graduates were called, some families would stand, cheer, and yell the graduate's name. When it was Leah's turn, most of the Fouron delegation hesitated, not sure whether to publicly cheer. Yvette had no such doubts. She was instantly on her feet. But the name she called out was not Leah's. Yvette shouted, "Haiti! Haiti! Haiti!" Leah's victory in obtaining a law school degree from a prestigious university in the United States was also Yvette's, and her extended family's, and Haiti's, and Haiti now existed wherever Haitians settled.

Yvette's close identification with Haiti resembles the long distance-nationalism of many Haitian women immigrants we have known, observed, or interviewed. It is both similar and different from Georges's, reflecting the different historical relationship that men and women have to the Haitian nation-state, as well as their different life experiences. Haiti has its own particular and mixed messages about gender that give to women and men both rights and responsibilities to family and nation. In societies such as Haiti, which celebrate patriarchal authority, women often simultaneously accept and critique constructions of gender.[2] The contradictions that propel women into struggle are especially potent among the Haitian poor. Despite their formal acceptance of a gender hierarchy, poor Haitian women who shoulder a disproportionate amount of the responsibility to ensure that children are fed, clothed, and educated continually contest the ideology of gender by the way they live their lives.

For generations, official accounts of the founding of the nation echoed and reinforced gender hierarchy through the tale of a woman who was present at the birth of the nation but as wife and mother, not as a leader or warrior. According to one widely known story, it was Claire Heureuse (also known as Félicité), the wife of Dessalines, the revolutionary leader and founder of the nation, who sewed the first Haitian flag. The design was said to be Dessaline's. The retelling of this story over the generations has taught both men and women about women's domestic relationship to Haiti. Georges learned the tale of Claire Heureuse as a schoolboy; a public elementary school for girls in his hometown was named for Claire.

For much of Haitian history, even the stories told by women portrayed women as a vital yet silent presence. The Vodou spirit Ezili Dantò, for example, is popularly known as a fierce mother, protective of her children, although easily enraged and punitive. But in most accounts she cannot speak. In one telling of the story, Ezili Dantò was present during the Haitian Revolution that founded the nation, but "in that war she was going to talk, to tell something, and then they go over and cut out her tongue because they don't want her to talk."[5]

There was, however, from the time of the Haitian Revolution another portrayal of women that acknowledged their importance to the nation but depicted them as without social status. Marie-Jeanne is said to have directly participated in the Haitian Revolution, but she is remembered as a slave woman without a last name or husband. There are also stories that place an unnamed woman in a key role at the Vodou ceremony which initiated the Haitian Revolution. This priestess assisted Boukman, a Vodou priest, by sacrificing a pig to the ancestral gods.[6] These alternative depictions highlight some of the tensions in Haitian notions of women's position in society. Embedded in the contrast between Marie-Jeanne, who gave her strength to the nation, and the heroine, Claire Heureuse, who was confined to the domestic sphere, is a tension over the construction of femininity in Haiti that continues to be lived within Haitian transnational space. This contradiction is embedded in the ways in which both Haitian women and men understand and identify with their national history.

Haitians took from eighteenth-century Europe a patriarchal idea of family as well as a civil code that gave men control of family life, wealth, and property. While successive nineteenth-century Haitian constitutions say nothing about women not being able to vote or not being able to own property, law codes and widely accepted practices restricted women's rights. For most of Haitian history, the father was by custom and law the head of the household. Women gained the right to vote in 1950;[3] they were defined as legal minors until 1979, and it was only in 1982 that married women could legally own property despite the fact that in the countryside, both men and women have obtained property through customary inheritance.[4] On the other hand, because women were seen as central to the reproduction of family, and the nation was portrayed as the extension of the family, women were inseparable from the reproduction of Haiti. Therefore, exclusion from formal rights did not mean that Haitian women were excluded from membership in the Haitian nation. As in many other states where women have been confined to domestic roles, from the time of the Haitian Revolution, women have been defined as contributors to the nation as mothers and wives.

From early in the history of Haiti, the citizenship laws have reflected the idea that women are part of the nation, but that their contribution is to help produce citizens. Haitian citizenship has been accorded to anyone who was born to either a Haitian mother or father who themselves were born Haitian. Until fairly recently, however, if a woman married a foreigner, she lost her Haitian citizenship and her children were thus not Haitian. In short, state officials and the literate elite envisioned women as able to reproduce the nation only in conjunction with a Haitian man. They were to have no independent relationship to the nation, but rather were intimately tied to their maternal role within the Haitian family.

Over the centuries, the Haitian upper class has been able to live by the dominant set of values which accorded prestige to women who remained within the domestic sphere. They legitimated their elite status along with their domination of Haitian society and politics on the basis of gendered cultural practices that most Haitian families could not afford to follow. The value system continues to endorse legal marriage and make a wife economically dependent on her husband. Those families who could live by these values gain in social status. They distinguished themselves from the poor in terms of the more decorous and homebound behavior of their women as well as the breadwinning capacities of their men. And many still believe that to live by these values is to uphold not only family but also national honor. These gendered cultural practices, unattainable for the majority of the population, have been part of the national narrative that is intimately linked to most Haitians' sense of self.

The restrictions placed on the mobility and economic independence of women by families aspiring to secure their position in the middle class were the source of Georges's mother's rejection of Haiti. Nanie had worked in a pharmacy before she married. Once married, though, she was prevented by her husband, Gilbert, as well as by her own interest in protecting their class position, from working outside their home. Yet Gilbert's position as the head of a vocational school brought prestige without a living wage. Nanie struggled to find ways to supplement her husband's income from her location within the household.

Different middle-class women experienced the restrictions on their mobility and the necessity of earning cash in different ways. Rolande's mother, faced with the similar limitations, began to run a small store from her living room. She bought herring, shortening, and sugar in bulk, and then sold them in small amounts. Man-Nana experienced her home-based retailing as a way of having her own income and gaining the prestige of having a business, however small. In contrast, Nanie became angry, bitter, and abusive, feeling trapped in her predicament. She had been forced into the marriage when, at the age of twenty-two and parentless, she became pregnant.

Her family insisted that she marry Gilbert, who not only was the father of the child but also was seen as a desirable match because he was a school-teacher.

Once married, Nanie began to do embroidery for other people. While Nanie took pride in her work, getting magazines from Paris with elaborate patterns, she felt that the household was confining to her energy, talents, and beauty, and there was not even enough money for food, much less the keeping of a proper household. Her husband's responsibilities, moreover, stretched into other households. In his mother's house lived two of his children by a previous relationship. Nor did Gilbert stop his relationships with other women after he married Nanie.

As the legal wife of a teacher, Nanie's situation differed from that of Gilbert's other women, who were unmarried town or rural women. Rural women, whether or not they are legally married, and town and city women without husbands, have always had more autonomy and responsibility than married women from the middle and upper classes. The freedom of these women comes from their lack of social status.

Contradictions of Gender

Until recently, people who have aspired to raise themselves into the middle class, as did Georges's parents, have found themselves caught between the family and mating practices of the poor that have given women a major economic role and the elite values that are said to embody the Haitian nation. Poor Haitian women and men live lives that stand in stark contrast to the dominant gender constructions.[7] From the time of slavery, the majority of Haitian women have been mainstays of the Haitian economy. Almost all West African societies, from which most of the Haitian population came, accorded women an important role in economic production and the marketplace, and offered spheres of autonomy within an extended family system. Throughout the Caribbean, women worked on slave plantations as field laborers, even if they were pregnant or nursing.[8] Even during slavery, women participated in a market system of selling food crops they produced in small gardens on or near the plantations. And when most of the population turned to the small-scale production of food crops after slavery, men took up the tasks of agricultural production while women continued to do most of the marketing of the crops. Consequently, despite the fact that legally and ideologically they were accorded subordinate status, poor Haitian women have always experienced a high degree of autonomy in terms of their movements outside the household and their control of the cash they earned through marketing. In Haiti, as elsewhere, class position as well as gender influences what a person is able to do to survive.

Although we were able to speak with more poor men than women, because the women were frequently engaged in some form of commerce and therefore out of the house when we conducted our interviews, those women we did interview were as comfortable as the men in talking about their love for Haiti and the continuing responsibility of the diaspora to Haiti. The majority of the women were long distance-nationalists. Yet they differed from men in their ardor, with women somewhat more despairing about the future. They were more convinced that the state had abandoned them, and they sounded closer to abandoning both state and nation.

In Port-au-Prince, where more than a million people have come in the past thirty years to escape the collapse of the Haitian rural economy, urban married women, including the wives of educated men, find themselves selling in the open market or along the side of the road. These women try to raise tiny amounts of cash by selling goods or cooked food, while their husbands stay at home doing some child care but basically idle. Women sell almost every kind of raw and cooked food, all kinds of used and new clothing and shoes, toiletries, cooking implements, containers, pots and pans, as well as dirty, heavy items such as charcoal. In Port-au-Prince, hundreds of women compete to sell the same thing. Women also wash clothes and work as domestics. Both of these occupations have very low prestige and command extremely low pay. Diana, age thirty, after being widowed with five children and without any family to send her remittances, turned to washing clothes:

> Where do I find money? I wash people's clothes. I do it in this neighborhood. For example, when they have dirty clothes, they give them to me to wash. And I iron them as well. I have so many that sometimes I can't even do it. Sometimes I can't. Every time I wash, I make six or seven dollars [U.S.$2 or $2.30 per load]. I buy water. I pay one gourde [U.S. 7¢] for a bucket of water.
>
> Women find work much more easily than men unless men have a specific trade such as that of a mason [bricklayer]. . . . When they can't find work, they can put a container on top of their heads and go

into the streets. And then you can buy a sack of charcoal and then sell it. Yes, women can do commerce. And women often feel most directly the responsibility to feed their children.

As one of the many women who shouldered the burden of the deteriorating Haitian economy, Diana's anger was palatable. She made the desperation of her situation graphic: "Nobody helps me. Take today. I didn't leave anything for the children [to eat]. If today I am lucky, I may find a spoonful of food for them to eat and tomorrow they may stay just like that. They are malnourished."

Thirty-year-old Josette is also the sole support for her children, whose fathers claim no responsibility for them. She expressed the rage that comes with having to support a family in a situation where employment options are few and men often leave for other women.

> The father of my children is around but I am the only one who is employed. I am responsible for everything. I make *paté* [meat pies] and I sell them in the streets. I don't have a husband. . . . He has other women. I don't see the guy anymore. I kicked the guys out, they came around and gave me the children and then they just sat around the house. If they stay around longer, I will have more and more children. . . . They do it a lot. Give you children and leave. That is all they go around doing. They have many girlfriends. To have so many children will just keep you in misery so I decided to stop and raise these children. The children's fathers are not working. I am the only one.

Men do some marketing but are confined by custom to selling a much more limited stock of items, many of which require more capital to obtain. They sell tires that they have repaired, sugarcane, and various imported items including batteries, machinery, cassettes for tape recorders, toiletries, and apples.[9] Nevertheless, women in the cities and towns generally supply the money to feed their families. The women we spoke with do what they have to yet are clear about the inequalities. As Josianne, who was weary and worn out at age thirty-five, explained: "I have had five children to feed for thirteen years, and my man has not been able to find work. Thirteen years he sits there. Some days I walk from downtown, all the way up here on foot. Sometimes, he meets me halfway and helps me carry the load. . . . When I am sick, I don't do it. We just all of us sit. He can't do anything."

Josianne also articulated for us the complexity of gender roles in Haiti—a complexity deepened and challenged but not yet altered through the process of migration. She told us that "men have double problems. [First,] they can't find jobs. They are doing *zenglendo* [violent criminal activities] and other things because they can't find anything to do. [Also,] there are those who manage to go to a higher class and they don't want to lose their dignity by coming down." Because of the gender division of labor, men compromise their self-esteem and masculine identity if they engage in petty commerce or follow the occupations of poor women, such as washing clothes or most forms of paid domestic labor. The very division of labor that continues to give men a superior status in the society actually restricts their freedom to fully participate in economic activities and obtain money without a woman.

From the view of a middle-class woman such as Nanie, the Haitian status system restricted the opportunities of women. But from the vantage point of a poor woman such as Josette, the contemporary status system limits the possibilities of men even more than women. Men who engage in women's roles in the economy lose everything—not only social standing but their claim to masculinity, which is their sole remaining claim to superiority over women and thus to social standing within the nation. Their sense of themselves as men and Haitian are one and the same. The national narrative draws a sharp and hierarchical line between masculine and feminine, and allows for only two genders.[10]

Sex as Women's Opportunity and Subordination

The necessities that Nanie faced in trying to earn money for her household and Gilbert's prohibition against her working outside the household reflected not just widely held concepts about gender roles and class but also the actual conditions of gender differences that women confronted and continue to face in their daily lives in Haiti. In a society where women are ultimately seen as responsible for their children, where men have more than one woman and family, and where male status has been measured through the number of children sired, there is a long-standing assumption that all women who are on their own are sexually accessible. The sexual component of almost all workplace experiences influences middle-class men's reluctance to have their wives work in Haiti, and has contributed to the high status that both men and women accord women who do not work outside the home. Unlike the many cultures where men see women walking alone as an invitation to rape, men in Haiti see women alone or in the workplace as willing and able to trade their sexuality for other things they need. Men may ask rather than take, but often they are making an offer that women cannot afford to refuse.[11]

Both women and men reported to us that women are pressured to exchange sex for both blue- and white-collar jobs, as well as access to goods for trading in the marketplace or for any assistance from Haitian officials. Impoverished men and women see the complexity of this practice. On the one hand, the sex demanded from women by men of greater means is a mark of women's subordination, and so a marker of the superior position of all men. On the other hand, because poor women can possibly exchange sex for work, the contacts necessary to get goods to sell in the marketplace, an education for themselves or their children, or other goods and services, poor women have greater means of surviving than poor men.

Of the forty-two women and men we asked, 71 percent acknowledged that requests for sex were commonly experienced by women looking for employment. Some spoke in general terms, while others reported about their own experience, although no one admitted in a formal interview that they themselves had accepted such a bargain. Those who did not answer the questions may have refrained from doing so exactly because they hit home, and talking about their experiences or those of family members would have been too uncomfortable and embarrassing. But most women we asked spoke forcefully about the problem: "Yes, it is not a lie. That's the truth. I went to ask for work in a factory and the guy there asked me to sleep with him, and because I refused I didn't get the job."

This exchange of sex for work allows some women to get hired, when men are not. This is especially true in the small industrial sector of Port-au-Prince where women are paid less than U.S.$2.50 a day to produce garments and other goods for large U.S. industries such as Disney. For example, we were told by a women, who had herself been a factory worker, about the demand for sex, although she reported not her success in obtaining work but her sister's history of unemployment: "I have personal experience; my youngest sister works in factories, but she doesn't last in factories because she refuses to sell her body for jobs. If you don't accept, they just expel you. They lay you off." A neighbor of hers remarked to us that "the only way you can avoid this problem is if a relative of yours is giving you a job. If you are not related to [an employer or business contact,] he will try to get sexual with you. If you refuse, you have problems. You won't get the job. And yet you want the job, so you give in."

It is because sexual transactions underlie women's participation in all kinds of economic activities, unless they are married and highly educated, that women who can live on remittances such as Yvette's sister-in-law, Mirelle, are reluctant to sell in the market. The pressure to exchange sex for employment also explains the anxiety experienced by Yvette when her niece, Lourdes, finished her secondary education. Lourdes, unable to obtain a visa to legally migrate, confronted the problem of supporting herself in Haiti. As Lourdes observed, "Women's lives are more difficult. Imagine yourself as someone who studied to be a secretary and goes to apply for a job in an office. If the boss is a man, then he makes it a point [to say:] "If you give me, then I give you." So therefore, it is more difficult for the women, while as for the man, if he goes to work in an office the boss will not say, "You give me and I will give you." . . . There are those who will tolerate it, but there are those who won't accept it. If you tolerate it, you will not have any problems but if you don't tolerate it, you will have a hard life and that is why I say it is harder for women." Lourdes finally obtained admission to the University of Haiti, which is free beyond the expense of fees and books. Yvette continued to support her with the hope that additional education would make her situation less difficult.

This is not to deny that immigrant women face sexual harassment and pressures to provide sexual favors to get or keep jobs in the United States. Factories where the production workers are women are known for this kind of sexual coercion. To obtain or keep a job, women workers are often obliged to provide sex to male supervisors and foremen.[12] Haitian women who work cleaning offices in New York have described to Nina sexual demands made on them by their U.S. supervisors. Undocumented women immigrants are especially vulnerable. The United States, however, offers more employment options, even for undocumented workers, than Haiti, and so the demands on women to exchange sex for employment are not as pervasive.

Gender and the Diaspora

Among immigrants entering with permanent resident visas, Haitian women and men have emigrated from Haiti and settled in the United States in approximately equal numbers.[13] During the 1970s and 1980s, women could often enter as tourists, obtain work as domestics or nannies, and on this basis, gain permanent resident status and then assist other members of their family to migrate. Yvette won her permanent resident visa in this way. Since then, changes in the U.S. immigration law, which now only allows visas for child care employment for European women working on contracts, have ended this possibility for Haitian women.

Arriving in the United States at the age of fifty-five, Georges's mother, Nanie, saw that she would have many more opportunities to earn money. With her own income, she would not be dependent on the will of her husband or son. She turned immediately to finding a way to earn her own living; she learned some basic English, took a quick course, and became a home attendant. Nanie picked up English much more readily than her husband, Gilbert, even though he had not only previously studied English but taught it. Gilbert, Georges's father, had arrived with Nanie and settled into Georges's household. Although he had wanted to come to the United States, Gilbert soon felt isolated, became depressed, and began to talk about returning to Haiti. For Gilbert, migrating to the United States meant not gaining a country but losing his life. He lost the respect he garnered from being the director of a school and a man who carried the name of a powerful family in Aux Cayes. His plans to return to Aux Cayes were first delayed by a mild stroke, and then canceled when he had a severe stroke that deprived him of the ability to talk, walk, or care for himself. His family had to put him in a nursing home since everyone, including Nanie, was working. She refused to give up her new independence and return to the position of caretaker to her husband. For Nanie, settling in the United States meant liberation from the constraints that women of her generation had faced in trying to make full use of their talents and potentialities.

Although Nanie declared her commitment to the United States, she did not at first actually abandon Haiti. In the beginning, Nanie remained connected to Haiti because she used her earnings to send money home to four of her children who were still there. Once she was able to earn a salary, she did not ignore her family obligations or the status benefits of being the one who sends money home. Only after Georges brought his brothers to New York, and his sisters built stable enough positions for themselves in Haiti that they were no longer dependent on remittances, did Nanie's ties to Haiti become attenuated. Her freedom from the burden of remittances was at the same time a loss. It was this lack of social obligation and responsibility that actually accounted for Nanie's loss of her relationship with Haiti.

And true to her word, she did not return to Haiti for the thirteen years she lived after coming to the United States. Yet the fact that she both verbally rejected Haiti and worked to get her U.S. citizenship does not mean that if she had lived longer, Nanie would not have eventually returned to her homeland. She knew that if she became a naturalized U.S. citizen, she would have been able to retire to Haiti and collect her hard-earned social security check.[14] She might have chosen to live her last years with her daughters in Haiti, not as a dependent but as someone who could dispense cash and knowledge of the United States.

Nanie's relationship to all her children was one based on duty, not warmth. They all bore the scars of the rage of her younger years, although Georges had shouldered the majority of the physical abuse. In later years, she and her daughter, Janine, were able to directly confront the fact that it was emotional rather than physical distance that kept them apart. "Why," Nanie asked Janine, who had come to New York for a visit, "do your letters from Haiti only contain a list of things you need without any expressions of love?" Janine's reply was direct: "Because in all those years of growing up in Haiti, Nanie, you never gave us any of your love."

On the other hand, Yvette, Rolande's cousin living in the United States, pours love and obligation on siblings, nieces, and nephews in Haiti whom she hardly knows. It is true that a sense of duty often compels her actions. In 1996, it was obligation that was foremost in her emotions when the phone rang in her basement room. Her older sister in Haiti, a sister she barely knew, had called to announce the death of Yvette's nephew. Although she received the call while the body was still warm, Yvette shook, not so much from the loss of the young man, whom she had met only once, but because it was Yvette who had to immediately find most of the money for an elaborate funeral in Haiti. But joy also came from Yvette's immersion in her transnational networks. The nieces whom Yvette has been supporting are in Haiti young women with whom she strongly identifies. Their ability to obtain an education was part of her life accomplishments, too.

Yvette, having invested in her extended family network, continues to remain invested in Haiti in ways that tie her to both family and nation. As she becomes enmeshed in the status system of Haiti, she reinforces patriarchal values and the gender hierarchy in Haiti while carving out a position of prestige and authority for herself within her own transnational social field. Even though the family members Yvette left behind benefit from her gifts, their needs remain great. Moreover, their sense of their own importance and expectations of what Yvette can produce grow with each gift that Yvette provides.

The money Yvette sends is employed in gendered ways. She makes legal marriages possible by sponsoring weddings that raise the prestige of her nieces. She provides remittances that allow her sister-in-law to differentiate herself from the neighboring women forced to sell in the marketplace. Yvette helps support her brother's efforts to earn money in their hometown of Tibouk, contributing to the capital-intensive occupations that are claimed by men. If Yvette sends money for this brother's projects, she obtains status and recognition. But if she then cuts back on these obligations, she not only loses her investment but also becomes the target of anger. By 1998, the need to maintain and continue the investment she had made led her to borrow money from her pension. When Candio succeeded in sending a car to Haiti to begin a family taxi business in Tibouk, Yvette went to Haiti for a three-week vacation, sponsored a wedding, and distributed money to family members and old friends.

Although Yvette became a U.S. citizen in 1999, she continues to see herself as part of Haiti. Her identification with Haiti is ongoing, immediate, and intimate. When her skin became gray from working overtime to pay the debts she had incurred sending money to Haiti, she told Georges, "My body is like Haiti. It is tired and without hope."

Her language resonates with the idioms of identity used by the women we spoke with in Haiti about family, the diaspora, and the nation. Women in both locations embraced the diaspora as part of Haiti, while criticizing the failure of the diaspora as a collectivity to fulfill its responsibilities to the nation. These ideas were echoed by the women we interviewed in Port-au-Prince who had neither employment nor education. Faced with the pressing task of feeding and educating their children, those women used the language of nation as well as the occasion of the interview to try to obtain assistance for themselves and their children. To them, a discussion about politics offered the occasion to ask directly for aid. At the same time, they were clear that their need for assistance was not a reflection on them as individuals but a political question that involved the past, present, and future of Haiti. And this Haiti was transnational. To assert that a person who emigrated to the United States and became a naturalized citizen was still Haitian was, for these women, to assert that such a person has an obligation to assist them in their desperate struggle to survive. They appealed simultaneously to Georges and the diaspora, using a language of nationalism.

Diana, for example, told Georges that Haitians who live in the United States "for a long time, . . . may become naturalized to another country, they may become American, they [may] become a citizen . . . [but] they are still Haitians, even if they naturalize." She also told him that she had not eaten that day and had left her hungry children to come speak with us.

But Diana, and many of the other women who spoke in this manner, were doing more than using the bond of nationality that they established with Georges to try to feed their children. Sometimes, they spoke to both of us about the state of the nation in ways that linked their immediate desire to support their children to demands for political change and social justice. Josette managed to sustain herself and her children by cooking and selling fried snacks. The dramatic increase in the price of food and fuel made her always difficult situation more precarious, and affected her ability to pay her children's school fees.

> Things have gotten worse. You can't feed your family with five [Haitian] dollars. You have ten dollars and you can't feed yourself from that. Day after day things are getting harder. You are sending kids to go to school without feeding them. You can't do anything for the kids. . . . If the government has some kind of conscience, they would see that people are suffering. That the Haitian people have a lot of problems.
>
> The one who is leading the country sees that food is expensive. The first thing he should have done was to lower the price of food. If you were really a good president, you should have been a president for the country and see all of those people who are poor, those who can't find a place to sleep, all of those who can't feed themselves, all those with problems. That's your job . . . that is your duty. Help those who can't help themselves.

Josette spoke not only of her own problems but of Haiti's. Although she had no schooling, she felt empowered to offer proposals for change. Her proposals would make the Haitian government even more engaged in the economic life of the country than in the past, but in a way that will serve the people. "There are many ways the government could help. They could buy things abroad and they wouldn't have to pay a lot of money, because they are the government. They wouldn't have to pay taxes and face red tape [the way private individuals do when they import goods], and that way they would help the country, but they don't want to." When she spoke of the future, she again moved from a discussion of her life to one of her country:

> For my children, I don't see the future for them. I would have loved to own a one-room house to live in. To have my two children with me. All my efforts that I made. I work hard; sometimes I go to bed and my whole body is aching. . . . I am trying to put together a thousand dollars to buy a piece of land from the state. I have been trying to do this for a long time. And things are so hard in the country. . . . When you see Haitians risking their lives to take a small boat [*kantè*] to go away, this is not what they would have liked for themselves. They would have loved to remain in their country and live in their country, but there is no life. I am young. I would love to stay and live in my country, but it is impossible.

Josette's reference to Haiti as "my country," a homeland where she wanted to live, if only the country would give her "life," echoes a transnational dialogue about the responsibilities of the state that has increasingly drawn women into political action.

Giving Voice to the Contradictions: Women as Transborder Citizens

The link between gender and nation within the Haitian national narrative has not offered Haitian women a fixed family portrait of women's relationship to Haiti. Instead, the imagery of the nation has taken the form of a moving picture, with women playing various roles at different times but always within a national landscape. During the U.S. occupation (1915–1934), women engaged in activities that defied the government. These women consciously saw themselves as acting in defense of the Haitian nation. After the occupation, urban elite and middle-class women turned to advocating women's suffrage and other legal rights for women.[15]

The 1950s marked a turning point in the way Haitian women officially were portrayed within nationalist rhetorics and the ways in which women of all classes experienced their relationship to the nation.[16] Soon after women finally obtained the right to vote in the 1950s, they found that they were being allocated a new position in the imagery of the nation. Duvalier depicted women not only as mothers of the nation but also as important political actors. He developed a female division of the Tonton Macoute, his paramilitary unit.[17] Duvalier called this unit Marie-Jeanne, after the slave woman remembered as an ancestress of the Haitian Revolution and whom Duvalier dubbed "a daughter of the revolution." Through these administrative and discursive moves, women became a vital part of the national political arena.

While Duvalier reenvisioned women as political agents, the nationalism he promoted did not challenge the upper-class ideal that the respectability of a family is judged by the behavior of its women and that decorous women are not independent economic actors. Yet the Duvalier regime set into motion other forces that have challenged the patriarchal order that rests on the subordination of women. During the Duvalier period, women were forced either to participate directly in activities that supported the dictatorship or be declared enemies of the nation.[18] Women found themselves subsumed in the political process. Those women who were not loyal to the Duvalierist cause were defined primarily as subversive, unpatriotic, and "unnatural."[19] Women who were "enemies of the nation" faced brutal political repression; they were arrested, tortured, raped, and murdered. Increasing numbers of Haitian women and men responded to the political terror and economic chaos that accompanied the Duvalier regime by emigrating, yet keeping their home ties. In so doing, they laid the groundwork for new ways to link gender and nation. They merged ideas about transborder citizenship, described in chapter 8, with the conception of women's liberation that emerged from the women's movements of the 1960s and 1970s in the United States, Canada, and France, and the realities of life for the majority of Haitian women in Haiti.

Haitian women who settled in the United States in the 1960s found an emerging civil rights movement, which demanded that the government protect the rights of its citizens of color. They also encountered and participated in a reemergent women's movement, which demanded protections from the state, and a New Left engaged in international struggles for liberation. Even though the Equal Rights Amendment to the U.S. Constitution was not passed, the campaign to win its passage popularized the concept that the government should accord women equal rights in employment, pay, and working conditions. Laws and rulings that allowed the government to more forcefully intervene in cases of domestic violence, and that prohibited sexual harassment, were passed and popularized. Meanwhile, the United Nations promoted women's rights all around the world and began to convene international conferences about the status of women. In addition, Haitian immigrant women learned that in the United States, women were often local community activists, advocating for children in parent-teacher associations and participating in local neighborhood groups. They also discovered that in the United States, as increasing numbers of women entered the workplace, patriarchal patterns in the family and responsibilities within the household were being debated and challenged.[20]

These varied experiences contributed to the emergence of a transnational Haitian women's movement in the 1980s. At first, activists in this movement were predominantly women intellectuals located in New York and Montreal. Many had come of age politically in the struggle to end the Duvalier regime, but they went on to organize around the position of women in Haiti and the Haitian diaspora. They gained new strength and inspiration in these efforts as the grassroots movement gathered steam in Haiti. This movement had its own transnational roots. Ideas about political empowerment, including women's rights, emerged within the context of various local development projects fostered by a wide range of nongovernmental religious and philanthropic institutions.

Poor and middle-class women in both Haiti and the United States have participated in large numbers in transnational grassroots organizations from churches to health clinics. In these settings, women sometimes obtain prestige and leadership positions through their activities, and confound older patriarchal values and patterns. Meanwhile, many transmigrant women who have received an education and achieved professional status abroad have returned to work for international agencies in Haiti or have opened schools, clinics, businesses, and offices in Haiti. While some Haitian upper-class women had always been able to obtain an education, the growth of a significant number of middle-class women professionals has fueled a new type of political activism. Some of these women have entered the political processes, either by participating in traditional politics or the international women's movement.

A report titled *Haïtian Women in Diaspora*, issued in 1986, captures the mood of the 1980s and the multiple influences that shaped a Haitian women's long-distance nationalism that spoke directly to concerns for social justice. The report was prepared by a committee of Haitian women who had come together as part of the preparation for the first UN Conference on the Status of Women in Nairobi in 1985. The women discussed the situation of Haitian women in the diaspora and Haiti. And they did not see the problems of women as separate from the struggles for profound changes in Haitian society. The preface stated that "the text we publish here reflects the duality of our experience. While our main objective is to expose our own problems as women, we also attempt to address the problem of Haitian society. . . . We have a country to rebuild. Problems of acute unemployment, of illiteracy, of health and sanitary services, to cite a few, need to be resolved."[21]

The strength of this transnational movement became evident in 1986 when thousands of women took to the streets of Port-au-Prince to demonstrate for political change. This protest brought together uneducated market women and highly educated transmigrant women to demand not only a new political leadership but also a redistribution of wealth and power. The ramifications of this demonstration and the growing political participation of transmigrant women of all classes led the Aristide government, which came to power in 1991, to create the Ministry of the Feminine Condition. This ministry, which was located in the building that formerly had been the central command of the Haitian military, received only token funding, thereby minimizing its actual programatic effect. When Nina interviewed the minister and her staff in 1995, the personnel with whom she spoke were primarily women educated abroad who had not been part of the grassroots women's organizations in Haiti. They were, however, linked with women's organizations around the world and did participate in the Beijing women's conference in 1996. The creation of a ministry devoted to the empowerment of women thus indicated a formal recognition of the reconfiguration of women's position in Haiti in the context of transnational migration and contributed to raising the profile of women's struggles for empowerment in Haiti.

The ministry, without adequate funds and devoid of the initial energy that marked the Aristide presidency, was continued under the Préval government as a symbol rather than a political force. Yet in the countryside, efforts to organize a grassroots movement centered on an alternative understanding of nation are ongoing.[22] This movement has attracted tens of thousands of women. The experience of poor men and women forced to live within the contradictions of a set of values that either restrict their life's possibilities or make them social pariahs, living outside the dominant values of society and nation, has proved a potent force for political struggles. While many women have become discouraged by the actions of political leaders and nongovernmental organizations that use politics for private gain, local grassroots groups continue to function. They inject their own understanding of nation into their local-level organizing, and utilizing the songs and slogans of the "peasant movement" (*gwoupman peyizon*) to instill a commitment to social justice into their use of nationalist rhetoric. The lyrics of the songs sung at meetings of women's organizations in the countryside articulate and promote this form of politics. They are fierce with a nationalism that demands respect and equality for Haiti within a world of nations, and places the demand for social justice at the core of the struggle. For example, the "Haitian Women's National Anthem" (*Im Nasyonal Fanm Ayisyen*) asserts the age-old demand for Haitian respect:

> We women of Haïti, we swear before the Lord.
> We'll struggle until this crisis is past us and
>   our country is liberated.
> We declare before the world that we are finished with being slaves!
> There is no nation of people in all the earth that is superior to another.[23]

This song from the peasant movement brings together the themes of history, honor, and respect.

> Let us not allow the visions of our ancestors to disappear
> Haiti is our own, we cannot remain uninvolved
> If we are liberated, it will be a victory and honor for us all.
> Women and men alike, teenagers, and children
> Let us consolidate our strengths
> So that all nations will respect us.[24]

The theme of building Haiti, voiced by Haitian women abroad in their 1986 report "Haïtian Women in the Diaspora," is echoed in the song "Where Are You, Women?" from the Haitian countryside in the 1990s.

> Where are you, women of Haiti, strong women, peasant women?
> Are you here with us? We're here!
> . . . .
>
> Women who recognize
> That we have to work together with men
>   with *all* true patriots
> To build a better society
> Are you with us?[25]

Women's Consent and Challenge

At first glance, this movement in the countryside that joins women's struggles for equality and empowerment with the broader movement for social and economic transformation of Haitian society seems to run counter to and be undercut by the migration of women such as Yvette. Originally from a small rural hamlet, Yvette's lifelong battle has been to obtain the resources to improve the lot and the social status of her family. To the extent that individuals such as Yvette seek social mobility in Haiti for themselves and their family through transnational migration, they reinforce values that underlie the Haitian gender hierarchy. Yet, when Haitian women become enmeshed in transnational ties that link them to gendered nationalist projects, they find themselves simultaneously challenging and reinforcing gender and class hierarchies. This contradictory process, in which women's efforts to gain social status reinforce structures of male domination, while at the same time eroding the foundations of these structures, needs careful research and analysis.

First of all, women such as Yvette are empowered to play significant roles as authority figures in rural and urban families. The empowerment of women within family networks challenges the basic assumptions of gender hierarchy: the natural authority of men and their right to speak for the family. Yet by competing for social status, women enter into a system of social statuses that endorses and emulates the culture of the dominant classes. With this comes the valuation of men over women. The daily transactions that reenact hierarchies of status and gender among kin become the ways in which the status hierarchies of the entire nation are experienced as natural and normal. The very effort to attain mobility within these hierarchies serves to normalize and naturalize the inequalities of wealth and power that allow the Haitian bourgeoisie to block all attempts by the vast majority of people in Haiti to improve the conditions under which they live. As kinship bonds extend transnationally, they reproduce gender relationships and status hierarchies, and enmesh immigrants and the kin they support back home in an ongoing structure of feeling.[26] Both compliance with and challenges to gender inequalities are experienced as part of the emotions that pervade transnational family interactions; love, obligation, jealousy, and ambition. This structure of emotion and desire, love and pride, reproduces relationships of nation, class, and status, as well as gender. Gender, status, class, and nation are not four separate systems of human relationships, nor are these systems of relationships bound by the geographic borders of Haiti.

Family migration strategies that cross national borders may be legitimated by and serve to reinforce values that link family to nation. Yvette's triumphant invocation of the Haitian nation on the occasion of Leah's graduation was an instance of long-distance nationalism. Rather than participating in explicitly political activities, long-distance nationalists often engage in impassioned politics within the domain of domestic activities and family rites of passage such as weddings, funerals, births, and graduations. Therefore, the political identifications of transmigrants are not disembodied sentimental imaginings but are rooted in the personal obligations of family and the enactment of gendered relationships. As transmigrant men and women experience these changes, their efforts to simultaneously maintain or improve their class positions in their home societies may enmesh them in actions that rebuild and enforce the dominant unequal constructions of gender in their homeland rather than unsettle them. These gender constructions are, in turn, implicated in nationalist constructions of the core norms and values of the state—in most instances, in ways that subordinate and disempower women. Such constructions of the nation become central to transnational nation-state–building projects that link diasporas to homelands through tropes of blood and family.

If women such as Yvette, through their transnational "kin work," directly participate in processes of social reproduction that re-create the gender hierarchy across borders, they also use a language of nation to confront not just gender hierarchy but the class structure of Haiti along with the power hierarchy that marks the relationship between the United States and Haiti.[27] Because projects to build the nation-state both include and exclude women in the language of the nation, the gendered foundations on which the inequalities of national patriarchy are built are always shaky.

The growing involvement of the same women engaged in transnational family relations in transnational grassroots organizations from churches to health clinics as well increases the potency of the challenge. The anger that Georges's mother, Nadine, directed at Georges and Haiti is being translated by a new generation of women into the courage and determination to transform Haiti. As these women obtain prestige and leadership positions through their activities, they confound patriarchal values and patterns. The changing roles for women that have emerged from their acting as transborder citizens who make claims to rights in both Haiti and the United States are producing a politics and a form of nationalism that calls class structures into question.

As long as migrant transnational social fields extend into two or more nation-states and persons located within these fields experience positioning within more than one national project, contradictions will abound on which struggles can be built. The gendered analysis of nationalism we have made in this chapter has revealed the internal contradictions within Haitian long distance nationalism, pinpointing the fault lines along which resistance is erupting and highlighting the alternative meanings contained within a shared nationalist rhetoric.

Our ability to make this analysis has been enhanced by the growth of the international women's movement, which has enabled women to enter into struggles on national terrains, and to raise global demands for social justice and economic equality.[28] Within this process, women who have lived as transmigrants and moved between the gendered constructions of various nations have played vital roles in bringing back home, to Haiti and the United States, political agendas that contest rather than reinforce gender hierarchies and systems of domination. All of these developments indicate that the changing positioning of women within the Haitian national narrative and the changing roles for women, based on their transnational connections, can produce a politics and a form of nationalism that confronts class structures globally.

The women's movement has survived betrayal and violence. Abandoned by formal political parties and political leaders, activists were targeted by the military coup of 1991 to 1994 which spread terror with a policy of systematic abduction and rape.[29] Since then, the movement has faced continuing political repression in the midst of ongoing chaos. Yet the efforts to organize a grassroots movement centered on a vision of a nation rebuilt on a foundation of social justice continues. Disenchantment with electoral politics has fostered organizations such as *Kay Fanm* (Women's House) and *Solidarite Fanm Ayisyen* (Haitian Women's Solidarity) that have attracted tens of thousands of women, many of whom have become discouraged by the actions of political leaders and nongovernmental organizations who use politics for private gain. In 2000, a platform of forty-three feminist organizations was created to support women's causes in Haiti.[30] These organizations helped collect 120,000 signatures to present to Kofi Annan, the UN Secretary-General, to urge the UN to support women's causes, not only in Haiti, but the world over. They are demanding "an equitable distribution of the world's wealth to minimize the effects of the neo-liberal economic policies which have particularly affected women's condition and a campaign to eradicate the violence against women."[31] The understanding of the nation that poor Haitian women bring into political struggles empowers a form of Haitian long-distance nationalism that is simultaneously a struggle for social and economic justice. Scholars of feminist politics have argued that as part of women's collective action, women have been "revamping and rewriting . . . histories . . . used to support . . . male domination that continue to be embedded in many of today's religious, national, and ethnic projects."[32] Nevertheless, more is at stake than a revamping and renegotiation of the representation of women within these projects. These struggles can instead redefine the nationalist project itself, placing it within a new context, so that people in disempowered locations struggle not against other nations but against a global structure of corporate wealth and power.

7

The Generation of Identity: The Long-Distance Nationalism of the Second Generation

When we didn't have enough to eat, we'd go out bird hunting. We'd use slingshots. When any of us caught a bird, we'd build a fire and grill it. Nothing I've ever eaten since tasted so good. Even though we were poor, in elementary school the contrast between those who had more means and how we lived was not that great. We went to the same school and played with all of the children. At that age, I didn't see the difference between mulatto and black, rich and poor. But later on, when I was finishing secondary school, I began to see things differently. The mulatto and black children from the richer families went off to Port-au-Prince to attend elite high schools and then the university. But what kind of future would there be for me? Then I began to wish I could leave Haiti. And when my father was offered a position with the United Nations in Africa, with benefits that included sending all his children to a university free of charge, I could not believe that he turned it down. He said he had a duty to stay in Haiti and contribute to his country, even though he barely got paid.

Georges's father taught his son a lesson about love of nation and its relationship to self when he decided not to accept the offer of employment with the

United Nations. At that time, people who left were politically suspect when they returned. Gilbert Fouron chose Haiti and the status he obtained as an educated man there over the much greater wealth that he could have secured had he become an exile and a wanderer. This lesson has resonated through Georges's life. Ultimately, Georges could find no future for himself without emigrating. Yet in his sense of self and in the way he has chosen to live his life, in some fundamental way, Georges has never left Haiti. Just as childhood experiences cut across divisions of class and gender to join Haitians together in a shared national identity, when transformed into lifetime memories, these same experiences bind those who grew up in Haiti. These memories have become a storehouse from which first-generation emigrants and members of their generation who remain at home draw sustenance.

In the past, the inculcation of national identity through the use of public institutions has connected people growing up in different classes and geographic locations in Haiti. Formal education has fulfilled an important role despite the fact that many of the young people of each generation have been unable to go to school.[1] As Georges's recollections of his childhood indicate, youth of different class backgrounds and with varying access to formal education often played with each other. As they enjoyed national holidays and public rituals together, and shared among themselves a sense of being part of the proud history of Haiti, they developed an identification that extended across class lines. Experiences in childhood included, of course, what one learned from one's parents.

As we saw in the previous chapter, a nationalist rhetoric that includes long-distance nationalism is utilized by Haitian women of different classes living in both the United States and Haiti. Carrying within it a transcript of the aspirations of women and the poor for social justice, as well as an endorsement for a national narrative that legitimates gender and class inequalities, it serves simultaneously to divide and unite. Here, we explore the experiences that unite and divide Haitian youth as they live their lives within transnational social fields. The formation of politicized identities among contemporary youth is a crucial one, if we are to understand the persistence of nationalism in a world closely knit by the economic penetration of the same corporations and financial institutions globally. We ask, What about this next generation, those born in Haiti in the wake of large-scale transnational migration and the children of Haitian transmigrants born in the United States? How do they understand their relationship to Haiti? Surrounded by radio broadcasts, which bring glimpses of a richer, more powerful, world beyond Haiti, they witness the apparent wealth of transmigrants and grow up in a context in which international organizations from all over the world dispense their largesse to impoverished Haitians. The generation of young people now coming of age in Haiti grapple with questions of national identity in a context quite different from that of their parents.

Meanwhile, young people of Haitian descent living in the United States, although much more familiar and comfortable with the pace and outlook of daily life than their parents, often seek ways to identify with Haiti. They are reclaiming Haiti by strengthening their ties with their ancestral land and reaffirming their Haitian identity. As Toufi, a young woman born in the United States, told Georges, "Haiti is me; Haiti is my pride." We argue that this new generation has been shaped by their parents' nostalgia for a sweet, prosperous, and proud Haiti, as well as by the enduring transnational connections maintained by many of their families. Together they constitute a new form of second generation, a transnational second generation, united by a shared long-distance nationalism.

At various conferences where we have discussed long-distance nationalism, some scholars have dismissed our work as only a "first-generation phenomenon" that will vanish with the coming of age of the immigrants' offspring. The children of immigrants are often called the second generation by U.S. experts on immigration, thereby reflecting and contributing to the notion of the incorporation of immigrants as a step-by-step irreversible process of Americanization. The term reflects a mind-set in which immigrants become part of their new country by a unidirectional movement from the culturally foreign to the acceptable and familiar.[2] We don't believe such a model of immigrant incorporation accurately portrays the identity of the children of transmigrants, and instead see long-distance nationalism as extending into the "second generation" and beyond.

Even if long-distance nationalism is a one-generation-deep political ideology it would clearly be significant. Long-distance nationalism affects the way migrants organize their daily lives, encourages and endorses the sending home of millions of dollars of remittances, shapes the life circumstances and possibilities of all those back home who live within transnational social fields, and propels the political strategies and rhetoric of migrant political leaders and Haitian officials. It is not confined to the identity politics of the migrant generation, however. Those who dismiss transnational migration and long-distance nationalism as confined to the first generation have not come to terms with the implications for future generations of the establishment of transnational social fields. We employ a transnational perspective to examine the second generation, looking at the effect of transnational migration on young people born in the United States of Haitian parentage and on young people living in Haiti within transnational social fields. We also examine the similarities and differences in identification with Haiti between children of Haitian parentage living in the United States and Haitian youth living in Haiti. Then we ask, if these fields persist as ongoing social relations as well as fields of dreams, how do we delimit the boundaries of the second generation?

Youthful Voices in New York

Her presence was not imposing; her rhetoric not fiery. She stood before the large lecture hall filled with people, mostly young, mostly Haitian, and spoke very quietly. But the audience hung on her words because she was Edwidge Dandicat, a successful author at the age of twenty-seven. "I am not a politician," she told them. "I am just a Haitian, and our community is in crisis." Her message was as much in her attendance at this meeting as in her specific words. She seemed the perfect symbol to open this conference, which had been called to initiate the Haitian American Community Action Network (HACAN).

HACAN was envisioned by the conference conveners as a means of "initiating a national network of community groups and individuals dedicated to promoting the well-being and the civil and political rights of Haitians in the United States."[3] But for many of the participants, the location of this Haitian community and the domain of community action were not stable. Dandicat stood as a symbol of Haitian American success, but on what grounds? Much of Dandicat's critically acclaimed fiction is located in both the United States and Haiti, carrying readers into the world of Haitian transmigrants who travel back and forth between the two countries.[4] Her life story, which was known to this audience, includes a childhood in Haiti, migration to the United States at the age of twelve, degrees from Barnard College and Brown University, and continuing ties to Haiti. Her English is flawless, although she addressed the conference in Kreyòl. Dandicat ended her speech by quoting the slogan on the Haitian flag, "*L'Union Fait la Force*" (Through union comes strength). The Haitian and American flags both decorated the speaker's podium.

At one point during the conference, the American flag fell down. Some in the audience cheered, but the youthful conference organizers and other members of the audience were visibly upset, quickly righting the flag and apologizing. The momentary disturbance made it clear that while the audience was divided in terms of their identification with the United States, they shared an identification with Haiti. The agenda of the conference included political concerns in Haiti as well as the United States. The meeting began with a session titled "Building Haitian-American Political Leadership," which informed conference participants that "in an increasingly hostile environment, let's have a broad overview of the sociopolitical environment in which Haitian Americans live." But the final session on the agenda, "Politics and Democratic Trials in Haiti," focused on Haiti and the responsibility of Haitian Americans to Haiti. The organizers asked those assembled, "How can Haitian American communities honestly contribute to Haiti's democratic well-being?"[5]

Not all the organizers and participants at the conference were equally comfortable with the transnational scope of the agenda. There was a noticeable difference between the older generation and the youth, a second generation that had come of age within families structured by transnational migration and in the context of efforts by Haitian leaders to portray Haiti as a transnational nation-state. Those who spoke for an older generation of leadership saw the goal of the community action network in terms of the traditional U.S. paradigm of immigrant settlement: the development of immigrants as an ethnic "community" that celebrates its roots, yet attends to the business of carving out a place for itself within U.S. political and economic structures. For example, Jocelyn McCalla (Americanized as Johnnie), head of the National Coalition for Haitian Rights (NCHR), the organization that attempted to launch HACAN, urged the audience to speak in "American" rather than "Haitian terms," "because we are here and we are here to stay." He made no mention of Haiti per se. He called on Haitian professionals to help improve life for Haitian migrants. "We have more power than we think we have at the local, state, and federal levels. We should build strong lobbies. We should build alliances and we need to link up to other groups."

It should be noted that many in this older generation of leadership were, in fact, engaged in politics in Haiti. NCHR had recently established an office in Haiti to pursue the struggle for human rights on Haitian terrain. Nevertheless, these first-generation leaders had learned in the United States to separate political organizations linked to Haiti from efforts to create ethnic constituencies. They had found that foundations and churches that helped fund Haitian community organizing efforts, such as the proposed network, expected to see ethnic activities focused on the incorporating of immigrants into the United States.

The majority of the participants at this conference and a significant section of its leadership came from a second generation that was born or has lived since childhood in the United States. This generation has a different vision of the meaning of community. Young, confident, well educated, they felt comfortable building an organization committed to concerns and activities that connected them to the United States as well as Haiti. They simply did not acknowledge the boundaries. Their experience growing up in the United States convinced them that they needed to have a public identity. Public identity meant that they had a label and a culture they could claim as their own. This identity became Haitian, but for them Haitian was not confined to a concern for building a Haitian community in the United States. At one point, the assembled body was called on to chant, "A strong Haitian community equals a strong Haiti; a strong Haiti equals a strong Haitian community." Their ability to use "community" as a flexible referent that could be applied to Haitians in Brooklyn, the New York metropolitan area, or the United States, to the entire Haitian diaspora, and to all Haitians abroad and in Haiti, gave the slogan many layers of meaning.

In the course of three decades of Haitian incorporation in the United States, we have found long-distance nationalism to be common among persons of Haitian descent born in the United States. In certain ways, our findings resemble the work of other researchers who describe a sector of second-generation Caribbean youth, including Haitians, who maintain an identification with the homeland of their parents.[6] Yet such research explains variations in identity as solely a product of a U.S. milieu without a transnational perspective on migration. A transnational perspective provides a different reading of these responses, one that points to a second generation of long-distance nationalism. To make this point, we draw on eleven lengthy interviews that Georges conducted in 1996 with college seniors who were born in the United States, but whose parents had immigrated from Haiti. These interviews reflect patterns we have observed developing in the course of thirty years of working with Haitian young people. They resonate with the interviews of leaders of Haitian youth organizations that we conducted in 1985. We hasten to add that not all young adults of Haitian descent embrace their origins. For example, Georges's two children differ in the way they relate to Haiti. Both speak Kreyòl well and will publicly identify with Haiti. But Leah, now a lawyer, took a renewed interest in Haiti in the course of our 1996 visit, while Georges's son Jacob, an engineer, has no desire to maintain home ties. Jacob, who spent his preschool years living with his grandparents in Aux Cayes, did return to Haiti in the summer of 1998, yet the disorder and disarray of the country only increased his sense of distance and alienation.

All of the students that Georges interviewed spoke some Kreyòl but not all were fluent, so Georges conducted the interviews in English. These young people were more educated than many second-generation Haitian migrants. Education, however, is highly valued by the Haitian migrant population and a significant segment of Haitian young people in the United States have some form of postsecondary schooling.[7] The students we interviewed did not come from elite backgrounds, either in Haiti or the United States; in the United States, their parents worked as nurses aids, office cleaners, and mechanics. Although these students were U.S. citizens, none of them identified themselves as Americans.[8] The exchanges sounded like this:

Georges: Do you classify yourself as Haitian American, African American, or Haitian?
Toufi: Haitian.
Georges: Haitian, no hyphen?
Toufi: No, no hyphen. I am a Haitian.

Sandra, age twenty-two, discounted the influence of her birthplace on her identity: "I know I say I'm Haitian because I have a Haitian background, my family is from Haiti, and the only thing I have from here is that I was born here. I picked up the American culture, but at the same time, I think that about 60 percent of me, if not more, is Haitian. . . . I automatically say I'm Haitian."

Sandra maintained that she has always thought of herself this way, but several of these young people spoke of their identity with Haiti as something that they consciously adopted as they grew older. Carline saw herself as growing up "more as an African American . . . but as of late incorporating more of the Haitian culture into my daily life." As Toufi explained it, "When I went into high school, I started to realize a little bit more of who I was and started getting more in touch a little more with my Haitian side, and that is the only side I have ever seen since then. And that is the side I want to help."

These students are treated by the larger society as if they are African American youth, and they experience discrimination because of this identification. Still, by the time they were teenagers, they were not able to easily identify as African American. African Americans often treated them as different and sometimes inferior. Meanwhile, their parents continued to teach them to differentiate themselves from African Americans. By the time they were college seniors, they chose to be Haitian, at least occasionally. We have observed this maturing of a sense of Haitian identity among many young adults of Haitian parentage. Many second-generation Haitian students begin to publicly identify with Haiti during college.[9] We want to stress that a decision to embrace a Haitian identity does not mean that these second-generation Haitians are antagonistic to African Americans, nor do they reject an overarching identity politics that unites them with other blacks and places them within an African diaspora. To the contrary, many see their Haitian heritage as part of a broader experience of blackness.

The decision to publicly identify as Haitian also seems linked to participation in the workforce and the racial discrimination that the second generation encounter in their work lives. All of the Stony Brook students held jobs as well as attending school, and it was in the workforce that they had their most direct experiences of discrimination. Being viewed as black was for them an experience of both differentiation and subordination that defined them as not fully American. They reported that they had learned that despite their citizenship and fluency in English, the United States "is not your country." In addition, events in the larger society that focus public discussion and debate around the Haitian presence in the United States serve to highlight or reinforce identity issues for the second generation. For example, the false labeling of Haitians as carriers of AIDS brought Haitian young people into political action. The mobilization against the AIDS stigma that brought Haitian youth into the streets of New York in 1990 was followed by many of these same young people supporting transnational projects to rebuild Haiti. Nine years later, Manouchka, a Haitian student in Nina's course on the Caribbean recalled the 1990 demonstration as a turning point in her life: "We shook the Brooklyn Bridge and demanded justice and respect." Although she had been only twelve when she marched through the streets, she began to be proud of her Haitian identity from that point and now sees her future as helping to rebuild Haiti.

Whether they viewed themselves as partly or completely Haitian, all of the Stony Brook students expressed pride in being Haitian. As these young people matured, they learned to turn to their Haitian origins as a wellspring of strength that allowed them to live their lives in the United States. In fact, they defined Haitian as "being proud." When one student, Claudia, was asked, "What does it mean to you to be Haitian?" she responded, "A lot of pride, a lot of history, strength."

This pride in Haiti is linked to a catalog of Haiti's historical accomplishments that were recited or referred to in each of the interviews. Among those achievements mentioned were that Haiti was "the first country to defeat slavery"; it is a country that maintained "an African religion," "a country with its own language," "a country that fought for its independence," and "the first black republic to defeat a white army." Given the fact that one of the forces that impel youngsters of Haitian descent toward identifying as Haitian is their racialization in the United States as black, the statement that Haiti "defeated a white army" is highly significant.

Without a transnational perspective, these students' specification that they were Haitian can be interpreted as evidence of the persisting importance of ethnicity within U.S. life. Pride in Haiti can be construed as a politics of cultural roots within a discourse about membership in a multicultural United States. Or continuing identification by a second generation with their ancestral homeland can be perceived as solely a reactive response to the racialization that the second generation experiences. And certainly, several of the students told us that the discrimination they faced convinced them that they should "go back to some place where they expect something of you, where they appreciate you, where they don't discriminate against you." That place becomes your true home, no matter where you were born.

Any adequate interpretation of the identities of the second generation must consider the significance of their transnational ties and experiences. The students we interviewed were raised within transnational social fields. All but one had visited Haiti, and that one young woman's plans had been abruptly canceled in 1991 when the military coup against Aristide made the prospect dangerous. Yet direct experience in Haiti was only one aspect of their ongoing relationships to Haiti. The daily events and rituals of their childhood were shaped by their families' efforts to send money and gifts to

Haiti, the arrivals and departures of family members, and the constant buzzing gossip and news exchanged with family and friends in Haiti. Sandra provided a description of the taken-for-granted interchange of visiting. "My grandmother has come here . . . I think only twice, but that's because she was sick. My cousins have come from time to time, and I think all of them have come once or twice, but I think there are one or two . . . different cousins and aunts who haven't been here yet." All of these young people also grew up with and continue to confront their parents' relationships to Haiti. Two had parents planning to return to Haiti to live, one to establish a business and the other to retire.

For most of these students, the transnational context of their lives makes it logical for them to see themselves as not only identifying with Haiti but also assuming some responsibility for it. For instance, Carline linked her ability to confront racism in the United States with her duties to Haiti: "My strength derives from my Haitian nationality. I feel I have an obligation to Haiti." Sabrina had returned the previous year from her first trip to Haiti with a commitment to assume part of the burden of supporting kin in Haiti that had previously been carried by her mother: "What I do once a month is send money to my family, because they are so much in need."

Haitian youth born in the United States and living within transnational social fields come to believe that identification with a homeland is a matter of action as well as words. Therefore, when they speak about their Haitian identity, they speak about future plans as well as their sense of self. All of the students Georges interviewed had plans that ranged from the personal to the political. But of course in this context, the personal was political. To identify with another nation as part of a personal sense of self and plan to take some action in relationship to that nation provides a base for Haitian political leaders seeking to rally persons living in the United States on behalf of Haiti.

Personal plans included everything from visiting to working in Haiti. Sabrina mentioned becoming a doctor and possibly opening a private practice in Haiti. "It would be good if I go back, and as far as helping my country and my people, that's something I would always do." In their discussions of education, the students made a link between their Haitian identity and education. They also told us that their obtaining an education reflected on Haiti and provided them ways to assist Haiti. Two students envisioned playing a directly political role. Toufi told us: "I want to be involved in politics in Haiti. My father always tells me no, because I may never be able to go back to Haiti, which would be a problem. True, but I just think I can go back and volunteer and do things." Carline took this plan the furthest: "Well, one of my biggest ambitions is to get involved in politics in Haiti. And even one day, run for president. . . . Even though I was born in America . . . even with or without [Haitian] citizenship, I still have patriotism for the country, so!"

In 1969, young men who were born in Haiti, but had emigrated to the United States often told Nina that they intended to become president of Haiti. Thirty years had not eliminated the possibility that a young Haitian living in the United States would have transnational political ambitions, yet the passing years had also made it possible for the presidential ambitions to be voiced by a young woman who was a U.S. citizen by birth.

It is important to note that Carline differed from the other students that Georges interviewed in the degree to which she herself had been a transmigrant, living her life across borders and incorporated in both countries. Although born in the United States, she had been sent back to Haiti for part of her education. Carline's experience is far from unique, however; many children born in the United States spend at least part of their childhood in Haiti, living within transnational households. Young people with a great deal of direct experience in Haiti frequently form a cohort within a school population, pressuring other young people of Haitian descent to identify themselves as Haitian and become involved in activities linked to Haiti. All the students we spoke with described such pressures within the Haitian Student Organization at Stony Brook, to which all but one of these students belonged.

In the past, many Haitian student clubs in New York, including the one at Stony Brook, have been active in transnational politics. Even when political repression in Haiti made it difficult for organizations in the United States to actually maintain or develop ties to Haiti, we found Haitian young people defining their activities in organizations in the United States as contributing to Haiti and as being part of Haitian life. In 1985, we interviewed the leaders of four Haitian student clubs, as well as a Caribbean Youth Association composed of Haitians and a Haitian soccer club for young people. All but one of the persons interviewed told us that their organization contributed to Haiti. They argued that activities that took place in the United States ensured that "people from Haiti lived a better life." U.S.-based Haitian youth groups participated in the movement against the Duvalier regime and in Aristide's Lavalas movement. By 1997, there was a political lull and those students who had not recently visited Haiti seemed removed from the political discourse of that country. Nonetheless, even in this period of political disarray, Carline stated, "I have to defend Haiti. . . . I feel at times I am the voice of the country." It is also crucial to note that many of the young people engaged in building the Haitian American Community Action Network, who were also immersed in transnational political activities, had come out of Haitian student clubs.

At least a core of the members of this second generation envisioned themselves as a force to "rebuild Haiti." As Claudia put it: "I have a lot of people who are just like me who are getting their education here but who want to go back. . . . It can be, you know, a very fulfilling future as far as Haiti is concerned because a lot of us who are getting our education here plan to go back and to build the country. So I see, in a few years, Haiti will be a good country again to live in." Carline concurred: "I can see my future in Haiti. It could be here and helping over there or totally there. Definitely my eyes will be focused on Haiti."

These young adults took into their vision of the future not only their own experiences in the United States but also their parents' imagery of a beautiful Haiti that once was. Sabrina, for example, used the word "rebuild" in discussing her own future plans: "I hope for the best for my future, and as far as Haiti, it's my country and I will definitely be going back. . . . It can be rebuilt." Georges asked, "What do you mean rebuilt? Was there a time when it was beautiful?" She replied: "That's all I heard, when I went to Haiti. All I heard was, 'You came at the wrong time. Haiti's at its worst. This was once a beautiful place.' " Most of the students we interviewed were familiar with this projection of Haiti's past, the same imagery of Haiti that haunts Georges's dreams. Past becomes linked to the future. Politics and nostalgia meet in the concrete organizations, practices, and plans of the second generation to reconstruct and reclaim Haiti for their generation and the future.

Youthful Voices in Haiti

In 1996, on our first day in Aux Cayes, Georges turned on the radio and found himself in an airspace that the young people there claimed as their own. A team of young women and men, most of them in their early twenties, were broadcasting a daily radio program, specifically designed to speak to youth. The program was aired on *Men Kontre* (Hands Together), a non-commercial station sponsored by the Catholic Diocese of Aux Cayes. Men Kontre originated under the Duvalier dictatorship as part of a broad-based social movement that led, in 1986, to the toppling of the twenty-nine-year-old regime. While many of the radio stations that contributed to the struggle had been silenced since that time, Men Kontre continued to serve as a forum to educate and inform the people of Haiti, and to provide political information and critique. Consequently, the young people who participated in the station's daily broadcasts for other young people were linking themselves to a particular history of resistance against political repression as well as a particular discourse about the Haitian nation and state that has been shaped by the past decades of struggle.[10] They were also part of a transnational organization. The priest responsible for the program travels between the United States and Haiti. In the United States, he runs Catholic retreats for Haitian young people that strengthen their identification with Haiti.

When we went to visit the radio station, we found that the broadcasters were successfully encouraging an ongoing dialogue among the youth of Aux Cayes. They called on their listeners to participate through telephone calls that were aired live. If the listeners did not have access to a phone, which was generally the case, they were encouraged to write to the station, become "pen pals," and receive personalized answers. Hundreds of young people responded to this offer, writing to the station and in this way joining in these regular on-air discussions.

We spoke to six members of the radio staff, one man and five women.[11] Two of those interviewed have the same mothers, but different relationships with Haitians abroad. They ranged in age from eighteen to twenty-nine; their average age was twenty-three. All six were born in the rural area that surrounds Aux Cayes where people continue to live by cultivating the land. Four of the six had fathers who worked the land as cultivators, selling crops to support the family. Only one had a father with any formal training or profession.[12] Four have mothers who were *commerçante*, small-scale retailers who sold agricultural products, cooked food, and a broad array of new or secondhand manufactured goods.

These young activists were as convinced as their parents' generation that children of Haitian parentage born abroad remain Haitian. They were among the many who readily used the language of blood as part of their long-distance nationalism. Marjorie (the young woman whose passionate nationalism generated in the midst of the public disarray that plagues Haiti startled and inspired us) told us, "I believe if the parents are Haitian, and always speak with her or him and say who s/he is and what nationality s/he is, that person is not totally [American]. S/he has Haitian blood in her or his veins." Carmel took up this theme, differentiating between legal definitions of citizenship and questions of political loyalty by using the language of blood: "According to the constitution of the foreign country, once you naturalize, you adhere to their nationality and reject your native one, but for me, regardless of what the other country says, you have Haitian blood in your veins."

Because they fervently embraced the idea of a transnational Haiti, all six members of the radio staff were against the concept of dual nationality. They felt that you can never stop being Haitian. The ties of blood were not seen as an abstract claim of identity—they came with an agenda. These young people saw those abroad as key to both their own future and that of Haiti's. They also were uniform in their acceptance of the morality of knowledge. As Anna explained: "It is an obligation because they know the conditions the country is in and the sufferings that exist in Haiti. If the country was good, they would never have left. They know what they left behind. They know that they left these people in the same conditions that existed prior to their departure. How can they ignore them and not lend a helping hand?"

Given the worsening living conditions and tenuous political situation, the staff of the radio program saw their personal future and that of the country as being very much connected to the Haitian diaspora. Yet the members of the radio staff differed in their personal degree of inclusion in transnational social fields. All had family living abroad, but not all received support from these families.

Whether the United States was a destination or desire, it emerged more as a land of possibilities than restriction. These youth knew something of the racial discrimination in the United States. Tonya reported, "My aunt and boyfriend told me that they are mistreated a great deal because they are black. They reserve the harder, dirtier work for them." But she and the others wanted to go anyway. Without employment or educational opportunities in Haiti, these young people saw no choice but to leave. They viewed the type of discrimination that they faced in Haiti from the rich and powerful who were still mainly mulattoes as more insurmountable barriers to their aspirations. Only with a foreign education and money could they overcome the prejudice based on color and class background that they encounter in Haiti.

These young people saw themselves living in the United States and even obtaining U.S. citizenship, if that would assist them in their goals. But their aims were linked to their expectation that they will always remain Haitian and connected to Haiti. By migrating to the United States and gaining an education, they would be able to give back to both their family and nation. Their achievements will belong and contribute to a brighter future for Haiti.

Coming of age within a Haitian political landscape that extends from Haiti to the United States, these young people experienced the Haitian diaspora as a political force within Haiti. Carmel remarked that those abroad "keep a keen eye on what is going on in Haiti." Added Anna: "This is our country. This is their country, too." As they embraced the diaspora as part of the future of Haiti, these young people made references to Haiti's past. They told us, "You see, whatever used to be is falling into disrepair, is being destroyed. . . . The country is going backward." In this nostalgia for the past, these youth who had never left Haiti invoked the same imaginary that had made Georges laugh with delight in his dreams. The vision of a sweet, prosperous bygone Haiti joined young people in Aux Cayes with the second generation in New York whose commitment to Haiti was filtered through the nostalgia they learned from their parents, imparting strength to the rhetoric of rebuilding Haiti that we found among this second generation. All invoked an image of a past Haiti that was better, stronger, and more beautiful than the Haiti that exists now.

In their nationalism and their inclusion of those abroad within the Haitian nation, the political activists from the radio program differed little from the thirty-six young people we interviewed who were less politically active, many of whom had less education and fewer life opportunities. Of those thirty-six, eight were youth in Aux Cayes and twenty-eight were in Port-au-Prince.[13] Isolated from the rest of Haiti by poor roads and a grossly inefficient telephone service, they were connected to Haitians who lived in other nation-states. These young people understood that they inhabited a global terrain of settlement that included the United States (Miami, New York City, Chicago, and Boston), Guadeloupe, and France. This knowledge shaped their definition of the term *Haitian*.

The youth in our sample who were not political activists varied widely in wealth, education, and ties to the diaspora. They ranged from the son of a prominent capitalist who held both a U.S. and Haitian passport, and had a home in both Miami and Port-au-Prince, to a homeless young man who supported himself by helping persons in an impoverished neighborhood illegally tap into the electric lines. Twenty-one (60 percent) classified themselves as poor, thirteen (37 percent) as middle class, and one (3 percent) as a member of the bourgeoisie. Twenty-eight were students at the time of the interview, although among these some reported only a few years of schooling. Thirty-four percent received remittances regularly or were in frequent contact with family abroad.

Despite the differences in their backgrounds and levels of education, the majority of these young people (69 percent) expressed some degree of nationalist sentiments, although they were not as fierce in their nationalism as the radio staff. Most believed that those who had emigrated and changed their nationality remain Haitian, and therefore remained within the Haitian nation. Most knew the word *diaspora*, and saw a role for the diaspora both politically (53 percent) and economically (42 percent) in contributing to the future of Haiti.

All of the youth were socialized in the midst of the fierce political struggles that took place within a transnational terrain. Previous generations of Haitian youth had learned patriotic sentiments from nationalistic rituals embedded in school curriculum, public ceremonies, and national holidays. While much of this had been abandoned by the 1990s, the Lavalas's slogans calling for the rebuilding of the nation were all around them, as graffiti on the walls of houses, churches, and schools, in discussions on the radios that played incessantly in Haiti, and in the Catholic masses of liberation theology priests. These youth witnessed or participated in street demonstrations with similar slogans. Then, between 1991 and 1994, they experienced the coup that sent Aristide into exile and the transnational resistance to the Haitian military dictatorship that followed.

The vantage point of this generation was one that extended far beyond their neighborhood or city. They grew up in a media age, dramatically different from the era of their parents' youth. With the advent of cheap transistor radios and inexpensive tape recorders, even people in rural Haiti can now listen to radio programs and exchange audio cassettes.[14] Without electricity in rural areas, television is not available, but poor households in cities such as Aux Cayes sometimes have black-and-white sets, and households living on remittances often have color television, VCRs, and compact disc players. Television and radio not only introduce U.S. and European lifestyles, music, and items of consumption; they also link Haiti with the diaspora.

Despite this uniform socialization, however, not all youth held the same opinions. We found some evidence that differences between young people were linked to their differing relationships within transnational social fields. There was some variation between those who had strong ties with family members abroad and those who did not. We define strong family ties as households that either receive regular remittances from family abroad or are in regular communication accompanied by assistance if needed. Except for political activists, young people with strong ties to family living abroad tended to be the most vehement in their identification with Haiti, and the Haiti with which they identified was transnational.

All over Haiti, different degrees of connection with family abroad provide sharply different life prospects for young people in Haiti, shaping not only their daily standard of living but also their sense of the future for themselves and Haiti. The young people who received money and gifts from family abroad appeared more positive and self-confident. From such kin, these young people expected either assistance in obtaining education in Haiti or sponsorship to go abroad and study. Indeed, they preferred to study abroad.[15] Giselle, whose parents were both in the United States, informed us that "Haiti doesn't offer any real university education. I have been calling my mother regularly, asking for my mother to send for me so that I can attend college in the United States."

In contrast, those without such prospects were already bitter, although still in their twenties. Their sense of frustration was deepened by the widespread belief in Haiti that kin have an obligation to help their family. As Carmel, age twenty-three, stated, "I used to hear people say that it is a comedy to be in philo [the last year of high school], but the tragedy begins when you pass the exam. I am now realizing that it is true. I want to study, but the tragedy of the reality is that I can't."[16] Even though Carmel had abandoned her dream of becoming a doctor or obtaining clerical skills, she still found herself without a job or future. Emilia, looking at her older sister's fate, was even more despondent than Carmel. She expressed the feelings of hopelessness of young people without transmigrant kin able to help them when she observed, "There is no future for me."

Most of those who voiced little or no nationalism had no contact with family living abroad. Only among the radio staff members, who were part of a political organization, did persons without strong transnational family ties display a fierce nationalism. The link between Haitian nationalism and transnational ties among the youth is an important area for further investigation.

The Second Generation: A Redefinition

Our research on the establishment of transnational terrains that encompass several generations has implications for concepts of the second generation that extend far beyond the specifics of the Haitian case and unsettle the very notion of the "second generation." Far more is at stake here than academic definitions. Categories can illuminate or obscure political processes, and the second generation is just such a category.

The scholars who first spoke of immigrant incorporation using a terminology of generations made several assumptions.[17] First of all, they assumed that the immigrants who settle in the United States arrive prepared to make a new life and abandon the old. These immigrants may remain nostalgic for their old country, but are committed to becoming part of the new land. Nonetheless, members of the first generation are unable to become fully Americanized. Their English will always be accented, reflecting their incomplete acculturation into the U.S. mainstream. Secondly, according to the long-standing scholarship of immigrant incorporation, members of the second generation, born in the United States, grow up in somewhat of a bind. At home they may live in somewhat of an old world culture, but outside the home they are able to fully claim the culture of their native land. Insecure because of their family background, some of these persons may go out of their way to display a U.S. identity and knowledge of U.S. culture. In contrast, members of the third generation are assumed to have no such limits or conflicts. Fully American, they may be relaxed enough to claim their cultural roots, yet they are culturally and socially fully part of the United States.

As we have indicated, this model of immigrant incorporation never fully fit European immigrants who arrived at the end of the nineteenth and early twentieth centuries. Large numbers of immigrants were transmigrants—they and their children lived in a world linked socially and culturally to the homeland until two world wars, the depression, and an aggressive Americanization campaign led them to sever or at least downplay their home ties. The old ideas about the second generation certainly don't seem to fit children of the migrants who began to come in significant numbers in the 1960s from Latin America, the Caribbean, and Asia. Young people growing up in contemporary migrant households do not automatically assume an "American" identity, although they are culturally different from their parents and often go through a stage where they try to distance themselves from their parents' culture and identity.[18] Some second-generation youth, who are racialized as black, do assimilate rapidly but take on an African American identity. The adoption of this identity by a sector of second-generation young persons constitutes a rejection of white mainstream culture and values that, through processes linked to race and class, marginalize black youth. In contrast, another sector of second-generation youth respond to racialization by joining with their parents in embracing the national identity of their country of origin.[19] As they mature, young people develop multiple, overlapping, and simultaneous identities, deploying them in relationship to events they experience at home, school, and work, and in the country of their birth as well as that of their ancestry.

Often, researchers and educators who debate the identities of the second generation assume that immigration is a one-generation-long phenomenon. They speak as if migration stops after the first generation so that the old country is represented in the United States only by an aging population of immigrants; a second generation grows up as a cohort surrounded by people their ages who were also U.S. born and bred. But this view of immigration was inspired by a pre–World War I migration stream that was abruptly cut by immigration restriction, depression, and world war. If contemporary attacks on immigration do not succeed in halting the flow of newcomers, and if the current pace of family reunions remains stable, young people born in the United States will continue to find in their households, and all around them, compatriots of their age who recently have arrived from the home country.[20] These young people mutually influence and socialize each other. In addition, transmigrant households constantly play host to relatives of various generations who engage in a circuit of visiting.

Once a migration is firmly established, child rearing is also a transnational process.[21] This means that in research on the second generation, we cannot assume that adults who have immigrated and settled in the United States will have children born and raised in the United States. This is a question for empirical investigation. For example, many Haitian parents have children born in Haiti who are brought to the United States only when they are teens, children born in the United States after their parents have migrated but sent home to be raised in Haiti, and children born and raised in the United States. Consequently, households contain children with many different degrees of knowledge about Haiti.

A transnational gaze provides a missing piece of the puzzle of why children born or raised in the United States may perceive an ancestral homeland as one of their multiple identities and become long distance nationalists. We suggest that the children of migrants living in the United States make their choices and move between different identities in relationship not only to their experiences of racialization within the United States but also in relationship to the degree to which their lives are encompassed within a transnational terrain. Those young people who grow up within such a setting develop a sense of self that has been shaped by personal, familial, and organizational connections to people "back home." At the same time, the production of self in terms of race, ethnicity, and nation is part of a political process, and these political processes extend transnationally. Participation in transnational social fields can link U.S.–born young people to broader processes that define them as a political constituency that can act on behalf of this "home country." In turn, their siblings, cousins, and cousin's cousins in Haiti see in the U.S. second generation hope for their own future and Haiti.

To be sure, there is much in the Haitian experience that is unique, so that long-distance nationalism among migrants' children must be explored cross-culturally. The tendency of Haitians to conflate self, family, blood, race, and nation is the product of a two-hundred-year history of nation-state building. Many migrants who create transnational spaces come from states that have less established and accepted nationalist ideologies, and their young people may learn more from their elders about a hometown identity than about a national one.[22] And even in the Haitian case, whether or not personal transnational connections are translated into long-distance nationalism varies. Still, the attraction to young people born in the United States of the appeal to return and rebuild a homeland is a force that extends from beyond the particularities of Haitian history and deserves systematic cross-cultural exploration. Nina certainly felt the tug when, as a teenager, she was urged by her synagogue's Zionist youth group to "build spiritual bridges" and contribute to the rebuilding of Israel. Myriads of Jewish youth born in the United States enthusiastically spend summers or years abroad in Israel, becoming lifelong participants of the long-distance nationalism promoted by the U.S. Zionist movement. This movement flourishes within a well-organized transnational institutional framework that builds long-distance nationalism for Israel among people whose traceable ancestors never lived in Israel. Two of Nina's cousins sent their sons to Israel in these kinds of programs. What surprises us is that there is little public or academic discussion of certain instances of long-distance nationalism among young people that seem almost taken for granted, yet when we mention the long-distance nationalism of Haitian youth born in the United States, we upset many scholars.

The Transnational Second Generation and the Continuation of Long-Distance Nationalism

It is time to redefine the second generation so that it encompasses those born in the homeland and the new land (or lands) after a large-scale transnational migration has been established and taken root. Such a migration establishes multiple social fields which span borders and connect persons who have family and friends abroad to those who do not. Young people growing up in either the homeland or a new land—after such a migration has been established—learn from the constant flow of information, goods, and resources brought by transmigrants.

Our definition of a transnational second generation begins with the fact that migrants, as they live their lives across borders, develop networks and households that are transnational, but we do not limit the second generation to only the young people in these households. The children who live within transnational households influence friends and neighbors who are not themselves part of transnational households. In this approach to defining and delimiting a transnational second generation, we stress that ongoing transnational social relations serve to personalize and, in a certain sense, nationalize flows of ideas and images, shaping the way in which media, ideas, and commodities are understood and utilized. The media that surround these youth include both radio, television, and newspapers produced for adults who constantly reiterate their long-distance nationalism, as well as forms of media specifically aimed at youth. Media are only part of a range of transnational forces that shape the perceptions of young people. For example, religious leaders form transnational youth organizations that can foster long-distance nationalism. In addition, the dress and music of the members of a transnational second generation are shaped by the flow of commerce conducted within transnational social fields. Because of this range of experiences, a transnational second generation differs from young people who grow up exposed to global media but without the context of a transnational migration that filters and refashions broader trends.

Not all members of a transnational second generation become long-distance nationalists. However, as we have seen by examining the experiences of second-generation Haitian youth in the United States and Haiti, some members of this generation do identify with and become committed to building a nation-state which extends beyond the territorial borders of Haiti. Their long-distance nationalism is not the same as their parents'. Nor can we say that the long-distance nationalism of the youth living in the United States is the same as the young people who have remained in Haiti. Although members of Haiti's second generation in the United States share with their peers in Haiti a transnational space, they have traveled to this place by a different path and experience it in different ways. Young adults living in Haiti in the wake of a massive out migration were grappling with the disappointments of a bleak, unpromising future and looking to the Haitians of the diaspora for assistance in creating a brighter one. Faced with the barriers of class, color, gender discrimination, political turmoil, and the lack of economic opportunity, they see migration to the United States and the Haitian diaspora as the hope for both themselves and Haiti. At the same time, the members of the second generation in the United States see connection with Haiti as a way to escape racial barriers and economic opportunities made uncertain by economic restructuring.

Young Haitians in Haiti and the United States hold different and disjunctive conceptualizations of both these locations. By arguing that Haitians born and living in the United States and people born in Haiti who live within transnational fields are equally members of a second generation, we are not denying the very different experiences these two sets of people have or the quite different adults they become. Young people born or brought up in the United States experience multiple assimilative pressures. They are extremely different culturally from people who have never lived in the United States.

Yet this second generation is a single cohort because, although they are not pursuing the commitment to a transnational Haiti by following the same path, they believe they are traveling toward the same destination. Located in different daily realities, the members of this second generation do not share an "imagined community" in the present but in the past and future.[23] Besides sharing a claim to a Haitian homeland, members of this second generation share a nostalgia for the Haiti that never was and a commitment to a Haiti that will be. Georges's nocturnal dreams and the daydreams of the young people he interviewed in at Stony Brook and those we interviewed in Aux Cayes and Port-au-Prince share a single vision. Underlying their disjunctive images of Haiti and the United States is a common vision of a sweet Haiti of the past and a prosperous, peaceful Haiti of the future.

Even young people of Haitian descent such as Georges's son, twenty-four-year-old Jacob, who rejects present-day Haiti, may do so in terms of the failure of Haiti to rebuild. Jacob retains his idea of a proud bygone Haiti and he is proud of that past. Such nostalgia serves as a tie with previous generations as well as between the various sectors of Haitian youth who live in different presents. This shared destination binds Haitians across national borders and generations.

We do not hold that long-distance nationalism reaching across generations is an inevitable outcome of transnational migration. Even if politicians in emigrant-sending countries pass laws that extend forms of dual nationality into future generations—as they have in the Dominican Republic, Mexico, and Colombia—the long-distance nationalism on the part of future generations is not assured. To the contrary, the situation we have observed provides us with an indication of how nationalist fervor can rapidly turn to cynicism. The paralysis of the political leadership in Haiti in 1998, a leadership that contained members recruited from the diaspora, created cynicism and a loss of nationalist passion in members of the second generation in both the United States and Haiti.

Our efforts to delineate transnational migration, long-distance nationalism, and the development of a transnational second generation should not be taken as either a celebration or denigration of these forms of interconnection across the borders of nation-states. The merits and problems of the emergence of phenomena such as a transnational second generation can only be judged in terms of the goals and concrete achievements of a specific nationalist project. Transnational social fields as well as life experiences generate a long-distance nationalism that can take people in many directions.

8

"The Responsible State": Dialogues
of a Transborder Citizenry

I got home at 11:45 last night. Although the snow was coming down heavily and the wind was howling, the students stayed after the class ended at 9:40 P.M. to continue the discussion. And I was so excited that it didn't matter to me either that I was going to have to drive home in a snowstorm. They told me that no one else has ever taught them these kinds of things. One student began the conversation by saying, "I lived a sheltered life. I never read the Constitution and I never looked at the legal system and the government the way we do in this class." Because that class is part of the state requirement for certification as a public school teacher, a great many of the students are studying to be teachers. But even though they are in college, they have never read the Constitution of their country and they don't know anything about U.S. laws. The course is also open to the whole campus, and so we have 186 people enrolled in my class. Another student said, "You should hear my father. I talk about this class at home and he says, 'What kind of crap are you learning?'" I invited the student's father to come to class. He came and then he apologized, saying, "You taught me something about my own country."

Georges is constantly surprised by how little interest people born in the United States have in their Constitution and laws. In his experience, one that we found reflected in our interviews, many people in Haiti readily discuss the constitutionality of the actions of their political leaders. Consequently, when Georges teaches his university classes about U.S. court rulings that affect education, he brings with him a stance toward government that reflects his Haitian upbringing. Georges's ideas about the state, however, are not based solely on his experiences in Haiti. Speaking in a U.S. classroom, Georges brings to students an understanding of the United States and its laws that reflects the past and current U.S. presence in Haiti, as well as the Haitian experience in the United States.

We argue that long-distance nationalists become a new form of citizenry—a transborder citizenry. As all other citizens, they claim rights and privileges from government, but transnational citizens claim a relationship to more than one government. We explore transborder citizenship by examining the Haitian assertion of their membership in two different, although intimately connected states—the United States and Haiti. Many Haitians have been functioning as substantive citizens of both polities, irrespective of whether they are legally citizens of Haiti or the United States.

When Haitians assert citizenship rights, they do so with an understanding of the state forged through their experience with both the Haitian and U.S. political systems.[1] Out of their combined experiences with distinct governments that have dramatically different expectations about the relationship between a state and its citizens, Haitian transborder citizens create new ways to think about and respond to the governments of both countries. They build on their experiences with the laws and day-to-day government practices in both states to develop something new.

If concepts of citizenship are being constructed across borders, then we have all entered a new and challenging political arena, one in which states remain insignificant. Yet people who live in transnational social fields raise new questions about the purpose and uses of government, pose new political agendas, and contribute to new struggles against oppressive conditions. In cities with a large influx of new migrants such as New York and Miami, newspapers carry headlines with stories such as "For Immigrants Dual Nationality Offers Advantages but Stirs Questions."[2] The questions raised are not only for migrants, though. The search for the meaning of nationality and citizenship in an epoch of globalization is an inquiry that confronts us all.

The United States and Haiti define the rights and responsibilities of citizenship quite differently. These political systems differ in the way they allocate citizenship, the expectations that citizens have of their government, and the obligations that the governments place on their citizens. These differences translate into how people see themselves as members of a particular state. John Kennedy famously captured some of these differences when he encouraged Americans to "ask not what your country can do for you but what you can do for your country." This patriotic statement rings true to persons raised within the U.S. political ethic because it portrays a government that is an object of loyalty rather than a source of services. The pronouncement makes no sense to many Haitians when they arrive in the United States. As Georges explained:

We almost had a riot in class the night I told my students that Kennedy's statement was one of the dumbest things I had ever heard. Of course I put it that way to provoke the students to speak out. I told them that to hear that from the president, when daily in the 1960s, if you were a poor black, Hispanic, or white, people didn't respect you or give you opportunities, makes no sense. And it is still true today that the poor and members of minority groups need the government. The government should be there giving you the support you need to protect your rights and provide the services that give you equal access to opportunities. Of course you should ask your government to do this for you. I pay my taxes to the government, so why can't it do something for me?

In expecting that the government should "do something for me," Georges is expressing a widely held Haitian view. Haitians generally believe that a good government is one that takes "responsibility" for its people and provides for their needs. In this respect, Haitians tend to hold a view of the relationship between a people and its government that differs from the prevailing political opinion in the United States. Haitians of all class backgrounds that we talked to in Haiti were able to speak readily and eloquently about the "responsibilities of the state." In contrast, we have found that the college students Georges teaches in New York and Nina teaches in New Hampshire, like most people raised in the United States, place fewer demands on the state.

"Oh Yes, The State"

Some political theorists have assumed that when people experience the state as repressive or intrusive and evade contact with government officials, they don't see themselves as part of that state.[3] But our research in Haiti and the United States shows the situation to be more complex. When we developed our questionnaire for our 1996 research, Georges suggested asking people, "What do you think about the state [*leta*]? Not the particular government now in office but the state?" Nina thought such a direct question would only be understood by educated persons and might intimidate most individuals. Actually, because she grew up in the United States, she couldn't even imagine asking such a question in an interview. She was surprised with the results when Georges persisted and began to ask about the state.

Most people didn't hesitate for a moment. Even those with only a few years of schooling felt quite at home with a discussion of the state. "Oh yes, the state," they would say, take a deep breath, and proceed to explain why they needed a responsible state. Vico, twenty-one years old, was supported by his mother, who works as a baby-sitter in Miami. Vico gave us a careful explanation of Haiti's problems and the responsibilities of the government: "Sometimes the parents are living in the countryside and they send their children to the city, where they have no supervision, face problems, don't have enough to eat, are left on the streets, beg, and sometimes have to steal to survive. They have no leadership. The government should intervene to help these kids, but the government has given up. There is no responsible state."

Louise looked old at the age of thirty-five. She was worn-out from her struggles to pay the rent on a one-room house and support eight other people (including her five children, husband, and cousins) from her earnings as a market woman. She sat in Mirelle's yard and instructed Nina about the relationship between the failures of the government and problems of the poor. "The government doesn't know anyone's problems but we don't say that it could not have known our problems. . . . There is too much misery. . . . I can't say anything because when the state tells you not to touch the government, you better not, because if you touch it, they will beat you up."

For Louise, as for so many others we spoke with, government authorities are persons to avoid. Yet Louise can envision a state that responds to the suffering of the Haitian poor. Despite her knowledge that she would face repression if she tried to change the regime, she holds onto an expectation that the state should take charge, face up to its responsibilities, and solve Haiti's problems. Of the ninety-five people we asked about the state, 75 percent told us that the state should take responsibility for the people. In discussing this, most people focused on education and employment opportunities as services the state should be providing. Others stressed public safety and security as the primary responsibility of the state—a growing concern in Haiti, where the rich drive the streets with private armed body guards, cell phones, and two-way radios, and all other citizens are at the mercy of armed robbers and brigands.

Poor citizens have developed their own theories about their relationship to a government that doesn't serve their needs. They distinguish between the government and a particular regime. In this way, they are able to continue to link themselves to the state, while distancing themselves from the actions of government officials who disregard the needs of the people. This distinction between a regime and government emerged in our interviews. Many strangers were afraid of sharing their views of the current political leaders of Haiti with us. They would speak only when we made it clear, "We are asking about leta [the state], not the gouvènman [the regime]."

Memories of Things Past: The Haitian State and the People

The founders of Haiti, the United States, and the first French republic all were influenced by the political theory of republicanism, which holds that "the people" are the ultimate source of legitimacy for the state and justifies the overthrow of an oppressive government "by the people." The officials and political leaders of all three revolutionary states were faced with the task of gaining acceptance from their own populations and the international community for a new system of government. They also had to determine what responsibilities the government would have toward the people and define just what was meant by "the people."

Despite these similarities, Haitian revolutionaries faced tasks that made Haitian political development distinct from that of France and the United States. First of all, because the revolution overthrew plantation slavery, Haiti's new leaders had to immediately create a whole new system of production. In addition, at a time when black people were judged by the world to be incapable of personal or political sovereignty, the leaders of Haiti also confronted the challenge of forging a black nation and justifying its governance by a black state. The new Haitian government was boycotted, disregarded, and ridiculed by most governments in the world. For fifty-eight years, the United States refused to recognize the independence of Haiti, only establishing full diplomatic relations in 1862.

The two tasks that burdened the Haitian revolutionaries were interrelated. Without worldwide political recognition of their status as an independent state, they were not accorded full rights to regulate their banking, trading, and borders, all necessities for building their economy. Given their restricted options for economic development, as well as the prevailing wisdom of the times, the new leadership attempted to restore the sugar plantations on which the colony's wealth had been based. Haiti's new leaders used the power of their new state to try to force the formerly enslaved population to continue to work in the sugar fields. When much of the population resisted, the leaders initiated the fissure between the governed and the government that exists to this day.

Haiti's new leaders next turned to the state as a base for their wealth and power. They began to use the military and government to extract wealth from the people through taxes on all marketing activities, imported goods, and land transactions. Thus, the state became and has remained the central route to wealth in Haiti.[4] Political leaders pocketed most of the revenues collected by the government, and allowed an emerging commercial and social elite to profit from various state monopolies. Those with power also extracted wealth by rents and various sharecropping arrangements on state lands. As a result, successive governments became separated by a chasm of fear and distrust from the majority of the people. Except for the short period when Aristide was president in 1991, that gap has never even begun to be breached.

In the nineteenth century, Haitian leaders alternated between the new ideology of republicanism, which claimed that the state embodied the people, and the old politics of the state, in which the right to govern was accorded to an emperor and his nobility. The succession of leaders in postrevolutionary Haiti followed the same pattern as in postrevolutionary France. Nineteenth-century France had two Napoleons who declared themselves emperor and a renewed reign of kings before it returned again to republican rule; Haiti had one self-declared king, Henry I, and two emperors interspersed between republics headed by presidents. Whatever the form of government, Haitian leaders generally took four related steps to legitimate their rule: they declared their government legal by promulgating a new constitution; they invoked the nation as a unit of kinship, describing themselves as the head of a family with the responsibility as "father" to defend national sovereignty and honor; they created government-owned enterprises and regulated the prices of basic goods with the promise that this was of benefit to the nation; and they developed symbols and patriotic rituals that linked the state to the nation.

All of these themes run through not only our interviews in Haiti but Georges's memories of the Haitian state of his youth:

Before the U.S. occupation in 1915, only important people bothered to wear shoes. But with the U.S. occupation and continuing when I was a youngster, there was a rule that people should not walk the streets without shoes. Haiti had an epidemic of hookworm so it was both a public health measure and a civilizing measure. The government didn't do it in the rural areas. The peasants used to come down from the mountains with their shoes dangling around their neck, and right before entering town, they would put on their shoes. If they were walking the streets without shoes, they were rounded up and taken to jail. This was a form of vagrancy law. This continued under Presidents Magloire and Duvalier. They had paddy wagons circulating in town looking for people without shoes.

But even during the 1950s when I was young, especially during the summer school vacation, you wouldn't wear shoes. You went barefoot. So the cry would go up, "Chalan dèyè-ou!" (Paddy wagon behind you!), and we would all flee. If kids wanted to tease their friends, they would yell, "A paddy wagon!" and all the boys and girls would scatter. Those were beautiful times. It was fun running away from the police and having these aged men run after you. They would huff and puff, and you made fun of them. Of course, if they recognized you, they would complain to your parents. But if you were middle class, as I was, they would not come down too hard, and our parents could make sure that we had something to wear

on our feet. It was the peasants and the poor who really suffered from this policy.

The expectation that the symbols and rituals of the state will pervade daily life shape the ways in which Georges and many other Haitian migrants experience both the U.S. and Haitian states. As people in Haiti answered our questions, they made casual reference to the Constitution, the responsibility of the state to take care of them, and symbols of the nation-state such as the flag. Complaining about the constant rise in the price of food, one young man said, "In Haiti, the only thing that goes up and comes down again is the flag."

Legitimating the State

A well-known Haitian proverb tells us that "constitutions are made of paper; swords are made of iron," reflecting the fact that Haitians have seen numerous constitutions written and disregarded. Most regimes have paid scant attention to the legal structure they promulgate. Yet new leaders seizing power through military coups or controlled elections have consistently written new legal charters. Each new constitution has attempted to obtain recognition of the legitimacy of the leadership from the Haitian people and the outside world. In each successive constitution, the state has promoted a set of positive rights by guaranteeing certain things to the population. The most recent Haitian Constitution, written in 1987, follows this tradition. It specifies that "the state has a compelling obligation to guarantee the right to life, health, and respect for the individual to all citizens without distinction, as stipulated in the Universal Declaration of Human Rights."[5] It goes on to assert that "the state guarantees the right to an education and the state assumes the responsibility for the physical, intellectual, moral, professional, social and civic development of the individual."[6] The Constitution functions less as a guide to government procedures than as evidence that the state is responsible for providing services such as education and health care.

From the time of the Haitian state's founding, leaders have spoken of their nation as a family, popularizing and endorsing the conflation of individual, family, and nation that we traced in chapter 5. The first Constitution of independent Haiti—which transformed its first leader, Dessalines, from governor-general to emperor—declared that Haitians were all the children of the same family and "the head of state is the father."[7] Successive generations of Haitian leaders have appealed for support and obedience by portraying themselves as the father of the nation. Political leaders have depicted themselves as patriarchs who have the right to both punish and reward. Many people responded by viewing citizenship as membership in a patriarchal family with the government acting as the patriarch. As the patriarch, the government can punish you. Yet the state should also take care of you. As a citizen, you respect the state and in turn the state provides for you. The father, although sometimes punitive, can supply certain things to his family. Through the gaze of memory and longing, Georges's recollections of his childhood in Haiti include experiences with a state that was punitive yet "paternal." The paddy wagons that roamed the street to ensure that the public wore shoes symbolized the state and enforced its discipline, but also guarded the health of the people.

In Haiti, "Papa" has long been an appellation of the head of state.[8] To the Haitian ear, this has been a term of respect rather than endearment. Even in situations of genuine affection, fathers have been a source of power. This Haitian view of state authority and political leadership became more visible to the rest of the world under the Duvalier regime. François Duvalier, who ruled Haiti with a bloody and iron fist, was known in Haiti as Papa Doc. (The title doctor referred to his training as a medical doctor and anthropologist.) A complex mixture of avoidance and desire for a strong government has marked the two hundred years of Haitian nation-state building. Georges's concepts of state and nation reflect the particular history of Haiti. He and other Haitian long-distance nationalists bring these notions to their transnational politics.

A strong leader, for example, has been equated with a strong military defense. Despite the exploitative activities of the state, all classes in Haiti have seen the need for a state that is militarily powerful enough to defend their national sovereignty. Haitians have constantly been reminded by their leaders that Haitian independence was won only through bloodshed. And through bitter experience throughout their history, Haitians have learned that their national sovereignty has always been at risk. For most of the nineteenth century, Haitians, as descendants of slaves, lived in an international environment where neither their personal freedom nor right to have their own nation was respected. Some U.S. political leaders referred to Haitians as "rebel slaves."[9] Slavery did not end in the Caribbean until the late nineteenth century; it was not abolished in Cuba until 1886. Moreover, the end of slavery did not put a stop to the ideology that black people were incapable of governing themselves or a state. These ideas justified the continuance of colonial rule in the Caribbean, Africa, Asia, and the Pacific until the middle of the twentieth century. There was a widespread and well-founded belief among Haitians through much of Haitian history that either the U.S. or European states were interested in recolonizing Haiti.[10]

This external context has made it clear to the vast majority of Haitians that their own freedom and sense of worth are enmeshed in the sovereignty of their state. The personal and political become linked so that as individual Haitians conflate family and nation, they link their personal self-esteem to their state's sovereignty. For Haitians, the sovereignty of the Haitian state as a black state among powerful white nations has, from the moment of the Haitian Revolution, proved that black people are equal to all others.[11] As Haitian leaders maintained and taught the logic of the paternal state, they accompanied their words with deeds. They implemented state policies that, while often authoritarian and sometimes brutal, officially took responsibility for the lives of the people. Although throughout much of its history Haiti has lacked some of the basic accoutrements of the modern state, such as efficient bureaucracies and roads to rural areas, until recently the government did maintain certain highly visible public services in the major towns. These services, as well as the continuing public rhetoric of political leaders, account for the fact that many poor people, including those raised in rural Haiti, still uphold the ideal of the responsible state.

The public services that were provided functioned as public rituals that linked delivery of state services to respect for the state.[12] From the time of the first U.S. occupation of Haiti (1915–1934) through the Duvalier regime, people who lived in towns experienced public sanitation, health clinics, public health campaigns, education, and entertainment.[13] The reasons behind the delivery of these services were complex. At that time, governments in many regions of the world began taking a more active role in guarding public health. State and local governments in the United States set up public sanitation systems, and began to monitor water and food. Colonial powers instituted various health measures in their colonies as part of an effort to increase the productivity of the labor force. During its occupation of Haiti, the United States participated in the worldwide trend of disseminating public health measures. The Haitian governments that followed the occupation maintained many of these public services. The

United States continued to contribute to these efforts even after the occupation, expanding the distribution of food and development projects in the 1970s. When Georges was young, these programs caused people living in his hometown of Aux Cayes to feel that the state did act responsibly toward the people. The streets of Aux Cayes, if not paved, were regularly swept and the open sewers that run down the sides of the streets were cleaned. Outhouses were inspected and offenders to the sanitary code were fined. As Georges noted:

We timed getting up to go to school by the sound of people cleaning the sewers. They cleaned them every day at 5:00 in the morning. And of course, your outhouse was regularly inspected and sprayed with some type of disinfectant, and you were told when to empty them. And there was a public health clinic for young children. Regularly you would go to the health center, free of charge. The doctor there was wonderful. There were also canteens where at dinnertime they would send you cooked food for the entire family. Because there was low status in getting this food, my mother would send the servants, as if it were for them. But we all ate it when my parents didn't have money to cook food for that day. They gave you powdered milk and cheese in school. It was from the United States.

There were free movies projected in the parks some Sundays, and there was a band concert performed by the military band every Sunday. They played John Philip Sousa's music like "Stars and Stripes Forever," which I thought was Haitian music until I came to the United States. Imagine that! I learned to respect the Haitian state and to believe in a responsible state to marching band music written to evoke patriotic American fervor. They would also play Haitian popular music. And you would sit in the park and talk to your friends. There were also public libraries. There was one in Aux Cayes, built in 1954.

And when you went to take your final exams, the last two years of secondary school that we call rheto and philo, the government would pay your transportation to Port-au-Prince and give you room and board while you were there. They would turn the high schools into barracks and you would stay there. You would get your breakfast, lunch, and supper. I ate better that week than ever before. And it was a source of adventure and excitement. That was the first time I saw Port-au-Prince. It was an enticement to continue school and take the exam. Those were fun times.

When I left in 1969, all these things were in place in Aux Cayes. I don't know what happened in the rural areas or Port-au-Prince but I know when rural people came to Aux Cayes, they could see the clean sewers and had to flee from the paddy wagon, if they had no shoes. So we all expected that, at least in cities, there were things that the government did, even under a brutal dictator such as François Duvalier. So you had health, food, education, recreation. You had everything you could imagine. And the government gave all these things to you. But all these things have disappeared. Now all of this is totally abandoned. Now you have garbage in the streets.

When these services dramatically diminished in the wake of the military juntas of the 1980s and 1990s along with the pressures by international lenders on elected officials to reduce state expenditures, public discussion of the regimes focused on the lack of public services and state-sponsored national rituals. On the radio, in newspapers, in conversations among family and friends, in Haiti and New York, people talked about the garbage in the streets of Port-au-Prince, untended open sewers, the chaos in the Haitian schools, and the abandonment of public respect for the flag. People also complained about the price of food and blamed the state.

Until 1995, while the state imposed various fees and taxes, it also kept the cost of certain products stable by stipulating the price at which they could be sold. Flour, cooking oil, sugar, gasoline, and cement prices were fixed. In the twentieth century, most of these products began to be processed by state-owned factories or imported from abroad by the government. This policy of price stabilization came to a halt by mandate of the consortium of banks providing loans to Haiti. Using the rubric, "free market," they also demanded that the government processing plants be sold.

Because of the history of government control of prices of some basic goods, most people in Haiti hold the government directly responsible for the rise in prices. Rather than blaming some abstract concept such as "inflation" or a poor "economy," they blame the leaders of the country. The dramatic rise of the price of rice was a constant theme in our interviews, and most people held the state responsible. People now measure the increased misery of their life by the much higher price of a *mamit* (an empty aluminum can used to measure out rice) filled with the grain. Tara, for one, directly linked the high cost of living to the inaction of Haiti's president. The twenty-four year old, whose mother had been a laundress and whose older female relatives did "commerce," told us: "The way I see Haiti, I don't see any improvement. Because almost every president who comes to power works for themselves. Take, for example, the new president who has been in power almost seven months, and nothing. Life is becoming more expensive. We used to buy a mamit of rice for four gourdes and then six [U.S. 36¢] gourdes. . . . So life is becoming more and more expensive."

Although in the past the Haitian government implemented certain state policies that met some of the people's needs, it never made more than a token effort to deliver free education from grade school through college. There have never been enough public schools to serve more than a handful of Haiti's population. Parents were also expected to provide uniforms and books, expenses that are beyond the budgets of most rural families.[14] The majority of the Haitian people have had little or no formal education. To attend a good high school, you have to live in a town. Except for schools of law, the only public university is in Port-au-Prince. This state university can only accommodate a small percentage of the students who pass the difficult exams necessary to graduate secondary school and enter college. Nonetheless, there are public schools and a free public university. The failure of successive governments to supply enough schools does not undermine the widely shared expectation that the state is responsible to educate the people. The authority of each government is eroded by its failure to provide education; belief in the state is maintained.

Those few men and women who received a university education in Haiti also obtained both social status and employment. Currently, there is competition for employment from people who have studied abroad, and the University of Haiti confers less status. It is still true that if you graduate from the state university in the fields of medicine, nursing, agronomy, or education, you are given a government job. Despite all its inadequacies, therefore, the state system of education serves as an example of what the state can offer. In addition to providing education, until recently the schools engaged students in patriotic practices such as flag raising and the celebration of various national holidays. These students disseminated this knowledge to family and friends who did not attend school. "Now that I think back," mused Georges,

they were teaching us not only to love the nation but to respect the state. They did it when officials of the government raised the flag every day. They did it through lessons in civics classes, where they made you recite every day, "Voler l'état c'est voler" ("To steal from the state is to steal"). When Duvalier went on the radio every morning to personally lead us in reciting the creed he wrote, in which we pledged loyalty to him, our love of Haiti and respect for the state were being linked together. At first, we believed in him because he promised to use the state to make life better for the people, and to restore the honor and prestige of the country. When it became clear that he was using the state to steal and was murdering anyone who questioned his actions, our opposition to him was fueled by the fact that he betrayed the respect for the state that he himself had taught us. The Duvalier government pocketed the state money as well as foreign aid and sent it off to Swiss bank accounts. The state was like a parent who says, "Do what I say, not what I do." So you learned to respect that parent and to want the things that parent could give you, and yet you were learning two contradictory messages at the same time. Because you couldn't trust your parent.

The poor and middle-class people we interviewed had learned the same lessons as Georges about the state. While many also distrusted and feared the regime, they expected the state to act on their behalf. Although only twenty, Josaphat, a student supported by remittances from his parents, was clear in his assertion that the state was responsible for the economy and the high price of commodities: "Yes, the state knows the problems of the poor even though they don't do anything for them. They always tell you they are trying to solve the people's problems. For example, they say they are fighting to get the price of rice down, but even though they say that, it never goes down. To the contrary, the price goes up. Like the price of gasoline. . . . The people expect the state to address their problems and to make life a little less costly for them. Only God can tell whether it will come true." Franck, age nineteen, resides in Aux Cayes and is also a student. He lives in a household supported by remittances and is equally sure that the government has responsibilities to the people. As Franck stated: "If the Haitian government does not know the conditions in which the masses are living, who else will know? They are there and they see the condition in which the masses of people are living, how life is becoming more difficult; they know and they feel how the problems are. If they don't do anything there will be a big catastrophe in Haiti, people will die of starvation, so they must do something to help. They are obligated to help the masses so that they don't suffer too much."

It is interesting to note that many people wanted the government to ensure security to people and their property. This is true despite the fact that in the history of Haiti, violence has most often been state sanctioned, coming from the military or armed forces. Part of the fury of the popular uprising against the Duvalier regime in 1986 was directed at the Ton Ton Macoute, the regime's militia. Individual macoute could arbitrarily seize property and beat people, throw them in jail, or kill them. The uprising against Duvalier was not against the state but against his regime. Many in the countryside and among the urban poor wanted an uprooting not only of Duvalier but also of the powerful persons who had used the state for personal advantage and to protect the Haitian bourgeoisie. They called for the state to stand with the poor and oppressed.

Aristide's campaign for presidency represented the effort of the grassroots movement in Haiti to use the electoral process to take charge of the state. Aristide employed colorful, powerful Kreyòl slogans and proverbs to give the rural cultivators and urban poor confidence in their potential as history makers. Previously, Aristide said, the ballot box had been a means to legitimate governments that were called democracies, but actually only served the interests of the rich and powerful. In his election campaign, he put this critique aside and instead emphasized that the state could be utilized to further the interests of all the people, including the elite. Aristide began to endorse and champion the reform of Haitian society through mass participation in the formal electoral process.

After he was elected with 67 percent of the vote, Aristide launched a classic nation-state–building political project. He proposed a "marriage between the army and the people."[15] He also advocated "reconciliation" among the various Haitian classes, using the language of family and nation that was familiar to all. Underneath the shared language of nation, though, members of different classes both in Haiti and the diaspora heard different things. The poor in Haiti began to feel that the state was theirs at last. Both poor and middle-class people in the diaspora felt embraced by a state that was acknowledging their continuing ties to Haiti.

Those with entrenched economic and political interests in Haiti were threatened, however. The threat to the status quo united the Haitian bourgeoisie, U.S. corporations profiting from Haitian cheap labor, and sections of the U.S. political and military establishment who have traditionally supported political stability rather than human rights. These forces did not want to address the issues of poverty and inequality, and responded by supporting a coup that ousted President Aristide. During and after the coup, poor people clung to their demand for a state that would be responsible for their needs, including security. Yet when Aristide returned, he no longer took steps to empower the majority of the people. Increasingly since 1995, poor and middle-class individuals have become cynical about the prospects of any Haitian government acting responsibly.

The people we interviewed blamed the state for the insecurity and danger they felt. Both young and old remembered an earlier time without gangsters, often forgetting that past violence had come from the government itself. Brigitte claimed that the government doesn't help the people: "In the past you used to see certain things, but now you are seeing them every day, in front of your eyes. If the state helped, if they gave security, these things wouldn't happen. Sometimes you may be lying in your bed and they kill you. If the state provided security, those things wouldn't happen."

It is far too simplistic to dismiss the Haitian view of the state as authoritarian and nondemocratic, as U.S. observers tend to do.[16] These observers measure democracy by periodic elections of political officials. Any government that is legally elected is seen as democratic and legitimate, whether or not it serves the interests of the majority of the people or ensures that the basic needs of all citizens are met. Because Haitians assume that a state must be responsible to the people, a state that does not take up that responsibility is no longer seen as legitimate. Haitians expect the state to be responsible for the people rather than to the people. Nonetheless, citizens are perceived as direct political actors. There is a foundational belief that the Haitian people are empowered to judge the acceptability of any particular regime; if a regime does not take responsibility for its citizens, then the people have a right to resist, avoid, and even overthrow it. Each day, people's actions provide a daily plebiscite on the legitimacy of a particular administration. This view of democracy is not just Haitian. Thomas Jefferson believed that ongoing revolution might be needed to keep government in the hands of the people.[17]

The Birth of a Transborder Citizenry

As Haitians have begun to emigrate to the United States and live as transmigrants, they have continued to build on their conceptualization of the responsible state. They actively contribute, as transborder citizens, to the transformation of concepts of state and citizenship in two political systems that interpenetrate in multiple ways. The stance toward both Haiti and the United States taken by Father Desormeaux, a Haitian Catholic priest based in Miami, illustrates the emerging political consciousness of many Haitian transborder citizens. On 14 March 1999, in Delray Beach, Florida, Father Desormeaux delivered a fiery oration at the funeral of Michaelee Dieujuste. Michaelee was one of the approximately forty people who were lost at sea on 6 March while trying to get to the United States in a small boat.[18] In a desperate effort to join her husband, Michaelee had paid several thousand dollars to smugglers who promised her a visa and safe passage to the United States. She left behind her children, house, and the business that her husband had built for her with the money he earned as a laborer in Florida.[19] Her husband explained, "She complained that I spent too much time here, away from her. She died because she wanted to be with me."[20] Michaelee, like many of the wives left behind in Haiti whom we interviewed, may have felt that the only acceptable future for her was to join her husband and live in the United States. She may also have known that some Haitian men take new wives when the U.S. immigration restrictions separate them from their wives and children in Haiti.

The day after the funeral, the priest's oration was the centerpiece of an article by a Haitian reporter published in the *Sun Sentinel*, a southern Florida newspaper. The funeral became an occasion for a Haitian priest to communicate his views about the relationship of Haitians to Haiti and the United States. Because of the article, his words reached not only the hundreds of Haitians who had come to mourn the tragedy of Michaelee but also the multiethnic readership of the *Sun Sentinel*. The message from Father Desormeaux was a potent mix of long-distance nationalism and demands on the Haitian and U.S. governments to act responsibly. To the accompaniment of sobs and sighs of grief, Desormeaux called on Haitians in the United States "to continue the fight not only for the rights of brethren still in Haiti but also for those in America who are suffering the indignities of substandard work and lack of civil rights."[21] After the service, he responded to the senseless loss of life by elaborating on his transnational message. Echoing the theme we heard in Haiti about the unbreakable ties between the diaspora and Haiti, he said, "We may be naturalized citizens but we are still Haitians." He went on, according to the *Sun Sentinel*, to "call on Haitians to take control of their destiny both here and in their economically and politically embattled homeland."[22]

Desormeaux's plea was founded on the understanding of many Haitian migrants that acting in support of their homeland is part of what it means to be American. He stressed the example of the American Jews who support the Israeli state, asserting, "Haiti is our little corner of Israel."[23] And Merle Augustin, the Haitian reporter, chose this statement for his story, noting that the priest was "drawing on the close bond of American Jews with Israel."[24] Both the priest and reporter had examples of this bond all around them because Delray Beach contains a large number of retired Jews who are second-generation immigrants and supporters of Israel, including Nina's mother, Evelyn, and Evelyn's partner, Warren, who sent Nina the *Sun Sentinel* article.

As we argued in chapter 2, Haitian long-distance nationalism resembles the homeland loyalties of many other contemporary and past migrants, including American Jews. Haitian transmigrants are aware of this. Aristide, who had studied in Israel, was one of many Haitian leaders who made this point when he used the example of Zionism to encourage Haitians to see the Haitian nation as transnational.[25] While many migrating populations retain their home ties, however, each brings into the U.S. political milieu its own understanding of the meaning of citizenship. Haitians demand that the government take responsibility for its citizens. They read the U.S. Constitution through this lens. It was in this spirit that Father Desormeaux's sermon made reference to civil rights and implored listeners to make demands on the U.S. government. Through the newspaper story written by a Haitian reporter, these ideas were made accessible to the U.S. public.

Thus, Haitian transmigrants infuse the U.S. political system with a call for the state to be responsible for the people. In addition, their actions contest the notion that citizenship means belonging to a single political system, and that political systems are confined within the territorial boundaries of states. Although not legally dual citizens, because the Haitian Constitution does not allow such a legal status, they are nonetheless actively participating in both political systems in ways that introduce new political conceptions into both systems. These actions implicitly acknowledge the intertwining connections between the two states; yet the connection is rarely made explicit.

Father Desormeaux's funeral oration did all this and more. He urged his listeners from their location in the United States to claim rights from both the Haitian and U.S. states. He also encouraged Haitian migrants to struggle for the rights of persons still in Haiti. In so doing, he was acknowledging that while Haiti and the United States have separate political systems, the two systems are intertwined as well. Still, Father Desormeaux did not address the question of unequal relationships between the two systems—a relationship we analyze in the next chapter.

By the 1990s, the U.S. press, with the assistance of a growing cadre of "Haitian American" reporters, had begun to portray Haitian migrants as persons of courage and determination who boldly struggle for their rights. In some ways, this new image has enabled Haitians to reclaim their own self-portrait as heroic rebels capable of taking on the most powerful nations of the world—and winning. The public image of Haitians as collectively confronting public authorities is a recent development.[26] During the first decade of large-scale Haitian immigration, in the 1960s, Nina wrote that because so many Haitians in the United States were undocumented, they would not demand their rights. At that time, the undocumented immigrants who Nina knew never protested or made claims on the state. They accepted unheated factories and apartments, salaries below minimum wage, and no overtime pay. By never claiming their income tax refunds, they paid more than their share of taxes, in addition to staying away from welfare or any other public benefit. One of Nina's friends was hit by a car and, although badly hurt, fled the scene of the accident. In another family Nina knew, the whole bedroom ceiling collapsed, but the parents filed no complaint against the landlord, even though they and their children had been injured.

That was 1969. Nina and others who studied immigration assumed that by allowing so many undocumented people to enter the country, the immigration system functioned to create a quiescent labor force.[27] The next three decades proved us wrong. Increasingly, sectors of the immigrant population began to engage in forms of political action. We had not considered that immigrants are influenced by the context of political struggles in which they are immersed and that this context is transnational. Haitians, for example, in both the United States and Haiti, began acting as transborder citizens with their own unique view of the U.S. and Haitian Constitutions and the responsibilities of both states. They saw the United States as a place with a constitution that promised that the state was responsible to protect the rights of the people and where such rights could actually be won through struggle.

The community organizations whose rise, as we chronicled earlier, received an impetus from U.S. federal, state, and local governments, proved to be a training ground in community empowerment. These organizations gave their members direct experience in struggles to defend the rights of poor people and migrants in the United States. For instance, in 1970, Nina traveled with busloads of Haitians to Washington, D.C., to join poor people from all over the country to protest cuts in federal antipoverty programs. Because of these experiences, increasingly significant numbers of Haitians, whether they were living in the United States or Haiti, began to view the United States as a political system in which people had to collectively struggle for state-guaranteed freedoms. Haitian Catholic priests, a number of radio broadcasters, and Haitian newspapers echoed this message. The Haitian understanding that life is a struggle merged with a realization that the poor and oppressed could politically mobilize in the streets, demand that the state assume its constitutional responsibilities, and win. In the 1980s and 1990s, these lessons were transformed into Haitian political action in both the United States and Haiti.

By the beginning of the 1980s, Haitians had begun to take to the streets in New York City and Washington, D.C., to demand that Haitians fleeing the Duvalier dictatorship be given political asylum, as were Cuban refugees. They protested the harsh treatment that these Haitian refugees, whose boats were landing in south Florida, were receiving: detention in prison camps (some located on the icy U.S.–Canadian border and others in the deserts of the Southwest), hearings and deportation without access to lawyers, food laced with drugs that led men to grow breasts, and the imprisonment of children.[28] Although a large proportion of Haitians had still not gained permanent resident status, they held militant public demonstrations and pickets. As a result of these protests, Haitian refugees were finally granted the temporary refugee status, "Entrant," and for a short while much of the imprisonment and deportations stopped.

Further lessons were learned as these Haitian community organizations began to work closely with U.S. advocacy groups, such as the Center for Constitutional Rights, committed to constitutional rights for immigrants. In the 1980s, with the understanding that legal battles are also waged in the domain of public opinion, busloads of Haitians again made their way to Washington, D.C., for demonstrations to support the fight in the court.

Meanwhile, a militant grassroots movement grew in Haiti in the face of the Duvalier dictatorship. This movement, which ultimately brought the dictatorship down, was built within the transnational social fields that Haitians had established. It reflected a form of grassroots organizing that Haitians were learning in both the United States and Haiti. During this same period, both international and foreign aid organizations, funded by the United States and a number of European governments, created organizations throughout the Haitian countryside.[29] These organizations helped rural people form producer cooperatives, build wells for drinking water, and develop local crops. This transnational organizing was officially apolitical and the projects functioned independently of the Haitian government. In reality, however, many of the projects empowered the rural population. People in the countryside felt they were not alone in their needs and demands. Because they understood that the funding for these organizations came from other countries, the belief of many Haitians that governments should take responsibility for the needs of their people was strengthened. They thought that the Haitian government should follow this example. The fact that some of the foreign organizations were nongovernmental and private, while others were directly funded by the U.S., French, Canadian, Dutch, or German governments, was not meaningful to many Haitians. They tended to believe that unlike the Haitian states, other states took responsibility for the health, education, and welfare of poor people.

When Jean-Claude Duvalier fled Haiti in 1986, the streets of Port-au-Prince, New York City, and Miami were filled with celebrating Haitians, glorying in a shared victory and sharing an experience of citizenship. At that moment, the political activism that had been confined to a vocal, although influential minority of Haitian migrants became a mass movement. In a march down Eastern Parkway in Brooklyn, we watched Haitians decorate Grand Army Plaza with Haitian flags and saw people who had never previously attended a demonstration dance in the streets. Teenagers who spoke only English at school and tried to pass as African Americans joined the chanting in Kreyòl. Elderly Haitians who had recently arrived walked hand in hand with their grandchildren born in the United States. Even Haitian Protestant ministers who preached against any engagement in politics came to celebrate with their congregants, as *vaksen* (hollowed bamboo musical instruments), drums, and other instruments used to welcome the *lwa* (vodou spirits) provided music for the festivities.

Crossing the Brooklyn Bridge to Save Haiti

As the paths of communication between Haitian migrants and people in Haiti grew dramatically, lessons learned in one terrain of struggle were popularized transnationally. Transmigrants who returned to Haiti to visit, set up businesses, or retire contributed to the new and shared political understandings that developed. People who lived in Haiti, but had permanent U.S. resident visas because their kin have become citizens, visited the United States frequently and carried back to Haiti ideas about social and political rights. Radio programs that were either transnational or contained information about Haitian political mobilizations in both Haiti and the diaspora became an important source of news.

By the end of the 1980s, a sector of the Haitian population in the United States, shaped by the previous decade of political mobilizations in both Haiti and the United States, had learned to take direct political action when they felt that Haitians as a group were being threatened. Even people who did not have permanent resident visas had become vocal and willing to demonstrate when Haitians were facing discrimination or ill-treatment. When Haitian migrants did protest, they generally directed their demands toward public authorities. While divisions of class and distrust of the motives of compatriots made it difficult to build broad-based community organizations, these barriers did not impede the short-term mobilization of thousands of individuals on behalf of "the Haitian community." By the 1990s, Haitians had begun to initiate their own lawsuits to expand immigrants' rights. In New York State, Haitians sued the state over the inadequate implementation of programs for bilingual education. The political clout of Haitians was recognized by the New York State education establishment when it decreed in 1997 that Haitian Kreyòl was one of the official languages students could use to take the New York State Regents Examinations, the most prestigious form of high school degree.[30] This action, although it was not of great assistance to Haitian children, since most Kreyòl speakers don't read and write Kreyòl, was a crucial symbolic victory because it acknowledged the Haitian presence.

The Haitian conflation of self, family, nation, and race historically served to involve people in political actions that confront the state. It now contributes to political actions that can shake a city as big and sophisticated as New York. This is what happened on 10 April 1990. As Georges described it:

At five in the morning, the strident rings of the phone pulled me out of a deep sleep. Still half asleep, I picked up the receiver. "Surely, you are not going to work today!" It was Alex, my boyhood and best friend, who immediately began to chastise me for still being in bed. The urgency of his tone made me feel that something very important and even life threatening was taking place, something only I had failed to remember.

Then I realized that he was talking about the demonstration that had been called to protest the Centers for Disease Control's and Food and Drug Administration's portrayal of Haitians as natural "carriers of the HIV virus" and a "group at risk" for AIDS, the dreaded Acquired Immune Deficiency Syndrome. Curious about the intensity with which he demanded to know my plans, since Alex was not one to go to demonstrations, I answered nonchalantly, "Of course not, why?" He reacted, "Man, don't you know that the entire Haitian community will be in Manhattan today? I thought you listen faithfully to all the Haitian radio programs in New York? Didn't you read the Haitian newspapers during the past few weeks?" Abruptly, he spoke in Haitian Kreyòl: "Today is the day that all Haitians must let their blood boil to respond to the Americans' accusa-

tions. The reason why they treat us the way they do here is because the United States is not our home. Get up! Get dressed! Get ready! Let us all participate in this patriotic koumbit *[collective work project]!" He again reverted to English and said: "We must go to Manhattan to rescue and save the honor of our country."*

That day, New Yorkers found that lower Manhattan had come to a halt. An estimated fifty thousand Haitians streamed across the Brooklyn Bridge into lower Manhattan and surrounded city hall.[31] Provoked by the actions of the U.S. Food and Drug Administration, which continued to link all Haitians to the AIDS crisis despite scientific evidence that clearly refuted the claim, Haitians took to the streets to protest against the U.S. government and this labeling.[32] Traffic did not move. Taxis were scarce because so many of the drivers were Haitian and they had taken the day off to march in the streets. Haitians were putting their collective foot down against the continuing affront to their sense of Haitian pride and self-worth. Simultaneous demonstrations were staged in Miami and in front of the U.S. embassy in Port-au-Prince. Leaders and activists also went to Washington, D.C., to meet with U.S. officials, and some months later, U.S. agencies stopped describing Haitians as an AIDS risk group.

When Aristide was ousted from his presidency in 1991 after only seven months in office, the Brooklyn Bridge and lower Manhattan once again became the scene for a demonstration. Again tens of thousands crossed the bridge. The U.S. government was the target of the protest because U.S. political leaders had never wanted Aristide to be elected, and trained and armed the Haitian military that staged the coup.

Our research revealed that the political lessons that Haitian migrants were learning in the United States were also being learned in Haiti. We were not surprised to find that transmigrants who had resettled in Haiti and continued to live their lives across borders knew about the demonstrations and pointed to Haitian political mobilization in the United States as evidence that the diaspora was part of Haiti. Marco, for example, was one of dozens of businesspeople who had grown up and been educated in the United States, but had returned to expand his family fortune in Haiti. He returned to invest in export processing factories, a hotel for visiting foreign consultants and advisers, and a business importing old and unsold clothes. Sitting in front of his computer linked to the Internet, in the office of his

small, continental-style hotel in Petionville, he told us about the AIDS demonstration. "Whenever they have to come together, like we've seen them do
in New York when we had that bad rap for AIDS or whatever . . . it works.
It was probably one of the largest marches ever in New York. We heard
about the Haitians abroad who can vote [in the United States]. They're
putting that into practice, and I think it worked, I think the Tenth Department reacted as a Tenth Department. The concept was first elaborated by
then-candidate Aristide, that this was a way to attach everybody to the
homeland. And the concept worked—it worked emotionally, it worked financially, and now it is working legally. They have a Minister of Haitians
Living Abroad."

We were somewhat surprised to find that the knowledge of the diaspora's political activism extended far beyond the return migrants. People who
lived in Haiti were not only imagining Haiti as a transnational nation-
state; they were experiencing it. Descriptions of the demonstrations for
Aristide in the United States punctuated our interviews. People with varying levels of social experience and political sophistication repeated the same
phrase: "The demonstration was so big that the bridge shook!" And the
bridge that they were talking about was the Brooklyn Bridge in New York,
not a bridge within the territorial boundaries of Haiti. The diaspora was
not only seen as an extension of Haiti but also understood to be the sector
of the nation that could actually have an impact on who controlled the Haitian state.

Franck grew up in Port Salut, a tiny sun-drenched town along a strip of
sand and palm trees in southern Haiti. He lives with his aunt in a household supported by remittances from her husband in the United States.
Even from this remote location, he had learned all about the diaspora, both
from his family ties and the radio. He was able to describe the political action taken by Haitians abroad, including events that had taken place five
years earlier, when he was only fourteen:

> The *Dizyèm* [the Tenth Department] is a leta [state] that the Haitians
> occupy, and that is where they collaborate together to help Haiti. To
> work in the interests of Haitian people who live in the United States.
> To help Haiti and to work for those Haitians who live abroad. To
> help them defend their own interests. . . . I used to listen to Radio
> Tropical and I heard especially the program "Haiti Reality," and they
> talked about the work that the diaspora did to send Haiti upward.

How they helped both groups: those Haitians who are abroad who don't have means of attending a university and Haitians who are in Haiti. If there is a group of people who played a greater role to help Aristide to return, I don't know it. The people of the diaspora are the ones who made it possible for Aristide to return after the Haitian people became martyrs. They stood up, they shook up the leadership of the American government to take action to save Haiti.

Those who had no contact with family abroad were as aware as those who lived on remittances of the actions of the diaspora, including its demonstrations on behalf of Haiti, because they speak to people who do have transnational family ties and because they have access to the radio. Miriam and her child lived in Port-au-Prince in a "cousin's" one-room house, which also provides shelter for eight other people. Although she spends most of her days scrambling to feed herself and her child, she was aware of the diaspora. She told us that the diaspora "helped Aristide return. They organized manifestations, they went on the radio, they joined their voices with the voices of the Haitian people, they saw the necessity, and they did bring him back."

As Haitians in the United States have become active and vocal in struggles for justice in the United States and Haiti, they have begun to regain their reputation, forged in the Haitian Revolution, as a people who will stand up against all odds. Key white and black New York politicians approach them as a people with a genius for political protest who do not allow themselves to be trampled. This image of Haitians reinforces the self-image of the Haitian migrants and people in Haiti. It also serves to expand the opportunity for Haitians to enter into U.S. politics, return to Haiti to participate in political activities there, or participate within the political domains of both states.

After the AIDS demonstration in 1990, Nina attended an elegant banquet staged by a Haitian Community Health Organization based in Brooklyn. As with many "community events," the attendance by community members was actually fairly sparse; most who attended were Haitian professionals. Still, the room was filled almost to capacity with diners. New York City political leaders and official representatives from their offices made their appearance, convinced that Haitians in New York were a force with which to reckon. While only a few Haitians have been elected to political office, they have been increasingly active in local- and state-level political campaigns in Florida, New York, New Jersey, and Massachusetts. In 1998, five Haitians ran for local or state office in south Florida, and one ran in New York. In addition, beginning with Louis Brun who ran for a seat in the New York State Legislature in 1970, and subsequently returned to Haiti, Haitians active in local politics in the United States have taken that experience back to Haiti and participated actively in the Haitian political system.

Haitian efforts to lobby the U.S. Congress and president are best understood as the actions of a transborder citizenry.[33] Beginning in the 1970s, the anti-Duvalierist forces set up their own Washington Office on Haiti, which became a strong political voice effectively disseminating information about Haiti and the plight of Haitian refugees to the Congress. The office also served as a vehicle for community organizing, popularizing a conceptualization of transnational citizenship to the Haitian media and various Haitian migrant groups. The person who headed that office, Fritz Longchamps, returned with Aristide in 1994 and stayed on to become foreign minister under Préval in 1996. By 1998, the Washington Office on Haiti had become a highly professional lobby with ties to Haiti as well as Haitians in the United States. It was using mailings and e-mails to inform Haitians and "friends of Haiti" about actions pending in Congress that would affect Haitians wherever they resided. It claimed credit for eliciting 10,000 letters to key U.S. legislators in a campaign to change U.S. tariff barriers on goods produced in Haiti. Its director informed the e-mail list that "when Senators and Representatives go back home to listen to constituents, Ahem . . . that means you!"[34]

One organization, the National Coalition for Haitian Rights (NCHR), emerged as emblematic of the Haitian claims for rights and services from both the U.S. and Haitian state. Although this organization was never built on a mass membership, since its founding in 1982, it has articulated and shaped the developing Haitian understanding of the relationship between government and the governed. Established in New York City by Michael Hooper, a white American immigration lawyer, as the National Coalition for Haitian Refugees, NCHR participated as a plaintiff in key U.S. court cases that sought constitutional protections for Haitian refugees. By the time it was featured in the *Wall Street Journal* in 1999, NCHR had changed its name to signal its new focus on Haitian rights, and become a transnational organization with offices in New York City and Port-au-Prince.[35] The organization, funded by U.S. foundations interested in the incorporation of new immigrants into the U.S. electoral process, provided clinics to help immigrants become naturalized citizens. NCHR also sponsored a foundation-funded initiative to create a nationwide organization of Haitians in the United States.[36] It joined coalitions of other migrant groups to obtain more favorable legislation. In 1998, NCHR helped win the passage of a bill that allowed 40,000 persons who fled the 1991 military coup to apply for U.S. permanent residence. At the same time, in Haiti, NCHR supported the struggle to prosecute those who had violated human rights in Haiti during the years of the military dictatorship. It become enough of a presence on the Haitian political scene that the head of the Haitian office was the target of an assassination attempt in 1999.

Through transnational organizations such as NCHR, Haitians graft together Haitian concepts of the responsible state, U.S. notions of civil rights, and the language of universal human rights popularized by United Nations declarations. The various political mobilizations of the past two decades—efforts to demand rights in the United States for Haitian refugees, protests against the Centers for Disease Control's linking of Haitians to AIDS, attempts to oppose the 1991 military coup and restore Aristide to the presidency, the campaign to oppose the U.S. congressional attack on immigrants' rights by convincing Haitians to become naturalized U.S. citizens and participate in the electoral process, and protests against police attacks on Haitians in New York City and Port-au-Prince—have contributed to the emergence of a Haitian transnational citizenry. This citizenry demands that states take responsibility for protecting and providing for their citizens. The fact that tens of thousands of Haitians have begun to act politically across the territorial borders of states does not indicate that the state is no longer a significant player in their lives. On the contrary, the long-distance nationalism that connects those in Haiti with their diaspora means that many Haitians act and speak as if they belong to two states simultaneously.

At first glance, much of Haitian political activity in the United States might seem to be part of an old and ongoing story of immigrants coming to America, adopting the political values of their new land, and entering into the U.S. political process on their way to "making it." But as we have seen, the old story was only a fable. Many past immigrants were in fact transmigrants who organized lobbies, voted, and demonstrated in defense of their distant homeland. They became part of the United States, but not all their political activities were U.S. based.[37] Transmigrants also participated in political processes back home, either to build up those states or to foster movements for autonomy, independence, and the establishment of new states.

A significant sector of migrants today are again acting as long-distance nationalists who contribute to the political life of two states. Nonetheless, while certain of their transnational political practices and concerns resemble those of past generations of migrants, there are significant differences in the ways in which contemporary migrants relate to more than one nation-state. To a much greater extent than in past generations where politics was a transnational activity, U.S. government agencies, foundations, philanthropic organizations, and the financial institutions such as the World Bank and Inter-American Development Bank in which the United States is a major actor are all playing a direct role in the homelands of these migrants. Haitians are among the myriad migrant populations that seek power and influence within the United States in order to influence the actions that the U.S. government takes within their homeland.

We have examined the origin and contents of the outlook of the Haitian transborder citizenry in this chapter. While this citizenry's perspective builds on both the U.S. and Haitian concepts of the state, the emerging Haitian political culture cannot be seen as a hybrid because the stance of the Haitian transnational citizens toward institutions of government was not produced through the interbreeding of two unrelated historical experiences.[38] The Haitian experience of the state did not develop isolated from the founding ideals of the American Revolution or the actualities of U.S. power. There is a long history of direct intervention by the U.S. state and U.S. corporations in Haiti. Haitian transmigrants bring to their engagement in U.S. politics, and then back into their participation in Haitian politics, a legacy of the Haitian experience with the state. It is one forged by Haiti's position as a black nation; it is also an experience that reflects the very significant engagement of the United States in Haiti for almost two hundred years. The militancy and political activism of Haitians in the United States in the 1990s can only be understood if we remember that Haitians have become public actors in the context of their transnational experiences.

The presence of the United States runs through Georges's reminiscences of Haiti. It was to the strains of an ode to the U.S. flag, "Stars and Stripes Forever," that Georges learned to both respect the Haitian state and love the Haitian nation. The Haitian transnational citizenry is a product of two centuries of experience with the U.S. and Haitian states. At the end of the century, these two states had been brought together in new ways by the possibility and necessity of Haitians struggling for justice and equity in a transnational terrain. Despite two centuries of disappointment in which the governments have been repressive rather than representative, and constitutions have only been honored by being breached, many people in Haiti still expect the state to be responsible and care for the people, who are the nation. They also expect that on its own terrain, the U.S. government lives up to its promises of equal justice and equal rights. These expectations, developed within Haitian transnational social fields, became incorporated into Haitian long-distance nationalism.

9

The Apparent State: Sovereignty and the State of U.S.–Haitian Relations

And this is where the shame comes in, when I think of what those clowns—those
politicians who are running the country—have done to Haiti. They know better.
All these people I thought I could rely on to renew Haiti after thirty years of dicta-
torship have become the enemies we must oppose. They have become dangerous.
They act like the Haitian proverb says, "The stupid one gives; only the imbecile
doesn't take" ["Se sòt ki bay; enbisil ki pa pran"]. *And meanwhile the people*
are living in deplorable conditions–no jobs, no schools–and yet everybody in the
government is getting rich.

Georges was in a state of rage. In June 1997, the Haitian prime minister and
most of the cabinet resigned. They left the country with no working government, and for months Haiti seemed to drift. President Préval and the
Haitian legislature were deadlocked; the Haitian legislators did not ap-
prove of anyone that the president nominated to replace the departing
prime minister. The resignations had been precipitated, in part, by the fact
that the Haitian government was forced to follow the free market policies
mandated by the international lending bodies led by the United States. If
the policies were not followed, then the billions of dollars promised in
loans would not materialize. There would be no money to run the govern-

ment or pay the debts that Haiti had already accrued. If the policies were adhered to, the political movement that had brought the government to power promising that the state would finally be responsible for the people would be publicly betrayed.

Although Georges recognized that the activities of the Haitian government were constrained by its reliance on international lending bodies, he directed his anger and frustration primarily at the political leaders of Haiti. He criticized them for their incompetence. As the months passed, the government limped on without a prime minister and many cabinet ministers as news of rampant corruption in the Haitian government spread. Georges's anger turned to despair. The majority of Haitians in Haiti and the diaspora shared this feeling. Yet most people, whether they voiced their opinion on a call-in transnational radio program or simply discussed the situation with their families, did not acknowledge that the Haitian government does not have full control of its destiny. They continued to speak and act as if Haiti were a sovereign state, even though many people, including Georges, realize that this is not actually true. The momentum of the rhetoric of Haiti as an independent nation-state seems to win out. As in many situations in which we experience contradictions between political rhetoric and our actual experience, the rhetoric continues to assert its own logic.

For example, Leopold, an elderly transmigrant living in Haiti, was intent on blaming Haitian leaders for all of Haiti's problems when Nina intervened and asked whether Haiti was actually an independent country. Leopold answered using an analogy, rather than directly criticizing the United States: "My dear, I will tell you the truth. As long as you depend on someone for survival, 'your belly belongs to some else' [*vant ou se nan men moun-sa-a li ye*]. If s/he tells you to pick up this sack and you don't do it, you are rebelling against him or her and tomorrow you won't have anything to eat. Whatever s/he tells you is what you have to follow. S/he is giving to you. You depend on him or her. If s/he can't get anything out of you, s/he won't give you. . . . It is only when you are self-sufficient that you can say that you are an independent person."

Up until this point, we have not questioned the assumption of national sovereignty that underlies so much of the discussion of how to rebuild Haiti, nor have we fully addressed the relationship between the United States and Haiti. Here, we argue that long-distance nationalism and the emergence of a transborder citizenry contribute to and revitalize the illusion of national sovereignty. This provides an entryway to the exploration of the role of states in the current global econonomy. A state can only be considered sovereign when it has the power to control its internal political affairs, its economic affairs, and its relationships with other states. Our conclusion is that like a growing number of states in the world today, Haiti is an *apparent state*.

At the end of the Cold War, so-called world leaders proclaimed that now the world was finally composed of sovereign nations, each free to pursue their own destiny through democratic means. The U.S. and Western European governments began to fund programs to promote "democratization." Widely disseminated by the media, nongovernmental organizations, and the United Nations, the rhetoric of democracy reached into the countryside of Haiti and encouraged even those who felt alienated from the structures of their government to assume that their state was a sovereign entity.[1]

At the same time that this image of a world made up of independent nation-states was being propagated, political leaders signed treaties such as the North American Free Trade Agreement and the General Agreement on Trade and Tariffs. These trade agreements, together with international bodies such as the World Trade Organization (WTO) and regional ones such as the European Union, actually function to countermand the decisions made by democratically elected legislators. The WTO, in particular, is poised to override the legislation and regulations passed by individual governments to control working conditions and protect the health and safety of the citizens of their states.[2] The new international agreements augment the power and interests of international conglomerates and financiers who control large amounts of capital, and wish to reduce regulation of their activities as well as limit any barriers to the global flows of currency, material, and products.[3]

In their discussions of globalization, scholars debate the long-term significance of these developments for the future of nation-states.[4] They question whether, in the wake of the emergence of new international organizations, trade agreements, multinational corporations, and worldwide financial institutions, states continue to hold any power. The debates about globalization and the future of states seem abstract, however, removed from the day-to-day lives of people, and their continuing struggles to raise their families while finding some sense of meaning and self-worth in the effort. Citizens of the various states generally enter into these debates about the sovereignty of states in the global economy only when one of the international agreements directly affects their livelihood or a particular protest makes the international news. When a group of French farmers trashed a McDonald's restaurant over a ruling that allows genetically altered crops to be sold in France, dramatic photographs of golden arches downed by a barrage of rotten apples were broadcast globally.[5] The demonstrations staged by an alliance of environmentalists, labor unions, and human rights activists from around the world at the 1999 WTO meetings in Seattle also brought the question of the global economy to the attention of the public for a few days. But on a daily basis, the citizens of states in many regions of the world have yet to confront whether or not they continue to live in sovereign states. Even in states that have a long history of foreign penetration such as Haiti, most people still speak as if the fate of the country were in the hands of its own government.

The Concept of the Apparent State

As we sat writing this book, we struggled for a way to describe the real and pervasive limitations on independent action actually faced by any and all Haitian governments, and the actual relationship between the United States and Haiti. We decided that the constraints on the Haitian government are so severe, they call for a reevaluation of our understanding of the meaning of the term *state*. Our use of the phrase *apparent state* signals our position that the governments of many countries today have almost no independent authority to make meaningful changes within their territorial borders.

At first we were tempted to evoke the older language of colony and colonizing power to explain the relationship of Haiti and similar countries to the United States.[6] But there are several problems in applying the older language of imperialist power and colonization to the contemporary situation. In the first place, the government of Haiti is not a puppet administration. The political leaders of Haiti are not directly controlled by United States. As we will show, the U.S. government and other powerful "donors" can do little to ensure that any Haitian government implements the U.S. agenda. This is why Haiti seems to be a sovereign state. Even with U.S. troops on Haitian soil from 1995 to 1999, and despite the fact that foreign loans, principally from the United States, fund the day-to-day operations of the Haitian government, the Haitian governments of Aristide and Préval refused to march in the direction set by the United States. There are, therefore, clear differences between a colony and an apparent state. Haiti is not a colony of the United States because the Haitian government can resist an imposed agenda, and control enough force to repress and otherwise limit the actions of its own citizens.

Apparent states have all the fixings of a state. Haiti has its own political system that includes a president, prime minister, legislature, voting citizenry, government ministries, and officials. It also has its own dominant classes, who for two hundred years, have presented their agendas as if they speak for the Haitian nation.

But the formal apparatus of a government and the very real struggles for power that continue to take place within it do not tell the whole story. While governments may be able to repress their citizens and curtail dissent, as well as refuse to implement aspects of imposed policies, their political actions as well as all their financial activities are monitored and constrained from abroad to such an extent that national leaders are left with no domain from which to take any action that will benefit the majority of their people. The more powerful states and global lending institutions can ensure that the Haitian government doesn't implement an alternative agenda. The result is that the government does little or nothing. As the citizens of Haiti discovered when they elected Aristide, if a leader is chosen through democratic elections who does not please the international community of lenders, that leader may find his or her government destabilized and is likely to be overthrown. Sovereignty is effectively a facade if Haiti's leaders do not have the power to set their own course and respond to the needs and demands of the Haitian people.

When we say that a state is apparent, we do not deny its own history, political traditions, class struggles, or domains of autonomy. Different cultural histories do matter. Because of this, the U.S. penetration of countries such as Haiti, the Dominican Republic, Panama, El Salvador, and the Philippines has produced different results in each of these states. The United States does not have the power to make all of these states fit into a single mold. And as we have demonstrated, Haitian transmigrants, acting as transborder citizens, have used their own particular political traditions to contribute to the form and substance of the U.S. processes of penetration.

Apparent states exist almost as a form of virtual reality: a set of images that appear to have real strength and force, but consist of two-dimensional projections that only simulate power and authority. In distinguishing apparent states from other ones we do not mean, however, to imply that any state is fully sovereign. No modern state has ever been able to conduct its political, economic, and social affairs completely apart from the influence of other states and the large financial conglomerates that control more capital than most of the world's states. By the 1990s, nation-states had become "strategic actors, playing their interests and the interests they [were] supposed to represent, in a global system of interaction, in a condition of systematically shared sovereignty."[7]

Sovereignty, moreover, has always been more a political ideology than a description of political realities.[8] First of all, the actions of all modern states have been constrained by the balance of power between strong states as well as by alliances, transnational financial interests, and treaties. And poor and weak states have always faced more constraints. Second, within any state, most of the people do not actually "rule." Debates on national sovereignty and discussions about violations of national honor and pride encourage citizens to feel that "the state" does belong to all the people. Yet, members of different classes within a state clearly have different degrees of political power. In the United States, the question of campaign financing periodically focuses attention on the mechanisms by which billionaires and heads of corporations fund political campaigns, make possible and shape the careers of politicians and presidential candidates, and extract political favors. In countries such as Haiti, powerful families who control the economic life of the country have ensured that the political system works to their advantage.[9]

If we dwell on the mythical aspects of national sovereignty in the past, however, we can miss the transformations of the status of states in the contemporary age of globalization. We are facing a fundamental change in the location and deployment of power, and this change is happening with very little discussion although it effects us all. Today, we need a new political language with a different set of images and metaphors even to begin to describe the way the world is organized. We need a way to acknowledge the fact that all states are now linked together financially by banks and corporations, which are owned primarily by private interests. As well, we need new terms that enable us to think about how and why processes of nation-state building continue to survive in different locations around the world. Within our new vocabulary, we must be able to differentiate between states such as the United States, which serve as staging areas for capitalist enterprises operating globally, and states such as Haiti, which play quite different roles in global relations of power. Haiti and many states like it now sustain only the formal apparatus of a state without any possibility of setting an economic direction that can begin to meet the needs of the populations they claim to represent. They appear to be more than what they are.

We use the term *apparent state* as a means of exploring why people around the world still regard their countries as independent and therefore place the blame for their countries' disastrous conditions solely on the corruption of their political leaders, whereas they see the United States and the "lending community" as sources of assistance. We ask what combination of conditions adds to the perception that such aid is a lifeline, when it could just as readily be interpreted as a leash, if not a noose? Our answer is that in apparent states, citizens mistake the rituals and symbolism of nation and the political apparatus of a state for actual control over the economic activities and transactions. Once this is understood, it becomes clearer why, in the midst of a furiously globalizing economy, powerful transnational financial actors from banks to foundations place so much emphasis on the formal procedures of democratic elections and "democratic institution building" within specific states.[10] There may be a direct relationship between the degree to which the institutional structures of a state—its courts, police, and electoral processes—are reinforced with the help of foreign aid and loans and the reduction of that state's actual sovereignty. Certainly, such projects contribute to the illusion of the citizens of apparent states that they belong to sovereign states and their elected representatives hold the power to shape the future of their country.

Past Foreign Penetration of the Haitian Economy and Politics

Although the past forty years have marked a new stage in the history of the Haitian state, Haitian governments, beginning shortly after the Haitian Revolution, have found their ability to act severely restricted by the power and direct interference of other states. During the period in which European states and the United States focused on developing their own strong national economies, Haiti, although officially an independent state, was kept from controlling key sectors of its economy by other militarily powerful states. To obtain diplomatic recognition from France, in 1825, Haiti promised to pay a huge indemnity and reduce by half the customs fees it levied on French imports. To repay the debt and finance government activities, successive Haitian governments began to borrow money from foreign banks.[11] Banking itself, including the issuance of currency and management of loans, was soon controlled by foreign interests. In 1905, a consortium of French, German, and American capital functioned as the National Bank of the Republic of Haiti.[12]

The tentacles of foreign power also reached into Haiti's political process. England, France, and Germany supported various contenders for the Haitian presidency. Some presidents came to power and remained there as a result of foreign intervention. Each time a president was elected, his government granted economic privileges and protections to the nationals of the foreign powers that had helped put him in office. Measures such as these prevented the Haitian government from erecting adequate tariff barriers to protect fledgling Haitian industries, even though it was standard procedure for states to impose stiff taxes on imports to allow domestic industries to develop.

When foreign nationals suffered economic loss, European powers either used threats of force or actually deployed warships to make sure that their investments in Haiti were protected and any losses compensated. In 1872, after the British bombarded Haiti to prevent an insurrection against a Haitian president they supported, German frigates seized two Haitian ships to protest damage that the British did to property in Haiti owned by a German businessperson. To resolve the dispute, Haiti was forced to pay £3,000 in compensation.[13]

Although the United States did not officially recognize the independence of Haiti until 1862, by the 1820s, U.S. consuls were ensconced in Haitian towns. From these towns, the United States monitored and worked to protect U.S. commercial interests.[14] The trade between Haiti and the United States had grown to $4.2 million in the years 1820–1821.[15] As early as 1869, Haitian leaders were suggesting that they counter the European influence by developing ties with the United States, and in the following years, the United States actively began to compete with European powers for investments and political influence in Haiti.[16] The U.S. ambassador to Haiti wrote in 1903 that the goal of the United States "was to control the resources of the little country."[17]

Foreign domination of Haiti became complete in 1915, when the United States militarily occupied Haiti. Even as the United States took direct control of the Haitian political process and economy, the occupation was not described as colonization by either U.S. or Haitian political leaders. Some semblance of Haitian sovereignty was preserved. The United States portrayed its occupation as tutelage; the supposed goal was to teach Haitians how to run their country. Even as U.S. officials dismantled the laws and institutions designed to limit foreign intervention, the language of the U.S. military occupation declared that Haiti belonged to Haitians. The National Bank of the Republic of Haiti was completely taken over by the National City Bank of New York; the gold reserves of the bank were removed from Port-au-Prince to New York City. A new Haitian president who would do the bidding of the occupying forces was elected. Haiti was allowed to maintain its own constitution as if it were a separate state, but the Constitution was rewritten so that it became legal for foreigners to own land in Haiti. When the Haitian legislature refused to accept the imposed Constitution, the U.S. governors dismantled the assembly and held a "plebiscite" in which only five percent of the population voted. The new Constitution passed. With foreign landholding legalized, U.S. corporations took possession of prime agricultural lands owned by the Haitian government. They dispossessed Haitian cultivators who had worked the land yet had never been given legal title by the Haitian state and converted it into plantations. U.S. investors replaced most of the German investment in sugar refining and utilities. Roads were built, a railroad constructed, and public health measures instituted as part of a program to increase the productivity of U.S. investments in Haiti. The disempowered population was forced to provide the intensive labor necessary for these projects.

The economic interests that underlay the U.S. occupation were stated clearly in the memoirs of Smedley Butler, a general who had been a major in the occupying forces. Butler wrote:

> I spent thirty-three years and four months as a member of . . . the Marine Corps. And during that period I spent most of my time being a high-class muscleman for big business, for Wall Street, and for the bankers. . . . Thus I helped make Mexico . . . safe for American oil interests in 1914. I helped make Haiti and Cuba a decent place for the National City Bank to collect revenues. . . . I helped purify Nicaragua for the international banking house of Brown Brothers in 1909–1912. I brought light to the Dominican Republic for American sugar interests in 1916. I helped make Honduras "right" for American fruit companies in 1903.[18]

In each of these countries, the United States maintained its economic interests in what appeared to be externally independent states. As part of making

Haiti "a decent place for the [U.S.] National City Bank to collect revenues," the U.S. occupying forces established and trained the Garde d'Haïti, an armed force that became the Haitian military. Throughout the occupation, however, the U.S. military was actually in control of Haiti. They brutally suppressed the armed opposition to the U.S. presence that arose in the Haitian countryside.

Haitian intellectuals responded to the U.S. occupation by asserting the value of Haitian culture. They promoted Haitian folklore, dance, and music, and articulated a fierce Haitian nationalism based on the widely shared nostalgia for Haiti's proud past. At the same time, Haitian intellectuals contributed to the transnational Negritude Movement, which asserted the full equality and humanity of black people.[19] Some Haitian writers also denounced U.S. imperialism, and sought to address the long-term penetration of foreign capital and political influence in Haiti.

When the U.S. Marines withdrew in 1934, Haitians assumed that their sovereignty was being restored. President Vincent was labeled by Haitian nationalists as the "Second Liberator of Haiti" because he arranged for the withdrawal of U.S. troops. In fact, U.S. domination continued. President Vincent had been selected by the United States, and his regime still protected and courted foreign economic interests that impeded the economic development of Haiti. A majority of the directors of the National Bank of the Republic of Haiti were Americans appointed in New York City, and the Haitian dollar stayed linked to the U.S. dollar. Until 1991, the Haitian paper currency, which invoked the Constitution as a symbol of a sovereign Haiti, read, "This bill, produced in conformity with the Constitution of the Republic of Haiti, is payable to the bearer in the legal money of the United States of America at the rate of 5 Gourdes to a Dollar." U.S. companies controlled major Haitian exports such as sugar, sisal, bananas, and bauxite.[20] Profits from these U.S. businesses were not invested back into Haiti. Capital also flowed out of Haiti to pay back U.S. foreign assistance, which often took the form of loans. The Haitian government attempted to break free of U.S. penetration by soliciting the intervention of other foreign powers. In 1936, the Haitian government negotiated unsuccessfully with Hitler's Third Reich to allow German companies to take over all public works in Haiti.[21]

In 1943, 5 percent of Haiti's best lands were transferred directly to a U.S. company called the Haitian-American Society for Agricultural Development. It bulldozed peasants' houses and crops, and destroyed one million food-bearing trees in order to establish rubber plantations. For a limited period of time, thousands of jobs were created. Ultimately, however, the plantations produced only five tons of rubber before natural rubber was replaced by chemical substitutes produced in the United States. The devastated lands in Haiti were abandoned.[22] Meanwhile, the Reynolds corporation was given a sixty-year monopoly on the extraction of bauxite. Haitian rural producers once again lost thousands of acres of land and their homes.[23]

During the 1950s, the Haitian government took twenty-seven million dollars in loans from the U.S. Export-Import Bank and thirteen million dollars in loans from Haitian sources to fund a dam and hydroelectric plant in the Artibonite Valley. Once more rural people lost their lands and livelihood, and the country received no lasting benefits. Improper drainage and dropping river levels produced little irrigation and an inadequate supply of electricity. By 1957, the Haitian government was facing over thirty-three million dollars of debt, almost all of which had been used to facilitate foreign investments that only drained resources and profits from Haiti.[24]

Throughout the entire period of distorted development that accompanied and followed the U.S. occupation, Haitian political leaders maintained and elaborated the rituals of the nation that Georges remembers from his childhood. The Haitian Revolution was proudly commemorated in 1954 in a *Tricinquantenaire*—the commemoration of one hundred and fifty years of independence. As part of the celebration, the Battle of Vertières, the final battle of the Haitian Revolution, was elaborately reenacted.[25] Statues of founding ancestors were erected outside the National Palace in Port-au-Prince.

During this period, the United States participated in rituals that celebrated the sovereignty of Haiti. Paul Eugene Magloire, the Haitian president from 1950 to 1955, was invited to the United States to address a joint session of the Congress and meet with President Eisenhower. He was accorded all courtesies extended to an important head of state. President Magloire responded by acknowledging the connection between the United States and Haiti, but avoided describing it as a form of U.S. domination. He informed the Congress that "no doubt, from time to time, clouds darken the atmosphere of confidence between the two countries. . . . But for better or for worse, we believe our destiny is closely linked with that of the great American democracy."[26] Magloire was then given a ticker tape parade down the streets of New York City. The message transmitted through public ceremonies was that although the United States was rich and powerful, and Haiti poor and weak, each was an independent country, freely choosing to be good neighbors.

Yet while Haiti's sovereignty was constantly being diminished during the country's first one hundred and fifty years, some domains of autonomy remained. Much of the profits from Haitian coffee production stayed in Haitian hands, although they were the hands of the Haitian merchant and business classes. Haitian cultivators also produced food crops for local markets and Haiti was able to feed itself. The Haitian government was the majority owner of certain key industries—the electric company, the flour mill, and sugar refineries—and monopolized the distribution of cooking oil, milk, herring, codfish, wheat, soap, detergents, and cigarettes. Today, however, almost all domains of economic autonomy have been destroyed.

Connected but Unequal: The Intertwining of the United States and Haiti

Beginning in the 1950s, but with growing intensity in the decades that followed, countries considered "underdeveloped" were offered large sums of money for "economic development" by the United States and various international lending institutions in which the United States was an influential player. In the context of the cold war, this "assistance" was meant to keep the debtor nations within the sphere of U.S. influence and capitalist development. The problem for many countries such as Haiti was that the loans led to further loans to pay back the initial debt, rather than sustainable development. The debt trap in Haiti began in 1957 when Duvalier, supported by the USAID representative in Haiti, took power through fraudulent elections that were accepted as legitimate by the United States.[27] Duvalier used the context of the cold war to gain access to millions of dollars in "foreign aid." A significant portion of the loans from the United States and various "multilateral" financial organizations went directly into the pockets of the Duvalier family. Duvalier used much of the rest of the money to run the Haitian government.

Alex Dupuy, a Haitian scholar who studies the sources of Haitian underdevelopment, has summarized the relationship between Haiti and the United States as follows: "The United States assumed the responsibility for financing the Haitian government through foreign aid, despite its knowledge of the widespread fraudulent practices and misappropriation of public aid monies by government officials. In return for this support, the Haitian government would follow a pro–U.S. policy and open the country to U.S. capital and U.S. products. Moreover, . . . the support of the regime by foreign capital made it more dependent on and subservient to foreign capital."[28] Three U.S. companies controlled 40 percent of all Haitian imports by 1963.[29] Beginning in 1967, U.S. companies began to look to Haiti to take advantage of its cheap labor and politically repressed, quiescent workers as part of the project of corporations in the capitalist core to move their production plants overseas. Yet a whole new level of initiatives directed toward Haiti began in 1971, when Jean-Claude Duvalier inherited the regime from his father. Economic funds described as "development assistance," but oriented toward facilitating the use of Haitian labor by transnational corporations kept increasing in size. In the 1970s, Haiti received $384 million. Between 1972 and 1981, $540 million flowed into Haiti. In the period between 1981 and 1985, right before the fall of the Duvalier regime, Haiti received $657 million in aid.

Most of this money was either directly from the United States or from funders such as the World Bank's International Development Association and the Inter-American Bank, in which the United States figures prominently.[30] In 1982, a USAID report summarized the goal of development aid. It did not describe the goal of a strong, independent, prosperous Haiti as envisioned in Haitian nationalist rhetoric. Rather, the United States sought through its aid a "historic change toward deeper market interdependence [of Haiti] with the United States."[31] Haiti became progressively poorer as repayments of the loans combined with the extraction of wealth from the population by the Duvalier regime drained the country of money for economic development. In 1976, 48 percent of the people were said by outside monitors to live in "desperate poverty."[32] By 1986, this number grew to 70 percent.

It was in the context of this vast penetration of U.S. funds into Haiti during the Duvalier regime that the large-scale Haitian migration from the countryside to Port-au-Prince and abroad began. There is a direct relationship between the financing of the Haitian government by the United States and other members of the international community, as the loan agencies call themselves, and the flood of Haitian immigrants to the United States. The growth of Haitian transnational family networks is linked to the role that the United States has played in Haiti during the past forty years; because the United States purposely reduced the few remaining autonomous domains of the Haitian economy, increasing numbers of Haitians were forced to go elsewhere to find employment. Analyses of U.S. development policies in Haiti at that time revealed that "USAID proposed the 'gradual but systematic removal' of domestic crops from 20 percent of all tilled land and their replacement with export crops such as coffee and cocoa."[33] Haiti was flooded with millions of dollars from Food for Peace and other food assistance programs. Haitian farmers were not able to compete with the donated or cheap imported food, made possible by government subsidies to U.S. and European farmers. As a result, each year, Haiti, a country where the majority of the people are cultivators, imports increased amounts of food. The donated food "assistance" served to clear the way for U.S. agricultural corporations to find markets in Haiti. While Haitian farmers were unable to get their crops to market without adequate roads or means of transportation, imported apples from Washington State were hawked on the streets of Port-au-Prince. Meanwhile, the importation of secondhand clothing and other used goods almost completely obliterated many forms of craft production. The results of the policies imposed on Haiti in the name of development assistance have been economic dislocation and destruction of Haitian economic life. A million people have fled the countryside and arrived in Port-au-Prince, desperate to earn a living by any means necessary. Up to a million more have left Haiti altogether. They are all refugees from the apparent state.

Despite the realities of domination and penetration, the semblance of Haiti's independence leads Haitians both at home and abroad to believe that the problem is solely one of leadership. For almost thirty years, all Haitian political activity focused on the overthrow of the Duvalier regime. Most Haitians in Haiti and the diaspora assumed that if the Duvalier regime could be overthrown, then the Haitian economy could be rebuilt and Haiti could resume its rightful place as a leader among black nations. The transnational grassroots movement that forced Duvalier to flee to France on a U.S. military jet in 1986, and then pushed aside the various military juntas that replaced him, reinforced the idea that the Haitian people could take possession of their state and determine its direction. This sense of self-determination was strengthened in 1990 when the grassroots movement elected Aristide, a leader of the movement, to the presidency, rather than the former World Bank official preferred by the United States.[34]

In assessing the sovereignty of the Haitian state, it is important to remember that much of the accoutrements of democracy in Haiti are made in the United States and paid for by the American people. In 1990, the United States called for showcase elections. Through supporting open and democratic elections, the U.S. government distanced itself from its support for the repressive Duvalier dictatorship. The United States along with allied funding organizations and governments spent at least fifty million dollars administering, facilitating, and observing the electoral procedures. They expected their candidate to be elected rather than Aristide, a radical priest. While with all their money, the donors could not determine the outcome of the elections, they could severely restrict the actions of the new Haitian president. As soon as Aristide was elected, he and his newly appointed ministers began to learn about the constraints that came along with all the support for Haitian democracy.[35]

The Aristide administration had to ensure that government activities were still carried out. Because many agencies were already funded by foreign capital, and often assisted by foreign "advisers," their agenda usually closely complied with the strictures "not just of the World Bank, but of the entire donor community."[36] Aristide found that to keep the country solvent, he had to continue to rely on foreign loans. Ultimately, he made arrangements with the World Bank, which imposed harsh restrictions on the assistance Aristide had promised to the Haitian poor. Aristide, for example, had pledged to raise the minimum wage significantly so that the Haitian people could move, in his words, "from misery to poverty." This initiative was countermanded by the lenders.[37]

Despite the fact that Aristide's initiatives were already undermined, the United States saw his government as threatening and worked to discredit the president and his administration. The U.S. Central Intelligence Agency strongly encouraged Haitian generals to overthrow Aristide, and seven months after he came triumphantly to office, President Aristide was indeed ousted by a military coup.[38] During the three years that the Haitian military ruled the country, it waged an all-out campaign to murder, destroy, and demoralize the grassroots movement that previously had taken control of the state. There is evidence that the Haitian generals who led the military junta and the leaders of the paramilitary organization responsible for the murder of activist priests, grassroots leaders, and their supporters worked closely with representatives of the U.S. government.[39]

Only after a meeting in Paris orchestrated by the United States and World Bank officials at which Aristide signed an agreement to endorse their economic policies was he restored to the Haitian presidency. After he was put back in office by a 1994 UN military operation in which the United States was the major player, Aristide faced even more restrictions than before on his direction of the Haitian economy. The World Bank and United States insisted even more forcefully than before that all industries owned by the Haitian state be sold to private investors and that government expenditures for services be reduced.

Speaking in Paris for the Haiti Consultative Group, an organization of representatives of governments and banks, USAID Assistant Administrator Mark L. Schneider announced, "Thanks to contributions from the United States Government and the Governments of Japan, Sweden, Mexico, Switzerland, France, Canada, Netherlands, Argentina, and Haiti—$81,474,605 in arrears to these three financial institutions were cleared and, in so doing, removing the most serious obstacle to the use of $260 million in frozen funds from these three institutions."[40] In the same speech, Schneider reported that the World Bank was committing forty million dollars to Haiti, while the Inter-American Development Bank (funded by the U.S. government) was providing another seventy million dollars. Translated into more straightforward language, this meant that the taxpayers of ten governments, including Haiti, repaid eighty-one million dollars in loan payments to banks that represent the richest governments in the world, including a U.S.–financed development bank. These same banks would in return lend Haiti more money, which would also have to be repaid. What is described as "development assistance" can just as easily be understood as a burden of debt that makes any meaningful development of the Haitian economy impossible.

When President Préval came to office in 1996, the multilateral "aid" agencies committed much vaster sums to Haiti, putting the country in even greater debt. Money also came from the U.S. government, as well as from Canada, France, Germany, and Japan. These "donors" pledged to provide more than $ 2 billion.[41] In return, the international financial institutions were to monitor the Haitian political and economic developments to ensure that there was the political and economic stability suitable for further investment of foreign capital.

The Haitian government was required to institute the economic agendas of these lending agencies. It was forced to end price controls on basic foods, devalue the Haitian currency, "streamline" the government, reduce public services, reorient agriculture to produce export crops to repay the foreign debts that the Duvalier regime had accumulated, place foreign experts inside Haitian government ministries, keep the minimum wage at a level lower than that of neighboring countries, and sell industries owned by the Haitian government. In other words, the Haitian government was compelled to accept an economic program that facilitates foreign investments in Haiti, raises unemployment, and allows for little investment in desperately needed public services, such as sanitation, health care, and education.

While some of the loans and aid went to create new jobs, the jobs supported by this aid were explicitly designed to be temporary. The Haitian government was instructed by lending agencies to reduce drastically the number of people employed by the government. Vast sums of money were allocated to create a climate of law and order suitable for the investment of foreign capital, with the assumption that attracting private corporations was the only possible way to develop Haiti. The connection between the U.S. investment in the Haitian judicial system of courts and police and the agenda of establishing a good climate for U.S. investors was publicly acknowledged by members of Congress in 1996 when partisan wrangling in the United States held up some of the funds.[42] Finally, eighteen million dollars was allocated to the Administration of Justice Program.[43] But there was little evidence of systemic change to ensure that in the future, the poor would have more access to justice than in the past. It was somewhat more evident that the Checchi Company, the U.S. corporation that received the USAID contract for the Administration of Justice Program, had made a profit.

There is little proof that the U.S.–led development strategy for Haiti has done anything at all to improve the standard of living of the vast majority of people in the country. The inflation rate was 17 percent in 1997.[44] By most measures, the misery of the Haitian poor increased. Four years after Aristide had been returned to power by U.S. and international forces, unemployment and malnutrition were higher, real wages were lower, clean water and health care were more costly, and the price of food had risen dramatically.

Massive corruption has also become the order of the day. The rich pay few or no taxes, the state continues to be used as a means of taxing the poor, and international aid goes into the pockets of government officials. Most of the over two billion dollars the United States had expended on Haiti was not invested in programs that would raise the standard of living of the majority of the Haitian population.

In 1969, during the Duvalier dictatorship, Georges's father wrote him to explain that he had not received his salary for his government position for six months. Money was scarce, and access to the basic necessities of life was difficult. There was no money to pay for the medical tests the doctor had ordered for Georges's father, who suffered from hypertension and diabetes. Thirty years later, in 1999, government employees still wait months for their paychecks. Now the requests go out to transmigrants as before, not only as letters but as cassette tapes and phone calls, begging family members abroad to "remember what they left behind" and fulfill their obligations. As we have seen, it is family abroad rather than foreign aid that sustains life for a large number of individuals in Haiti. This fact was acknowledged in 1998 by the U.S. State Department in a report on Haiti that stated, "Remittances from abroad now constitute a significant source of financial support for many Haitian households."[45]

Despite the Haitian government's efforts to meet its foreign debt obligations, a point of contention arose between international lenders and the Haitian government in the late 1990s. The problem was not that Haiti had failed to develop an economy that could serve the needs of impoverished people but rather that the Haitian government had failed to implement a key part of the imposed agenda: privatization of all government-owned industries. While some of the industries, such as the cement plant and the flour refinery, were sold and others were not even functioning, foreign investors wanted the big prizes: TELECO, the telephone company, and EDH, the electric utility. Even in their antiquated and undercapitalized current condition, these industries are immensely profitable. TELECO, for example, earns more than twenty million dollars profit a year for the Haitian government and is one of the few sources of cash that the Haitian government is able to spend without foreign directives.[46] When sold to a private corporation, this vital source of funds will be gone. Since the government is not likely to collect taxes from corporations and the rich, tax revenue will not replace any income lost from the transfer of the telephone company to foreign hands.

It gradually became clear, during the delays in implementing the privatization of Haitian industries, that U.S. and international aid organizations desired the transfer to private hands of the few profit-producing industries in Haiti. The Haitian Constitution specifies that these industries cannot be sold without the approval of the Haitian legislature. Some members of the Haitian Parliament at first refused to sell the companies. Eventually, IMF

Director Michel Camdessus personally visited Haiti to clarify that the country would forfeit millions of dollars in assistance unless the legislature fully complied with the sale. Finally, as a result of his visit, the Parliament passed the laws. Haiti subsequently received IMF approval, and soon after, the U.S. State Department issued a series of "Points for Haiti" providing its own ultimatum: unless the various Haitian politicians agreed to provide privatization, political order, and elections there would be no more money. The document reads: "The high-level of donor attention and support that Haiti currently enjoys will not last forever. If the government cannot satisfy the basic conditionalities necessary to ensure prudent use of resources, donor money will go elsewhere. . . . The steps that the international donors are expecting in the months ahead—privatization, civil service reductions, continued budget austerity—will be politically difficult but . . . to turn back now on economic reforms would be disastrous for Haiti's long-term development."[47]

In 1998, the U.S. Congress laid down the law. The Foreign Operations, Export Financing, and Related Programs Appropriations Act stated that "none of the funds appropriated or otherwise made available by this Act may be provided to the Government of Haiti unless the President reports to Congress that the Government of Haiti . . . has made demonstrable progress in privatizing major governmental parastatals, including demonstrable progress toward the material and legal transfer of ownership of such parastatals. . . . As used in this section, the term 'parastatal' means a government-owned enterprise."[48] By the spring of 2001, the phone and electric companies were still not privatized, the various political parties in Haiti were engaged in a fierce Constitutional dispute over the legitimacy of legislative and presidential elections, and internal party competition in the United States continued to struggle over whether loans and aid to Haiti should be cut.

U.S. Institutions and the Haitian Apparent State

In the United States, any interference by foreign powers, interests, or individuals in the workings of U.S. political parties is seen as a particularly egregious breach of U.S. national sovereignty. Yet organizations linked to the U.S. Republican and Democratic Parties have directed and funded political activities in Haiti with the purpose of influencing the outcome of Haitian elections. Both U.S. Republicans and Democrats have worked to shore up those political forces they found most appealing by large infusions of foreign money, technical assistance, and political advice, all in the name of strengthening democracy and civil society. The International Republican Institute (IRI) claimed to "promote a level playing field."[49] Just what this means becomes clear when we examine the parties that IRI supported. Members of these organizations were connected to the Duvalier regime and the military juntas that followed, including the one that overthrew Aristide; they are directly linked to state sponsored terrorism.[50] The groups supported by IRI included an organization whose name reflects the rhetoric of its sponsors: the Advancement and Progress of Haiti (FRAPH). FRAPH is a paramilitary group linked to murder, torture, rape and other forms of antidemocratic activity.

In a further demonstration of the U.S. role in the Haitian political process, the Federal Bureau of Investigation (FBI), a U.S. domestic crime-fighting organization, was called into Haiti in 1995 to investigate the assassination of two figures linked to the Haitian Right. In the view of William Perry, the deputy assistant director of the FBI, the investigation was "unusual" because "the FBI was investigating a violation of foreign law . . . in a foreign country."[51] This example raises the question of whether the United States really considers Haiti a foreign country with a sovereign government.

This question is rarely addressed in the ongoing debate among Haitians of all classes about what is wrong with Haiti. They struggle to come to terms with the bitter experiences of the past decade, particularly the evidence that the Haitian government seems to enrich itself in the midst of an ever-deepening degree of misery for most of Haiti's people. The questions of the day are "What went wrong?" and "What is wrong?" The terms of the debate, as it is waged by a transnational citizenry, echo the themes of the past. Most Haitians hold onto the goal of a strong, independent Haiti, even though most are living within transnational terrains, and witness the penetration of the U.S. government and foreign capital into all aspects of Haitian political and economic life. They fail to examine the centuries-long penetration of the Haitian economy by foreign banks and the contemporary impotence of the Haitian political system in the face of agendas set by the United States and international lending agencies. Most people we interviewed in Haiti, as well as most of the transnational Haitian media and our

Haitian friends and acquaintances in New York City, see the problems of Haiti as stemming from weaknesses within the leadership of its people, its culture, or the people themselves.

It Is Not a Question of Country, It Is a Question of Pocket (Yo Pa Patryòt, Yo Se Patri-pòch)

The idea that Haiti cannot advance primarily because of the selfishness and corruption of its leaders is widespread among all classes in Haiti. This is the belief of urban professionals who personally work for the government as well as uneducated people who grew up in the countryside. This syndrome of blame became a constant refrain after the "transition to democracy" that followed the ousting of Duvalier when the governments of Aristide and Préval continued the same policy of personal enrichment as the dictators who preceded them. Both U.S. government experts on Haiti and Haitians in the United States and Haiti discussed the idea of a culture of corruption that kept Haiti from advancing.

Esmeralda, who had worked in the Presidential Palace, described for us the mind-set of government officials:

> When they have connections with foreign governments, they don't come to defend the interests of the masses. They come to defend the interest of the government, their pocket, and their own interests. . . . They are there to get money to purchase the sports utility vehicles and beautiful houses. They have nothing to do with the masses and the disfavored. They come to protect their own interests and those of their relatives. [But] to get to power, they say they are coming to defend the interests of the masses. You see a guy like Aristide: watch him. That is what we call a hypocrite [*rat mòde soufle*], meaning a rat bites you and then it blows the wound to soothe you so it can bite you again. . . . So he puts you to sleep and he takes everything you have. So that is why they are denouncing his wealth right now. He stole like nobody before him. He bought a mansion and the people are dying of hunger. He owns millions and millions of dollars. That is a scandal, a priest who came to defend the interests of the masses. The people feel betrayed.

Mathilde, a woman who worked as a secretary at the University of Haiti, took up a similar theme: "Before 1986 there were struggles. In the course of the struggle that ended in 1986, the people thought they would reach a point where things would be better, and even the youth were also saying that things would change. They were going to have elections and new leaders. And then 1986 came and nothing happened. The crowds were mobilized and Aristide was president, and [still] nothing happened. Everything happened and nothing happened. So now people are playing the role of an observer. The are just observing, they are just watching. They are looking, they are watching. . . . The future is very grim."

People who had no experience with the state other than that of political repression were equally critical and dismayed by what they saw. Claudia, a young woman whose mother sold goods in the marketplace and whose father was a cultivator, told us: "There is a saying in Haiti that says a person near power is not the same as a person in power. During election time, people come and promise you all sorts of things and sweet talk you, but when you vote for them and they get into power, they forget about their promises, and what they promised they don't deliver. They don't have a will to help. That doesn't mean that they don't have the capacity. I don't want to generalize, but most of them when they get into power are only making money. The country is falling apart."[52]

Even when people acknowledged the interference of foreign powers, they often did not address the power that foreign states, corporations, and banks hold in Haiti. Instead, their identification with the Haitian nation and its crowning achievement, the establishment of a sovereign state, led many in Haiti to place most of the responsibility for its condition on the failure of Haitian leaders to act responsibly toward the people.

Many in the diaspora who had put their hopes in the grassroots movement were even slower to acknowledge the corruption. In 1996, when both rich and poor in Haiti were already denouncing the widespread corrupt practices of the democratically elected officials, there were many in the diaspora still willing to defend the leaders and deny or overlook the corruption. Tempers flared in the course of transnational radio call-in shows. From Haiti came statements of dismay: "The Lavalas leaders are now living in mansions." From the diaspora came the irritated rebuttal, "So what if they are stealing? They are rebuilding Haiti."

Eventually, however, the verdict was strongly critical of the leaders of the Lavalas movement. The Aristide and Préval governments, even though they had gained their position through the heroic struggle of a grassroots movement against dictatorship and had supported the masses' demands for justice, were as corrupt as previous regimes. And they were not building the strong, egalitarian, prosperous Haiti that had been the goal of the struggle. Only a few voices acknowledged that in effect Haiti is an apparent state because Haitian leaders, except for corruption, have almost no sphere for economic action independent of the strictures of international lending institutions.

We Are No Good (Se Nou Ki Pa Bon)

In the current debacle, many Haitians became critical of their own capacities to rule. Disappointed and demoralized by the actions of their leaders, we heard Haitians of all classes fall back on a logic of self-blame. They thus echoed the constant refrain of European and U.S. political leaders and intellectuals since the days of the Haitian Revolution: "The Haitians as a black people are incapable of self-government."

This theme often emerges at moments of crisis. It was voiced by Haitian nationalists in New York City at the time of the 1994 U.S.–led invasion and occupation. Georges sat in his home in Queens, New York, the day after President Aristide had returned to Haiti, and listened to a special program on Radio Tropicale aired transnationally. The broadcasters and invited guests angrily denounced those who called the radio station to express suspicions about the motives of the U.S. government in returning Aristide to Haiti. One of the guest speakers shouted: "During the past two hundred years we have been criticizing others, [and] what have we accomplished? Nothing. Now we have foreigners who want to help us. The time to philosophize is over; we must participate in this new attempt to make the country work."[53]

During the next few months, similar statements were broadcast every day on the Haitian media in the United States. This theme became a widespread consensus by 1996: the problem in Haiti was the corruption of its leaders, and fundamentally, the responsibility for the failures of Haiti rested with the Haitian people. On the occasion of "an open conversation with the Haitian community" broadcast on Radio Tropicale in September 1996, many listeners called the animator, complaining, "We are no good [Se nou ki pa bon]; since Duvalier's overthrow, Haiti has received enough foreign aid to fix the country; it is all of us who are no good, we are defective." This logic ignores the full extent to which Haitian development in the past and present has been constrained by foreign states and international loans.

We heard the same contention in Haiti. Yvette's niece, Lourdes, expressed her love of Haiti through a torrent of self-hatred. "I don't see any future for this country. It needs to be reformed. Drop a bomb and kill everybody in it. Just erase it from the face of the earth and bring another nation in it. That is what I see for the future of Haiti. I don't see anything for Haiti to make it a better country. I don't see how the change will occur. I don't see it."

Haitians are not alone in placing full responsibility for the poverty of Haiti on the actions of Haitian leaders. The U.S. government and U.S. foundations have promoted scholarship that comes to the same conclusion. For example, the U.S. Army War College and Ford Foundation funded a small conference in 1996 about Haitian economic development. Haitian scholars based in both Haiti and the United States joined with U.S. academics, lawyers, and pundits to summarize the Haitian situation. In the published proceedings, the editor of the volume, Robert Rothberg, reported on the consensus of the conference: that President Préval had "the opportunity . . . of reconstructing and remolding the Haitian state, raising Haitian living standards, and creating a new political culture of democracy and tolerance."[54] So when Préval failed, according to this point of view, the responsibility lay with the Haitian leadership and Haitian people. And although these experts were active participants in the process of foreign penetration of the Haitian economy, they spoke as if the Haitian people were free to blaze their own path. They and the impoverished people we interviewed both stated clearly that the full responsibility for the future of Haiti was in the hands of Haiti's leaders.

Hometown Realities and Apparent States

I called a colleague of mine who teaches in the public school where I used to teach to see if it would be possible to place a student teacher in his school. But what he was mainly interested in talking to me about were the activities of his hometown association. He mentioned that his hometown association was having a fund-raising marathon and he asked me for money. And I am not even from that town.

Hometown associations have emerged as an alternative means of development in Haiti, a way of connecting the Haitian diaspora with various towns and rural areas and channeling funds into small-scale local projects. Beginning in the 1980s, persons from small village hamlets in Haiti often came together in the United States to form hometown associations, known among Haitians as "regional associations." Since that time, many Haitian hometown associations have flourished in both the United States and Canada. While the guiding force of these organizations is often a few professionals or well-established transmigrants abroad, the fund-raising is done among networks that extend beyond individuals from the hometown. They may involve people who otherwise would not be sending money to Haiti and thus pull them into the concerns of long-distance nationalists. Georges, who is already committed to Haiti, finds himself contributing directly to development projects in the hometowns of his friends.

Haitian migrants are not alone in their enthusiasm for supplementing the home ties of family with organizational activities that build a semblance of transnational community. In both the past and present, hometown associations have formed an important part of the ways in which immigrants settle in a new society.[55] As a teenager, Nina accompanied her grandmother to meetings of her hometown association and met Russian Jewish immigrants who had emigrated from her grandmother's hometown more than fifty years previously.

Hometown associations seem to be a domain of political activity that functions outside the state. At first glance, they appear to embody the concept of civil society, a sphere of public life that is independent of the state. It is possible to interpret the development of contemporary hometown associations as a repudiation by local people of broader national identities. Their homeland is their local land. Scholars studying the hometown organizations of Mexican and Dominican migrants in the United States have been struck by the way in which migrants seem to live within a "transnational community," rather than identifying with either their home country or the United States.[56]

We argue, however, for an alternative interpretation of the flourishing of hometown associations. While these organizations contribute to the erosion of the economic sphere of government action, states may be able to remain the acknowledged political master. This seems to be the case in Haiti. We conclude our examination of the apparent state with a discussion of Haitian hometown associations because these organizations maintain a complex dynamic relationship with the Haitian state.

As in the Europe of the past and many areas of the world today, many Haitians certainly identify with their hometowns. Georges identifies with Aux Cayes, although he has not been an active member of the Association of Aux Cayes and knows little about its activities beyond the repair of the town cemetery wall—an achievement we inspected while in Haiti. But he is often invited to contribute to associations in which his friends or acquaintances are members. The meetings, dances, and fund-raising activities offer immigrants a chance to mingle with old friends and make new ones in the midst of dealing with the pressures of living in a new land. Nevertheless, the official purpose of most of these Haitian organizations and their activities is to contribute to the development of the hometown. Dances, parties, and fund-raising marathons all raise money for projects in the specific town.

Haitian hometown associations, together with a broad range of other "nongovernmental" associations, have begun to provide whatever services exist in rural areas. Clinics, schools, electrification, water, roads, and firefighting equipment come not from the central government but from organizations based outside Haiti, and hometown associations must be counted among these transnational "donors." Haiti on every level has become a society that lives off donations. But the state has not yet faded away. It is possible that eventually this form of development will become so routine that people will no longer look to the state. Presently, however, this type of fund-raising is experienced as a critique of the state, a form of remonstrance against the state for not doing what needs to be done.

We first became aware of the extent of the activities of these hometown associations in the 1980s while studying Haitian organizations in the New York metropolitan area. A quiet, intense, quite formal gentleman named Monsieur Le Blanc contacted us to ask for help in drawing up a charter for a coalition of hometown organizations. He was trying to bring these groups together for joint action in the name of Christianity, Haiti, and social justice. We learned that in the midst of the repression of the Duvalier regime, people from small towns in Haiti—places so small that in the past, immigrants were ashamed to claim such backward areas as their hometowns— were organizing transnationally to help reconstruct Haiti. At the time, Monsieur Le Blanc seemed to be a dreamer. A grassroots movement for

change in Haiti springing up from rural areas outside the conventional political forces of either the Right or Left seemed impractical and far-fetched,
if not straight-out utopian. A few years later, of course, the grassroots
movement exploded into public view and brought down the Duvalier regime. Hometown associations, in their scattered and strangely apolitical
way, contributed to a movement that directly took on the regime and addressed demands to the state. Yet after the grassroots movement had splin-
tered and subsided, hometown associations once again appeared to be removed from Haitian politics.

Emigrants from particular localities who have settled in the United
States and Canada gain prestige back home by investing in various projects
ranging from rehabilitating a local graveyard to supplying electricity or
water for the town. During both the 1980s and 1990s, these projects were
designed to circumvent the corruption and political intrigues of the Haitian government and link localities directly to emigrant associations. By the
end of the 1990s, Haitian businesspeople interested in transnational investment strategies began to show more interest in building on the connections
between emigrants and their hometowns. And Haitian hometown associations had become significant enough that their activities were covered in
the pages of the *New York Times*.

An article in the *New York Times* in May 1998 captured the contradictory
currents that come together in hometown associations. In the accompa-
nying photo, seven men and one woman, all fairly young, are standing on
a paved road in front of a signpost in Jacmel, a small coastal city in southeast
Haiti. The signpost not only points to the four cardinal directions but also
to Mexico, Panama, Miami, and Surinam. The transnational positioning
of Haiti is graphically acknowledged. The title under the picture reads
"Haitian-Americans in Jacmel, where they met last month with Haitian
mayors to discuss economic development." The focus of the story was on
Tiburon, described as a "dusty outpost" in southwest Haiti.

Tiburon is the hometown of Fritz Martial, the founder of Moment Créole, a long-running radio program on WLIB, a radio station owned by African American and Caribbean leaders in New York City. Despite the fact that
Martial helped found the Committee to Help and Develop the Parish of
Tiburon in 1976, he has at various times adamantly argued that Haitian
migrants should focus their energies on the United States, rather than continue to be engaged in Haiti. Yet by the 1990s, he was speaking as a long-
distance nationalist, fully caught up in the question of how the diaspora

WALL PAINTINGS: U.S.- HAITI RELATIONS

Although euphoric about the return of Aristide by U.S. forces, this grassroots artist questioned whether the relationship between the two countries would lead to peace. Wall painting, Port-au-Prince, Haiti, 1994. Photo from collection of Georges Fouron.

The U.S.-led occupation of Haiti in 1994 that returned Aristide to office, symbolized here by the American eagle carrying the Haitian flag, was thought by many people to signal the beginning of a better day for Haiti. Wall painting, Port-au-Prince, Haiti, 1994. Photo from collection of Georges Fouron.

It was hoped that the U.S. military, represented here by a soldier and his dog, would disarm the Makout, an aspiration that was not realized. Wall painting, Port-au-Prince, Haiti, 1994. Photo from collection of Georges Fouron.

Haitian nationalism is linked to the people's aspirations for peace, love, sincerity, and justice. Wall painting, Port-au-Prince, Haiti 1994. Photo from collection of Georges Fouron.

Wall Paintings: Aspirations and Nationalism of the Grassroots Movement

"Life is strange," reads this painting. The tire in the foreground labeled "Justice and Freedom" reminds us that poor people took justice into their own hands. Oppressors were executed by crowds who burned tires around the necks of the individuals they targeted. Wall painting, Port-au-Prince, Haiti, 1994. Photo from collection of Georges Fouron.

The artist sees in Haitian nationalism a cry for justice carried out without vengeance, violence, or provocation. Wall painting, Port-au-Prince, Haiti, 1994. Photo from collection of Georges Fouron.

Wall Paintings:
Nationalism "From Below"

The common man carries the heavy burden of supporting Haiti, as the rooster, symbolizing Aristide, watches and waits on the sideline, poised to step into the fray. Wall painting, Port-au-Prince, Haiti, 1994. Photo from collection of Georges Fouron.

The Haitian people cry out for justice, linking death to the Leopards, a Makout elite presidential guard trained and equipped by the United States under the Duvaliers. Wall painting, Port-au-Prince, Haiti, 1994. Photo from collection of Georges Fouron.

could help develop Haiti. He explained his efforts on behalf of Tiburon by telling the *Times* reporter, "We could not stay here [New York], live well and let that happen to the place of our ancestors." The article notes that when Martial left Haiti in 1969, Tiburon had "one elementary school, no hospital and no potable water to serve the town's 50,000 residents."[57] The hometown association, according to the article, had provided the town with six schools, including two high schools, and one of the best irrigation systems in Haiti.

The article went on to cover a meeting, the first of its kind, that had brought together "mayors, private business owners, and potential investors from overseas." One of the goals of this meeting, as the organizers explained, was to "help bolster the power of the elected mayors whose positions have been rendered largely ceremonial because officials in the capital make important decisions without consulting them. Economic alliance with Haitians living abroad, they said, would give the mayors the financial clout to direct aid to their municipalities as they saw fit." Such an arrangement would allow organizations like Martial's to construct not only schools but factories. Indeed, several mayors brought proposals for projects such as restoring maritime ports and building food processing plants that would not only help meet the domestic need for food but also begin food exports of tropical produce, such as mangoes and avocados.

Rural development projects of this nature are fraught with contradictions that can undermine their success. Local established interests in Haiti often see the ambitious members of the diaspora who come home to build both industries, social status, and a political constituency as a threat, and so can sabotage the development projects. In addition, many past projects have foundered because transmigrants were more interested in boosting their personal prestige than in promoting economic development. The differences between those in Haiti and the diaspora are especially apparent in actual projects that involve joint participation. The article on Tiburon, written by a Haitian transmigrant who was a *New York Times* reporter, pointedly raised these issues. The headline read: "In Haiti, Not All Gifts Well Received: Émigrés Help Keep Homeland Afloat, but Loyalty Is Questioned." But even as these issues are debated, the question of the actual power or sovereignty of the Haitian state is obscured.

The Haitian government has encouraged the efforts of hometown associations, although no financial or technical support has been forthcoming. Such local efforts fit well with the World Bank/USAID agenda that stresses "decentralization." Decentralization is a political program to remove power from the central government and capital city, and develop democratic institutions in the countryside, giving decision-making authority to local mayors. The question still remains as to how much political power there is in Haiti to centralize or disperse. Nowhere in these projects is the power of the handful of Haitian families who control most of the wealth of Haiti and the support for their position from the U.S. government ever addressed.

If these projects are successful, they could undercut the broader national identification that transmigrants have with Haiti. Political and economic energies could be channeled into particular locales in Haiti. This has yet to happen. Because of the strong identification of Haitians in Haiti and abroad with the two-hundred-year-old project of building a strong and independent Haiti, local development projects are often explained and justified as aspects of the rebuilding of Haiti. Haitian transmigrants have not seen their local identities as separate from or antagonistic to the identification with Haiti.

Even those who work around the state do it with a view that government is corrupt, rather than from an acknowledgment of the apparent state or in an effort to defy the state system. They are seeking less of an alternative development than a way to get around the current regime. Their language remains nationalist. They see themselves as part of a transnational body politic and they, too, participate in the language of rebuilding a strong democratic Haiti. Their vision is not local but national. Their critique is of the regime and not the "regime of truth" that constrains all visions of global encroachment of capitalism into state systems.[58]

If the experiences of constructing transnational social fields has created a new politics, there are still aspects of this politics that maintain or reinforce previous political assumptions. New terrains of struggle have developed. At the same time, those who are engaged in long-distance nation-state–building projects and act as transnational citizens still think and act in ways that limit their abilities to speak to the issues of justice, equality, and equity that their struggles have raised. This is because despite their transnational experiences, most Haitians still think of both Haiti and the United States as sovereign and autonomous. At particular moments, egregious acts of intervention—the U.S./UN occupation, or USAID and World Bank policies that continue to support corrupt and repressive regimes—have been vociferously critiqued by specific Haitian organizations and mass mobilizations.

This critique, however, has never been transformed into a politics that recognizes the interpenetration of the two countries. Without this, it is difficult to address the structure of class inequality that exists within both the United States and Haiti, and to analyze the ways in which the Haitian elite's wealth is sustained through its connections to the United States. It is equally difficult to understand that financial institutions and U.S. policies affect every aspect of daily life in Haiti. As long-distance nationalists debate the role of the diaspora in Haiti and their rights to dual citizenship, the actual powerlessness of the Haitian government recedes from view.

The Haitian experience of the apparent state should raise questions about the meaning of democracy and citizenship that are relevant for all of us, no matter what our country of citizenship. To the extent that increasing numbers of states have less control over the institutions and finances that affect their citizens, what is the meaning of democracy? If political leaders must respond to external agendas that meet the interests of global financial institutions and the more powerful states in which they are based, how can citizens have any control over their economy and polity? If transborder citizens of countries such as Haiti find that the power to control their state's destiny lies in the centers of capital in which global financial institutions and corporations are based, such as the United States, then a new form of politics develops in which political battles about the future of countries around the world take place in the core capitalist countries. Nevertheless, with the growth of organizations such as the WTO that have the power to supersede decisions made by citizenries in states around the globe, and with the development of direct corporate investment in the coffers of political parties and candidates in the capitalist centers such as the United States, Germany, and Japan, we may have to face up to the fact that all states will share the fate of Haiti. They are or will become apparent states with decisions made outside of democratic processes and the reach of the majority of the citizenry. The states will have the power to police individuals, not corporate and financial wealth and power. We will return to this question in our final chapter. First, we take a closer look at the political directions and class interests contained within long-distance nationalism. Long-distance nationalism can serve to shore up the illusion of sovereignty of apparent states. It can also contribute to global movements to challenge the global alignment of power that underlies the current state system.

10

Long-Distance Nationalism as a Debate: Shared Symbols and Disparate Messages

I called into the radio station and they invited me to come speak. Rolande doesn't see why I bother. But the announcer went on and on about the benefits of privatization. How, if the telephone company and the electricity company are sold to international corporations, we will finally have good services in Haiti and the country will advance. They made it look like anyone who opposed these plans was against rebuilding Haiti. And they broadcast these shows in Haiti so that people get the message that the diaspora, who are experienced in these things, all support privatization. But if you listen to the people calling in, then you see that there is not agreement, there is debate. And everyone speaks in the name of the nation.

Although they use the same metaphors of blood and nation, those who are disempowered sustain a vision of a different future for Haiti than the Haitian elite and political classes who control substantial wealth and influence in Haiti. The disempowered, who make up the disparate vast majority of the population, utilize a nationalist ideology to critique oppression and legitimate struggles against it. Yet in so doing, they find themselves in a terrain of multiple meanings and ambiguous messages that simultaneously facilitate and inhibit their ability actually to build a sustained movement to change their world. The situation is less one of polyvocality—the cacophony of many voices—than the use of a single message to mean contradictory things.

It is important to look in more depth at the ways the poor, women, sectors of the Haitian diaspora, and others who are disempowered, employ public debates around issues that affect the nation as a means of articulating their own political agenda. They are able to do this because the core symbols and key words of nation are "extremely volatile, liable to manipulation and misprision in equal measure."[1] Because it also continues to employ the volatility and ambiguity of the language of nation, long-distance nationalism contains multiple political agendas, including one that opposes all forms of oppression.

Throughout this book, we have examined both the shared rhetoric of nation and its different meanings. We have argued that family networks, which extend across time and space, are sanctioned with a language of blood that connects people with diverse experiences to the nation. Yet underneath the shared ideology of nationalism, the diverse experiences of class and gender lend differential meanings to the common nationalist rhetoric. The experience of migration and dispersal adds further complexities to the differentiation that underlies the metaphors of community and nation. Large-scale emigration from Haiti is creating new lines of social and economic differentiation. Those who survive on remittances have greater resources than those who receive no assistance from family abroad. The diaspora differs from the population in Haiti, and is itself divided by the vast differences in income, education, and lifestyle that separate business people, professionals, white-collar workers, and service and domestic workers.[2] Nonetheless, because all these differences, antagonisms, and jealousies coexist with a shared devotion to the Haitian nation, struggle between those with very different interests and perspectives is contained within an ongoing discussion of the fate of the Haitian nation. All sides contend using a common vocabulary of family obligation, blood ties, and loyalty to the nation.[3]

A Running Commentary on Oppression

Nationalist discourse is not the only instance in Haiti or other locations in the Caribbean of the widespread utilization of core cultural symbols as "floating signifiers." In Caribbean cultures, which developed in the context of the extreme oppression of chattel slavery, African people have developed

forms of speaking that made ambiguity and the signaling of multiple contradictory meanings by a single work or phrase into an art form.[4]

This broader cultural practice has been shaped in Haiti by the two-
hundred-year experience of oppression in which all Haitians struggled
against the domination of more powerful states, while the Haitian poor
contended with exploitation by the dominant class. Our interviews were
filled with folk sayings, whose meanings and politics, like the Kreyòl language in which they were stated, always must be understood in context.
Standing on their own, a myriad of folk sayings seem to endorse selfish behavior or see injustice and exploitation as inevitable parts of a social order.
One hears, "If you give you must be stupid; if you don't take you must be
an imbecile" (*Se sòt ki bay; enbesil ki pa pran*); "The donkey works so that the
horse can run around" (*Bourik travay pou chwal galonnen*); "What the poor
say has no worth; the stupidities of the rich are considered wisdom" (*Sa
malere di pa janm gen valè; betiz gwo nèg se bon pawòl*).[5] We were told repeatedly, "Each firefly lights its own lamp" (*Chak koukouy klere pou je li*). This
particular saying seems to endorse individualism, including selfishness, expressing the wisdom of a resource-poor society in which everyone has to
look out for her- or himself. Rolande's godchild, Murielle, living in Haiti
on the tiny salary of a cashier, provided us with an evaluation of the political
leaders that began with this folk saying.

> "Each firefly lights its own lamp." . . . They are patriots of the pocket
> [*patri pòch*]. Through that many people will suffer. We have the right
> to demand that the government provide work. . . . [They] could cre-
> ate work, paved roads, pave all the streets everywhere, build sew-
> ers. . . . The problem is that they don't [do it]. There is too much
> dirt, we inhale too much dirt when we walk around. I would like
> jobs for everybody, and for Haiti to be luxurious, and for all the un-
> employed people to find jobs so they will not kill people, hold up
> people, take what they possess. For everyone to be able to live so that
> all people will have a life. I for one am not living. I do not have a life.
> I would like Haiti to be like any foreign country, but I know it will
> never be like one. Because there is no unity. I would like to see a bet-
> ter Haiti. For Haiti to become more beautiful, to have all the
> streets paved.

When made by Murielle, the observation that each firefly looks after its
own affairs becomes a reproach not an endorsement of selfishness and op-

portunism. Murielle's longing for a "better Haiti" is based on a vision in which life improves for "everyone." She uses the folk wisdom that sees individual pursuit of wealth as natural—not to justify such behavior but to critique it. She describes the greed of the political leaders by using the phrase "patriots of the pocket"—drawing the line between the true patriot who sacrifices for the common good and the behavior of the political leadership. As in many other instances in which folk sayings describe the behavior of the rich, by taking note of this behavior, she implies another set of values without verbalizing them. These alternative values, ever-present even when unvoiced, critique the rich and invoke a more collective, egalitarian vision. This vision is not one of absolute equality but of mutual support between those who have and those who have not, coupled with a redistribution of resources. As we have seen, to speak about the relationships between hierarchy and communality, people told us, "You have your five fingers; they are not of the same height."

Lourdes, Yvette's niece, who is living on remittances, took the occasion of talking to Nina to echo Murielle's critique of selfishness, but to direct her criticism toward the diaspora. Again, the endorsement of individual self-interest is followed by an evaluation of current behavior that contains within it assumptions about other possible forms of political action. As Lourdes maintained, "'Each firefly lights its own lamp.' That is the situation we are living in now. Everybody sees their own interest. [The diaspora] . . . can help their relatives, but they can't put their heads together to help Haiti. If they could have done it, they would have done it by now and Haiti would have changed by now. They promise to do this and to help, but deep down it is not true. They are just patriots of the pocket."

Taken as a national dialogue conducted through folk sayings, the discussions by the poor of the current situation in Haiti contain an alternative nationalist agenda and vision for a future Haiti. According to this viewpoint, only when Haitians unite to achieve both social justice and collective prosperity will Haiti's promise and heritage be realized. In asserting this, we want to emphasize that there is certainly no single unified "view from below."[6] Neither the poor, nor men and women, nor rural or urban people, nor the diaspora maintain only one viewpoint or see the world through a single lens. Dominant and alternative meanings and messages interpenetrate and alternate in the perspective of various disempowered and disparate sectors of a transnational Haiti. Nonetheless, there is an alternative and coherent perspective that is available, accessible, and accessed in the context of the continuing exploitative conditions that make up the daily life of the majority of Haiti's people. This alternative perspective is known, and it shapes the practices of transborder citizens and the political life of the Haitian diaspora. Most clearly voiced in the songs, slogans, and speeches of the grassroots movement in Haiti, this alternative viewpoint also pervades the interviews we did among the poor in Port-au-Prince and Aux Cayes.

At first glance, it seems extraordinary that despite two hundred years in which Haitian leaders have consistently betrayed the goal of building a nation where there is equality between all people, Haitians should continue to maintain this ideal. Yet, as we have shown in our examination of survival through grapiyaj, and as other careful and unromanticized ethnographies of the Haitian rural, urban poor, and Haitian migrants have documented, many people face daily decisions in which they must choose between collective and individualistic values. Collective work groups, household arrangements, extended family households, and neighborhood activities are aspects of many Haitians' life experiences, and contribute vitality to a social vision that merges one's individual fate into a broader collectivity.[7]

The transnational grassroots movement fostered by the Catholic Church has served as a locus and catalyst for articulating an alternative agenda within a discourse of God and nation. In speaking of this movement as a flood of the oppressed, Aristide was able to bring together peasants, soldiers, and the urban poor into a movement of change and vindication led by the Lord.

> Alone we are weak.
> Together we are strong.
> Together we are the flood.
> Let the flood descend, the flood of
> Poor peasants and poor soldiers,
> The flood of the poor jobless multitudes (and poor soldiers),
> Of poor workers (and poor soldiers) and
> The church of the poor, which we call the children of God!
> Let the flood descend!
> And then God will descend and put down the mighty
>   and send them away,
> And he will rise up the lowly and place them on high.[8]

Using rhetoric such as this, Aristide was able to voice the aspirations of the poor and clothe them in nationalist idioms. He invoked God and employed biblical prophecy to validate the nationalism of the poor. Typical of Aristide's mix of religion and nationalism is his statement that "the church of the poor is under the protection of the flag of liberation theology, which cannot be disconnected in Haiti from the nationalist courage that manifests itself in actions, good actions, and in the organization that brings those actions to pass. So let us sing the national anthem."[9]

In church sermons, and at religious meetings, demonstrations, and retreats, Haitian priests and grassroots leaders place the language of the Haitian national anthem, the "Dessalinienne," in the context of building a "church of the poor." Here, the national anthem, named after Haitian revolutionary leader Dessalines, becomes a hidden transcript that speaks to the oppressed. The lyrics, which call on people to remember their ancestors and dedicate themselves to the country as the "sole masters of the soil," can express a social agenda in which the mighty are removed from power and the poor will take the matter in their hands to "end corruption," end "insecurity in the streets," win justice, "bring down the enemies of the people, Duvalierists, Macoutes, criminals," feed the people, and provide education.[10]

Dual Nationality or Dual Citizenship

One of the areas of fissure behind the common language of love of nation and demands on the state is sharp disagreement about whether all who share Haitian nationality should have legal rights to citizenship. In chapter 6, we noted that Haitian transmigrants and the persons in Haiti with whom they share transnational social fields are forming a transborder citizenry. They participate in the political process of both Haiti and the United States, and in so doing, forge new concepts of what it means to be a member of a state. In that discussion, we looked at this dual participation in terms of what people are actually doing, putting aside for further consideration whether they had a legal right to be citizens of two or more countries. We observed that the practices of transborder citizenship have developed despite the fact that Haiti does not allow dual citizenship, and the United States both disallows and allows it, since the courts have overturned all aspects of the citizenship laws that bar dual citizenship.

Underlying the debate in Haiti over dual citizenship are conflicting interests and perspectives that divide the diaspora from those in Haiti, notwithstanding a shared rhetoric of long-distance nationalism that defines all persons of Haitian descent as part of the nation. Transmigrants living in the

United States have been actively organizing for dual citizenship. Those who have joined in this effort come to it out of several different kinds of transmigrant experiences. Members of the diaspora argue that Haitian citizenship rights would allow them to travel to Haiti without paying the twenty-five U.S. dollars required of all noncitizens. They also feel that since they are asked to support the country financially, they should have the right to participate in political decision making by electing local officials, the national Parliament, and the president. Those with aspirations for leadership want the possibility of serving as government ministers or elected representatives in Haiti. Aristide had, in fact, promised to institute dual citizenship. Technically, to make such a law possible, the Haitian Constitution would have to be amended. But when Aristide abolished the army without constitutional authority, the diaspora also pressed him to institute dual citizenship, despite its prohibition by the Constitution.

Within the territory of Haiti, however, opinion is divided about whether Haitians who have become citizens of other countries should be allowed to remain Haitian citizens with the right to vote and hold office. Those who oppose dual citizenship offer different arguments depending on their social and political position in Haiti. People who stayed in Haiti and have some level of education and training have seen the diaspora as competition for scarce jobs. This influences their views about whether members of the diaspora should be granted dual citizenship. Jerome, a mechanic, one of the minority of people who have full-time employment, expressed the fears of many. He put forward the case not in terms of what was good for him but what was good for Haiti: "I cannot envision something like that being good for Haiti. They [the diaspora] could have helped, but they came in, they got the jobs, they got the positions, they were well placed, yet they did not do anything. . . . They all come to enrich themselves."

Because the state continues to be seen as one of the few sources of employment or avenues to wealth, granting citizenship rights to the diaspora is perceived as increasing their ability to compete for government jobs and opportunities provided by public office. It is not just the urban professionals or elite who fear such competition. They have allies among people in the provinces who are upwardly mobile and use remittances to raise the social positions of their families. Even women such as Rose, with a husband in the United States and aspirations to migrate so that her children can be educated in the United States, worry about the competition for government employment if the diaspora wins dual citizenship. She told us, "I am against it [dual citizenship]. Since they changed their nationality, they can't occupy high office. . . . They shouldn't be able to take those jobs [because] Haitians need those jobs to live."

As so many of the people in Haiti who argued against dual citizenship, Rose made it clear that she accepted the diaspora as part of Haiti. She was a long-distance nationalist. To justify her stance, though, Rose joined with those who distinguished between nationality and citizenship. For Rose, "Even if s/he doesn't speak Kreyòl, s/he is always Haitian." She did not claim that the diaspora could not understand Haiti. In fact, she remarked that "if the problems are explained, the diaspora can understand." And she believed that not only Haitian emigrants who settled abroad and became naturalized U.S. citizens but also the children of these emigrants who became naturalized as Americans remained Haitian, because "if they are born of Haitians, they are Haitians. They are made out of Haitian blood."

Many other people we spoke to, however, especially the poor who struggled for the state to understand and respond to their misery, were against extending citizenship rights because they felt that those who lived abroad were even less likely to respond to the demands of the poor. This was the view of Mary-Jo, a former factory worker who had five children to support and a husband who only found occasional work as a truck driver. "The person who should be elected president should know the miseries of the masses. When you tell her/him you are hungry, s/he will know that hunger is something that burns right through you. Then s/he will be able to do something. But if you tell her/him I am hungry so give me five gourdes [U.S. 33¢ (and s/he is a person from the diaspora)], the person may say no, whereas you are dying of hunger."

Many of these people saw in the efforts to grant the diaspora citizenship just a further extension of the invitation to profit from government office that made the state a source of personal profit rather than public good. According to Lourdes, Yvette's niece, "Maybe there are some who may work well, who understand, but there are many also who will just come to defend their business, their money. They come here to make tons of money."

The debate in Haiti around dual citizenship convinces Haitians that they do continue to have a sovereign state. No matter what side they take in the debate, persons who become engaged in it make the assumption that the Haitian government can make decisions that affect the shape of the Haitian economy and can take on the responsibility of creating a democratic, prosperous Haiti. States have the power to determine who has citizenship rights by birth, who is able to become naturalized, and who is an alien. The debate also contributes to a widespread consensus that Haiti shares a transnational nation, as well as a state. As poor people in Haiti oppose citizenship rights because the diaspora may not understand their obligations to the impoverished majority, struggling to survive, they reaffirm that those settled abroad do continue to have obligations and so remain part of Haiti. At the very same time, as poor people question the contributions of the diaspora to Haiti, they give voice to a very different agenda for their nation. As a young activist in Aux Cayes stressed: "To see something different in Haiti, people must stop exploiting the masses, the leaders must stop thinking that they can exploit the masses [*gwoup defavorize-yo*], everybody must have the opportunity to feed themselves."

Privatization and the Repackaging of Globalization as Part of Long-Distance Nationalism

The different agendas and visions of the world contained within Haitian nationalism cannot be reduced to a division between haves and have-nots within Haiti, or between those in Haiti and the diaspora. Georges heard a resonance to his own nationalism in the voices of some of the poor, illiterate people we interviewed. He found other of our interviewees using the same nationalist rhetoric, but taking from the unity of self and nation only the message of self-advancement. To explore and highlight the complexity of the crosscutting divisions that underlie the shared nationalist rhetoric of "rebuilding Haiti"—a rhetoric invigorated and nurtured along by the recent development of long-distance nationalism—we explored the ways in which people of all classes, both in Haiti and the diaspora, were approaching the proposal to privatize all of Haiti's national industries as well as most government services. To privatize state-owned enterprises means to sell industries such as the telephone and electric companies as well as the state university to private investors who make the best offer, whether these investors are local capitalists or international conglomerates.

In these debates, the Haitian government, which came to power under the mantle of the Lavalas movement, and vocal members of the diaspora have been using nationalist rhetoric to undermine the concept of the responsible state and the demand of the Haitian poor that, as Murielle put it, "the government provide work" and a better Haiti. Others in Haiti and abroad have used the call to rebuild Haiti to critique privatization. In both cases, sharply different political visions undergird the common language of nationalism, whether in its more traditional territorially based version or its emergent long-distance guise.

The debate over privatization in Haiti reflects Haiti's relationship to the United States and to global financial institutions such as the World Bank and other institutions of finance capitalism. Privatization is only one piece of a philosophy of development labeled by economists as "neoliberalism" to identify its ideological lineage with ideas about free markets and free trade that first emerged with the initial triumphs of British capitalism in the eighteenth century. According to neoliberals, in the age of global capitalism, states should abandon their efforts to develop national economies through regulations, tariffs, and protection. They should also abandon their attempts to address issues of social inequality within their nation. Development will instead come to countries all around the world if states implement policies that allow for the free flow of capital. Such policies include the elimination of protective tariffs, so that goods from multinational corporations can be readily imported into all countries. Rather than try to feed their own populations or develop national industries to produce for national needs, economically weak states are told to devalue their currencies in order to make the prices of their products—which are mostly raw materials and crops raised for export—cheaper on the world market. Neoliberal wisdom also advocates creating a proinvestment environment via low wages to entice foreign investors to establish industries.

In states such as Haiti that were already in debt, the neoliberal policies never took the form of good advice, but rather a list of demands that accompanied the loans offered to keep the governments afloat. These demands have their own neoliberal language. They are called "structural adjustment policies." Privatization is often one of the key demands of structural adjustment policies, and this has been the case in Haiti.

As we have seen, the poor and middle class in Haiti attributed much of the difficulties of their life circumstances—the high cost of food, the reduction in the already low level of government services, the lack of employment and a living wage—to the corruption of their political leaders. They spoke of the failure of the state to be responsible to the people without linking that failure to the constraints imposed by foreign governments and the international financial establishment. When this lending establishment continued to demand that Haiti's state-owned telephone and electric companies be sold to private investors, however, a debate over privatization ensued. This debate has been articulated within a rhetoric of nationalism. No matter what their social or geographic position, whether the speaker looked down on Port-au-Prince from a villa in the hills of Haiti or sat in a Brooklyn barber-shop, all sides defended their point of view in terms of their love of Haiti. We found that the struggle for more equitable distribution of resources and so-cial justice continued to be present as a hidden transcript, encapsulated within this discussion about whether privatization would be good for Haiti and encoded in the polysemous rhetoric of nationalism.

We should also note that Haitian support for privatization adds a twist to the neoliberal agenda. As this agenda becomes absorbed within Haitian nationalist rhetoric and placed by Haitian transborder citizens within their own understanding of the role of the state, it becomes fundamentally al-tered. Even people who were convinced that Haiti should sell its public holdings to corporations did not abandon the idea that the state should be both responsible and accountable to the people. This means that Haitians uphold, for example, government regulation of corporations at a time when the free market ideologues are trying to remove government regula-tions. Typical of the Haitian version of neoliberalism were the comments of a lawyer, trained in the United States yet living in Haiti, who told us, "There must be some regulation also, but it must be more open."

When we were in Haiti in 1996, the television and airwaves were filled with a campaign to sell privatization to the Haitian people. Some of the dismantling of state enterprises had already taken place. There had been some disquiet about the selling of the public cement and flour companies. But it was the electric and phone companies that were the real money-making enterprises, and public debate centered on these two industries. The government alleged that selling these industries to private interests would bring more jobs, improved services, and a better Haiti. When vari-ous forces mobilized political opposition to privatization, the government used different words to present the same economic agenda by utilizing a discourse of "modernization." The government set up a Commission on the Modernization of Public Enterprises, equating the selling of public re-sources to private corporations with the building of a modern Haiti. Popu-larizing the agenda imposed by international banks, government officials purported that selling the telephone and electric companies to private in-vestors, even if they were foreign corporations, was a critical step in ending Haiti's backwardness and poverty.

Our interviews revealed that poor people also learned about privatization from grassroots neighborhood organizations, political parties,
churches, and schools. Many people, however, told us that they felt they
had not been given enough information to make an intelligent choice.
Given the very real political pressure to go along with the government's
program, and the fact that we were strangers, it is likely that the statements
about a lack of information were a form of dissent. As we listened to the debate and questions raised about privatization, we found we were given another glimpse at the different political agendas that underlie the steady reit-
eration of nationalist themes.

We discovered that there was some support for privatization and some
opposition among all classes, but for different reasons. The situation was
not straightforward. You could not simply say that wealthy businesspeople
were for privatization and poor people were against it, or that the diaspora
supported privatization and persons in Haiti were opposed to it. Some
prominent members of the Haitian elite, who have been able to channel the
profits of Haitian state-owned businesses into their own pockets through
government corruption, emerged as aggressive critics of the plans to sell the
electric and phone companies to private corporations. Some of the poor
and many of the rich have been able to obtain services without paying the
state-owned companies. As Robert White, a former U.S. ambassador to El
Salvador and head of the Center for International Policy in Washington,
D.C., pointed out, "The electric company's ten biggest corporate cus-
tomers do not even pay the company for electric service, let alone pay taxes
on earnings."[11] Such people have formed a militantly nationalist opposition to the agenda of the World Bank. Often staunch and public supporters
of dictatorship as the solution to Haiti's problems, they have relentlessly
ridiculed the elected leadership for not representing the interests of the
Haitian people. On the other hand, other members of the Haitian bourgeoisie saw business opportunities from privatization and the possibility of
an even more luxurious lifestyle.

Persons living in the United States have tended to be for privatization.
Better telephone service would mean easier contact with Haiti. The dedica-
tion of so many Haitian immigrants to maintaining their family ties and
obligations made them an ally of the forces pushing for selling the phone
company. The commitment of those abroad to ease the life of family in
Haiti, as well as the constant pressure for status and social recognition back
home, also played a role in convincing many in the diaspora to support sell-

ing the electric company. Without adequate electricity, Rolande can provide her parent's house in Aux Cayes with a refrigerator and fan, but they usually don't work. Yvette can send a stereo tape player with high-powered speakers and a color television to her nieces, yet the constant blackouts in Port-au-Prince limit the entertainment value of the glossy electronic equipment.

So Rolande, trying to assist her aging parents, could find herself supporting plans for Haiti made by international bankers. And Yvette, struggling to maintain her self-esteem within a U.S. racial climate that demeans her blackness, could become an ally of multinational corporations and the World Bank as she tries to improve her social status by acting as the benefactor of her large network of kin in Haiti. Some Haitian transmigrants have clearly and publicly taken this position. Fritz Martial, the founder of a long-standing AM radio program in the New York metropolitan area, whom we met in the last chapter raising money for his hometown in Haiti, has typified the voice of those in the diaspora who have endorsed a program of selling state companies to private interests. As Martial argued, "Forget about ideology, we live in a global capitalist system and we must go along. Private profit is what makes the world work. Look at the United States. If there is electricity and telephones in the United States, and if there are roads and huge buildings made of concrete, this is because these industries have all developed through the pursuit of private profit. It is private profit that makes the country strong." For Martial, who was well established in the United States, privatization becomes a way to further the plans of the Tiburon hometown association to turn a rural hamlet into a thriving metropolis.[12]

As neoliberal ideology has become more entrenched within the foreign aid policies of the United States, many in the business and professional strata of the diaspora have served as a chorus that reproduces and disseminates the "wisdom" that health, education, sanitation, water, transportation, road construction, and communication, as well as services to the poor, should all be provided by either nongovernment charitable institutions or private for-profit businesses. Some members of the diaspora have also become the agents of this foreign policy, working directly for or with U.S. lending agencies and foreign aid providers to preach that development in Haiti should be privatized, while others have become part of corporations and businesses interested in selling services to Haiti. Impressed with the availability and efficiency of electric utilities and telephonic communications in the United States, these people accept the equation that as large corporations profit from Haiti, they will provide more employment and also develop Haiti. They do not address the probability that the fact that the sale of public resources at bargain-basement prices has provided windfall profits for international corporations in Latin American countries and that any improved services these corporations subsequently provided were beyond the reach of most of the people in these countries.

Many of those supporting or actively working for the privatization of Haiti merge their desire for personal gain with nationalism. All of the Haitian businesspeople we spoke with had lived abroad and returned to Haiti to begin various enterprises or to work in family businesses. Transmigrant businesspeople in Haiti who find their businesses hampered by the lack of basic services may support privatization by cloaking their pragmatism in a concern for the nation. They tended to equate privatization with the opportunity for transmigrants to invest in businesses in Haiti and the reconstruction of the Haitian nation. One young man, who had spent part of his youth in the United States, gone to college there, and then served in the army, remarked: "The diaspora really wants it, because they see an opportunity for them to invest, for them to help Haiti. . . . [P]rivatization is good."

Businesspeople in Haiti need reliable electricity and additional phone networks to expand their business enterprises. For decades, Port-au-Prince and all other localities that have electricity have faced severe blackouts. Electric services have been routinely unavailable for much of the day in the capital and often completely absent in small cities like Aux Cayes. The rural areas in Haiti have yet to be electrified. Many business people don't see the capital for development coming from inside Haiti and feel that although they would rather get a piece of the action from this immensely profitable business, they would be better-off with an "imported solution" than continued government ownership. Milo at various times had run factories that assembled garments for U.S. corporations using cheap Haitian labor, and had also imported new and used clothing to sell in Haiti. He explained his position, "If you need imported money, then you're going to have to go through some of the imported solutions. . . . It's a very tricky thing and I don't know if we have the upper hand to deal with it the way we should, or if it is going to be forced down our throat or whatever. This is the answer that I don't have, but . . . the time has come for Haiti to make a deal. . . . [L]ong term, it looks good."

Many people who had not lived abroad, had steady employment in Haiti, and could pay for a phone, but were unable to obtain one, accepted privatization as well. This position was also sometimes taken by people who lived on remittances and felt that family abroad would pay the bills. They needed the electricity to fuel the expanded lifestyle that remittances made possible and a phone to remain in communication with kin abroad. A person with a secure remittance income told us that the phones "need to be privatized. I applied for a phone and still don't have one. People all over are waiting for phones. Unless I go to a friend on top, I won't get it." Yet most of those in Haiti who supported privatization for reasons of personal convenience and comfort, justified their position in nationalistic terms. An employed mechanic maintained, "I think that it is good for the country. First of all, the country has no roads. It has no schools, it has no telephone, electricity. From the perspective of its infrastructure, the country has zero. There is no potable water. It is only in the first class that you can say they have these things and the low class has nothing. [After privatization] . . . if I apply for a telephone, I will get a telephone. If I make an application for electricity, I will get it. I will have good schools for my children. And if I have a trade, I will be able to work. Therefore, it will be good for the country. The government must privatize."

Most of the people who supported privatization believed that both telephone and electric services would actually become more expensive if they were privately owned. They still argued that this type of "modernization" would be good for Haiti, however. In this case, the equation of self, family, and nation allows those who speak in the voice of the nation to discount the needs of the majority of the Haitian population, whose daily income is considerably below any commonly accepted standards of poverty. One woman whose husband was a government employee, and who herself ran a small dress shop, claimed that "God never closes a door without opening a window. If it becomes more expensive, God will show them [the poor] a way to pay for it."

Poor people without remittance income and even some who were supported from abroad saw the question differently. If the utility companies were private, while services might be better, prices would be higher, and the various arrangements that poor neighborhoods had made to obtain access to phones and electricity would be disrupted. Poor people did not own telephones, but they knew that this lack did not separate them from most middle-income people. Phone lines in Haiti are hard to get unless you know someone who has political influence and can arrange a line for you as a form of patronage. Those who did have phones tended to share them. By making their phone lines available to neighbors, those with telephones increased their social standing in their neighborhood and reduced the jealousy of neighbors. Access to a phone was necessary to contact family members who resided in the diaspora. Many expressed the fear that if privatization were to occur so that phone service was readily available to those who could pay, there would be increased pressure on everyone to have their own telephone, and those without money to purchase the service would be left entirely without access. Lourdes, Yvette's niece who lives on remittances from abroad, responded by saying, "[Privatization] won't be good for us Haitians. When they privatize, the person now will say no, I can't let you use the phone because it is privatized so now you can get your own. But we won't have money to get a phone because we are not working, we are a bunch of unemployed people. What are we going to do? So we won't go at all [to get access to a phone]. Many times we have problems at night and have to use someone's telephone to call. When we need to call our relatives abroad, we won't be able to do it."

The most adamant opposition to privatization on the part of the urban poor was addressed to the plans to transfer the electric company from public to private hands. Poor urban men and women felt that the plan to sell the inefficient state-owned electric company would literally push them into the dark ages. For them, the politicians' use of the word "modernization" to describe the selling of the state electric company was a bitter joke. Most people in those locations obtained electricity illegally, a practice called taking *priz* (tapping the line), paying only the person who illegally connected them to an electric line. Privatization would end the practice of tapping the lines of the electric company. Some tapped into a neighboring household's line, paying something for the service, but less than the going rate. Many of those who received electricity legally subsidized the expense by selling priz to other residents who do not have the means to pay for a legal connection. As many asserted, "We have a little priz. I get it from someone else and I give them 10 gourdes [U.S. 66¢] a month."

One of the many ways of living by your wits in Haiti was to perform this service for your neighbors, and we interviewed people who made a living by jury-rigging the power lines that crisscrossed their neighborhood. These services are offered to the residents of their shantytowns for a connection charge and monthly fee to maintain the connection in place. On average, a family pays U.S.$1.70 for the initial connection and a similar sum per month for maintenance. Often the priz taken provided only enough wattage for a single lightbulb, but some also ran a radio, an iron, or even a small black-and-white television. For those who had no job, education, or skill, privatization threatened to disrupt a lifestyle that allowed them access to some of the amenities of life they would not otherwise enjoy. And since most of the urban poor would be unable to afford the rate the companies would charge for their services, they would also be deprived of electricity altogether. As for the rural poor, they lived without electricity, and persons who looked beyond the label of modernization could see that a private company would not make any profits by extending electricity to rural people who could not pay the bills.

Like those in other classes, many of the poor who spoke against privatization did so in terms of the nation. Bienaime, who lives by grapiyaj and has little education, told us, "Privatization would be good for outsiders [the diaspora], for the whites, for the foreigners who are coming to amass their fortune. . . . And if they [the current government] can't defend the nation's interests, we are going to mobilize because they [the diaspora, whites, foreigners] come to enjoy Dessalines's land. . . . The reason it has reached this point is because we are not united as a nation. . . . If they don't want to give us consideration, and we decide to take to the streets, it will be bad for whites. . . . A nationalist is a person who loves their country, someone who loves their nation. That is what defines a nationalist."[13] Although he can barely keep himself going physically, Bienaime is politically alive. He actively participates in a neighborhood organization that meets to make small improvements in an area that has neither sewers, streets, nor water.

There is a sector of people among the poor, students, and professionals in Haiti and the diaspora who had been involved with political organizing and used their nationalism directly to challenge the hegemony of global capitalism. The people we spoke with in this group were aware that similar debates over privatization had taken place in other countries and saw the efforts to impose a neoliberal agenda as part of a worldwide struggle. A young secretary who works at the university and had attended workshops on privatization argued, Privatization will not help the country develop, but the state is doing it anyway and there has not been any public debate. People have not been informed. Those who are looking for ways to inform themselves can attend seminars, read books, listen to the news. . . . You will know what privatization did to the other countries and you will know what it is. But there has not been a national debate among the masses of the people. In all the countries that embrace privatization, I don't see a brighter future for them. During the first three or five years of privatization, you may see some improvement, you will see some activities taking place, but that won't mean anything. On the contrary, things will get worse."

Standing in an open-air garage of a minidevelopment project that trained impoverished young men to be auto mechanics, Larco, one of the project's leaders, reminded us: "I don't say no, I don't say yes [to privatization] because the real problem is not there. The real problem is not whether to privatize or not. The problem is in the relationship that should exist between two countries and two people. Privatization is just a detail, bullshit. It is a distorted mirror. It is something that they want you to be preoccupied with while they are dealing with other business that exploits countries around the world."

Beyond the Debate: The Continuing Struggles for Equality

Underlying the privatization debate, which is waged within the shared national narrative, is another debate, one that is more fundamental than whether or not to sell a few badly administered industries. The debate interpenetrates, but goes far beyond the issues of privatization. It is a debate about the meaning of the Haitian nation and its future. The concern to build a strong and prosperous Haiti seems to unite all Haitians and fuels long-distance nationalism. But as we listened, it was clear that although they speak of shared blood and ancestors, of nostalgia for the past and hopes for the future, Haitians with very different lifeways have extremely different views of the direction in which Haiti should develop. As is so often the case in Haiti, and in so many other locations around the world where populations survived slavery and centuries of political repression, one has to look at double meanings and constantly be aware of the alternative messages that underlie statements of the obvious. There are, nevertheless, alternative narratives, and the one voiced by the grassroots movement is both widely known and compelling. It stands rooted in the love of nation and yet also stands with global movements for social justice.

Despite their poverty, many of the poor and unemployed people we interviewed were not isolated from recent global social movements of women, workers, and all poor and oppressed people. The grassroots movements in Haiti in the 1980s and 1990s foreshadowed the protest that became visible globally in Seattle, Washington, at the end of the millennium, when people assembled from around the world to challenge the WTO and its neoliberal agenda. Haitian transnational connections provide links not only between families but to organizations and social movements that build a collective vision of social justice as well.[14] We found some people from all classes in Haiti influenced by global movements, although sometimes the evidence presented to us took the form of a shared rhetoric rather than a public acknowledgment of organizational connections. And since under the government of the generals who had ousted Aristide, people were beaten, raped, tortured, and murdered for their participation in organizations that advocated social justice, we did not specifically ask.[15] But repeatedly, as we listened to the responses that people gave to our questions about long-distance nationalism, an alternative vision emerged. Many impoverished people feel they have equal rights to be human beings, and as such, to claim prosperity, security of mind and body, and dignity. And they claim these rights in the name of all oppressed people.

The sources of their vision are multiple, and there is not a single, clearly organized set of ideas or a single leadership. The entire Haitian landscape is filled with billboards that advertise not products, but the projects of international organizations working in Haiti with the stated goal of improving the lives of the poor. While most of these projects provide only token improvement, the promise of a brighter future remains tangible for impoverished people in Haiti. Development projects make it obvious that the poor of Haiti live within a world where others live well and prosper. The particular others that most have in mind are people in the United States.

The movement within the Catholic Church that preaches a theology of liberation has had a profound impact on Haiti and among poor Haitians in the United States. Because he used the electoral process to propel himself into the Haitian presidency, Aristide became the most prominent member of this movement, but he was only one priest among many. While several of the most dynamic priests who emerged from this movement have been murdered, and the Catholic Church itself has done much to derail the power of this movement, the movement continues. It has schooled hundreds of thousands of people in the struggle for social justice in Haiti and among the Haitian diaspora. Haitian women and men arose as lay leaders, as well as nuns and priests, and many continue their efforts.

Haitian transmigrant women are also serving as leaders in the struggle to forge an alternative agenda for Haiti, one that places the fight to reshape the Haitian nation within worldwide movements against corporate globalization. Their presence is felt both within the church-led grassroots movement as well as in the multitude of transnational organizations dedicated to the empowerment of the poor and oppressed.[16] These women build on their life experiences in Haiti and abroad to embrace long-distance nationalism, but imbue it with a commitment to resist all forms of injustice. Meanwhile, in the United States, their day-to-day experiences with barriers of race give Haitian men and women of all classes who settle there reasons to respond to calls to end oppression. They carry their opposition to racism into their long-distance nationalism.

Poor people in Haiti have historically used a narrative of nation, and now use long-distance nationalism, simultaneously to mask and express a politics that opposes those who dominate and exploit them. The alternative political goals contained within long-distance nationalism are strengthened by the continual changes in the composition of the Haitian diaspora as Haitians experienced in the struggle for social justice migrate to the United States. Individuals, shaped by the struggle in the Haitian countryside, who find themselves in the United States, with a telephone and perhaps even Internet connections, are vocal in pressing for a different future for Haiti. A view-from-below form of nationalism—a subaltern nationalism that reflects the experience of poor and rural people, yet influences the understanding of the nation of people of other classes—has emerged within a transnational Haiti.[17] This counterhegemonic politics resonates with the Haitians' quotidian encounters with racism and sexism. It is a "grassroots" politics growing up outside and in opposition to the formal political leadership and their ideologies, even as it is framed within the same nationalist discourse.

II

The Other Side of the Two-Way Street:
Long-Distance Nationalism as
a Subaltern Agenda

I just can't understand why you don't feel an emotional tie to your homeland. I can't stop loving Haiti, no matter how bad things get and no matter what the leaders do. Haiti is me. No matter what the government does, I am still Haitian. No matter where I live and how hard I work to educate my students at Stony Brook to be responsible (American) citizens, I love Haiti.

Throughout our researching and writing, we struggled over our different views of nationalism. Nina was uncomfortable with Georges's nationalism when we began this book. Whenever we discussed nationalism, it was as if we were talking past each other. As Nina explained to Georges:

Nationalism has made me uncomfortable for a long time. I was very patriotic as a child. I participated in our neighborhood Memorial Day and Fourth of July parades. I loved the marching band and uniforms. And I scolded my parents for not having an American flag to decorate our house on appropriate occasions. I also felt very loyal to Israel and read every history of Israel I could find in our local public library. The library only supplied Zionist histories, which justified taking the land from the Palestinians. Then, during the war in Vietnam, I began to re-

ject devotion to country as an excuse to destroy the people and environment of an-
other nation. One day, standing ironing my clothes, I watched a televised speech
by an Israeli diplomat. In the most elegant English, he claimed Israel had the
right to annex the West Bank, although it made Palestinians virtual prisoners
in their own land. And something clicked. Nationalism, whether it was U.S. or
Zionist, localized or long-distance, became for me only a justification for the ex-
termination of people who were culturally different.

Up until that moment, I had felt myself to be part of both the U.S. and Jewish
people. Suddenly, I felt like a stranger in my own land and a stranger among
my own people because I didn't support what was being done in my name. Al-
though I have to admit that to say I repudiate genocidal actions done in my
name is to continue some sense of connection and responsibility. After all, I get
more upset about the U.S. bombing of Iraq or the Israeli settlements on the West
Bank than I did when England went to war with Argentina about the Malvi-
nas Islands.

Georges would counter:

Last month, I was stopped by the police again and given a ticket for speeding. These
things affect you. When the police officer stopped me, I thought, "Look at every-
thing I have achieved and yet because I am black, I will always be seen as some-
thing lower, something other than a full American." I went to court to set up a
date to protest the ticket. After all, I have my rights. The prosecutor looked at the
ticket and said: "Are you kidding me? Are you serious? I have never seen anything
like this in my life. I know that area well, and people drive over fifty-five miles an
hour and they don't get stopped. And you got a ticket for going forty-one miles an
hour in a thirty-mile-an-hour zone. Why did he stop you? Do you drive a flashy

car? Were you the only car on the road?" "No," I said, "there were many other cars on the road going faster than me and I have a black Toyota Corolla."

This was not a private conversation. There was a courtroom full of people listening to me. As the prosecutor was talking, I was saying to myself, "Didn't you ever hear of DWB [driving while black]?" but I didn't say it out loud. I adopted a meek demeanor, and he told me I should challenge the ticket. "Go home, man, don't think about it. You have more important things to worry about and this is ridiculous." But driving home I thought again, "Where is home? How can I stay in this country for the rest of my life? I have to return home to Haiti."

As we put the book together, we began to recognize why Georges continued to feel more intimately tied to a particular national identity, and why Nina could afford to feel estranged from both the United States and her Jewish roots. Although we were both speaking in English and using universally accepted understandings of the concept of nation and nationalism, we were actually talking about two extremely different kinds of experiences. We had distinct relationships to the nation-state in which we were born. At the heart of the matter were the questions of race and power.

Because of the position of black people in the United States and because Haiti is a black nation, Georges finds he is always on the defensive. He must present the evidence of his life accomplishments—the support he has provided for his family, his ability to speak French as well as Kreyòl, and his advanced degrees. It is as if the world has put him on trial, and with him, Haiti. The struggles of Haiti as a black nation to achieve honor and respect from the world of nation-states was part of his struggle to claim his humanity. When Georges responds to claims of kin and country that extend across international territorial borders, he does so as part of his effort to assert that Haiti is a nation worthy of respect in the eyes of the world, and that he, therefore, is an equal member of the human race.

Nina does not feel confronted by the court of world public opinion. She doesn't find herself under constant surveillance in a situation where the verdict on her being human is not yet in.

Usually, I don't think about my whiteness, but in the course of writing this book, I began to realize that I take for granted that I will be thought of as human, civilized, and capable of the highest cultural achievements. If I am not, it is because of my gender. But any problems I might have faced getting an education or employment, or when a university administrator disregards my efforts or a store clerk keeps me waiting, I don't see it as a slight to a whole race or people.

Nina's taken-for-granted sense of accomplishment and capability gives her a sense of empowerment that allows her to reach out to those who are not white from a position of privilege and patronage.[1] She has begun to realize that she can perpetuate the inequality by her unthinking acceptance of her racialization as white.

It was different for my parents. They grew up at a time when Jews in the United States were seen as racially different from white Americans, so while they weren't seen as black, they also were not seen as completely white, completely American. There were neighborhoods, they told me, where there were signs posted that said, "No Jews or dogs allowed." So their core identity linked them to other Jews and then to Israel. To defend Jews and Israel was a statement about their own humanity. At the same time, they saw the barriers to Jewish advancement in the United States diminish after World War II. Because the United States treated Jews better than other countries did, they identified with the United States. Furthermore, as part of their efforts to become incorporated into the U.S. mainstream, they moved into the white suburbs, and began to accept and enjoy the privileges of whiteness.

While I was brought up with these privileges, however, I never learned to judge the U.S. government through the lens of what was good for the Jews. Growing up in that white suburb, I assumed I was white, Jewish, and fully American. But the Jewish part of my identity was shaped by the fact that I grew up near

Bronxville, New York, where Jews were not allowed to buy houses and by the knowledge that my one of my brothers worked as a caddy in a local golf club that did not allow Jewish members. Perhaps beginning with that experience, for many years he felt that he could not be Jewish and white. Until recently, he did not publicly acknowledge to neighbors and medical colleagues that he is Jewish.[2]

Our ruminations about our life experiences with race and nation helped us understand the continuing pull of long-distance nationalism when migrants settle in the United States and are not fully accepted into the nation. It also allowed us to see another aspect of Nina's dislike of nationalism. In rejecting nationalism, she had been trying to distance herself from the normality of whiteness in the United States. For Nina to identify as simply "American" means to embrace a concept of belonging that accepts her unequal and better treatment from police, employers, and landlords on the basis of a white identity. If Nina identifies as an American, she adopts this whiteness and thus claims an identity that legitimates racial inequality.[3]

White citizens of the United States as well as western European countries with histories of slavery and colonialism face a dilemma in trying to find, within their own nationalism, an agenda for social and economic justice such as that voiced by the disempowered in Haiti. That is because the national identities of the United States and western European countries are deeply imbricated with concepts of white superiority. To identify with those nations is to accept the line drawn between white Christian civilization and the barbarism of all others.

Haitian nationalism presents a dramatic contrast. The Haitian sense of nation, embedded in the nostalgia for things past and the perpetuation of historical memory, is an expression of the struggle for Haitian equality in the world of nations. Haitian long-distance nationalists seek to restore the glory of Haiti so that Haiti and all Haitians can obtain respect, dignity, and justice in the world of nation-states. Haitian nationalism provides a wellspring for building a state that will stand with the poor and oppressed.

It is more difficult for Nina to find within U.S. nationalism a call for dignity and justice for all peoples or to discover in the U.S. experiences of government a long-standing tradition of the responsible state. Still, she has also come to realize that Haitian transborder citizens have found that there is much to build on in the U.S. experience, if one is struggling for a more just world. Concepts of empowering the poor, collectively struggling against racism and the oppression of women and gays, and demanding that the power of the state stand on the side of the people are all to be found within the U.S. experience. Many of these concepts, and the laws that turn them into daily U.S. political practices, are the result of fierce struggles in which migrants played an important role. We are only beginning to appreciate these contributions as part of a transnational migrant history. Nineteenth- and twentieth-century migrants fused their long-distance nationalism and identification with workers worldwide into struggles for political and economic rights that people in the United States sometimes claim as uniquely "American."[4]

Nina has not learned from this project that she should be a U.S. nationalist. But she has ascertained, as a result of this research, that long-distance nationalism may contain within it aspirations and agendas that contribute to global struggles for human dignity. We are not concluding our book with an endorsement of nationalism or long-distance nationalism in and of itself. It all depends.

Long-Distance Nationalism and the Shell Game of Migration

Stand on the sidewalks of New York City and you see a man with a folding table taking bets on a shell game. Where is the hidden object? You place your money and take your choice. His hands move the coverings with speed. "The hand is quicker than the eye," he says, "now you see it and now you don't." A crowd gathers, and someone steps forward and bets. Here is easy money. With a flourish, the man lifts the cover—and the object that should have been underneath it is gone.

To some degree, for many people who emigrate from their homeland in search of a better life, life becomes a shell game. While there are certainly those such as Georges's mother, Nanie, who have convinced themselves that they have won the game, in spite of the frustrations they may feel and indignities they face, many others feel as Georges does. Wherever these people happen to be, they tend to think that they have made the wrong choice. Happiness lies back home, but what is meant by home changes. If they are in the United States, then transmigrants may see home as the land of their ancestors. If they return to that land—whether to visit or resettle—

the home they dream of may again be abroad. The shell game of migration as a route to solving problems that flow from global contexts of inequality is an old one. Migrants throughout the generations have insisted that their stay is temporary, and as each new difficulty has confronted them, thought that perhaps the time had come to return home.[5] It is participation in this shared illusion that in some ways ties together those in the homeland and those abroad.

We began this book with Georges's dream of a dear, sweet Haiti that never existed because we believe that nostalgia is the knot that ties together the disparate threads of the aspirations of men and women, young, and old, first and second generation who identify themselves as members of the Haitian nation-state. We also have shown that an identification with the nation of Haiti can be shared by people who are settled in the territories of different nation-states, and are separated not only by geography but also by legal citizenship, class, gender, generation, language, and culture. Young people in Haiti, Haitian youth in the United States, and Georges all project a nostalgia for the past glory of their homeland. Nostalgia is a key ingredient in most nationalisms, and it has become part of the nationalism of Haitians, wherever they are living.

In the course of this book, we have tried to give voice to the dreams that contribute to and sustain the construction of a transnational homeland as well as explore the economic and political contradictions that underlie such dreaming. Nostalgia can serve as a form of amnesia that not only obliterates painful memories but makes it difficult to comprehend current realities. We saw that Haitian transmigrants and those left behind share between them a dream of a better life. It is this shared vision that builds for them a national identity in a transnational space, and provides the hopes and expectations that serve to connect their daily life to political projects that are the domain of nation-states. They share the act of dreaming and they call this dream Haiti, but in some ways their dreams are quite different.

People in Haiti, people facing a daily struggle to survive, see migration to the United States as a solution to all their problems. They believe that in the United States, they will have money, employment, security, housing, and education. They see the United States as a modern country, and count among the apparatuses of modernity not only modern conveniences but also democracy, justice, and the rule of law. There will be a government that follows the Constitution, and protects and provides for the people. Migration will be the solution to their problems, not just by offering them a better life but by allowing them to contribute to building a beautiful, sweet Haiti, and restoring to Haiti its pride and dignity among the nations of the world. Migration is seen as the solution for the individual, the family, and for Haiti.

At the same time, like Georges and Yvette, many Haitian migrants react to the stresses and strains of daily life in the United States by imagining that the solution to their problems is to return to Haiti. They don't find equal protection under the law. The rights that they have are often only obtained through community struggles. And while the United States may lend money for community development and civil society activities in Haiti, Haitians living in the United States find that the U.S. government is increasingly refusing to take any responsibility for poverty, low wages, hunger, and the lack of medical care or housing within U.S. borders.

From Shell Game to Empowerment

In certain ways, nostalgia for a past remembered as a time of righteousness, justice, and self-respect, a golden age that needs to be recovered, can be empowering. Nostalgia can generate "an energizing impulse, maybe even a form of knowledge. The effort to revalue what has been lost can . . . cast a powerful light on the present. Visions of the good society can come from recollections and reconstructions of the past, not only from fantasies of the future."[6] We discovered within the nostalgia that binds together Haitian long-distance nationalists aspirations for a world in which people can live without fear, gain the resources to live a life of dignity and respect, and be treated like human beings. And that there was a widespread belief that a responsible state is necessary to make this possible.

Acting on these beliefs, Haitian long-distance nationalists make claims on more than one state and see themselves as members of each of the states in which they participate. In so doing, they contest the notion of citizenship as a legal status and one that ties persons to one political system. They also challenge the belief that political systems are confined within the territorial boundaries of states. Long-distance nationalism, while it may build on nostalgia and emotion, is translated into political action in relationship to state institutions. Therefore, wherever Haitian long-distance nationalists think they belong, and however they identify, as transborder citizens they actually participate in *both* the Haitian and U.S. political systems. Their participation in the United States includes demonstrating, lobbying, suing for rights in courts of law, running for office, owning businesses, working to improve public institutions from schools to hospitals, joining and leading unions, and working for and speaking to U.S.–based media. Through all these means they help mold public opinion in the United States, contributing to the debates about globalization and the relationship between people and government. Georges in front of his several hundred students is part of a much broader phenomenon of transborder citizenship being enacted by long-distance nationalists from all over the world who live and work in the United States.

At the same time, long-distance nationalists participate in Haiti. They fund political candidates, hometown projects, and nongovernmental organizations, returning to Haiti as visitors, tourists, government consultants, employees, businesspeople, and educators, owning or working for Haitian transnational media, and of course, providing their families with financial support and information about the world outside Haiti. Through all these means they help mold public opinion in Haiti, too, contributing to the debates about globalization and the relationship between people and government. In exercising their membership in two political systems that are formally independent although integrally linked, long-distance nationalists contribute to new understandings of politics and new forms of political struggle in both locations.

Empowerment for Whom?

While we can speak of the entire body of Haitian long-distance nationalists as a single transborder citizenry, to do so is to lose sight of the divergent political paths that the experience of transborder citizenship is fostering. These paths lead in two opposite directions, although the oppositionality within long-distance nationalism is difficult to recognize and is complicated by the fact that they are both located on the same road under the signpost of nationalism. Nonetheless, we maintain that these two opposite directions can be identified, even though the road is not well marked, and there are many crosscutting intersections and overlapping positions. If the routes of the two opposing paths are traced, it becomes clear that they are distinctive, leading in different directions for Haiti and people around the world.

To even suggest that there are choices to be made from among different political directions puts us at odds with recent academic fashions that have celebrated the complexity and cacophony of cultural history and politics.[7] We have certainly built on the insights of a postmodern scholarship that reveals the polyphony of voices and perspectives contained within all cultural symbols and political narratives. On the other hand, in the face of the growing disparity of wealth and power throughout the world—a disparity played out in the grim figures of increasing infant mortality, malnutrition, shortened life spans, and mothers' deaths from childbirth in Haiti—we feel that to not search out a new political direction and advocate for it is itself a political position, and an unacceptable one. We believe it is imperative that we speak about alternatives and make choices.

In this book, we have argued that the nationalist rhetoric of any nation-state contains within it multiple messages and we have spoken of these messages as alternatives, focusing on nationalism as a debate. We have seen that there are different meanings within the shared rhetoric of long-distance nationalism because people experience their nationalism through the filters of gender, class, color, and legal citizenship. Yet we also found that underneath the multiplicity of meanings were two dramatically different political agendas and visions of the future. We learned from the disempowered in Haiti and the diaspora, from women, and from the poor that there are clear alternative directions within the rhetoric of Haitian long-distance nationalism, and that in one of those alternatives, there is the beginning of a path to a future that we can both embrace. An alternative politics for the restructured global economy can be found within the "recesses of national culture from which alternative constituencies of peoples and oppositional analytical capacities may emerge."[8]

If followed in one direction, long-distance nationalism can lead Haitian transmigrants to the broader neoliberal project of restructuring nation-states to serve global financial interests. In this project, nation-states persist within the global economy, fostered in many cases by long-distance nationalism, but their governmental structures are transformed so that they function as organizational tools of powerful transnational corporations and financial conglomerates.[9] States serve only as a means of protecting the holdings and rights of global corporations and their functioning. On the neoliberal side of the street, global capitalists support government policies that use long-distance nationalism to facilitate the workings of long-distance capitalism. They have been hell-bent on restructuring the global economy to maximize their opportunities to extract profits without regard to human or environmental costs. Their goal is not to eliminate states but restructure them to expedite the movement and operation of global capital. Transborder citizens who move in this direction serve as contributors to and spokespeople for these neoliberal states. If such states have large emigrant populations, the life possibilities of both those who emigrate and those who stay at home will remain seriously constricted by the burden that emigrants must carry. They face lives encumbered not only by the necessity of supporting themselves and their family in the new land but also by their obligations to family left behind and their homeland. Long-distance nationalists will continue to carry and justify this heavy transmigrant burden, while government resources are used to facilitate the operations of transnational capital. The contributions of transmigrants and nongovernmental organizations will increasingly replace state-sponsored development.

The road of long-distance nationalism offers another direction, however. It is a two-way street. Traveling on the same route, yet in a different direction, are a disparate cluster of people who have in common their subordination and disempowerment in relation to global capitalists. We summarize their position with the word "subaltern," a term that emphasizes the commonality of the disempowered. Subalterns share a position of subordination, but are situated in more than one class. In Haiti, they are rural cultivators with different amounts of land, town and urban people living by grapiyaj, factory workers, and those with some education struggling to keep self and family afloat. As women and men, rural and urban, uneducated and educated, they bring to their politics multiple "situated knowledges" and identities.[10] In the current conjuncture of globalization, however, subalterns share a certain positioning in respect to the global operation of capital. They find themselves increasingly unprotected from its ravages, and many are beginning to look for answers.

The message that emerged from Haiti's slave revolts, as well as from its rural and urban poor, is a clarion call to live in a world that allows all people to "live like human beings." To be human means having access to the resources to live a decent life. To be human means that people can adequately feed, shelter, and educate themselves and their children, that they can be spared the pain and suffering of curable diseases, and that they have security of person and personal property. That all people should be seen as equal means that they have a right to live in a system that makes it possible for all people to obtain all these things from their hard work. But all that is not enough, as Georges has come to realize. To live like human beings, we all need honor and respect. "Honor, Respect" is the way people in the Haitian countryside have traditionally greeted each other. Poor Haitians have understood the essentials of being human for a long time.

We are not, of course, saying that all poor people agree with each other or share a common set of political goals. In Haiti, as elsewhere, poverty brings with it jealousy of family and neighbors, anger, and desperate acts.[11] We have tried to highlight the tensions and bitterness that exist within transnational family networks, between men and women, between the diaspora and those they "left behind." At the same time, in a profound way, the majority of people we interviewed communicated through their love of Haiti a common set of commitments that we have called a subaltern "agenda"—an agenda of the disempowered. This agenda focuses on the demand to be treated as human beings.

And this demand is often voiced in relationship to the state. Those whose long-distance nationalism sets them in the direction of a subaltern agenda expect state structures in emigrant-sending countries and centers of financial, political, and military power such as the United States to serve the people. They call on states to protect their citizens from exploitation and oppression by being agents of responsibility within a global economy. In this version of state practices, the institutions of many states, organized to work in concert, could globally regulate, control, and redirect the actions of transnational corporations. States would become instruments of social responsibility.

Haitian long distance nationalists as transborder citizens can make contributions to the transnational struggles to fashion states that are instruments of public interests rather than private capital. They can infuse into politics at every level demands for a responsible state. In so doing, they build on the concept of citizenship and states that they have forged through the grassroots struggles for justice and rights, as well as against police brutality and discrimination in Haiti and the United States.

We conclude this book by sketching the elements of this alternative that we see emerging within Haitian transnational social fields, and the relationship between subaltern long-distance nationalism and other transnational social movements. Subaltern long-distance nationalism recognizes that people can move in a common direction from their own and disparate cultural and political roots. This form of nationalism is sustained by a pride in national differences, yet without resort to concepts of hierarchy of gender or nation.[12] That is to say, people are brought into political action through a collective identity that claims not superiority but equality. Subaltern long-distance nationalism is a political movement that extends beyond the borders of individual nation-states, but does not stand in opposition to states as instruments of political organization and power.

This alternative path is one that provides a global perspective. It can take from the transnational experiences of migrants an understanding of the current realities of life in the United States that would go beyond the shiny visions of the American dream currently being marketed by media around the world. It would allow people living in apparent states, such as Haiti, to better confront the source of the problems they face. A subaltern agenda would not limit political critique to the corruption of leaders and channel all dreams of a better life into the hope of migration. The transnational experiences of migrants can provide us all with a better idea of how the world is actually organized, allowing us to see beyond a model of the formal world system of independent states, and to confront the transformations being imposed on all these states by global corporations and financial institutions.

To organize the world differently and more justly than it is today, government remains a necessity, but governments must be rooted in local understandings and traditions. This does not mean, however, that persons need to make their demands on only one government. Haitian long-distance nationalists—whether they identify as Haitian, American, Canadian, or French—are active participants in more than one state and make their demands on more than one state. They offer all of us a workable model of citizenship in a transborder world. Their demands for responsible states contribute to the struggle of the poor and disempowered for responsible governments everywhere. The subaltern long-distance nationalism being developed by a section of Haitian transborder national citizens provides a broad vision of the world and the place of each nation-state within it.

Subaltern long-distance nationalism is intimately connected to other transnational social movements and grassroots uprisings, such as those that have taken place Chiapas, Mexico, and many other places where people have struggled for popular democracy and made demands on the state. It connects with the many other ways in which disempowered people are currently organizing to obtain social and economic justice. In the United States, a subaltern agenda often is voiced within demands for respect. When he leaves his university classroom to teach literacy classes to African American adults in Harlem, Georges hears the demand to be treated as a human being—an important theme among black youth in the United States.[13]

As a political activist in Cincinnati, Ohio, Nina heard the same call for a world where people could be fully human among white and black women on welfare, black women hospital workers, and trade union activists, black and white, men and women, who walked the picket lines. She heard it again when she worked as an ethnographer among the homeless in New York City and people with AIDS in New Jersey. She also often heard the desire for social and economic justice articulated as a demand for respect. Subalterns struggle to live as human beings by making states responsible for the well-being of their people.

The political agendas of subaltern populations translated into contemporary long-distance nationalisms represent a crucial component of global movements for social and economic equity and justice. Long-distance nationalism is not necessarily contradictory to revolutionary internationalism, or to ideologies of indigenous rights, women's rights, and human rights, or to the movement to protect the environment. These ideologies all have proved capable of motivating struggles that voice the aspirations of the "wretched of the earth."[14]

At first, the environmentalist movement, the international women's movement, and organizations for indigenous rights that became prominent at the end of the twentieth century seemed to stand apart from making demands on states. Some observers of these new social movements saw them as signs of a globalization from below that embraced the links between the local and global by repudiating all nationalisms. Noting that these social movements crossed state borders, scholars at first assumed that this form of globalization from below rendered nation-states and nationalisms obsolete. Social movements were portrayed as "nongovernmental," a form of civil society that defied the territorial boundaries of states. In contrast, the nation-state seemed to be a project of elites without resonance among the poor, women, and indigenous people. Nationalism was something that was used in various ways to disempower them.

The situation is proving itself to be much more complex.[15] A subaltern agenda can take on many guises so that territorially based and long-distance nationalism, local organizations formed to obtain rights and benefits from nation-states, and transnational social movements may be different means of obtaining the same ends. Taking up the agenda of the poor, subaltern movements are making demands on states for the regulation of corporate

greed. When they find that states serve the interests of corporate and financial capital, transnational movements are organizing to challenge global
capitalists and their control of governments. Many participants within the
global mobilization against the WTO—which brings together labor unions,
environmentalists, the international women's movement, religious leaders
committed to variations of liberation theology, and indigenous organizations—project responsible states as a means of regulating and dismantling
global capitalist forces. This global mobilization also demonstrates that
multitudes of people from around the world have developed a political program that resonates with subaltern long-distance nationalism.

As in the case of these other movements, subaltern long-distance nationalists don't rely on formal electoral processes. The expansion of transnational capital into political fund-raising makes it clear that electoral processes are structured to produce the best candidates money can buy. In
apparent states, electoral processes are penetrated not only by transnational
capital but also by the direct intervention of other governments. Consequently, in apparent states and states that are central to the global economy,
leaders elected legally and officially may have no relationship to the struggles of the vast majority of the people they claim to represent.

We understand that any alternative path is difficult to envision, much
less follow, and the situation around the world looks grim. There are certainly more questions than answers. Can any political movement gain
sufficient power to reverse the growing gap between rich and poor that has
resulted from the worldwide campaigns of structural adjustment and privatization? How do we counter the efforts of politicians to take up the rhetoric of social movements and use it in the service of corporate profits?[16]
How can we do anything to prevent genocidal wars waged in the name of
the superiority of one nation over another? We suggest that it is important
to look within nationalist rhetoric to find the motivations that can point
people around the world in an alternative direction and the sources for
global movements for empowerment. Our research has explored the possibilities that lie within long-distance nationalism. We have seen that people
as well as capital are transnational, extending into the domain of many
states. Within transnational movements for global justice, long-distance
nationalists are in a position to contribute to the struggle against the power
of transnational capital.

This means that transmigrants living in the United States whose nationalism embraces an agenda for social justice can make a significant contribu-

tion to any effort to develop an alternative politics to the one being offered by neoliberalism. They are essential allies of everyone who desires to set the world on an alternate path. Transmigrants located in key centers of capital such as the United States can provide networks that extend around the world. As long-distance nationalists, they can add to the grassroots movements for equity and justice. If this happens around the world, then the possibility of change becomes more than the sum of its parts. Long-distance nationalists become an important link to globally restructure the world in a very different way than the structural adjustment of the neoliberal agenda. On the other side of the street, people struggle for a world that makes human dignity possible.

While our mutual encounters in this book with each other and the people we interviewed in Haiti led us to ruminate about our roots and appreciate our differences, this was not and did not become the purpose of our project. Rather, our joint research and this book have been an effort to understand more clearly how the two of us are able to share a politics and identify with each other across the divides of gender, race, and nationality, and despite the fact that Georges sees the world through the filter of Haitian long-distance nationalism and Nina through a form of internationalism. Our hope has been that in finding the roots of our mutual sympathy, we might contribute to a global reconstitution of the world so that it is possible for all people to meet their basic human needs and to live lives of dignity and respect.

Notes

1 "At First I Was Laughing"

1 The notion of social fields has been used both in British social anthropology and by Pierre Bourdieu and those who built on his theory of social practice. See Barnes 1954 and 1979; and Bourdieu and Wacquant 1992. With its focus on human interaction and situations of social relationship, the concept of social fields facilitates an analysis of the processes by which international migrants become incorporated into a new state and maintain ongoing social relationships with persons in the sending state. Whether the relationships are egalitarian or exploitative, and whether they are with co-ethnics or others in the new society, is a matter of empirical investigation (see, for example, Basch, Glick Schiller, and Szanton Blanc 1994; and Glick Schiller and Fouron 1999).

2 For a sensitive account of situations in which Haitian immigrants in the United States cut their ties, see Richman 1992b.

3 Historically, in Haiti, people were more familiar with the term *patriotism* than *nationalism*. Those who used both words terms tended to see patriotism as devotion to country and nationalism as the struggle for the equality of Haiti in the world of nations. These distinctions have recently blurred, and so we speak of the contemporary Haitian transnational identification with Haiti as nationalism.

4 We adopted this term from Benedict Anderson 1993, 1994.

5 See Appadurai 1991; Featherstone, Lash, and Robertson 1995; Mittleman 1996c; and Soysal 1994.

6 See Appadurai 1993; and Canclini 1995.

7 The future of nation-states or even territorially based government has been debated recently by increasing numbers of scholars intent on spelling out the implications of globalizing processes. See Appadurai 1993; Camilleri and Falk 1992; and Mittleman 1996a, 1996b.

8   Such comments are reported in Haitian newspapers as well as on news programs on Haitian radio and television in Haiti.

9   Recent scholarship on whiteness traces the processes by which immigrants to the United States—first from Ireland, and then from southern and eastern Europe—were originally racialized as different from the dominant white culture, but over time were able to claim whiteness. See Brodkin 1998; Ignatiev 1996; Jacobson 1998; and Roediger 1991.

10   We have argued for a transnational perspective on migration in a series of earlier articles and books. See, for example, Glick Schiller and Fouron 1990; and the articles collected in Glick Schiller, Basch, and Blanc-Szanton 1992; and Basch, Glick Schiller, and Szanton Blanc 1994. See also Rouse 1991; and Kearney 1991.

11   Especially after World War I, Jewish hometown associations became "the chief benefactors of their less fortunate brothers and sisters still in the Old World" (Soyer 1997, 9). Daniel Soyer (1997, 1–2) reports that in the 1930s, the Yiddish Writers Groups of the Federal Writers' Project estimated that New York City contained three thousand of these associations with over four hundred thousand members, which represented a quarter of the city's Jewish population. When family members and lapsed membership are added to the total, "the number of individuals . . . connected directly or indirectly with a landsmannschaft may well be as high as one million."

12   See Bourne 1916; Warne [1913] 1990; and Roberts [1912] 1990.

13   See Portes and Rumbaut 1996; and Schermerhorn 1949.

14   See Cinel 1982, 47; Wyman 1993; and Morawska 1987, 1989.

15   See Anderson 1994; Appadurai 1993; and Brubaker 1996.

16   It should be noted that the immigration at the end of the twentieth century was far less significant in its demographic impact on the United States than the mass migration at the beginning of the century. Because the U.S. population had become much larger in the intervening sixty years, the new immigration in the 1980s represented a much smaller part of the whole. Hence, the 1980s influx made up only 2.9 percent of the population, as compared to the earlier peak that contributed 9.6 percent to the growth of the U.S. population (DeSipio and de la Garza 1998).

17   See Lamm and Imhoff 1985; Brimelow 1995; and D'Souza 1996.

18   See Ridgeway 1994, 60.

19   See Stepick 1998, 29–30; Dewind 1987.

20   See Duany n.d., 52.

21   See Guarnizo 1997.

22   In 1998, the *New York Times* ran a series of articles on transnational migration featuring Dominican, Indian, and Mexican immigrants (see Sontag and Dugger 1998; Dugger 1998; and Sontag 1998). Evidence of transnational connections and long distance nationalism often appears in the wake of political scandal such as the uproar about Chinese immigrants who raised funds for the Democratic Party. See, for example, Gerth and Sanger 1998; and Gerth 1998. There is also periodic reporting of support by immigrants in the United States for projects in their homeland. For instance, the Irish were featured in a story by John O'Farrell: "Ireland Fund Donors See Results: U.S. Benefactors View Projects Charity Aided" (1999).

23   See Adamic 1941; DeConde 1992; Glick Schiller 1999a, 1999b; and Paul 1981.

24   See Glick 1975; Fouron 1985a, 1985b; Glick Schiller et al. [1987] 1992; Glick Schiller and
       Fouron 1990, 1998, 1999; and Fouron and Glick Schiller 1997.

25   During our research in Haiti in 1996, we were joined at various times by Rolande, Leah,
       and Karen, each with a very different relationship to Haiti and the United States. Their
       responses, questions, and experiences deepened the investigation and contributed to
       the sensibilities we bring to the writing of this book. Rolande, Georges's wife, was born
       and grew up in the same town in Haiti as her husband. She, too, has lived for thirty
       years in the United States, and obtained her associate degree in business and a bachelor's
       degree in hotel management. Leah, their daughter, was born in the United States yet
       speaks fluent Kreyòl, the language of Haiti, as well as unaccented English. Cynthia,
       Leah's law school roommate, is African American and had not previously been abroad.

26   Kreyòl, a language with both African and European roots, is a language spoken by all
       Haitians who grew up in Haiti. Some people refer to it as patois, as if it is not fully devel-
       oped, and contrast it to French, which was Haiti's sole official language until 1987. Most
       anthropological linguists, however, note that Kreyòl has its own grammatical rules and
       vocabulary, and see it as a distinct language. It is not a dialect of French because it is not
       completely comprehensible to persons who know only French. Today, although both
       French and Kreyòl are the official languages of Haiti, the majority of Haitians speak
       only Kreyòl and do not understand French. French remains the prestigious language
       used for most official functions and important transactions.

27   The individuals we interviewed were practicing a type of indirect criticism and dialogue
       called, in Haitian Kreyòl, *pwen* (barb). Pwen are often "thrown" through the use of
       songs that indirectly criticize an individual's actions (Richman 1992b). This practice of
       struggling with people, especially those who are more powerful or could take action
       against you, indirectly through song, the use of folk sayings, or by metaphor, is wide-
       spread in the areas of the Caribbean where Africans had been enslaved. See also Bur-
       ton 1997.

28   A sense of the daily pulse of Haitian life, including Haitian transnational spaces, can be
       found in Brown 1991. We have drawn on the glimpses of daily rural life documented in
       Woodson 1990; Richman 1992b; and Smith 2001. During 1985–1986, we were part of a
       research team that interviewed ninety-six Haitian leaders in New York and fifty U.S. or-
       ganizational representatives about questions of Haitian identity and culture in the
       United States (Glick Schiller et al. [1987] 1992). In 1995, Nina traveled to Haiti to inter-
       view fifteen government officials and intellectuals about the links between Haiti and
       Haitian living abroad. Studies of Haiti and Haitian immigration that have been of par-
       ticular use in our work include Averill 1997; Anglade 1986; Buchanan 1980; Bellegarde-
       Smith 1990; Charles 1990a, 1990b, 1992; Dupuy 1997, 1989; Laguerre 1998; Nicholls
       [1979] 1996; Stepick 1998; and Trouillot 1990.

29   The term "cousin" is used for persons of the same generation who have some family
       connection. Often, the exact genealogical link is not known by the speakers who use
       the word.

2   Long-Distance Nationalism Defined

1   These definitions are based on the approaches to nationalism found in Calhoun 1997; Gellner 1983; Hobsbawm 1990; Kedourie 1960; and McCrone 1998. All of these approaches link the concept of nationalism to territory. They differ from uses of the term in notions such as Black nationalism, Arab nationalism, or Hindu nationalism. Logically, it makes sense to differentiate identities based on common historical origins and shared racialization or religion—the substance of "Black Nationalism"—from political ideologies linked to efforts to form, claim, or defend territorially based polities. Political usage is often not logical, however. As will be seen, we define long-distance nationalism as the political ideology of a population connected to a particular territory and state, although all those who maintain this set of beliefs and related political practices do not reside within the borders of that particular state.

2   Philip Abrams argued that the concept of the state obscures the class structure and myriad of institutional arrangements through which power is held. He challenged the literature that saw the state as an object rather than an ongoing myth that obscures relationships of subordination ([1977] 1988). Building on the work of Corrigan and Sayer 1985, Gupta 1995, and Joseph and Nugent 1994, we illustrate the ways in which relationships of power that embody the state are embedded in daily transnational activities in chapters 8 and 9 below.

3   Political scientists often refer to this model of the political organization of the globe as the "Westphalian system" and assert that it began in Europe in 1648 (Krasner 1999, 20–25).

4   The political theory that envisions each person as able to have only one nation is rooted in racialized views of the nation as well as the legal system of states and citizenship. This system was formalized after World War I.

5   On one hand, one can argue that Germany's current policy of recognizing as German citizens some persons of German descent whose ancestors settled outside of Germany is a continuation of a conception of the German nation glorified by the Nazis. In 1936, for example, at an occasion honoring the forty-eight flags of the Nazi Auslands organization, Rudolf Hess stated that "the German everywhere is a German, whether he [sic] lives in the *Reich*, or in Japan, in France or in China, or anywhere else in the world. Not countries or continents, not climate or environment, but blood and race determine the world of ideas of the German" (cited in Kamenka 1976, 11). On the other hand, many states also have linked citizenship to descent, including Haiti. See Dikötter 1997; Cinel 1982; Wyman 1993; and Glick Schiller 1999a.

6   Basch, Glick Schiller, and Szanton Blanc 1994.

7   See Berube 1991, 1288; Basch, Glick Schiller, and Szanton Blanc 1994; and Appadurai 1993, 424.

8   See Joseph and Nugent 1994.

9   See Balibar 1991; and Calhoun 1997.

10   In approaching long-distance nationalism as both words and action, we build on Craig Calhoun's work: "There is nationalism as discourse: the production of cultural understandings and rhetoric which leads people around the world to think and frame their as-

pirations in terms of the idea of nation and national identity. . . . [T]here is (also) nationalism as project: social movements and state policies by which people attempt to advance the interests of collectivities they understand as nation" (1997, 6).

11   Pamela Grahm 1996 provides a description of the role of migrants in the complex political dynamics that preceded the decision on the part of the Dominican government to grant citizenship rights to Dominican emigrants and their children who are U.S. citizens.

12   In this usage, we differ from those who have created a scholarship of diaspora studies that groups disparate examples of dispersal of populations through all periods of history under the term diaspora, whether or not they are engaged in nation-state building (Cohen 1997). We find such an approach fuels the assumption that in a world of global connections, states are increasingly irrelevant. This assumption cannot, in our view, be substantiated.

13   See Greenberg 1999.

14   See Feldman-Bianco 1992.

15   See Gerth 1998. In past years, U.S. citizens have been accused of spying or lobbying for Korea and spying for Israel with a similar uproar. For the long-distance nationalism of Kosovar immigrants, see Sullivan 1998; and Stewart 1999. Some kinds of transnational military activity by U.S. citizens has come to be taken for granted or endorsed by the U.S. government, such as the Cuban militias in Florida or efforts throughout the twentieth century to raise money and arms for the liberation of Ireland.

16   See Anderson 1993, 1994.

17   For a review of the variations in the concepts of citizenship, see Shafir 1998. For the contradictory legal and social statuses of immigrants, see Bauböck 1994.

18   A classic delineation of the ways in which legal citizens of lower social classes may not have access to all rights is found in Marshall 1964. More recent scholarship links the exclusion of legal citizens from full access to rights to racialized and gendered concepts of who belongs to a nation. See, for example, Haney-Lopez 1996; Lowe 1996; Hamilton and Hamilton 1997; Lister 1997; and Yuval-Davis 1997.

19   See Trouillot 1990.

20   See Bauböck 1994.

21   Some transborder citizens identify with more than one nation-state. This is especially true in the second generation. We want to make it clear that not all persons embedded in transnational social fields who claim citizenship privileges or rights in more than one state act as transborder citizens motivated by long-distance nationalism. Aihwa Ong 1993 has identified a quite different and pragmatic stance to states, historically practiced by elite sectors of "overseas" Chinese, that she terms "flexible citizenship."

22   Our concept builds on Michel Laguerre's notion of diasporic citizens (1998) and Rainer Bauböck's discussion of transnational citizens (1994). We have chosen to use "transborder citizens" rather than transnational citizens because we found that while long-distance nationalists tend to identify with one nation, they act as members of more than one state. The term "diasporic citizenship" seemed problematic to us for two reasons. While Haitians do use the term "diaspora" for emigrants who still make claims on the government of their ancestral land, the word has generally encompassed dispersed pop-

ulations who may have a historic homeland but do not have a homeland government. In addition, we wish to be able to include in our terminology people within an emigrant-sending country who make claims on the states in which their emigrants have settled.

23   Countries vary in the ways they allocate legal citizenship, and some differentiate between legal citizenship and another form of belonging called "nationality." If one is a U.S. citizen, one is said to be a member of the U.S. nation, a "national" of the United States. No difference is drawn between the two statuses. Persons who become naturalized citizens are required to renounce allegiance to all foreign rulers. Because of this oath, many people think that dual citizenship is illegal in the United States, although that is not actually the case. If the legal systems of other states allow dual citizenship or nationality, U.S. citizens may possess some form of membership in other states, even if they are U.S. citizens by birth or naturalization (Harrington 1982, 104–9). In the United States, one obtains citizenship by being born on U.S. soil, being born elsewhere but of parents who are U.S. citizens, or by living in a U.S. territory for seven years and then taking on the legal status of citizenship through a process called "naturalization." All persons who are granted permission to settle rather than for short visits are eligible to apply for naturalization. Even without becoming a citizen, as a "permanent resident," they have some of the rights and duties of citizens, such as paying taxes. Nevertheless, they can't vote in state or national elections. In locations such as New York City, noncitizens have been able to vote in elections for certain local officials, such as school board members.

24   Mexican nationals who are also citizens of other countries can't vote or hold office; their claims to a continued relationship to the ancestral homeland are, however, validated. Dual nationality sometimes allows emigrants certain economic advantages, such as easier access to buying property or exemption from certain taxes imposed on persons who are neither citizens nor nationals. This is the case in India and the Philippines, as well as in Mexico.

25   In 1999, the front page of the *New York Times* highlighted the implications of transnational citizenship by reporting about the plans of Israelis settled in the United States to vote in the Israeli election. To vote they had to return to Israel. Deeply discounted flights to Israel were advertised "in Israeli newspapers distributed in the United States, on a Web site, and in fliers in Hebrew and English posted in Jewish neighborhoods in Brooklyn and Queens" (Nagourney 1999).

26   A distinction between Eastern and Western nationalism has been made by scholars such as Hans Kohn (1994, 162–65) and John Plamenatz (1976, 22–36). Ernest Gellner (1983) differentiated between types of nationalism in his various works. See also his typology of Hapsburg nationalism, unificatory nationalism, and diaspora nationalism (1994, 111–12). The Left has a venerable history of distinguishing between good and bad nationalisms as well. Karl Marx and Friedrich Engels noted the difference between the "historical nations" of Europe—such as England, France, Italy, Germany, Hungary, and Poland—that possessed the right of self-determination, and "nationalities"—such as the Welsh—that were relic "remnants of people long gone" and had no such rights (Engels [1866] 1974, 382–83). Vladimir Ilyich Lenin distinguished between the nationalism of

the "oppressed, dependent and subject nations and the oppressing, exploiting, and sovereign nations" ([1920] 1967, 22).

27 As Michael Herzfeld has pointed out, "Any ideology, no matter how consistent its formal expression, may produce radically divergent applications and interpretations (1992, 14). Here Victor Turner's approach to symbols as resources deployed by social actors is useful. He asserts that symbols are "semantically 'open.'" Their meaning is not absolutely fixed so that it is not necessary for the symbol to hold the same meaning "for everyone who agrees that a particular signifier (outward form) has symbolic meaning" (1985, 171). The term "discursive formation" is Michel Foucault's (1969), and has been applied to nationalism by Herzfeld (1997) and Katherine Verdery (1993, 37–46). Craig Calhoun (1997) has applied Foucault's term "discursive formation" to the ideology of nation.

28 See Scott 1990, 18–19.

29 Floating signifier refers to a complex linguistic situation in which the meaning of the term varies with context, speaker, and situation. Our description of nationalism as a floating signifier has been developed from Henry Louis Gates Jr.'s discussion of the process of "double voiced" signification through which a symbol is assigned meaning and then "decolonized" (1988, 50). Gates, in turn, has built on Ferdinand de Saussure's and Mikhail Bakhtin's work on signification. As Drexel Woodson has indicated, many words in Haitian Kreyòl are polysemous. They have meanings that "can only be defined precisely in particular sociolinguistic contexts, because they comprise various senses which employ different levels or ranges of semantic contrast, and because the semantic contrasts themselves presuppose familiarity with a series of finely graded distinctions among human physical and behavior characteristics which have become socially significant during the course of Haitian history" (1990, 219). It is therefore appropriate that the approach to nationalism we are advocating builds on research conducted in Kreyòl. Our understanding of hegemony is influenced by the writings of Antonio Gramsci (1971), Jean Comaroff and John Comaroff (1991), Stuart Hall (1988), and William Roseberry (1989).

30 Benedict Anderson has argued that "the dawn of nationalism is the dusk of religion" (1996, 11). David McCrone (1998, 113) critiques the tendency of scholars of nationalism to separate it from the study of religious beliefs and practices.

31 Ronald Takaki (1993, 1989) exemplifies a scholar who has fought to expand the understanding of U.S. history to incorporate the contributions of different cultures. For a feminist statement of the dilemma of locating struggles against the oppression of women within the framework of U.S. nationalism, see Jones 1998. Despite the fact that some gay and lesbian activists speak of "the queer nation," the focus of much of their struggle is for rights and recognition within the legal framework and nationalist ideology of a particular nation-state (see Herrell 1996; and Dominguez 1996).

32 See Appadurai 1993; and Kearney 1991.

33 See Fanon 1967.

34 Noël Sturgeon uses this concept to demonstrate that essentialism can be taken up as a weapon by oppressed people in their struggles (1999, 257). Sturgeon adopts this term from Tsing 1997.

3   Delivering the Commission

1   Kowalski 1992, 37. See also U.S. Department of State 1998, 1–2.
2   This U.S. government agency funds development projects in countries all around the world.

4   "Without Them, I Would Not Be Here"

1   In the early 1960s, Haitians could travel to francophone Canada and stay for up to two weeks without a visa.
2   U.S. Department of State 1998, 1–2.
3   The scholarly literature on Haiti uses the term "peasant" to refer to persons who do small-scale farming. The people we interviewed used the word "*kiltivatè*" (cultivator), and we have adopted their term for this book.
4   For an analysis of U.S. development policy in Haiti, see DeWind and Kinley 1988.
5   The National Labor Committee 1994, 136.
6   Central Intelligence Agency 2000, 7.
7   Ridgeway 1994, 4.
8   Haitian Kreyòl does not distinguish gender in its use of pronouns. To indicate the meaning of what was being said, we use s/he or him/her.

5   "The Blood Remains Haitian"

1   By 2000, many in Haiti had become disillusioned about the possibility that Haitians abroad will rebuild Haiti, and increased anger was directed at the diaspora and individuals from the diaspora returning to Haiti. Nonetheless, the diaspora continued to be seen as part of Haiti.
2   The term "color line" was used to describe the legal and informal racial barriers that divided whites and blacks in the United States until the 1960s. While water fountains, restaurants, theaters, and other public facilities are no longer segregated, black people still experience a color line in the sense that they are policed or given more intense surveillance than whites when they enter certain neighborhoods or stores. In 1999, the New Jersey highway patrol was questioned for their use of training manuals with racial profiling that led officers to search the cars of black drivers much more often than those of whites (Peterson 1999).
3   See Dikötter 1997; Herzfeld 1992; and Balibar 1991.
4   Immigration and Naturalization Service 1996.
5   Between 1971 and 1981, more than 45,000 Haitians arrived by boat (Silk 1986, 16). Most of these people were held in detention camps, despite the fact that they had fled from a brutal dictatorship. Although relatively few Haitians have ever been able to obtain official refugee status, many who fled by boat eventually gained permanent resident status through a legal amnesty program passed by Congress in 1986. Beginning in 1981, however, the United States Coast Guard began intercepting Haitian boats on the high seas, destroying the vessels and returning Haitian refugees to Haiti. Because the Duva-

lier dictatorship granted permission for the interceptions, these acts were deemed legal. Otherwise, such actions would have been defined as piracy. The Coast Guard's interception of people fleeing Haiti continued, even when the democratically elected government of Aristide was overthrown in 1991 and the United States refused to recognize the military government that ruled Haiti from 1991 to 1994. As political violence and general insecurity worsened in Haiti in 1999, Haitians again began to flee Haiti in small boats.

6   See Stepick and Swartz 1982, 1986.

7   Immigration and Naturalization Service 1996, 65.

8   Until 1986, employers were not required to verify legal status. In the 1960s and 1970s, anyone who was working could obtain a social security card and pay into social security.

9   See Foner 1987, 1992.

10   Despite the increasing disorder and disarray in Haiti in the years that followed our 1996 visit, the airport waiting area was improved by 1999. Apparently those in power shared Georges's discomfort about the airport.

11   The Haitian experience of standing back and judging Haiti through the eyes of white Americans or Europeans is similar to what W. E. B. Du Bois, in writing about the African American experience, called "double consciousness, this sense of always looking at one's self through the eyes of others, of measuring one's soul by the tape of a world that looks on in amused contempt and pity" ([1903] 1989, 364). Michel-Rolph Trouillot (1987) pointed this out in "History, Power, and Ethnography in Haiti."

12   Kamenka 1976.

13   For a summary of the U.S. founding fathers' views on race and republican government, see Takaki 1990, 3–63. For a review of the French vacillation about persons of color, citizenship, and slavery, see Madiou 1991.

14   Symbols such as blood, race, and kinship drawn from the physical world are experienced as what Mary Douglas called "natural symbols," and as such have "surreptitious force" (quoted in Herzfeld 1992, 11).

15   As quoted in Madiou 1991.

16   Henry Louis Gates Jr. (1986) in his Introduction to *"Race," Writing, and Difference* summarizes the view of Enlightenment thinkers about race and civilization. Ronald Takaki (1990) addresses the stance of U.S. intellectuals at the time of the American Revolution. In the nineteenth century, a concept of citizenship as based on blood became popular in many states, such as Germany, that began to claim they were nations. As Walker Connor has pointed out, "Bismark's [sic] famous exhortation to the German people . . . 'to think with your blood' was [an] . . . attempt to activate a mass psychological vibration predicated upon an intuitive sense of consanguinity" (1994, 37).

17   Oriol 1992.

18   Ardouin [1853] 1958, 9.

19   Letter dated 26 August 1914, quoted in Schmidt 1971, 79.

20   See Schmidt 1971.

21   Déjean 1942, 3–4.

22   Ibid., 12.

23   Ibid., 12.

24 Heinl and Heinl 1978, 643.

25 See Brown 1991, 229.

26 Aristide, 1990, 90.

27 See Buchanan 1980; Dupuy 1997; and Nicholls [1979] 1996.

28 In this respect, Haitians and many contemporary migrants differ from those who came to the United States from rural Europe between 1840 and 1915 (see Connor 1990).

29 See Fouron 1985a, 1985b and Glick Schiller et al. 1987.

30 In addition, until the second half of the twentieth century, there was no Haitian tradition of permanent migration. Although some Haitians have been settling in the United States for two hundred years, most past Haitian migrants had sought, if poor, short-term work in neighboring countries, and if rich, education and cultural polish in Europe. Portugal and Greece were other countries that, until recently, defined emigrants as traitors to the nation (see Feldman-Bianco 1992; Klimt 2000; and Triandafyllidou n.d).

31 See Glick Schiller et al. [1987] 1992.

32 A typical example of these sentiments is the poem (quoted in Wyman 1993, 92) to "American Hungarians" by Emil Ábrænyi:

> I know with eager zeal you'd heed,
> The nation's call, and you will cross the seas
> To join our brethren here, to fight, to bleed,
> To die for Magyarland's sweet liberties.

33 Even the migrants who spoke Kreyòl, a distinct language with its own grammar, and knew little or no French identified themselves in the United States as French. Since only whites were recognized as having diverse cultural heritages, while all black persons were described only in racial terms, Haitians used a French rather than a Haitian identity to resist the U.S. racial structure. We want to make it clear that Haitian attempts to avoid racial discrimination by embracing other identities than black within a U.S. context is not a rejection of a more universal black identity or a rejection of African Americans. In general, most Haitians have tried to avoid the treatment that has been accorded to black persons in the United States even as they have struggled for the rights of all black people. For a discussion of the multiple and changing identities of Haitian migrants between 1957 and 1987, see Glick Schiller et al. 1987; 1992 [1987].

34 See Glick [Schiller] 1975; and Glick Schiller 1977.

35 Beginning in the 1960s, influential social scientists began to designate all immigrant groups except those from England as ethnic groups. In so doing, they negated the differentiation between immigrants such as the Italians, who were seen as white after World War II, and those from outside Europe, who continued to be viewed as people of color. In subtle ways, the attribution and celebration of ethnic difference has maintained the distinction between white Anglo-Saxon Protestants (WASPs) and all others. This differentiation was heightened from the 1880s to 1945 and has still not completely disappeared, as became evident in the excitement when Al Gore chose Joseph Lieberman, a Jew, as the Democratic Party nominee for vice president in 2000. Even as such identities acknowledge the validity of diverse cultural roots, they perpetuate the notion

that only those who can claim English ancestry are fully part of the U.S. mainstream and can qualify as real Americans. At the same time, the practice of designating immigrants and their descendants from Ireland, eastern and southern Europe, as well as immigrants of color as U.S. ethnic groups, negates the continuing significance of race in the United States. European immigrants are accorded and experience the social acceptance that accompanies whiteness that is not accorded those populations viewed as people of color, such as Haitians. An additional complication is the tendency to use the term *multicultural America* in a way that highlights racialized categories such as Hispanic, Asian, and black, contrasting these groupings with normative white America. The seminal work that popularized the concept of ethnic group for all multi-identity populations in the United States was Nathan Glazer and Daniel Moynihan's *Beyond the Melting Pot* (1970). Matthew Frye Jacobson (1998) discusses the changing ascription of whiteness in the United States. For a look at the continuing significance of race, see Bell 1993; Dyson 1997; Hill 1997; Harrison 1995, 2000; Lieberson 1980; Steinberg 1981; and Williams 1989.

36 Portes and Stepick 1993. For discussion of Haitian radio in South Florida, see Eugene 1998.

37 Solomon 1998.

38 Benjamin 1998.

39 United Haitian Association Newsletter, June 1982, 1.

40 Beginning in the 1990s, some U.S. politicians were actually encouraging a Haitian transnational identity. For example, in a 1996 statement to the Haitian community, Howard Golden, the president of the borough of Brooklyn, described Haitian Flag Day as an event that "will focus on social and cultural issues facing Haitians at home and in the United States, with particular attention to young people" (1997, 1).

41 See Buchanan 1980; Glick [Schiller] 1975.

42 Aristide 1990, 8.

43 Aristide n.d.

44 Richman 1992a, 196.

45 Jean-Pierre 1994, 59.

46 *Radyo Moman Kreyòl* 1991. *Moman Kreyòl* is a popular Haitian radio program aired on WLIB-AM every Sunday from 10:00 A.M. to 4:00 P.M. WLIB-AM is a minority-owned and operated business with roots in the Caribbean community in New York.

47 Aristide 1993, 195–96. It is important to note here that the English translation by Linda Maloney, which was completed during Aristide's exile in the United States, strays strikingly from the original French document. The translation's tone is less threatening and the language less militant.

48 Aristide 1993, 141–42.

49 See Americas Watch and the National Coalition for Haitian Refugees 1993; and Human Rights Watch and National Coalition for Haitian Refugees 1994a, 1994b, 1996.

50 Fifty-five thousand fleeing Haitians were intercepted by the United States Coast Guard on the high seas during the first year of the coup. Despite the fact that the U.S. government did not recognize the Haitian government after the coup as legitimate, at least thirty-five thousand of these refugees were forcibly sent back. In 1993, as a presidential

candidate, Bill Clinton stated, "I am appalled by the decision of the Bush administration to pick up fleeing Haitians on the high seas and forcibly return them to Haiti before considering their claim to political asylum. . . . This policy must not stand." When Clinton became president, however, he continued the policy of "interdiction." Many of those who were returned were beaten or imprisoned by the de facto military government (see Poppen and Wright 1994, 20).

51   See Dupuy 1997.

52   The Immigration and Naturalization Service reported that in 1996, the most recent year for which it had a full tabulation of immigrant naturalizations, 24,556 Haitian migrants became U.S. citizens. In 1985, only 2,545 Haitians became U.S. citizens (Immigration and Naturalization Service 1996, 141; 1999, 149). For a discussion of the increased rate of naturalization among all nationalities, see Dao 1999.

53   Darbouze 1997, 10. Bold in the original.

54   In the years 1992 and 1993, a period of intensive and well-documented repression of the Haitian grassroots movement, only 756 Haitians were granted political asylum (Immigration and Naturalization Service 1999, 86). In 1994, 3,284 applications were pending when the year began and 10,400 people applied. Of these, only 1,436 people were granted refugee status during 1994 (Immigration and Naturalization Service 1996, 79). Most individuals who fled Haiti were sent home without a chance to even formally apply for refugee status. In the same year, almost all of those who applied for refugee status from Iraq, Iran, Cuba, Laos, and Vietnam were approved.

6   "She Tried to Reclaim Me"

1   Bhabha 1990, 3. We use the word *narrative* in the sense of a story that changes over time.

2   See, for example, Abu-Lughod 1986.

3   Charles 1995, 8, 3. According to Ertha Pascal Trouillot (1983, 12), the law provided for a transition to full political rights, allowing participation in municipal elections first, and voting in national elections three years after that.

4   Trouillot 1983, 27.

5   Maggie, quoted in Brown 1991, 229. See also Chancy 1997.

6   In its hierarchy, Vodou still allows both men and women to play the role of officiant, but in the larger society, Vodou remains a stigmatized religion without social standing.

7   See Mireille Neptune Anglade's pathbreaking work (1986). This Haitian pattern is part of a broader Caribbean one of women as breadwinners. See Safa 1995. See also Lowenthal 1984.

8   See Beckles 1989.

9   It is possible that some of this rigid division of labor is breaking down. The vast influx of people desperate for work in Port-au-Prince live in close quarters with those returning to Haiti from the United States, Canada, Bahamas, or Dominican Republic. Each migrant experience brings a different sexual division of labor that influences the categorization of male and female jobs.

10   In Haiti, as in other Caribbean locations, male bisexual practices have been quietly accepted, and Vodou and Carnival make public cross-dressing or gender-blending

behaviors, but there has been no public acceptance of homosexuality. For a discussion of homosexuality, gender categories, and national identity in Martinique, see Murray 1996.

11   See Charles 1994.

12   When working with labor organizers in Cincinnati, Ohio, in the 1970s, Nina found that native-born black and white women faced sexual harassment when they tried to obtain or keep factory jobs.

13   In the 1990s, a larger number of Haitian women entered the United States with permanent resident visas than did men. In 1994, 7,506 women and 5,826 men were admitted as immigrants. In 1997, 8,122 women and 6,935 men were admitted as immigrants. Since the Immigration and Naturalization Service estimated that in 1996, there were 105,000 Haitians who were in the country illegally, most of whom had entered legally but overstayed their temporary visas, and these statistics are not broken down by gender, it is difficult to make precise statements about the proportion of men and women. The 1990 census figures indicated approximately equal numbers of men and women among Haitian immigrants. See Bureau of the Census 1993, 43.

14   Permanent legal residents collect the social security that they earn, but only by remaining in the United States.

15   See Labelle 1988.

16   See Charles 1995.

17   Duvalier also appointed a woman to head his entire paramilitary.

18   See Charles 1995, 137–41; and Chancy 1997.

19   Charles 1995, 139.

20   See Pierrette Hondagneu-Sotelo's description of "reconstructing gender through immigration and settlement" among Mexican immigrants in the United States (1994, 98–147).

21   Haïtian Women Ad Hoc Committee for the Decade 1986, 1.

22   For a discussion of the Haitian peasants' movement, see, for example, Smith 2001.

23   Quoted in ibid, 168–69.

24   Quoted in ibid, 169.

25   Quoted in ibid, 170.

26   See Luin Goldring's excellent essay, "The Power of Status in Transnational Social Fields" (1998).

27   Micaela di Leonardo develops the concept of kin work in her book, *The Varieties of Ethnic Experience: Kinship, Class, and Gender among Californian Italian-Americans* (1984).

28   See Wells 1999.

29   See, for example, Americas Watch and the National Coalition for Haitian Refugees 1993; and Amnesty International 1996.

30   Other feminist organizations such as *Enfo Fanm* (Women's Information Network), *Konbit Fan Saj* (Midwives' Association), and *Fanm Yo La* (Women Are Present) have entered the fray.

31   Reported in www.rehed-haiti.net/members/crad/sicrad/reperes/machmon2.html), accessed 20 October 2000.

32   Sutton 1992, 226.

7   The Generation of Identity

1   Many others who attended school for only a few years gained little from their schooling because instruction and written materials have been in French, and most children come to school speaking only Kreyòl. Although Kreyòl was recognized by the Haitian government as one of two official languages of Haiti in 1987, efforts to provide instruction in Kreyòl continue to be sporadic.

2   See Simpson and Yinger 1958; Gleason 1980; Gordon 1964; and Warner and Srole 1945.

3   HACAN conference packet 1996.

4   Her third book, a novel that explores Haitian settlement in the Dominican Republic and the 1937 massacre of Haitians by the Trujillo government, has served to fan Haitian nationalist sentiment among Haitian migrants in the United States, including the second generation (Dandicat 1998b). Published in English in 1998, its Haitian readership is the highly educated sector of the second generation in the United States, but its message is much more widely disseminated because the book has been discussed extensively on the Haitian radio programs that are broadcast every day of the week. See also her previous two novels, *Krick? Krak!* (1996) and *Breath, Eyes, Memory* (1998).

5   HACAN conference packet 1996.

6   See Stepick 1998; Rumbaut 1996; and Waters 1996, 1999.

7   The 1990 U.S. Census reported that 41 percent of Haitian immigrants have less than a high school education, 48 percent have at least a high school education, and 11 percent have college degrees or higher. Women are about as likely as men to obtain a high school or college education (Bureau of the Census 1993, 171–72).

8   Three of these students saw themselves as both Haitian and American at the same time, but more Haitian than American. They were generally not comfortable with seeing themselves as "hyphenated Americans," although one of the students explained that a high school teacher had instructed her that Haitian American was her proper identity. The one young women who identified herself as Haitian American went on to explain, "I think I'm Haitian before I'm American." Four others were adamant about the fact that they were only Haitian. Although we are examining the Haitian long-distance nationalist identity claimed by these U.S.-born students, we are not claiming this is their sole identity. We attribute some of their adamancy about their Haitian identity to their experiences on a college campus that demands an identity politics and to the fact that Georges, a faculty member on their campus who self-identifies as Haitian, did the interviewing.

9   We had assumed that the public identification we noted in the New York metropolitan area was prompted by the proliferation of various ethnic clubs on college campuses, which, according to their own accounts, had prompted Haitian students to form a Haitian club. At the University of New Hampshire, however, where there are only pan-ethnic clubs such as the Black Student Union, the handful of Haitians make it clear that they are Haitian through the public performance of Haitian dance and poetry.

10   In 1998, the clergy from Aux Cayes who led this program in Haiti participated in a retreat for second generation Haitian youth in the New York metropolitan area. In this

instance, the young people in Aux Cayes and New York were influenced not only by the same nationalist politics but also by the same religious leaders.

11   All six closely resembled each other in their knowledge of and interest in questions of Haitian identity, their understanding of Haiti as a transnational nation-state, and their desire to migrate to the United States.

12   The use of the word *cultivator* instead of *peasant* reflects the class aspirations of these young people, who have acquired a high school education. Only one of these young people had a parent with some social status. This father was a land surveyor, a powerful position in the rural area because surveyors must certify all land deeds and transactions.

13   Our total sample of young people ranged in age from sixteen to twenty-four.

14   Voice of America broadcasted a program in Kreyòl. Radyo Tropicale is a radio station that airs simultaneously in Haiti and the diaspora.

15   Going abroad to study may not necessarily mean to the United States. Many young people are sent to Mexico, the Dominican Republic, or Europe to study fields like medicine, agronomy, or engineering. With that diploma in hand, at a lesser cost than a U.S. education, they may then be sponsored or find a way to migrate to the United States, where employment prospects and remuneration for professionals is higher. Even if they can't enter the United States, their foreign degrees will help them find positions in Haiti or set up their own practices. They reenter Haitian society with the prestige of a foreign diploma as well as with the mystique of having lived abroad.

16   The young people at the radio station averaged 12.3 years of education. Haitian schooling consists of thirteen years of education. The twelfth year is called "rheto" and the thirteenth year "philo." You must pass a state examination in order to obtain either of these diplomas. To go to university, you need a philo diploma. Except for one who was still attending school, all the rest of the staff had completed their schooling, although two had only "rheto" degrees, and one had yet to pass the philo exam, half of those interviewed could not continue on to a university education in Haiti. In the United States, however, a rheto diploma is considered equivalent to a high school diploma. For young people in Haiti who have not been able to obtain the resources, or have not been able to pass the philo, the only hope for further education lies abroad.

17   There have been different versions of assimilationist theory, but all saw progression across generations toward structural integration and acculturation. See Park 1950; and Gordon 1964, 78–108.

18   See Stepick 1998; Portes and Zhou 1993; see Portes 1996, Portes and Rumbaut 1996; Rumbaut 1996; and Waters 1996.

19   See Alejandro Portes and Min Zhou's analysis (1993) of research that included Haitian youth in Miami. Alex Stepick (1998), working in Miami with Haitian young people, has reported the same type of variation. Mary C. Waters reveals a range of responses among Caribbean second-generation youth in New York City to the experience of racialization, including "identifying as [black] Americans, identifying as ethnic Americans with some distance from black Americans, or identifying as immigrant in a way that does not reckon with American racial or ethnic categories" (1996, 178). Milton Vickerman (1999) speaks of the fluidity of identity choices of the second generation. Nonetheless, this sig-

nificant rethinking of the Americanization process has not addressed the transnational social and political processes that shape the lives and identities of a significant sector of both transmigrants and their children.

20   Rob Smith (1998a) has made a similar critique of the research on the second generation.

21   In the past decade, increasing numbers of researchers on immigration have begun to ac-knowledge and study transnational households (see Laguerre 1998; Lessinger 1995; Pes-sar 1996; and Smith and Wallerstein 1992). Many children living in emigrant-sending countries depend for their sustenance, growth, and development on parents and other family members living abroad.

22   See Smith 1998b.

23   Anderson 1996.

8   "The Responsible State"

1   In fact, since Haitian transnational fields extend into more than two states, the resulting new politics of citizenship are even more complex. When interviewing political officials in 1995, Nina did find that persons who had returned to Haiti from different countries entered the Haitian political arena with very different political notions and styles, which reflected their various diasporic experiences. The officials who had lived in Venezuela, France, Canada, and the United States seemed to have different concepts of citizenship. In this book, we focus on the lessons learned as Haiti is experienced within the United States and the United States is experienced within Haiti.

2   Sengupta 1998. For a discussion of the contradictions that surround the legal status of transmigrants, see Bauböck 1994.

3   See Trouillot 1990; and Scott 1985.

4   Alex Dupuy, using terminology from the classic sociology of Max Weber, applies the word "prebendary" to describe the Haitian state. Dupuy defines prebendary as "a politi-cal regime in which those who held office or political power lived off politics. In addi-tion to their regular salaries, these officials received perquisites of office either as bribes or by siphoning (i.e., stealing) public money from various government agencies or state enterprises for private ends" (1997, 21). In our opinion, siphoning continues to be the primary activity of most Haitian officials.

5   Translated from Chapter 2, Haitian Constitution, 1987, Section A: Article 19, in Moïse 1990, 499.

6   Haitian Constitution (Chapter 2, Section F: Article 32), as cited in Moïse 1990, 502.

7   Moïse 1988, 33.

8   This imagery reinforces the patriarchal family as well as the subordination of women within the nation and family. Many male spirits of the vodou religion are also called papa.

9   Farmer 1994, 78.

10   See Nicholls 1985.

11   Since the Haitian Revolution, many African Americans have also viewed Haiti as repre-senting the demands of persons of African descent for equality. See, for example, the

writings of James Weldon Johnson (1920a, 1920b, 1920c, 1920d) and the contemporary defense of Haiti by leaders such as Randall Robinson of Trans-Africa (1994).

12   Building on Bruce Kapferer's seminal work *Legends of the People, Myths of the State* (1988), Michael Herzfeld (1992) has discussed the use of bureaucratic practices and language in creating a sacred aura of nationalism. Such practices and utterances also normalize the state.

13   Michel-Ralph Trouillot argues that one of the ways that the Duvalier regime obtained consent was through "the expansion of the role of the state as a mechanism of redistribution" (1990, 188).

14   Under the first Aristide and the Préval administrations, the costs of these items were kept low through government subsidies.

15   Aristide 1992, 112–14.

16   See, for example, Rothberg 1997.

17   See Jefferson [1787] 1984.

18   See Augustin 1999.

19   Recent changes in U.S. immigration law, such as the Immigration Act of 1990 (P. L. 101–649), have made the process of legally joining a spouse even more time-consuming and expensive than it had been. The Immigration and Naturalization Service routinely denies Haitians visitors' visas, as Georges and Rolande found out when Rolande's elderly aunt was denied a visa to come to Leah's law school graduation. Georges's brother's daughter was denied a visa to visit Georges on her way to begin a fellowship in Canada.

20   Augustin 1999, 6B.

21   Ibid.

22   Ibid.

23   Ibid.

24   Ibid.

25   The Préval government, which followed Aristide's regime in 1996, tried to research the ways in which U.S. Jews raise money for Israel, with the idea of encouraging the Haitian diaspora to take similar steps on behalf of Haiti (personal communication from Alex Stepick).

26   See Glick [Schiller] 1975.

27   See Sassen 1988.

28   See Simon 1998.

29   These are generally labeled "nongovernmental organizations" (NGOs), but they are often actually funded by governments, and frequently not the government of the country in which they work. Haiti has become a patchwork quilt of such organizations, which have stepped in to take up many public functions, such as health care, education, dental care, sanitation, and economic development. See, for example, Smith 2001; and Mathurin, Mathurin, and Zaugg 1989.

30   See the New York State Education Department Web site, http://www.nysed.gov:80/rscs/exams/regents.html, for copies of the regents exams in Haitian Kreyòl.

31   Estimates of the numbers of demonstrators made by newspapers, the police, and the organizers of demonstrations almost always vary dramatically. Both of us were at this

demonstration and are convinced that the numbers were in the tens of thousands rather than the three thousand reported in press accounts (see Walker 1990, 27).

3 2   Beginning in the 1980s, Haitians were falsely labeled as a risk group for HIV by the U.S. Centers for Disease Control. With some help from the media, this depiction served to communicate to the public at large that Haitians were a source of deadly contamination, responsible for transmitting the AIDS virus to people in the United States. Haitians were fired from their jobs, evicted from housing, and physically attacked. Children were ostracized by fellow students, teachers, and administrators.

3 3   Lobbying on behalf of Haiti was done as early as 1957 when the Duvalier government hired John Roosevelt, a son of Franklin Delano Roosevelt, for $150,000 to defend its interests. Such lobbying was more of the classic corporate version in which a person knowledgeable about Washington is hired to promote the interests of his or her employer (Heinl and Heinl 1978, 590).

3 4   Smith 1999.

3 5   See Valbrun 1999, A24.

3 6   For a description of the Haitian American Community Action Network (HACAN) that NCHR tried to build, see chapter 7.

3 7   See Higham 1982; and Adamic 1941.

3 8   The concept of hybridity has been embraced in some postmodern cultural theory as a critique of bounded homogeneous notions of culture that produce essentialist thinking and cultural politics. By positing a mixing of formerly pure types, the hybrid concept can also perpetuate essentialist approaches to culture. For discussions of the concept, see Werbner and Modood 1997; and Canclini 1995.

9   The Apparent State

1   See, for example, Smith 2001.

2   See Schaeffer 1997.

3   For an example of the limitations on national sovereignty that arise from international banking projects within various states, see Johnston and Turner 1999. Alicia Girón and Eugenia Correa have provided a useful discussion of the implications of financial deregulation, which "has made it gradually impossible for nation-states to control their money supply or credit" (1999, 183).

4   See Sassen 1995, 1988; and Camilleri and Falk 1992.

5   See Daley 1999.

6   For an alternative approach to the one advocated here that uses the concept of "coloniality" proposed by Peruvian sociologist Anibal Quijano to describe the current position of formerly colonized states and their migrant populations, see Grosfoguel and Georas 2000; and Quijano and Wallerstein 1992.

7   Castells 1997, 307. According to a basic textbook in international relations, sovereignty "means that a government has the right, at least in principle, to do whatever it wants in its own territory. States are separate, are autonomous, and answer to no higher authority (due to anarchy). In principle, all states are equal in status if not in power. Sover-

eignty also means that states are not supposed to interfere in the internal affairs of other states. Although states do try to influence each other (exert power) on matters of trade, alliances, war, and so on, they are not supposed to meddle in the internal politics and decision processes of other states. . . . This agreement only partially holds up in practice" (Goldstein 1994, 70). An alternative view of the world system has been argued by people such as Immanuel Wallerstein (1979).

8 Some scholars have contended that while governments and government policies and practices are real, "the state" is everywhere a mystification of the power of dominant classes (Abrams [1977] 1988). We find much of their argument convincing, yet have decided in this book to focus on the myth of national sovereignty that keeps us from addressing the vast differences in power and autonomy between states such as the United States and Haiti. For arguments about the autonomy of the state, see Poulantzas 1973; Mitchell 1991; and Domhoff 1996. In an entirely different set of assertions, dependency theorists such as Andre Gunder Frank (1969) and the world system theorists such as Immanuel Wallerstein (1979), who developed the argument further, posit a peripheral and subordinate role for Third World states. More recently, scholars such as Gilbert Joseph, Catherine Legrand, and Ricardo Salvatore (1998) have explored such relationships by writing the state's cultural history. Here we examine the continuing imagery of the nation-state as a local cultural construction.

9 See Broder 1999a, 1996b; Frantz 2000; Minutaglio 1999; and Fauntroy 1991.

10 See Carey 1998; House Committee on International Relations 1996; and USAID 1995.

11 See Dupuy 1997, 126.

12 Ibid., 127.

13 See Nicholls 1985, 108–9.

14 See correspondence of the American Consul, Yale University Archives.

15 See Bellegarde-Smith 1990, 52.

16 See Nicholls 1985, 108–9.

17 Quoted in Bellegarde-Smith 1990, 54.

18 Ibid., 68.

19 The culture wars were fought on two fronts. On the one hand, some Haitian intellectuals resisted the occupation by promoting and celebrating their "Latin and French culture," which from their perspective, was superior to the boorish, materialistic, and crass culture of the Americans. To speak French instead of English, to use French products instead of U.S. ones, and to play soccer rather than baseball became proof of patriotism and a form of resistance. Other Haitian intellectuals embraced the emerging global anti-colonial and anti-imperialist movement, which promoted self-determination for the dominated and colonial societies while reevaluating indigenous cultures and practices. These intellectuals began to show an interest in Africa. Negritude and black solidarity became new expressions of nationalism (see Hoffman 1984).

20 See Dupuy 1989, 141.

21 See Heinl and Heinl 1978, 521.

22 Ibid., 542.

23 See Dupuy 1989, 145.

24   Ibid., 144.

25   This is the same battle that is now being commemorated in the public schools of Broward County, Florida.

26   Quoted in Heinl and Heinl 1978, 570.

27   See Heinl and Heinl 1978, 582.

28   Dupuy 1989, 169.

29   Ibid., 166.

30   Ibid., 173.

31   USAID "Country Development" cited in Dewind and Kinley 1994.

32   See Hancock 1989, 180.

33   Poppen and Wright 1994, 25. See also DeWind and Kinley 1988.

34   There is disagreement among Haitian scholars about whether the Aristide government had a plan for a new direction for Haiti. See Dupuy 1997.

35   Between 1987 and 1999, the United States paid for a significant share of the activities of the United Nations, Organization of the American States, the Carter Center, and the International Foundation for Electoral Systems in Haiti (see Carey 1998). The U.S.–based National Democratic Institute for International Affairs and the International Republican Institute also directly intervened in political life in Haiti.

36   Burki 1997, 3.

37   The minimum wage was raised a token amount in 1991, from $3.00 to $4.80 a day (see Dupuy 1997). Without a system of legal protections or unions, even the low minimum wage is not enforced. Aristide used the phrase "from misery to poverty" in numerous speeches.

38   See Weiner 1993, A1; Dupuy 1997, 69; and Chomsky 1994. Careful documentation of the efforts of the military government to suppress the vibrant civil society of Haiti can be found in the report *Silencing a People: The Destruction of Civil Society in Haiti* (Americas Watch and National Coalition for Haitian Refugees 1993).

39   See Nairn 1994a, 1994b; and Weiner 1995.

40   Schneider 1995.

41   See U.S. State Department 1998, 6.

42   House Committee on International Relations 1996. At the very same time, the U.S. Congress was dramatically cutting legal services to poor people in the United States and attacking legal aid programs as outside the responsibility of government. Yet, U.S. programs such as judicial reform in Haiti sustain the beliefs of a Haitian transborder citizenry that the state should be responsible for providing services to the people. To the extent that Haitians in Haiti or the United States knew about the project, it strengthened their view that despite the failures of the program, the U.S. government does take responsibility for providing services to people.

43   The National Coalition for Human Rights 1997.

44   U.S. State Department 1998, 2.

45   Ibid., 6.

46   White 1997, 10.

47   U.S. State Department 1997.

48   U.S. House 1998.

49   Although IRI has strong links with the Republican Party, it bills itself as a nongovern-
      mental organization (NGO). One member of the U.S. Congress is on its board of direc-
      tors, while contributors make up some of the wealthiest corporations: Boeing, Coca-
      Cola, Ford, Eli Lilly, Texaco, Pfizer, Lockheed Martin, Chevron, and the Mortgage
      Bankers of America. IRI established a "party building program in Haiti . . . designed to
      strengthen the institutional structures and capabilities of the parties so that they can
      participate more effectively in the country's political life." They wished to "promote a
      level playing field for participation and competition" (Zarin 1998, 2).

50   Carey 1998, 12.

51   Perry 1996, 2.

52   In 1996, some of the poor still had hopes that their democratically elected leaders would
      respond to the needs of the majority of the people. And Aristide, although discredited
      in the eyes of many of his former supporters, was still seen as a voice of hope by people
      who were desperate for change. By 2001, the cynicism had grown, but so had the en-
      trenched political interests so that there were several factions competing for power:
      Aristide, the Préval forces, and the former military/Duvalierists. None seemed to care
      what happened to the country, and these factions made efforts to speak out against at-
      tacks on Haiti or Haitians more difficult in Haiti as well as the diaspora. These divisions
      undercut attempts to protest the deportation in 1999 of thousands of Haitians who were
      living or had been born in the Dominican Republic.

53   Radio Tropicale broadcast, 14 October 1994.

54   Rothberg 1997, vii.

55   For contemporary accounts of Mexican and Dominican hometown associations, see
      Levitt 1997; Smith 1994, 1998b; and Goldring 1996. For hometown associations at the
      beginning of the twentieth century, see Park [1925] 1974; and Cinel 1982.

56   See Smith 1994; Levitt 1997.

57   Pierre-Pierre 1998, B6.

58   Foucault developed the concept of a regime of truth, warning that the structure of polit-
      ical power always shapes our understandings of the world. For a discussion of this con-
      cept, see Reyna and Glick Schiller 1998.

10   Long-Distance Nationalism as a Debate

1   Michael Herzfeld (1992, 13) explores the changing and constantly contested meanings
      of symbolic forms, especially those embedded in the rhetoric of the state. These sym-
      bolic forms often build on an older language of kinship and blood. See also Hertzfeld
      1997.

2   Luis Eduardo Guarnizo (1999) has examined the internal fissures within the transna-
      tional social fields of Colombian immigrants.

3   Our argument differs from the many scholars who emphasize the heterogeneity of iden-
      tities and fragmentation of interests that underlie any national identity and ideology.
      See Gilroy 1993; Beckett and Mato 1996; Cohen 1997; and McLaren 1994. Other writ-

ers, such as Yasemin Nuhoglu Soysal (1994), have focused on the emergence of a language of universal human rights in a "postnational" world that extends beyond claims to the rights of citizenship in a particular state.

4   See the discussion of signification in chapter 2 and Gates 1988. Much of the analysis of Caribbean culture along these lines has been done in relationship to music, Carnival, and religion. See, for example, Averill 1997; Brown 1991; and Burton 1997.

5   Averill 1997, 7–8.

6   In order to highlight the experiences and perspectives of poor and working-class transmigrants, which differ in significant ways from those of national political leaders, some scholars of transnational migration have started to talk about "transnationalism from below" (Smith and Guarnizo 1998). The phrase "view from below" has become a shorthand way of discussing counterhegemonic politics that emerge from oppressed sectors of the population. It has the same sense as "grassroots," something that emerges outside and in opposition to the formal political leadership and their ideologies.

7   See Farmer 1992; Laguerre 1978, 1982; Richman 1992b; Smith 1998; and Woodson 1990.

8   Aristide 1990, 104.

9   Aristide 1990, 90.

10   Ibid., 107.

11   White 1997, 10.

12   We should note that just as we finished this book, Martial went to Haiti to head a private cellular phone company that was competing with the public phone service.

13   Dessalines was the revolutionary general who, in his founding of the nation, is said to have drawn the distinction between Haitian (black) and foreigners (white). Despite the transnational ties and growing definition of the diaspora as part of Haiti, impoverished people also employ this distinction between blackness and whiteness to criticize or repudiate Haitians who live abroad. The African American and Haitian American troops that came to Haiti as part of the U.S. occupation in 1994 were sometimes designated as blan (white) and occasionally described as *blan nwa* (white blacks). To make clear the social distance they felt from Haitian immigrants who return flaunting their prosperity through their dress and body language, people in Haiti may designate members of the diaspora as foreigners/whites. We found that when we first began an interview, people would identify both of us as *blancs*, categorizing us by this word that means white/foreigner. Georges found this exclusion troubling.

14   See Joint 1996. For description of the protest against the WTO in Seattle in 1999, see Battle in Seattle (1999, 3–28).

15   See Americas Watch 1993; and Human Rights Watch 1994a, 1994b, and 1996.

16   See, for example, the call to build the "World March of Women in the Year 2000" to which Haitian women's organizations contributed (World March of Women 2000).

17   We join the many other scholars who have adopted the term "subaltern" from Gramsci (1971) as a way to name the disparate groupings of people who come to share the perspective of the disempowered.

11   The Other Side of the Two-Way Street

1   There is a growing literature on white privilege. See McIntosh 1992; Lipsitz 1998; and Avakian 1999.

2   For a discussion of the concept of Jews looking different, see Brodkin 1998; and Jacobson 1998.

3   See Roediger 1994.

4   Transnational labor struggles, workers' internationalism, and long-distance nationalism contributed to European social democracy and Latin American labor movements, as well as to U.S. concepts of civil rights, workers' rights, and human rights. See, for example, the insightful paper by Donna Gabaccia and Fraser Ottanelli (1995).

5   See Wyman 1993; and Portes and Rumbaut 1996.

6   Lears 1998, 66.

7   For a straightforward exposition of this position in anthropology, see Rosaldo 1989. For a critique of this position, see Ahmed 1992.

8   Bhabha 1990, 3.

9   See Sassen 1995.

10   Haraway 1991.

11   See, for example, Farmer 1992; and Richman 1992b.

12   As Cynthia Enloe has pointed out, "It is worth imagining . . . what would happen to international politics if more nationalist movements were informed by women's experiences of oppression" (1990, 64).

13   See Canada 1995.

14   Fanon 1967.

15   See Flacks 1995; and Hunter 1995.

16   In the U.S. presidential campaign of 2000, Democratic candidates Gore and Lieberman—with personal holdings in and large contributions from oil companies, the insurance industry, and pharmaceutical corporations—declared themselves the champions of "working families" against corporate greed.

Bibliography

Abrams, Philip. [1977] 1988. Notes on the difficulty of studying the state. *Journal of Historical Sociology* 1, no. 1:58–89.

Abu-Lughod, Lila. 1986. *Veiled sentiments: Honour and poetry in Bedouin society.* Berkeley: University of California Press.

Adamic, Louis. 1941. *Two-way-passage.* New York: Harper and Brothers.

Ahmed, Aijaz. 1992. *In theory: Classes, nations, and literatures.* London: Verso.

Americas Watch and the National Coalition for Haitian Refugees. 1993. *Silencing a people: The destruction of civil society in Haiti.* New York: Human Rights Watch.

Amnesty International. 1996. *Haiti: A question of justice. Amnesty International Report.* AMR 36/1/96 January. www.amnesty.org/alib/aipub/AMR/236000/96.

Anderson, Benedict. 1993. The new world disorder. *New Left Review* 193 (May/June):2–13.

———. 1994. Exodus. *Critical Inquiry* 20 (winter):314–27.

———. 1996. *Imagined communities: Reflections on the origins and spread of nationalism.* Rev. ed. London: Verso.

Anglade, Mireille Neptune. 1986. *L'autre moitié du développement: À propos du travail des femmes en Haïti.* Port-au-Prince: Éditions des Alizés.

Appadurai, Arjun. 1991. Global ethnoscapes: Notes and queries for a transnational anthropology. In *Recapturing anthropology,* edited by Richard Fox. Santa Fe, N. Mex.: School of American Research Press.

———. 1993. Patriotism and its futures. *Public Culture* 5, no. 3:411–29.

Ardouin, Beaubrun. [1853] 1958. *Etudes sur l'histoire d'Haiti.* Edited by Dr. François Dalencour. Condé-s-Noireau, France: Condéenne.

Aristide, Jean-Bertrand. n. d. Pwojè Lavalas. Mimeograph, in files of Georges Fouron.

———. 1990. *In the parish of the poor: Writings from Haiti.* Maryknoll, N.Y.: Orbis Press.

———. 1992. *Théologie et politique.* Montreal: CIDIHCA.

———. 1993. *An autobiography.* Maryknoll, N.Y.: Orbis Books.

Augustin, Merle. 1999. Hundreds of mourners gather at a Delray church to memorialize Haitian refugees who drowned. *Sun Sentinel*, 14 March, 1B, 6B.

Avakian, Arlene Voski. 1999. Transgressing borders: Teaching about whiteness in women's studies. *Identities: Global Studies in Culture and Power* 6, no. 1: 145–74.

Averill, Gage. 1997. *A day for the hunter, a day for the prey: Popular music and power in Haiti*. Chicago: University of Chicago Press.

Balibar, Etienne. 1991. Racism and nationalism. In *Race, nation, class: Ambiguous identities*, edited by Etienne Balibar and Immanuel Wallerstein. London: Verso.

Barnes, John Arundel. 1954. Class and committees in a Norwegian island parish. *Human Relations* 7:39–58.

———. 1979. Networks and political processes. In *Social networks in urban situations*, edited by J. Clyde Mitchell. Manchester: Manchester University Press.

Basch, Linda, Nina Glick Schiller, and Cristina Szanton Blanc. 1994. *Nations unbound: Transnational projects, postcolonial predicaments, and deterritorialized nation-states*. Amsterdam: Gordon and Breach.

Battle in Seattle: Special WTO Issue. 1999. *Nation* 269, no. 19:11–28.

Bauböck, Rainer. 1994. *Transnational citizenship: Membership and rights in international migration*. Aldershot, U. K.: Edward Elgar Publishing.

Beckett, Jeremy, and Daniel Mato, guest eds. 1996. Indigenous peoples/global terrains. *Identities: Global Studies in Culture and Power* 3, nos. 1–2:1–13.

Beckles, Hilary McD. 1989. *Natural rebels: A social history of enslaved black women in Barbados*. New Brunswick, N.J.: Rutgers University Press.

Bell, Derrick A. 1993. *Faces at the bottom of the well*. New York: Basic Books.

Bellegarde-Smith, Patrick. 1990. *Haiti: The breached citadel*. Boulder, Colo.: Westview Press.

Benjamin, Jody. 1998. Observing Haitian holiday. *Sun Sentinel*, 19 November, 20B.

Berube, Margery S., ed. 1991. *The American heritage dictionary*. 2d college edition. Boston: Houghton Mifflin.

Bhabha, Homi. 1990. Introduction: Narrating the nation. In *Nation and narration*, edited by Homi Bhabha. London: Routledge.

Bourdieu, Pierre, and Loic Wacquant. 1992. *An invitation to reflexive sociology*. Chicago: University of Chicago Press.

Bourne, Ralph. 1916. Trans-national America. *Atlantic Monthly*, no. 118:86–97.

Brimelow, Peter. 1995. *Alien nation*. New York: Random House.

Broder, John. 1999a. Bradley relies on Wall Street to raise funds. *New York Times*, 24 October, A1.

———. 1999b. McCain and Bradley collect big money, but it isn't soft. *New York Times*, 16 December, A22.

Brodkin, Karen. 1998. *How Jews became white folks and what that says about race in America*. New Brunswick, N.J.: Rutgers University Press.

Brown, Karen McCarthy. 1991. *Mama Lola: A vodou priestess in Brooklyn*. Berkeley: University of California Press.

Brubaker, Roger. 1996. *Nationalism reframed: Nationhood and the national question in the New Europe*. Cambridge, U. K.: Cambridge University Press.

Buchanan, Susan. 1980. Scattered seeds: The meaning of the migration of Haitians in New York City. Ph.D. diss., New York University.

Burki, Javed. 1997. Closing statement. Consultative Group on Haiti, World Bank press release, 4 April, Port-au-Prince.

Burton, Richard D. E. 1997. *Afro-Creole: Power, opposition, and play in the Caribbean*. Ithaca, N.Y.: Cornell University Press.

Calhoun, Craig. 1997. *Nationalism*. Minneapolis: University of Minnesota Press.

Camilleri, Joseph and Jim Falk. 1992. *The end of sovereignty? The politics of a shrinking and fragmented world*. Aldershot, U. K.: Edward Elgar Publishing.

Canada, Geoffrey. 1995. *Fist stick knife gun: A personal history of violence in America*. Boston: Beacon.

Canclini, Nestor Garcia. 1995. *Hybrid cultures: Strategies for entering and leaving modernity*. Minneapolis: University of Minnesota Press.

Carey, Henry. 1998. Electoral observation and democratization in Haiti. In *Electoral observation and democratic transitions in Latin America*, edited by Kevin Middlebrook. San Diego: Center for U.S.–Mexican Studies.

Castells, Manuel. 1997. *The power of identity*. Vol. 2 of *The information age: Economy, society, and culture*. Malden, Mass.: Blackwell.

Central Intelligence Agency. 2000. *The world factbook 2000-Haiti*. http://www.cia.gov/cia/publications/factbook/geos/ha.

Chancy, Myriam. 1997. *Framing silence: Revolutionary novels by Haitian women*. New Brunswick, N.J.: Rutgers University Press.

Charles, Carolle. 1990a. A transnational dialectic of race, class, and ethnicity: Patterns of identities and forms of consciousness among Haitian migrants in New York City. Ph.D. diss., State University of New York at Binghamton.

———. 1990b. Distinct meanings of blackness: Patterns of identity among Haitian migrants in New York City. *Cimarron* 2, no. 3:129–38.

———. 1992. Transnationalism in the construct of Haitian migrants' racial categories of identity in New York City. In *Towards a transnational perspective on migration: Race, class, ethnicity, and nationalism reconsidered*, edited by Nina Glick Schiller, Linda Basch, and Cristina Blanc-Szanton, eds. New York: New York Academy of Sciences.

———. 1994. Sexual politics and the mediation of class, gender, and race in former slave plantation societies: The case of Haiti. In *Social construction of the past: Representation as power*, edited by George C. Bond and Angela Gilliam. London: Routledge.

———. 1995. Gender and politics in contemporary Haiti: The duvalierist state, transnationalism, and the emergence of a new feminism (1980 –1990). *Feminist Studies* 21, no. 1:135–64.

Chomsky, Noam. 1994. Democracy enhancement, part 2: The case of Haiti. *Z Magazine* (July/August). Electronic print-out.

Cinel, Dino. 1982. *From Italy to San Francisco: The immigrant experience*. Stanford, Calif.: Stanford University Press.

Cohen, Robin. 1997. *Global diasporas: An introduction*. Seattle: University of Washington Press.

Comaroff, Jean and John Comaroff. 1991. *Of revelation and revolution: Christianity, colonialism, and consciousness in South Africa*. Chicago: University of Chicago Press.

Connor, Walker. 1990. When is a nation? *Ethnic and Racial Studies* 13, no. 1:92–100.

————. 1994. A nation is a nation, is a state, is an ethnic group, is a. . . . In *Nationalism*, edited by John Hutchinson and Anthony D. Smith. Oxford: Oxford University Press.

Corrigan, Philip, and Derek Sayer. 1985. *The golden arch: English state formation as cultural revolution*. Oxford: Basil Blackwell.

Daley, Susan. 1999. French see a hero in war on "McDomination." *New York Times* (New England ed.), 12 October, A1, A4.

Dandicat, Edwidge. 1996. *Krick? Krak!* New York: Vintage.

————. 1998a. *Breath, eyes, memory*. New York: Random House.

————. 1998b. *The farming of the bones*. New York: Soho.

Dao, James. 1999. Immigrant diversity slows traditional political climb. *New York Times* (New England ed.), 29 December, A1, A20.

Darbouze, Roland. 1997. Vive le drapeau haïtien. *Builder's Journal*, 18 May, 3.

DeConde, Alexander. 1992. *Ethnicity, race, and American foreign policy: A history*. Boston: Northeastern University Press.

Déjean, Leon. 1942. Notre combat. *Chantiers* 1, no. 2 (15 July):3–4, 12.

DeSipio, Louis, and Rodolfo O. de la Garza. 1998. *Making Americans, remaking America: Immigration and immigrant policy*. Boulder, Colo.: Westview Press.

DeWind, Josh, and David Kinley. 1987. *The remittances of Haitian immigrants in New York City*. Final report prepared for Citibank, in the files of Nina Glick Schiller.

————. 1988. *Aiding migration: The impact of international development assistance on Haiti*. Boulder, Colo.: Westview Press.

————. 1994. "Export-led" development. In *The Haiti files: Decoding the crisis*, edited by James Ridgeway. Washington, D.C.: Essential Books.

Dikötter, Frank, ed. 1997. *The construction of racial identities in China and Japan: Historical and contemporary perspectives*. Honolulu: University of Hawaii Press.

di Leonardo, Micaela. 1984. *The varieties of ethnic experience: Kinship, class, and gender among Californian Italian-Americans*. Ithaca, N.Y.: Cornell University Press.

Domhoff, G. William. 1996. *State autonomy or class dominance: Case studies on policy making in America*. New York: Aldine De Gruyter.

Dominguez, Virginia. 1996. Engendering the sexualized state of the nation. *Identities: Global Studies in Culture and Power* 2, no. 3:301–6.

D'Souza, Dinesh. 1996. *The end of racism: Principles for a multiracial society*. New York: Simon and Schuster.

Duany, Jorge. n. d. Blurred frontiers: The socioeconomic impacts of transnational migration on the Hispanic Caribbean and the United States. Manuscript, in the files of Nina Glick Schiller.

Du Bois, W. E. B. [1903] 1989. *The souls of black folks*. New York: Bantam Books.

Dugger, Celia W. 1998. In India, an arranged marriage of two worlds. *New York Times*, 20 July, A1, B6–7.

Dupuy, Alex. 1989. *Haiti in the world economy: Class, race, and underdevelopment since 1700*. Boulder, Colo.: Westview Press.

————. 1997. *Haiti in the new world order: The limits of the democratic revolution*. Boulder, Colo.: Westview Press.

Dyson, Michael Eric. 1997. *Race rules: Navigating the color line*. New York: Vintage Books.

Engels, Friedrich. [1866] 1974. What has the working class to do with Poland? In *Karl Marx: The first international and after*, edited by David Ferbach. New York: Vintage.

Enloe, Cynthia. 1990. *Bananas, beaches, and bases: Making feminist sense of international politics*. Berkeley: University of California Press.

Eugene, Emmanuel. 1998. Transnational migrant media: A study of south Florida Haitian radio. Master's thesis, Florida International University.

Fanon, Franz. 1967. *The wretched of the earth*. Harmondsworth, U. K.: Penguin.

Farmer, Paul. 1992. *AIDS and accusation: Haiti and the geography of blame*. Berkeley: University of California Press.

———. 1994. *The uses of Haiti*. Monroe, Maine: Common Courage Press.

Fauntroy, Walter E. 1994. Haiti's "economic barons." In *The Haiti files: Decoding the crisis*, edited by James Ridgeway. Washington, D.C.: Essential Books.

Featherstone, Mike, Scott Lash, and Roland Robertson. 1995. *Global modernities*. London: Sage Publications.

Feldman-Bianco, Bela. 1992. Multiple layers of time and space: The construction of class, race, ethnicity, and nationalism among Portuguese immigrants. In *Towards a transnational perspective on migration: Race, class, ethnicity, and nationalism reconsidered*, edited by Nina Glick Schiller, Linda Basch, and Cristina Blanc-Szanton. New York: New York Academy of Sciences.

Flacks, Richard. 1995. Think globally, act politically: Some notes toward new movement strategy. In *Cultural politics and social movements*, edited by Marcy Darnovsky, Barbara Epstein, and Richard Flacks. Philadelphia, Pa.: Temple University Press.

Foner, Nancy. 1987. The Jamaicans: Race and ethnicity among migrants in New York City. In *New immigrants in New York City*, edited by Nancy Foner. New York: Columbia University Press.

———. 1992. West Indians in New York City and London: A comparative analysis. In *Caribbean life in New York City: Sociocultural dimensions*, edited by Constance Sutton and Elsa Chaney. Rev. ed. New York: Center for Migration Studies.

Foucault, Michel. 1969. *The archaeology of knowledge*. New York: Pantheon.

———. 1980. *Power/knowledge: Selected interviews and other writings, 1972–1977*. Edited by Colin Gordon. New York: Pantheon Books.

Fouron, Georges. 1985a. The black immigrant dilemma in the United States: The Haitian experience. *Journal of Caribbean Studies* 3, no. 3:242–65.

———. 1985b. Patterns of adaption of Haitian immigrants of the 1970s in New York City. Ed.D. diss., Teachers College, Columbia University.

Fouron, Georges, and Nina Glick Schiller. 1997. Haitian identities at the juncture between diaspora and homeland. In *Caribbean circuits: New directions in the study of Caribbean migration*, edited by Patricia Pessar. New York: Center for Migration Studies.

Frank, Andre Gunder. 1969. Latin America: Underdevelopment or revolution. New York: Monthly Review Press.

Frantz, Douglas. 2000. The 2000 campaign: The Arizona ties. *New York Times*, 21 February, A14, late edition.

Gabaccia, Donna, and Fraser Ottanelli. 1997. Diaspora or international proletariat? Italian labor migration and the making of multiethnic states, 1815–1939. Diaspora 6, 61–84.

Gates, Henry Louis, Jr. 1986. Editor's introduction: Writing "race" and the difference it makes. In "Race," writing, and difference, edited by Henry Louis Gates Jr. Chicago: University of Chicago Press.

——. 1988. The signifying monkey: A theory of African-American literary criticism. New York: Oxford University Press.

Gellner, Ernest. 1983. Nation and nationalism. Oxford: Blackwell.

——. 1994. Conditions of liberty: Civil society and its rivals. London: Hamish Hamilton.

Gerth, Jeff. 1998. Democratic fundraiser said to name China tie. New York Times (New England ed.), 15 May, A1, A20.

Gerth, Jeff and David E. Sanger. 1998. How Chinese won rights to launch satellites for U.S. New York Times (New England ed.), 17 May, 1, 18.

Gilroy, Paul. 1993. The black Atlantic: Modernity and double consciousness. Cambridge: Harvard University Press.

Girón, Alicia, and Eugenia Correa. 1999. Global financial markets: Financial deregulation and crisis. International Social Science Journal 160 (June):183–94.

Glazer, Nathan, and Daniel Moynihan. 1970. Beyond the melting pot. Cambridge: MIT Press.

Gleason, Philip. 1980. American identity and Americanization. In Harvard encyclopedia of American ethnic groups, edited by Stephan Thernstrom. Cambridge: Harvard University Press.

Glick [Schiller], Nina Barnett. 1975. The formation of a Haitian ethnic group. Ph.D. diss., Columbia University.

Glick Schiller, Nina. 1977. Ethnic groups are made not born. In Ethnic encounters: Identities and contexts, edited by George L. Hicks and Philip E. Leis. North Scituate, Mass.: Duxbury Press.

——. 1999a. Transmigrants and nation-states: Something old and something new in the U.S. immigrant experience. In The handbook of international migration: The American experience, edited by Charles Hirshman, Philip Kasinitz, and Josh DeWind. New York: Russell Sage.

——. 1999b. Transnational nation-states and their citizens: The Asian experience. In Globalisation and the Asia Pacific: Contested territories, edited by Peter Dicken, Philip Kelley, Lily Kong, Kris Olds, and Harry Wai-chung Yeung. London: Routledge.

Glick Schiller, Nina, Linda Basch, and Cristina Blanc-Szanton, eds. 1992. Towards a transnational perspective on migration: Race, class, ethnicity, and nationalism reconsidered. New York: New York Academy of Sciences.

Glick Schiller, Nina, Josh DeWind, Marie Lucie Brutus, Carrolle Charles, Georges Fouron, and Louis Thomas. [1987] 1992. All in the same boat? Unity and diversity among Haitian immigrants. In Caribbean life in New York City: Sociocultural dimensions, edited by Constance R. Sutton and Elsa M. Chaney. Rev. ed. New York: Center for Migration Studies.

——. 1987. Exile, ethnic, refugee: Changing organizational identities among Haitian immigrants. Migration Today 15, no. 1:7–11.

Glick Schiller, Nina, and Georges Fouron. 1990. "Everywhere we go we are in danger": Ti

Manno and the emergence of a Haitian transnational identity. *American Ethnologist* 17, no. 2:329–47.

———. 1998. Transnational lives and national identities: The identity politics of Haitian immigrants. In *Transnationalism from below*, edited by Michael Peter Smith and Luis Guarnizo. New Brunswick, N.J.: Transaction Publisher.

———. 1999. Terrains of blood and nation: Haitian transnational social fields. *Ethnic and Racial Studies* 22, no. 2:340–66.

Golden, Howard. 1997. Statement in honor of Haitian flag day. In *Builder's Journal*. New York: Flag Day Committee.

Goldring, Luin. 1996. Blurring borders: Constructing transnational community in the process of Mexico–U.S. migration. *Research in Community Sociology* 6:69–104.

———. 1998. The power of status in transnational social fields. In *Transnationalism from below*, edited by Michael Peter Smith and Luis Eduardo Guarnizo. New Brunswick, N.J.: Transaction Publishers.

Goldstein, Joshua S. 1994. *International relations*. New York: Harper Collins College Publishers.

Gordon, Milton M. 1964. *Assimilation in American life: The role of race, religion, and national origins*. New York: Oxford University Press.

Grahm, Pamela. 1996. Nationality and political participation in the transnational context of Dominican migration. In *Caribbean circuits: Transnational approaches to migration*, edited by Patricia Pessar. Staten Island, N.Y.: Center for Migration Studies.

Gramsci, Antonio. 1971. *Prison notebooks: Selections*. Translated by Quinton Hoare and Geoffrey Smith. New York: International Publishers.

Greenberg, Joel. 1999. Israeli court bars extradition of a U.S. youth. *New York Times* (New England ed.), 26 February, A12.

Grosfoguel, Ramón and Chloe Georas. 2000. "Coloniality of power" and racial dynamics: Notes towards a reinterpretation of Latino Caribbeans in New York City. *Identities: Global Studies in Culture and Power* 7, no. 1:85–125.

Guarnizo, Luis Eduardo. 1997. The emergence of a transnational social formation and the mirage of return migration among Dominican transmigrants. *Identities: Global Studies in Culture and Power* 4, no. 2:281–322.

———. 1999. Mistrust, fragmented solidarity, and transnational migration: Colombians in New York City and Los Angeles. *Ethnic and Racial Studies* 22, no. 2:367–96.

Gupta, Akhil. 1995. Blurred boundaries: The discourse of corruption, the culture of politics, and the imagined state. *American Ethnologist* 22, no. 2:375–402.

HACAN conference packet. 1996. Mimeograph, in the files of Nina Glick Schiller.

Haïtian Women Ad Hoc Committee for the Decade. 1986. Haïtian women in diaspora. Montreal: Centre International de Documentation et d'information Haïtienne Cäribéenne, and Afro-Canadienne.

Hall, Stuart. 1988. The toad in the garden: Thatcherism among the theorists. In *Marxism and the interpretation of culture*, edited by Cary Nelson and Lawrence Grossberg. Urbana: University of Illinois Press.

Hamilton, Dona Cooper, and Charles V. Hamilton. 1997. *The dual agenda: The African-American struggle for civil and economic equality*. New York: Columbia University Press.

Hancock, Grahm. 1989. *Lords of poverty: The power, prestige, and corruption of the international aid business*. New York: Atlantic Monthly Press.

Haney-Lopez, Ian. 1996. *White by law: The legal construction of race*. New York: New York University Press.

Haraway, Donna. 1991. *Simians, cyborgs, and women: The reinvention of nature*. New York: Routledge.

Harrington, Mona. 1982. Loyalties: Dual and divided. In *The politics of ethnicity*, edited by Stephan Thernstrom. Cambridge, Mass.: Belknap Press.

Harrison, Faye. 1995. The persistent power of "race" in the cultural and political economy of racism. *Annual Review of Athropology* 24:47–74.

———. 2000. Facing racism and the moral responsibility of human rights knowledge. *Annals of the New York Academy of Sciences* 925:45–69.

Heinl, Robert Debs, and Nancy Gordon Heinl. 1978. *Written in blood: The story of the Haitian people, 1492–1971*. Boston: Houghton Mifflin.

Herrell, Richard. 1996. Sin, sickness, crime: Queer desire and the American state. *Identities: Global Studies in Culture and Power* 2, no. 3:273–300.

Herzfeld, Michael. 1992. *The social production of indifference: Exploring the symbolic roots of Western bureaucracy*. Chicago: University of Chicago Press.

———. 1997. *Cultural intimacy: Social poetics in the nation-state*. New York: Routledge.

Higham, John. 1982. Leadership. In *The politics of ethnicity*, edited by Stephan Thernstrom. Cambridge: Harvard University Press.

Hill, Mike. 1997. *Whiteness, a critical reader*. New York: New York University Press.

Hobsbawm, Eric J. 1990. *Nations and nationalism since 1780: Programme, myth, and reality*. New York: Cambridge University Press.

Hoffman, Leon-François. 1984. *Essays on Haitian literature*. Washington, D.C.: Three Continents Press.

Hondagneu-Sotelo, Pierrette. 1994. *Gendered transitions: Mexican experiences of immigration*. Berkeley: University of California Press.

Human Rights Watch and National Coalition for Haitian Refugees. 1994a. Rape in Haiti: A weapon of terror. *Human Rights Watch Report* 6, no. 8.

———. 1994b. Terror prevails in Haiti: Human rights violations and failed democracy. *Human Rights Watch Report* 6, no. 5.

———. 1996. Haiti, thirst for justice: a decade of impunity in Haiti. *Human Rights Watch Report* 8, no. 7.

Hunter, Allen. 1995. Rethinking revolution in light of the new social movements. In *Cultural politics and social movements*, edited by Marcy Darnovsky, Barbara Epstein, and Richard Flacks. Philadelphia, Pa.: Temple University Press.

Hutchinson, John, and Anthony D. Smith, eds. 1994. *Nationalism*. Oxford: Oxford University Press.

Ignatiev, Noel. 1996. *How the Irish became white*. New York: Routledge.

Jacobson, Matthew Frye. 1998. *Whiteness of a different color: European immigrants and the alchemy of race*. Cambridge: Harvard University Press.

Jean-Pierre, Jean. 1994. The tenth department. In *The Haiti files: Decoding the crisis*, edited by James Ridgeway, Washington, D.C.: Essential Books.

Jefferson, Thomas. [1787] 1984. Letter to W. S. Smith, in *Writings: Jefferson*. Vol. 12. Selections, edited by Julian P. Boyd and Lyman Butterfield. Viking Press.

Johnson, James Weldon. 1920a. Self-determining Haiti: I. The American occupation. *The Nation* III, no. 2878:236–38.

———. 1920b. Self-determining Haiti: II. What the United States has accomplished. *The Nation* III, no. 2879:265–67.

———. 1920c. Self-determining Haiti: III. Government of, by, and for the National City Bank. *The Nation* III, no. 2880:295–97.

———. 1920d. Self-determining Haiti: IV. The Haitian people. *The Nation* III, no. 2882:345–47.

Johnston, Barbara, and Terrence Turner. 1999. The American Anthropological Association, the World Bank group, and ENDESA S. A.: Violations of human rights in the Pangue and Ralco dam projects on the Bío Bío River, Chile. *Identities: Global Studies in Culture and Power* 6, nos. 2–3:387–434.

Joint, Louis Auguste. 1996. *Education populaire en Haïti: Rapport des "ti kominote legliz" et des organisations poulariges*. Montreal: L'Harmattan, Inc.

Jones, Kathleen. 1998. Citizenship in a woman-friendly polity. In *The citizenship debates*, edited by Gershon Shafir. Minneapolis: University of Minnesota Press.

Joseph, Gilbert M., Catherine C. LeGrand, and Ricardo D. Salvatore, eds. 1998. *Close encounters of empire: Writing the cultural history of U.S.–Latin American relations*. Durham, N.C.: Duke University Press.

Joseph, Gilbert M., and Daniel Nugent. 1994. Popular culture and state formation in revolutionary Mexico. In *Everyday forms of state formation: Revolution and the negotiation of rule in modern Mexico*, edited by Gilbert M. Joseph and Daniel Nugent. Durham, N.C.: Duke University Press.

Kamenka, Eugene. 1976. Political nationalism—The evolution of an idea. In *Nationalism: The nature and evolution of an idea*, edited by Eugene Kamenka. New York: St. Martin's Press.

Kapferer, Bruce. 1988. *Legends of the people, myths of the state*. Washington, D.C.: Smithsonian Institution Press.

Kearney, Michael. 1991. Borders and boundaries of the state and self at the end of empire. *Journal of Historical Sociology* 4, no. 1:52–74.

Kedourie, Eli. 1960. *Nationalism*. New York: Praeger.

Klimt, Andrea. 2000. Enacting national selves: Authenticity, adventure, and disaffection in the Portuguese diaspora. *Identities: Global Studies in Culture and Power* 6, no. 4:513–50.

Kohn, Hans. 1994. Western and eastern nationalism. In *Nationalism*, edited by John Hutchinson and Anthony D. Smith. Oxford: Oxford University Press.

Kowalski, B. J. 1992. Dire straits in Haiti. *World Press Review* 39, no. 9:37.

Krasner, Stephen. 1999. *Sovereignty: Organized hypocrisy*. Princeton, N.J.: Princeton University Press.

Labelle, Micheline. 1988. *Idéologies de couleur et classes sociales en Haïti*. Montreal: Les Presses d'Université Montreal.

Laguerre, Michel S. 1978. Ticouloute and his kinfold: The study of a Haitian extended family. In *The extended family in black societies*, edited by Dmitri B. Shimkin, Edith Shimkin, and Dennis Frate. The Hague: Mouton.

———. 1982. *Urban life in the Caribbean: A study of a Haitian urban community*. Cambridge, Mass.: Schenkman.

———. 1998. *Diasporic citizenship: Haitian Americans in transnational America*. New York: St. Martin's Press.

Lamm, Richard D., and Gary Imhoff. 1985. *The immigration time bomb: The fragmenting of America*. New York: Truman Talley Books.

Lears, Jackson. 1998. In defense of nostalgia. *Lingua Franca* (December–January):66.

Lenin Vladimir Ilyich. [1920] 1967. Preliminary draft of theses on the national and colonial questions. In *Lenin on the national and colonial questions: Three articles*. Peking: Foreign Language Press.

Lessinger, Johanna. 1995. *From the Ganges to the Hudson*. New York: Allyn and Bacon.

Levitt, Peggy. 1997. Transnationalizing community development: The case of migration between Boston and the Dominican Republic. *Nonprofit and Voluntary Sector Quarterly* 26, no. 4:509–26.

Lieberson, Stanley. 1980. *A piece of the pie: Blacks and white immigrants since 1880*. Berkeley: University of California Press.

Lipsitz, George. 1998. *The possessive investment in whiteness: How white people profit from identity politics*. Philadelphia, Pa.: Temple University Press.

Lister, Ruth. 1997. Citizenship: Towards a feminist synthesis. *Feminist Review*, no. 57 (autumn): 28–47.

Lowe, Lisa. 1996. *Immigrant acts: On Asian American cultural politics*. Durham, N.C.: Duke University Press.

Lowenthal, Ira. 1984. Labor, sexuality, and the conjugal contract in rural Haiti. In *Haiti: Today and tomorrow*, edited by Charles R. Foster and Albert Valdman. Lanham, Md.: University Press of America.

Madiou, Thomas. 1991. *Histoire d'Haiti*. 8 vols. Port-au-Prince: Editions Deschamps. Originally published in 4 vols. from 1847 to 1904.

Marshall, Thomas Humphrey. 1964. *Class, citizenship, and social development: Essays by T. H. Marshall*. Garden City, N.Y.: Doubleday and Company.

Mathurin, Alliette, Ernst Mathurin, and Bernard Zaugg. 1989. *Implantation et impact des organisations non gouvernementales: Contexte général et étude de cas (Haiti)*. Geneva: Société Haïtiano-Suisse d'Edition and Centre Haïtien de Recherches et de Documentation.

McCrone, David. 1998. *The sociology of nationalism*. London: Routledge.

McIntosh, Peggy. 1992. White privilege and male privilege: A personal account of coming to see correspondences through work in women's studies. In *Race, class, and gender: An anthology*, edited by Margaret Anderson and Patricia Hill Collins. Belmont, Calif.: Wadsworth.

McLaren, Peter. 1994. White terror and oppositional agency: Towards a critical multiculturalism. In *Multiculturalism: A critical reader*, edited by David Goldberg. Cambridge, Mass.: Blackwell Publishers.

Minutaglio, Bill. 1999. *First son: George W. Bush and the Bush family dynasty*. New York: Times Books.

Mitchell, Timothy. 1991. The limits of the state: Beyond statist approaches and their critics. *American Political Science Review* 85, no. 1:77–96.

Mittleman, James. 1996a. The dynamics of globalization. In *Globalization: Critical reflections*, edited by James Mittleman. Boulder, Colo.: Lynne Reinner.

———. 1996b. How does globalization really work? In *Globalization: Critical reflections*, edited by James Mittleman. Boulder, Colo.: Lynne Reinner.

———. ed. 1996c. *Globalization: Critical reflections*. Boulder, Colo.: Lynne Rienner.

Moïse, Claude. 1988. *Constitutions et luttes de pouvoir en Haïti, tome i: 1804–1915. Lafaillite des classes dirigeautes*. Montreal: CIDIHCA.

———. 1990. *Constitutions et luttes de pouvoir en Haïti, tome ii: 1915–1987. De l'occupation étrangère à la dictature macoute*. Montreal: CIDIHCA.

Morawska, Ewa. 1987. Sociological ambivalence: The case of eastern European peasant-immigrant workers in America, 1880s–1930s. *Qualitative Sociology* 10, no. 3:225–50.

———. 1989. Labor migrations of Poles in the Atlantic world economy, 1880–1914. *Comparative Study of Society and History* 31, no. 2:237–70.

Murray, David. 1996. Homosexuality, society, and the state. *Identities: Global Studies in Culture and Power* 2, no. 3:249–72.

Nagourney, Adam. 1999. Jets are chartered for Israelis in U.S. to get out to vote. *New York Times* (New England ed.), 8 May, A1, A17.

Nairn, Allen. 1994a. Behind Haiti's paramilitaries. *The Nation*, 259, no. 13:458–60.

———. 1994b. He's our S. O. B. *The Nation* 259, no. 14:481–82.

National Coalition for Haitian Rights. 1997. *Institutionalizing human rights in Haiti*. http://www.nchr.org/hrp/nchrhrp.

———. 1999. *Haiti on the edge*. http://www.nchr.org/hrp/INLEHaiti99.

National Labor Committee. 1994. In *Haiti files: Decoding the crisis*, edited by James Ridgeway. Washington, D.C.: Essential Books.

New York State Education Department. 1999. *New York state regents examinations* (at http://www.nysed.gov:80/rscs/exams/regents).

Nicholls, David. [1979] 1996. *From Dessalines to Duvalier: Race, color, and national independence in Haiti*. Cambridge, Mass.: Cambridge University Press.

———. 1985. *Haiti in the Caribbean context: Ethnicity, economy, and revolt*. New York: St. Martin's Press.

O'Farrell, John. 1999. Ireland fund donors see results: U.S. benefactors view projects charity aided. *Boston Globe* (city ed.), 22 June, A2.

Ong, Aihwa. 1993. On the edge of empires: Flexible citizenship among the Chinese in diaspora. *Positions* 1, no. 3:745–78.

———. 1998. *Flexible citizenship: The cultural logics of transnationality*. Durham, N.C.: Duke University Press.

Oriol, Michel. 1992. *185 images de la révolution à St. Domingue*. Port-au-Prince: Henri Deschamps.

Park, Robert Ezra. [1925] 1974. Immigrant community and immigrant press and its control. In *The collected papers of Robert Park*, edited by Everett Hughes, Charles Johnson, Jiotsvitchi Masuoka, Robert Redfield, and Louis Wirth. New York: Arno.

———. 1950. *Race and culture*. Glencoe, Ill.: Free Press.

Paul, John. 1981. The Greek lobby and American foreign policy: A transnational perspective.

In *Ethnic identities in a transnational world*, edited by John Stack Jr. Westport, Conn.: Greenwood Press.

Perry, William E. 1996. Opening statement by Deputy Assistant Director William E. Perry. House of Representatives Committee on the Judiciary, Subcommittee on Crime/Haiti: Human Rights and Police Issues. 4 January, 1–4. http://www.US.net/cip/perry.

Pessar, Patricia. 1996. *A visa for a dream*. New York: Allyn and Bacon.

Peterson, Iver. 1999. Whitman says troopers used racial profiling. *New York Times*, 21 April, section A1.

Pierre-Pierre, Garry. 1998. In Haiti, not all gifts well received. *New York Times*, 11 May, B6.

Plamenatz, John. 1976. Two types of nationalism. In *Nationalism: The nature and evolution of an idea*, edited by Eugene Kamenka. London: Edward Arnold.

Poppen, Cinny, and Scott Wright, eds. 1994. *Beyond the mountains, more mountains: Haiti faces the future*. Washington, D.C.: *Ecumenical Program on Central America and the Carribean*.

Portes, Alejandro, ed. 1996. *The new second generation*. New York: Russell Sage.

Portes, Alejandro, and Rubén G. Rumbaut. 1996. *Immigrant America: A portrait*. 2d ed. Berkeley: University of California Press.

Portes, Alejandro, and Alex Stepick. 1993. *City on the edge: The transformation of Miami*. Berkeley: University of California Press.

Portes, Alejandro, and Min Zhou. 1993. The new second generation: Segmented assimilation and its variants. *Annals of the American Academy of Political and Social Sciences* 530 (November): 74–96.

Poulantzas, Nicos. 1973. *Political power and social classes*. London: New Left Books.

Quijano, Anibal, and Immanuel Wallerstein. 1992. Americanity as a concept, or the Americas in the modern world system. *International Journal of Social Sciences* 134:583–91.

Radyo Moman Kreyòl. 1991 WLIB-AM, 5 January.

Reyna, Stephen, and Nina Glick Schiller. 1998. The pursuit of knowledge and regimes of truth. *Identities: Global Studies in Culture and Power* 4, nos. 3–4:333–41.

Richman, Karen. 1992a. "A *Lavalas* at home/a *Lavalas* for home": Inflections of transnationalism in the discourse of Haitian president Aristide. In *Towards a transnational perspective on Migration: Race, class, ethnicity, and nationalism reconsidered*, edited by Nina Glick Schiller, Linda Basch, and Cristina Blanc-Szanton. New York: New York Academy of Sciences.

———. 1992b. They will remember me in the house: The pwen of Haitian transnational migration. Ph.D. diss., University of Virginia.

Ridgeway, James, ed. 1994. *The Haiti files: Decoding the crisis*. Washington, D.C.: Essential Books.

Roberts, Peter. [1912] 1990. Restrictions on immigration are necessary. In *Immigration: Opposing viewpoints*, edited by William Dudley. San Diego, Calif.: Greenhaven Press.

Robinson, Randall. 1994. Haiti's agony, Clinton's shame. *New York Times*. 17 April, section 4:17.

Roediger, David R. 1991. *The wages of whiteness: Race and the making of the American working class*. London: Verso.

———. 1994. *Towards the abolition of whiteness: Essays on race, politics, and working-class history.* London: Verso.

Rosaldo, Renato. 1989. *Culture and truth: The remaking of social analysis.* Boston: Beacon Press.

Roseberry, William. 1989. *Anthropologies and histories: Essays in culture, history.* New Brunswick, N.J.: Rutgers University Press.

Rothberg, Robert I., ed. 1997. *Haiti renewed: Political and economic prospects.* Washington, D.C.: Brookings Institution Press.

Rouse, Roger. 1991. Mexican migration and the social space of postmodernism. *Diaspora* 1 (spring): 8–23.

Rumbaut, Rubén G. 1996. The crucible within: Ethnic identity, self-esteem, and segmented assimilation among children of immigrants. In *The new second generation*, edited by Alejandro Portes. New York: Russell Sage Foundation.

Safa, Helen. 1995. *The myth of the male breadwinner: Women and industrialization in the Caribbean.* Boulder, Colo.: Westview Press.

Said, Edward. [1978] 1995. *Orientalism: Western conceptions of the Orient.* Harmondsworth, U. K.: Penguin.

Sassen, Saskia. 1988. *The mobility of labor and capital: A study in international investment and labor flow.* New York: Cambridge University Press.

———. 1995. *Losing control: Sovereignty in an age of globalization.* New York: Columbia University Press.

Schaeffer, Robert. 1997. *Understanding globalization: The social consequences of political, economic, and environmental change.* Lanham, Md.: Rowman and Littlefield.

Schermerhorn, Richard A. 1949. *These our people: Minorities in American culture.* Boston: D. C. Heath and Co.

Schmidt, Hans. 1971. *The United States occupation of Haiti, 1915–1934.* New Brunswick, N.J.: Rutgers University Press.

Schneider, Mark L. 1995. Speech for the Haiti Consultative Group, 31 January, Paris (at www.info.usaid.gov/press/spe__test/speeches/speech.252).

———. 1998. Statement before the House International Relations Committee, 6 May.

Scott, James C. 1985. *Weapons of the weak: Everyday forms of peasant resistance.* New Haven, Conn.: Yale University Press.

———. 1990. *Domination and the arts of resistance: Hidden transcripts.* New Haven, Conn.: Yale University Press.

Sengupta, Somini. 1998. Immigrants in New York pressing drive for dual nationality. *New York Times*, 30 December, B1, B4.

Shafir, Gershon, ed. 1998. *The citizenship debates: A reader.* Minneapolis: University of Minnesota Press.

Silk, James. 1986. *Despite a generous spirit: Denying asylum in the United States.* Washington, D.C.: U.S. Committee for Refugees, American Council for Nationalities Service.

Simon, John. 1998. Refugees in a carceral age. *Public Culture* 10, no. 3:577–601.

Simpson, George, and J. Milton Yinger. 1958. *Racial and cultural minorities.* New York: Harper.

Smith, Jennie Marcelle. 2001. *When the hands are many: Community organization and social change in rural Haiti.* Ithaca, N.Y.: Cornell University Press.

Smith, Joan, and Immanuel Wallerstein, eds. 1992. *Creating and transforming households: The constraints of the world economy.* New York: Cambridge University Press.

Smith, Merrill. 1999. Campaign for trade relief. E-mail correspondence to Haiti advocacy general list (advocacy@bellatlantic.net), 15 August.

Smith, Michael Peter, and Luis Eduardo Guarnizo, eds. 1998. *Transnationalism from below.* New Brunswick, N.J.: Transaction Publishers.

Smith, Robert C. 1994. Los ausentes siempre presentes: The imagining, making, and politics of a transnational community between Ticuani, Puebla, Mexico, and New York City. Ph.D. diss., Columbia University.

———. 1998a. Comments delivered at the Second Generation Conference, April 4, 1998, Harvard University, Cambridge.

———. 1998b. Transnational localities: Community, technology, and the politics of membership within the context of Mexico–U.S. migration. In *Transnationalism from below,* edited by Michael Peter Smith and Luis Eduardo Guarnizo. New Brunswick, N.J.: Transaction Publishers.

Solomon, Lois. 1998. History of Africa, holocaust in classes. *Sun Sentinel,* 2 August, 1B.

Sontag, Deborah. 1998. A Mexican town that transcends all borders. *New York Times,* 21 July, A1, B6–7.

Sontag, Deborah, and Celia W. Dugger. 1998. The new immigrant tide: A shuttle between worlds. *New York Times,* 19 July, 1, 28–30.

Soyer, Daniel. 1997. *Jewish immigrant associations and American identity in New York, 1880–1939.* Cambridge: Harvard University Press.

Soysal, Yasemin Nuhoglu. 1994. *Limits of citizenship: migrants and postnational membership in Europe.* Chicago: University of Chicago Press.

Steinberg, Stephen. 1981. *The ethnic myth. Race, ethnicity, and class in America.* Boston: Beacon Press.

Stepick, Alex. 1998. *Pride against prejudice: Haitians in the United States.* Boston: Allyn and Bacon.

Stepick, Alex, and Dale Swartz. 1982. Haitian refugees in the U.S. *Minority Rights Group Report,* no 52.

———. 1986. Flight into despair: A profile of recent Haitian refugees in south Florida. *International Migration Review* 20, no. 74:329–50.

Stewart, Barbara. 1999. Crisis in the Balkans: Volunteers signing up in Yonkers to fight for Kosovo. *New York Times,* 12 April, on-line archives.

Sturgeon, Noël. 1999. Ecofeminist appropriations and transnational environmentalisms. *Identities: Global Studies in Culture and Power* 6, nos. 2–3:255–80.

Sullivan, Stacy. 1998. From Brooklyn to Kosovo, with love and AK-47s. *New York Times,* 22 November, on-line archives.

Sutton, Constance. 1992. Some thoughts on gendering and internationalizing our thinking about transnational migrations. In *Towards a transnational perspective on migration: Race, class, ethnicity, and nationalism reconsidered,* edited by Nina Glick Schiller, Linda Basch, and Cristina Blanc-Szanton. New York: New York Academy of Sciences.

Takaki, Ronald. 1989. *Strangers from a different shore: A history of Asian Americans.* Boston: Little, Brown and Co.

———. 1990. *Iron cages: Race and culture in nineteenth-century America*. New York: Oxford University Press.

———. 1993. *A different mirror: A history of multicultural America*. Boston: Little, Brown and Co.

Triandafyllidou, Anna. n. d. Immigration, nationalist discourse, and the rhetoric of exclusion: The case of Greece. Manuscript, in the files of Nina Glick Schiller.

Trouillot, Ertha Pascal. 1983. *Analyse de la législation révisant le statut de la femme mariée*. Port-au-Prince: Imprimerie Henry Deschamps.

Trouillot, Michel-Rolph. 1987. History, power, and ethnography in Haiti. Paper presented at the 86th Annual Meeting of the American Anthropological Association, 20 November, Chicago.

———. 1990. *Haiti: State against nation*. New York: Monthly Review Press.

Tsing, Anna. 1997. Environmentalists: Transitions as translations. In *Transitions, translations, environments: International feminism in contemporary politics*, edited by Joan Scott, Cora Kaplan, and Debra Keates. New York: Routledge.

Turner, Victor. 1985. *On the edge of the bush: Anthropology as experience*. Tucson: University of Arizona Press.

United Haitian Association. 1982. Patriotic appeal to the community. *United Haitian Association Newsletter* (June).

USAID. 1995. Democracy enhancement project: Project no. 5210236, 20 March, Port-au-Prince.

U.S. Bureau of the Census. 1993. *1990 census of population: The foreign-born population in the United States*. Washington, D.C.: Department of Commerce.

———. 1997. The foreign-born population: 1996. *Current populations reports* (March):20–494.

U.S. House. 1998. *The foreign operations, export financing, and related programs appropriations act*. CV Cong., First sess., H.R. 2159.

U.S. House Committee on International Relations. 1996. Hearings of the house international relations committee, 27 September (at www.us.net/cip/hearning).

U.S. Immigration and Naturalization Service. 1996. *Statistical yearbook of the immigration and naturalization service, 1994*. Washington, D.C.: Government Printing Office.

———. 1999. *Statistical yearbook of the immigration and naturalization service, 1997*. Washington, D.C.: Government Printing Office.

U.S. State Department. 1997. Points for Haiti. 1–2 August (at www.us.net/cip/white).

———. 1998. Background notes: Haiti. March 1–12 (at www.state.gov/www/background_notes/haiti__0398__bgn).

Valbrun, Marjorie. 1999. Former ragtag immigrant organization evolves into coalition pushing Haitian-American rights. *Wall Street Journal*, 4 February, A24.

Verdery, Katherine. 1993. Whither "nation" and "nationalism"? *Daedalus* 122, no. 2:37–46.

Vickerman, Milton. 1999. *Cross currents: West Indian immigrants and race*. New York: Oxford University Press.

Walker, Adrian. 1990. FDA ban on blood donors disputed; policy aimed at Haitians. *Boston Globe* (city ed.), 5 April, Metro/Region section, 27.

Wallerstein, Immanuel. 1979. *The capitalist world economy*. Cambridge, U. K.: Cambridge University Press.

Warne, Frank Julian. [1913] 1990. Restrictions on immigration are not necessary. In *Immigration: Opposing viewpoints*, edited by William Dudley. San Diego, Calif.: Greenhaven Press.

Warner, Lloyd, and Leo Srole. 1945. *The social systems of American ethnic groups*. New Haven, Conn.: Yale University Press.

Waters, Mary C. 1996. Ethnic and racial identities of second-generation black immigrants in New York City. In *The new second generation*, edited by Alejandro Portes. New York: Russell Sage Foundation.

———. 1999. Black identities: West Indian immigrant dreams and American realities. Boston: Harvard University Press.

Weiner, Tim. 1993. Key Haiti leaders said to have been in the C. I. A.'s pay. *New York Times*, 1 November, A1.

———. 1995. Haitian ex-paramilitary leader confirms C. I. A. relationship. *New York Times*, 3 December, A6.

Wells, Diane. 1999. Re-dyeing the cloth: The women's political platform and Trinidad and Tobago's general election of 1995. *Identities: Global Studies in Culture and Power* 5, no. 4:543–68.

Werbner, Pnina, and Tariq Modood. 1997. *Debating cultural hybridity: Multi-cultural identities and the politics of anti-racism*. London: Zed Books.

White, Robert E. 1997. Haiti: Democrats vs. democracy. In *International policy report*. Washington, D.C.: Center for International Policy (at http://www.ciponline.org/democrac).

Williams, Brackette. 1989. A class act: Anthropology and the race to nation across ethnic terrain. *Annual Reviews of Anthropology* 18:401–44.

Woodson, Drexel. 1990. *Tout mounn sé mounn, men tout mounn pa menm*: Microlevel sociocultural aspects of land tenure in a northern Haitian locality. Ph.D. diss., University of Chicago.

World March of Women. 2000. Advocacy to women's world demands action sheets, 8 March–17 October. http://www.ffq.qc.ca/marche2000/en/cahier/c-03.

Wyman, Mark. 1993. *Round-trip to America: The immigrants return to Europe, 1880–1930*. Ithaca, N.Y.: Cornell University Press.

Yuval-Davis, Nira. 1997. Women, citizenship, and difference. *Feminist Review*, no. 57 (autumn):4–27.

Zarin, Michael. 1998. IRI's response. 16 October (at http://www.us.net/cip/iri2).

Index

eign aid, 230; and Haitian long-distance
nationalism, 118, 204; Haitians and
AIDS, 291n
Men: as husbands, 138; poor, 140, 149; prob-
lems of, 139; self-esteem of, 139; and ur-
ban employment, 138
Middle class, Haitian, 170, 184, 191–93
Midwives' Association (*Konbit Fanm Saj*),
287n
Migration: of 1880s-1930s, 9; of 1960–1996,
10; as solution, 265
Military coup. *See* Aristide, Jean-Bertrand;
Cedras, Raoul
Military dictatorships, growth of, 10;
Haitian, 73, 170. *See also* Duvalier,
François; United States: relationship to
Haiti
Military occupation. *See* United States: occu-
pation of Haiti
Ministry of Haitians Living Abroad
(MHAVE), 12, 202
Ministry of the Feminine Condition, 149
Modernization. *See* Privatization
Moment Créole, 234, 285n
Morality of knowledge, 33, 78
Morality of obligation, 82, 79, 84
Moun andeyò, 25
Mulatto, 65, 101–5, 108–10, 113, 155, 168
Multiculturalism, 114, 285n
Multinational corporations. *See* Corpo-
rations

Nation, 17, 101, 114, 129; and class, 132; and
diaspora, 132–33; as family, 90, 91, 94,
133, 184–85, 200; French concept of, 102;
and gender, 132–35; transnational concept
of, 94
National Bank of the Republic of Haiti, 215–
17
National Coalition for Haitian Refugees
(NCHR), 285n, 287n
National Coalition for Haitian Rights
(NCHR), 159–60, 204–5

National City Bank of New York, 216–17
National Democratic Institute for International Affairs, 294n
National identity, 4, 25, 110, 157
Nationalism, 3, 8, 13, 15–19, 28, 34–35, 127,
132, 145, 169–71; authoritarian regimes,
28; and critique of oppression, 238; and
debate over privatization, 248; definition
of, 275n, 279n; Eastern, 280n; exclusion
of religion, 29; fundamentalist, 29; Haitian in contrast to United States, 262;
link to territory, 278n; localized, 22, 29,
152; nationals, 26; polysemous, 28; progressive, 28; reactionary, 28; rhetoric of,
267; sacred aura of, 291n; United States,
258; Western, 280n; and women, 150. *See
also* Black: nationalism
Nationalist, definition of, 254; discourse,
and floating signifiers, 239
Nationality, definition of, 280n
National narratives, Haitian, 132, 135, 139,
146, 255
Nation-state, 4, 5, 17–19, 92, 110, 152–53, 169,
176, 177; post-World War II understanding of, 110
Naturalization, to the United States, 123–27,
143–45, 168, 205, 286n; and Haitian citi-
zenship rights, 245
Nazis, 6, 278
Nèg, 103–4
Negritude, 217, 293n
Neoliberalism, 247, 250, 254, 267, 273
Newspapers, Haitian, 197, 200, 276n
New York Times, 122, 234–35, 276n, 280n
Nongovernmental organizations (NGOs),
38, 148, 150, 153, 198, 266, 268; definition
of, 291n; dissemination of democratic
rhetoric, 210; and hometown associa-
tions, 233
North American Free Trade Agreement
(NAFTA), 210
Nostalgia, 1–2, 14, 121, 127, 129, 157, 166, 169,
172, 176, 177, 255, 262, 264–65

ment, 147–49; identity, 285n; migration, 3, 45, 32, 149, 157–59, 175–77; nation-state, 17, 19–23, 27, 33, 122, 123, 144; organizations, 167; politics, 9, 165–66, 186; processes, 30; social fields, 3, 25, 35, 57, 73, 76, 92, 143, 153, 156, 158, 163–64, 168, 171, 174–79, 198, 207, 236, 269, 279n; space, 129, 176, 264, 277n; "view from below," 296n. *See also* Obligation; Social movements; Transborder citizenship

Undocumented immigrants. *See* Immigrants
Unemployment, Haitian, 64, 149, 224, 255–56
United Haitian Association (UHA), 115–16
United Nations, 18, 33, 121–22, 148, 153–54, 205; conference on the status of women, 148; dissemination of nationalist rhetoric, 210; Haitian military operation, 223; and Haitian political life, 294n. *See also* United States: occupation of Haiti
United States: amnesty program of 1986, 73; Army War College, 231; campaign financing, 213; census, 288n; Coast Guard, 282n, 283n, 285n; Congress, 73, 126, 282n, 294n; economy, 76; Export-Import Bank, 218; foreign policy and Haiti, 5; Immigration Act of 1990, 291; immigration laws, 67, 87, 90, 141–42, 194; industrial development, 105; Marines, 217; occupation of Haiti, 5, 105–6, 122, 127, 146, 215–17, 230, 236; permanent residency visa, 141–42; presence in Haiti, 5; and racial segregation in Haiti, 105; relationship to Haiti, 5, 183, 209, 211–12, 215, 218; scholarship on Haiti, 231; trade with Haiti, 215. *See also* Constitution: of the United States; Corporations; Immigration and Naturalization Service (INS); International lending bodies; Nationalism; Naturalization to the United States
Universal Declaration of Human Rights, 185

University of Haiti, 141, 190, 228
USAID, 219–21, 224, 235, 236

Vietnam War, 258
Vincent, Stenio (Haitian president), 217
Visas, for permanent United States residence, 199, 205, 282n, 287n
Vodou, 10, 104, 106, 107, 134, 286n, 290n
Voodoo, 128
Voye Ayiti Monte (VOAM), 120

Wall Street Journal, 204
Walter, Littleton (Colonel), 105
Westphalian system, 278n
White: Americans, 261; mainstream culture, 173; as normative group, 285n
White Anglo-Saxon Protestants (WASPs), 284n
White-collar workers, 239
Whiteness, 109–10, 125, 261; as critique, 296n; link with "civilization," 103; scholarship on, 276n
White privilege, literature on, 296n
Whites, in Haiti, 254
WLIB (New York City radio station), 234, 285n. *See also* Radio
Women: diaspora, 148–49; Duvalier regime, 146–47; education, 149; female domain, 69; feminist struggles, 147; grassroots movement, 148–50; Haiti, 130–54, 239; Haitian legal history, 134; Haitian women's movement, 146–50; identification with Haiti, 132; international movement, 271; legal rights of, 146; long-distance nationalism, 137, 149; middle class, 135–36, 146, 148; nationalist rhetoric, 147; political action, 146; poor, 135–36, 137, 140; rural, 135–36; sexual availability, 139–40; sexual transactions, 140–41; single, 139, 141; suffrage, 146; upper class, 135, 146, 149; urban employment, 137–38
Women are Present (*Fanm Yo La*), 287n

Women's House (*Kay Fanm*), 153
Women's Information Network (*Enfo Fanm*), 287n
Women's movement, 146–50, 153
Women's rights, 148
World Bank, 206, 247, 250; and Aristide, 222–23; and decentralization, 235; and Haitian elections, 221; and intervention, 236. *See also* International lending bodies
World system theorists, 293n
World Trade Organization (WTO), 210;

global mobilization against, 272; 1999 meetings (Seattle), 211, 256, 296n
World War I, 276n, 278n,
World War II, 284n

Youth: Black, United States, 271; Haitian, 155–77, 229

Zenglendo (violent criminals), 139
Zionism, 15, 111, 174, 195, 258
Zionist youth groups, 174

Earlier or different versions of sections of some chapters have appeared in journal articles and book chapters. These include: "'I Am Not a Problem without a Solution': Poverty, Transnational Migration, and Struggle," in *New Poverty Studies: The Ethnography of Politics, Policy, and Impoverished People in the U.S.*, edited by Jeff Maskovsky and Judy Good (New York: New York University Press, forthcoming); "All in the Family: Gender, Transnational Migration, and the Nation-State." *Identities: Global Studies in Culture and Power* 7, no. 4 (2001); "The Generation of Identity: Redefining the Second Generation within a Transnational Social Field," in *Migration, Transnationalization, and Race in a Changing New York*, edited by Héctor R. Cordero-Guzmán, Robert C. Smith, and Ramón Grosfoguel (Philadelphia: Temple University Press, 2001); "Transnational Lives and National Identities: The Identity Politics of Haitian Immigrants," in *Transnationalism from Below*, edited by Michael Peter Smith and Luis Eduardo Guarnizo (New Brunswick, N.J.: Transaction, 1998); "Haitian Identities at the Disjuncture between Diaspora and Homeland," in *Caribbean Circuits*, edited by Patricia Pessar (Staten Island, N.Y.: Center for Migration Studies, 1997): "Laços de sangue: Os fundamentos do estado-nação transnacional," in *Globalization, State, Identities*, special issue of *Revista Crítica Ciências Sociais* 48 (June 1997), reprinted in *Identidates: Estudos de Cultura e Poder*, edited by Bella Feldman-Bianco and Graça Capinha (São Paulo, Brazil: Hucitec, 2000).

Nina Glick Schiller is an associate professor of anthropology at the University of
New Hampshire and coordinator of the Race, Culture, and Power minor. She is
the author (with Linda Basch and Cristina Szanton Blanc) of *Nations Unbound:
Transnational Projects, Postcolonial Predicaments, and Deterritorialized Nation-
states* (1994). She is the editor (with Linda Basch and Cristina Blanc-Szanton) of
*Towards a Transnational Perspective on Migration: Race, Class, Ethnicity, and Na-
tionalism Reconsidered* (1992).

Georges Fouron is chair of the Social Sciences Interdisciplinary (SSI) Program at
the State University of New York at Stony Brook, where he is an associate professor in both the SSI Program and the African Studies Department.

Library of Congress Cataloging-in-Publication Data
Glick Schiller, Nina.
Georges woke up laughing : long-distance nationalism and the search for home /
Nina Glick Schiller and Georges Eugene Fouron.
Includes bibliographical references and index.
ISBN 0-8223-2781-3 (cloth : alk. paper)—ISBN 0-8223-2791-0 (pbk. : alk. paper)
1. Haitian Americans—Ethnic identity. 2. Haitian Americans—Social condi-
tions. 3. Immigrants—United States—Social conditions. 4. Transnationalism.
5. United States—Emigration and immigration. 6. Haiti—Emigration and
immigration. 7. United States—Relations—Haiti. 8. Haiti—Relations—
United States. 9. Fouron, Georges Eugene. 10. Haitians—Interviews.
I. Fouron, Georges Eugene. II. Title.
E184.H27.S35 2001   305.896'97294073—dc21   2001033752